LIBRARY OF HEBREW BIBLE/ OLD TESTAMENT STUDIES

448

Formerly Journal for the Study of the Old Testament Supplement Series

THE PERFORMATIVE NATURE AND FUNCTION OF ISAIAH 40–55

Jim W. Adams

NEW YORK • LONDON

T & T Clark International, 80 Maiden Lane, New York, NY 10038

T & T Clark International, The Tower Building, 11 York Road, London SE1 7NX

T & T Clark International is a Continuum imprint.

Library of Congress Cataloging-in-Publication Data
Adams, Jim W.
The performative nature and function of Isaiah 40-55 / Jim W. Adams.
p. cm. -- (Library of Hebrew Bible/Old Testament studies ; 448)
Includes bibliographical references (p.) and index.
ISBN-13: 978-0-567-02582-1 (hardcover)
ISBN-10: 0-567-02582-9
1. Bible. O.T. Isaiah XL-LV--Criticism, interpretation, etc. I. Title.
BS1520.A525 2006
224'.1066--dc22
2006019653

06 07 08 09 10 10 9 8 7 6 5 4 3 2 1

Printed and bound in Great Britain by Biddles Ltd., King's Lynn, Norfolk

In Loving Memory of Sam F. Middlebrook

(6 November 1933 – 26 June 1992)

אבי מורי רעי

CONTENTS

ACKNOWLEDGMENTS

This present study represents a revised version of my doctoral dissertation, which was submitted to Fuller Theological Seminary in June 2004 and entitled "Speech Act Theory, Biblical Interpretation, and Isaiah 40–55: Exploring the Use and Value of the Philosophical Notions of Speech Act Theory for Biblical Interpretation and Specifically for Isaiah 40–55," conducted under the supervision of Dr. John Goldingay and Dr. Colin Brown. What is presented in this work is not a revision of my basic thesis, but a narrowing down of the former study, refinement of selected arguments, and one additional section which contains a summary review of Old Testament interpreters applying speech act theory into their research.

Over the years the book of Isaiah has become a sort of testing ground for scholars to explore the viability and applicability of numerous interpretive methods. Consequently, a massive amount of work has been done on the book. I want to express my humble thanks to all those who have spent far more countless hours and years than I studying and interpreting this book, and specifically chs. 40–55. I hope it will become apparent in the pages that follow that I have learned much from each and every one of these scholars, maybe more so from the ones with whom on occasion I disagree. As well, I have learned a great deal from the biblical scholars who have explored speech act theory and its hermeneutical use. I am especially indebted to the work of Richard S. Briggs and Anthony C. Thiselton.

In the production of this work I want to thank the editorial board, Dr. Andrew Mein, Henry Carrigan, and T. & T. Clark, for bestowing on me the honor of publishing this work in this prestigious series. I want to especially thank Dr. Duncan Burns for his kindness towards and patience with me, impeccable work, attention to detail, and perseverance through the various untimely trials in seeing this work reach publication on time.

Along my journey many people have profoundly influenced my life and learning. I want to thank my teachers over the years who include Dr. John Amstutz, Dr. Scott Bauer, Dr. Sheri Benvenuti, Mark Duzik, Dr. Jack Hayford, Dan Hicks, Dr. Lynn Losie, Dr. Ralph P. Martin,

Don McKenzie, Chuck and Barbara Middlebrook, Dr. Don Pickerill, Larry Powers, Dan Stewart, Rachel Shivers, Dr. Tom Wymore, and Dr. William Yarchin. I must thank the Administration at LIFE Pacific College who supported and encouraged me during my doctoral studies. I would also like to thank all of my students over the years who have significantly impacted my understanding of the Bible and especially Isaiah.

I would also like to thank those who have had a special impact on my life and studies. I would like to thank Dr. Sam F. Middlebrook, to whom I dedicate this work and who God took all too soon. Thank you, Sam, for fostering in me a love for the Old Testament and the Jewish people. You will always be my spiritual father, teacher, and friend. Thank you, Dr. John E. Hartley, for your great teaching skills and integrity, your constant challenge to think harder, your companionship in life, and for deciding for me that I would do my doctoral studies in the Old Testament. Thank you, Dr. Colin Brown, for your kind, humble, and gentle way, for introducing me to speech act theory, your vast treasury of knowledge, for your timely encouragement concerning my doctoral research, and your friendship. I would also like to thank Dr. Anthony C. Thiselton who in private discussions and through his work helped me significantly to formulate my understanding of speech act theory and how it applies to Isa 40–55. Also, I need to thank Dr. Roy F. Melugin for his stimulating critiques and suggestions concerning my dissertation which have made their way into this present study. Most importantly, I would like to thank Dr. John Goldingay. Spending time with you, John, during and after my doctoral studies has left an indelible mark upon my life and my thinking about God and Scripture. Your commitment to God encourages me; your brilliance with interpreting the biblical text challenges me; your graciousness towards others and especially your students inspires me; your undying faithfulness and love to your wife Ann is truly holy, *otherthan*. Thank you for all your time, insight, guidance, encouragement, and friendship over the years!

I must also thank my family and friends. Specifically, thank you, Mom and Dad, for always supporting me in my life, my studies, and my vocation. I wish you were still here, Dad! Mom, I am never in need of love or encouragement so long as you are around. Thank you, Sheri, Brew, Nathan, Emily, and Lily for always loving and supporting me. I am especially thankful that you are always forcing me to ask the question, "So what?" Last, but by no means least, I want to thank the love of my life, my wife, Audry, and our two children. Audry, without you I would be lost; you are truly my compass. I cannot express how thankful I am for your loving support and all that you have given up on my behalf. In the years to come I will strive to prove that your sacrifice was worth it. Thank you, Brady and Michaela, for your unwavering patience, long-standing forgiveness, and unconditional love. Through your youthful resilience, may you never show signs of doctoral scars. I love you both more than words can say.

ABBREVIATIONS

α′	Aquila
θ′	Theodotian
σ′	Symmachus
1QIsa[a]	Isaiah Scroll A from Qumran Cave 1
1QIsa[b]	Isaiah Scroll B from Qumran Cave 1
4QIsa[d]	Isaiah Scroll D from Qumran Cave 4
AB	Anchor Bible
ABD	*The Anchor Bible Dictionary*. Edited by D. N. Freedman. 6 vols. New York: Doubleday, 1992
AHw	*Akkadisches Handwörterbuch*. W. von Soden. Wiesbaden: Harrassowitz, 1959–81
AJSL	*American Journal of Semitic Languages and Literatures*
Akk	Akkadian
AnBib	Analecta biblica
ANET	*Ancient Near Eastern Texts Relating to the Old Testament*. Edited by James B. Pritchard. 3d ed. Princeton: Princeton University Press, 1950
ANETS	Ancient Near Eastern Texts and Studies
AOAT	Alter Orient und Altes Testament
Arb	Arabic
BASOR	*Bulletin of the American Schools of Oriental Research*
BBET	Beiträge zur biblischen Exegese und Theologie
BBR	*Bulletin of Biblical Research*
BDAG	Bauer, W., F. W., Danker, W. F. Arndt, and F. W. Gingrich. *A Greek–English Lexicon of the New Testament and Other Early Christian Literature*. 3d ed. Chicago: University of Chicago Press, 2000
BDB	Brown, F., S. R. Driver, and C. A. Briggs. *A Hebrew and English Lexicon of the Old Testament*. Oxford: Clarendon, 1907
BETL	Bibliotheca ephemeridum theologicarum lovaniensium
BEvT	Beiträge zur evangelischen Theologie
BHS	*Biblia hebraica stuttgartensia*
Bib	*Biblica*
BibB	Biblische Beiträge
BibInt	*Biblical Interpretation: A Journal of Contemporary Approaches*
BJRL	*Bulletin of the John Rylands University Library of Manchester*
BJS	Brown Judaic Studies
BKAT	Biblischer Kommentar: Altes Testament
BN	*Biblische Notizen*
BSac	*Bibliotheca Sacra*
BSO(A)S	*Bulletin of the School of Oriental (and African) Studies*
BT	*The Bible Translator*

BTB	*Biblical Theology Bulletin*
BWANT	Beiträge zur Wissenschaft vom Alten und Neuen Testament
BZ	*Biblische Zeitschrift*
BZAW	Beihefte zur *ZAW*
CAD	*The Assyrian Dictionary of the Oriental Institute of the University of Chicago*. Edited by I. I. Gelb et al. Chicago: Oriental Institute, 1964–
CBK	Calwer Bibelkommentare
CBQ	*Catholic Biblical Quarterly*
CDA	*A Concise Dictionary of Akkadian*. Edited by J. Black, A. George, and N. Postgate. Santag 5. Wiesbaden: Harrassowitz, 2000
CJT	*Canadian Journal of Theology*
ConBOT	Coniectanea biblica, Old Testament
COS	*The Context of Scripture*. Edited by W. W. Hallo. 3 vols. Leiden: Brill, 1997–2002
CRBS	*Currents in Research: Biblical Studies*
CTJ	*Calvin Theological Journal*
CThM	Calwer Theologische Monographien
DCH	*The Dictionary of Classical Hebrew*. Edited by David J. A. Clines. 6 vols. Sheffield: Sheffield Academic Press, 1993–
EdF	Erträge der Forschung
ETL	*Ephemerides theologicae lovanienses*
EvQ	*Evangelical Quarterly*
EvT	*Evangelische Theologie*
ExpTim	*Expository Times*
FAT	Forschungen zum Alten Testament
FDVNF	Franz Delitzsch Vorlesungen Neue Folge
FL	*Foundations of Language*
FOTL	The Forms of the Old Testament Literature
FRLANT	Forschungen zur Religion und Literatur des Alten und Neuen Testaments
FTL	Forum Theologiae Linguisticae
FzB	Forschung zur Bibel
GBH	*A Grammar of Biblical Hebrew*. P. Joüon. Translated and revised by T. Muraoka. 2 vols. Rome: Pontificio Istituto Biblico, 1993
GBS	Guides to Biblical Scholarship
GKC	*Gesenius' Hebrew Grammar*. Edited by E. Kautzsch. Revised and translated by A. E. Cowley. Oxford: Clarendon, 1910
HALOT	*The Hebrew and Aramaic Lexicon of the Old Testament*. Edited by L. Koehler et al. 5 vols. Leiden: Brill, 1994–2000
HBT	*Horizons in Biblical Theology*
HCOT	Historical Commentary on the Old Testament
HeyJ	*Heythrop Journal*
HKAT	Handkommentar zum Alten Testament
HTR	*Harvard Theological Review*
HUCA	*Hebrew Union College Annual*
IB	*Interpreter's Bible*
IBHS	*An Introduction to Biblical Hebrew Syntax*. B. K. Waltke and M. O'Connor. Winona Lake, Ind.: Eisenbrauns, 1990
IBS	*Irish Biblical Studies*
ICC	International Critical Commentary

Int	*Interpretation*
JANESCU	*Journal of the Ancient Near Eastern Society of Columbia*
JAOS	*Journal of the American Oriental Society*
JBL	*Journal of Biblical Literature*
JBR	*Journal of Bible and Religion*
JNES	*Journal of Near Eastern Studies*
JNSL	*Journal of Northwest Semitic Languages*
JP	*Journal of Pragmatics*
JQR	*Jewish Quarterly Review*
JSOT	*Journal for the Study of the Old Testament*
JSOTSup	Journal for the Study of the Old Testament: Supplement Series
JSS	*Journal of Semitic Studies*
JTS	*Journal of Theological Studies*
K	Kethib
KAT	Kommentar zum Alten Testament
KJV	King James Version
LSJ	*Greek–English Lexicon*. H. G. Liddell, R. Scott and H. S. Jones. 9th ed. Oxford: Clarendon, 1968
LUÅ	Lunds universitets årsskrift
LXX	Septuagint
LXX[A]	LXX, MS Alexandrian Codex
LXX[B]	LXX MS, Vatican Codex
MT	Masoretic Text
NASB	*New American Standard Bible*
NCB	New Century Bible
NEB	*New English Bible*
NIB	*New Interpreters Bible*
NIBC	New International Bible Commentary
NICOT	New International Commentary on the Old Testament
NIDOTTE	*New International Dictionary of Old Testament Theology and Exegesis*. Edited by W. A. VanGemeren. 5 vols. Grand Rapids: Zondervan, 1997
NIGTC	New International Greek Testament Commentary
NIV	New International Version
NJB	*New Jerusalem Bible*
NRSV	New Revised Standard Version
OBO	Orbis biblicus et orientalis
Or	*Orientalia*
OTG	Old Testament Guides
OTL	Old Testament Library
OTS	*Oudtestamentische Studiën*
P&BNS	Pragmatics & Beyond New Series
PhEx	*Philosophical Exchange*
PhQ	*Philosophical Quarterly*
PhR	*Philosophical Review*
POS	Pretoria Oriental Series
POT	De Prediking van het Oude Testament
Q	Qere
QJS	*Quarterly Journal of Speech*
RB	*Revue biblique*

RelS	*Religious Studies*
RelSRev	*Religious Studies Review*
RevQ	*Revue de Qumran*
RSV	Revised Standard Version
SBB	Stuttgarter biblische Beiträge
SBLDS	Society of Biblical Literature Dissertation Series
SBLMS	Society of Biblical Literature Monograph Series
SBLSBS	Society of Biblical Literature Sources for Biblical Study
SBLSCS	Society of Biblical Literature Septuagint and Cognate Studies
SBLSP	Society of Biblical Literature Seminar Papers
SBLSS	Society of Biblical Literature Semeia Studies
SBS	Stuttgarter Bibelstudien
SBT	Studies in Biblical Theology
SBibT	*Studia Biblica et Theologica*
SJ	Studia judaica
SJOT	*Scandinavian Journal of the Old Testament*
SM	Scripta Minora
SJT	*Scottish Journal of Theology*
SOTSMS	Society for Old Testament Study Monograph Series
SSN	Studia Semitica Neerlandica
ST	*Studia theologica*
STDJ	Studies on the Texts of the Desert of Judah
Syr	Syriac
TBü	Theologische Bücherei
TDOT	*Theological Dictionary of the Old Testament*. Edited by G. J. Botterweck and H. Ringgren. 14 vols. Grand Rapids: Eerdmans, 1974–2004
Tg	Targum
TLOT	*Theological Lexicon of the Old Testament*. Edited by E. Jenni and C. Westermann. Translated by M. E. Biddle. 3 vols. Peabody, Mass.: Hendrickson, 1997
TQ	*Theologische Quartalschrift*
TRu	*Theologische Rundschau*
TynBul	*Tyndale Bulletin*
TZ	*Theologische Zeitschrift*
UF	*Ugarit-Forschungen*
Ug	Ugaritic
USQR	*Union Seminary Quarterly Review*
Vg	Vulgate
VT	*Vetus Testamentum*
VTSup	*Vetus Testamentum*, Supplements
WBC	Word Biblical Commentary
WMANT	Wissenschaftliche Monographien zum Alten und Neuen Testament
WTJ	*Westminster Theological Journal*
ZAW	*Zeitschrift für die alttestamentliche Wissenschaft*
ZTK	*Zeitschrift für Theologie und Kirche*

INTRODUCTION

Speech Act Theory

Speech act theory has emerged within the field of the philosophy of language as a primary way of thinking about how language functions and conveys meaning. In short, the discipline illuminates the fact that speaking something does not merely constitute description or the conveying of information; it may also involve the performing of an action. This is evident in the most basic of utterances, such as when a person says, "I do" during a marriage ceremony; or promises to another, "I will come tomorrow"; or declares, "You are fired"; or announces, "I name this ship the Queen Mary"; or states, "I bet you ten dollars that the Lakers will win next week." As the biblical interpreter G. B. Caird observed, such types of utterances "are none of them reporting an action which has been accomplished by non-verbal means, but doing with words exactly what they say they are doing."[1] More technically, certain utterances include an illocutionary force or forces that personally involve a speaker and/or hearer in extralinguistic actions prescribed in the propositional content that brings about a state of affairs in the world.

This phenomenon of communicative action leads to the fact that meaning does not solely derive from ascertaining the propositional content of a sentence; it also includes determining what type of speech act a speaker utilizes in expressing an utterance. In a recent collection of essays on performative utterances, Savas L. Tsohatzidis justifies the linguistic importance and study of illocutionary acts by stating that they "constitute the primary subject matter of speech act theory" and

> that they appear to be *meaning-determining acts*, in the sense that the identification of what a speaker means in uttering a sentence of his language is not possible, even after the proposition he thereby purports to express has been identified, unless it is further determined which one among the various types of acts of this kind he is engaged in performing

1. G. B. Caird, *The Language and Imagery of the Bible* (Grand Rapids: Eerdmans, 1997), 21.

> by means of his utterance. If this is so, and if the study of what speakers of a natural language mean by uttering sentences of that language is, as it is generally acknowledged to be, a central object of linguistic and philosophical investigation, it is no wonder that the study of illocutionary acts should be acknowledged as an indispensable component of the study of meaning.[2]

Hence, the concept of speech acts provides a crucial element in understanding any type of communicative action. Despite the clear importance of speech act theory, Anthony C. Thiselton remarks that it "has suffered undeserved neglect in biblical interpretation, in systematic theology, and in discussions of 'religious language' in textbooks on the philosophy of religion."[3]

The concept of performative language also provides, in part, an answer to the hermeneutical problem. In general, the problem revolves around the endeavor to understand anything whenever meaning is in doubt. In biblical interpretation, the problem arises by the fact that the interpreter and the ancient text are separated by time, language, and culture. Simplistically stated, the hermeneutical task attempts to close this gap in order for meaning to transpire. According to the philosopher Hans-Georg Gadamer, understanding takes place when the horizons of the interpreter merge with those of the text and thus realize a "fusion of horizons" (*Horizontverschmelzung*).[4] Thiselton has focused much of his attention on the area of hermeneutics and has devoted himself to identifying interpretive strategies whereby the interpreter can progress towards such a fusion.[5] For Thiselton, speech act theory, particularly the concept of self-involvement, provides one of the most promising ways for actualizing this fusion of horizons. In fact, Thiselton argues that "self-involving

2. Savas L. Tsohatzidis, "Ways of Doing Things with Words: An Introduction," in *Foundations of Speech Act Theory: Philosophical and Linguistic Perspectives* (ed. Savas L. Tsohatzidis; London: Routledge, 1994), 1–25 (1–2).

3. A. C. Thiselton, "Speech-Act Theory and the Claim that God Speaks: Nicholas Wolterstorff's *Divine Discourse*," *SJT* 50 (1997): 97–110 (97). In his recent survey of speech act theory and biblical studies, Richard S. Briggs ("Uses of Speech-Act Theory in Biblical Interpretation," *CRBS* 9 [2001]: 229–76 [229–30]) arrives at this same conclusion.

4. Hans-Georg Gadamer, *Truth and Method* (trans. and rev. J. Weinsheimer and D. G. Marshall; 2d ed.; New York: Continuum, 2000), cf. 306–7, 374–75.

5. Thiselton's key discussions on hermeneutics are located in his two books, *The Two Horizons: New Testament Hermeneutics and Philosophical Description* (Carlisle: Paternoster; Grand Rapids: Eerdmans, 1980), and *New Horizons in Hermeneutics: The Theory and Practice of Transforming Biblical Reading* (Grand Rapids: Zondervan, 1992).

hermeneutics remains fundamental to the larger hermeneutical enterprise."[6] Generally speaking:

> In the case of *promises* or *authorizations*...*something is at stake in the extra-linguistic attitudes and commitments of the speaker or writer*. In the case of *prayers*, *confessions*, or utterances of repentance or of faith, *something is at stake in the extra-linguistic attitudes or commitments of those readers* who participate in the speech-act character of the texts as a speech-act.[7]

Certain types of communicative action draw in the reader as a self-involved participant with the text. In some instances the reader is the recipient of a promise, or a warning, or is commissioned to a task. In other cases, the reader becomes the speaker who confesses, prays, laments and so on. Such self-involvement includes extralinguistic action expressed in the propositional content of the utterance. Prescribed entailed action extends beyond the world of the text and thus has transforming implications for the reader/speaker and reality. As a self-involved participant in the text, the reader becomes an essential and indispensable factor in the process of interpretation.

Speech act theory is laden with a host of complex and intricate concepts found in a vast amount of dense material that does not lend itself to a casual perusal. A number of inherent ambiguities along with differing opinions exist in the philosophical literature. Due to this, misunderstanding and misapplication typically mark the non-specialists' use of speech act theory, specifically in biblical studies. In addition, very little dialogue has occurred among biblical interpreters who have utilized speech act theory.[8] In order to address these concerns I will present an overview of the central concepts and issues in speech act theory while in dialogue with particular biblical interpreters.

Regarding the transferability of speech act theory to biblical interpretation, much work has already been done to demonstrate that the notions of speech act theory can be applied to written texts. For speech act theorists, the relationship between the performative utterances of a

6. Thiselton, *New Horizons*, 274.

7. Ibid., 598 (emphasis in original).

8. David Hilborn makes this observation as he remarks that despite the importance of speech act theory for the analysis of liturgy, "it has been appropriated only sporadically by those working on such discourse, and even then, there has been very little dialogue between those concerned" ("From Performativity to Pedagogy: Jean Ladrière and the Pragmatics of Reformed Worship Discourse," in *The Nature of Religious Language: A Colloquium* (ed. Stanley E. Porter; Roehampton Institute London Papers 1; Sheffield: Sheffield Academic Press, 1996), 170–200 [173]).

speaker/hearer and the writer/reader is a natural one. As Richard S. Briggs correctly concludes, "Broadly speaking, speech-act theory is well suited to any communicative action."[9] Briggs has most recently re-examined the now-famous debate between the philosopher/literary critic Jacques Derrida and speech act theorist John R. Searle—whether a theory that focuses on speech acts between a speaker and hearer can in turn be applied to communicative acts embodied in texts which pass from writer to reader—and further demonstrates that the discipline legitimately and logically applies to texts.[10]

A number of biblical interpreters have recognized the hermeneutical value of speech act theory, but tend only to theorize its usefulness rather than actually incorporating it in the exegetical process. A volume of *Semiea* in 1988 was devoted to discussing how speech act theory relates to biblical criticism, and more specifically, literary criticism.[11] The majority of the essays follow this theoretical angle.[12] In his contributing essay, Martin J. Buss confirms this assessment by initially noting that the "potential contribution of speech act theory can be viewed either in terms of a theoretical reconceptualization of the process of exegesis or in terms of a refinement of exegetical procedures in their application to specific passages." Buss concludes that like most in the field, even the two essays presented by the biblical scholars Hugh C. White[13] and Daniel Patte[14] discuss the theory in terms of the former agenda.[15] Buss's assessment remains true today, as Briggs most recently confirmed.[16] Somewhat connected with this goal is the philosophical endeavor incorporating speech

9. Briggs, "Speech-Act Theory," 236.

10. Richard S. Briggs, *Words in Action: Speech Act Theory and Biblical Interpretation* (Edinburgh: T. & T. Clark, 2001), 73–86; see also idem, "Speech-Act Theory," 236–38.

11. Hugh C. White, ed., *Speech Act Theory and Biblical Criticism* (Semeia 41; Decatur: Scholars Press, 1988). For the basic focus of the collective essays, see idem, "Introduction: Speech Act Theory and Literary Criticism," *Semeia* 41 (1988): 1–24.

12. Thiselton notes that the volume is generally thought, "with the exception of one or two articles, to be like an orchestra tuning up for a concert which was never played" ("God Speaks," 97 n. 3). For a brief analysis of the main thrust of the volume, see Briggs, "Speech-Act Theory," 255–57.

13. Hugh C. White, "The Value of Speech Act Theory for Old Testament Hermeneutics," *Semeia* 41 (1988): 41–63.

14. Daniel Patte, "Speech Act Theory and Biblical Exegesis," *Semeia* 41 (1988): 85–102.

15. Martin J. Buss, "Potential and Actual Interactions between Speech Act Theory and Biblical Studies," *Semeia* 41 (1988): 125–34 (125).

16. Briggs, *Words in Action*, 103.

act theory in the quest to demonstrate how God continues to speak through ancient and diverse texts. Thiselton has done some work in this area,[17] but for Kevin J. Vanhoozer and Nicholas Wolterstorff this enterprise has been a primary concern.[18] In general, these two scholars use speech act theory to provide conceptual paradigms for understanding the ongoing function of the biblical text as divine communicative action. These philosophical undertakings have proven insightful and valuable on a number of levels, but they do not necessarily explore how speech act theory can be utilized in the interpretation of biblical texts. The aim of this study is to address Buss's second proposal. It joins with the efforts of Thiselton and Briggs in exploring the relevance of speech act theory for hermeneutics in general, and specifically in the interpretation of Isa 40–55.

Concerning limitations, speech act theory is often considered a means for viewing all language comprehensively and as applicable to every type of literature. Quite the contrary, the discipline is not a hermeneutic in and of itself and cannot account for all types of language as it comprises only a part of the larger concerns of the philosophy of language. In fact, speech act theory is an interpretation of how language functions and thus, as Stanley Fish concludes, "If speech act theory is itself an interpretation, then it cannot possibly serve as an all purpose interpretive key."[19] In addition, as with any reading strategy, speech act theory most appropriately and obviously applies to particular texts that express or correspond to certain types of speech acts.[20] Consequently, the interpreter must utilize it critically. Further, speech act theory does not provide a method that by-passes the hermeneutical issues of interpretation but rather equips the interpreter with specific tools for analyzing uses of language. At the most basic level of exegesis one must still execute all the different aspects of translation and more broadly engage in the questions

17. See, in particular, A. C. Thiselton, "Authority and Hermeneutics: Some Proposals for a More Creative Agenda," in *A Pathway into the Holy Scripture* (ed. P. E. Satterthwaite and David F. Wright; Grand Rapids: Eerdmans, 1994), 107–41; see also idem, "Communicative Action and Promise in Interdisciplinary, Biblical, and Theological Hermeneutics," in *The Promise of Hermeneutics* (ed. Roger Lundin, Clarence Walhout, and A. C. Thiselton; Carlisle: Paternoster; Grand Rapids: Eerdmans, 1999), 133–239; idem, *New Horizons*, 17–18.

18. For Vanhoozer's and Wolterstorff's work, see the Bibliography.

19. Stanley Fish, "How to Do Things with Austin and Searle: Speech-Act Theory and Literary Criticism," in *Is There a Text in This Class? The Authority of Interpretive Communities* (Cambridge, Mass.: Harvard University Press, 1980), 197–245 (244).

20. So Briggs, *Words in Action*, 9–12; Thiselton, *New Horizons*, 32–33.

of genre, literary structure, historical, literary, and cultural contexts, and so on. Speech act theory will refine the interpretive process and contribute additional tools to exegesis but does not single-handedly provide answers for every hermeneutical question.

In my opinion, speech act theory should also not be considered as another type of reading criticism; nor should it be subsumed or equated with other interpretive methods. In contrast, Buss suggests viewing "biblical form criticism as a version of speech act theory."[21] In particular, Buss sees similar interests and goals between Gene Tucker's form-critical method and speech act theory.[22] First, Buss parallels *genre* with Searle's illocutionary taxonomy. As will be discussed below, Searle proposes a classification of different types of illocutionary forces. Searle notes how genre can impact the function of a particular illocutionary act, but illocutions are never equated with genre as envisioned by form critics. With this adjustment in mind, determining a particular genre does include the analysis of the language and imagery employed. The terminology used may express an overarching illocution and thus could impact how one conceives and categorizes a unit's genre. Conversely, genre can also provide clues for identifying types of illocutions expressed within a particular unit. In addition, genre does possess a certain force or overall aim and in this way the two ideas can be related.[23] Buss also sees *setting* in line with J. L. Austin's concern for social context. The social aspect of a speech act can clarify the function of an illocution, but isolating a particular setting within these two approaches is completely different in orientation and purpose. Finally, Buss sees an affinity between *intention* and Austin's illocution and rarely his perlocution. This parallel raises at least two problems. First, the goal of seeking the text's intention in form criticism is essentially a historical endeavor. Second, as will be discussed in the following chapter, Buss displays Austin's imprecision in distinguishing between illocutions and perlocutions.[24] Buss also sees a

21. Buss, "Actual Interactions," 129.

22. Gene M. Tucker, *Form Criticism of the Old Testament* (GBS; Philadelphia: Fortress Press, 1971), cf. 11–17.

23. Without appealing to form criticism, Vanhoozer goes beyond Searle and sees genre and illocutions related, but more in the sense of the ongoing intention or function of a genre as communicative act (see Kevin J. Vanhoozer, "Semantics of Biblical Literature: Truth and Scripture's Diverse Literary Forms," in *Hermeneutics, Authority and Canon* [ed. D. A. Carson and John D. Woodbridge; Carlisle: Paternoster; Grand Rapids: Baker, 1995], 53–104; idem, *Is There a Meaning in This Text? The Bible, the Reader, and the Morality of Literary Knowledge* [Grand Rapids: Zondervan, 1998], 340–42).

24. See Buss, "Actual Interactions," 130.

relationship between ritual actions, speech, and extralinguistic action,[25] but he does not explicitly link these ideas to the form-critical method. A definite correlation exists between performative and liturgical language, which has been explored primarily from a New Testament and ecclesiastical perspective.[26] Further, the goal of determining the intention or asking what a particular passage intended to *do* in a particular setting does find some affinity with speech act theory. Nevertheless, form criticism, along with other historically oriented methods, primarily focuses on language in a descriptive sense that views it as representational—the purpose of language is simply to represent states of affairs or describe facts—whereas speech act theory views language as performative and self-involving.

As will be discussed below, speech act theory proves its unique contribution to interpretation when used to identify performative utterances or strong illocutionary acts that include linguistic and/or non-linguistic convention, self-involving extralinguistic stance and/or action, and entail transformative effects in the world. In contrast, it has been argued that speech act theory aligns with the concepts and goals of rhetorical criticism. Theorists include in their discussion on speech acts the aspect of perlocutionary effects; however, the central feature of speech act theory is the illocutionary act. Further, perlocutionary effects are dependent upon illocutionary acts, not vice versa. According to speech act theorists, meaning is found in the linguistic illocutionary act whereas the perlocution occurs outside of language and concerns the non-linguistic psychological effects of illocutionary acts transpiring within the listener/reader. Hence, the actual study of meaning centers on illocutions, not perlocutions. Attempting to determine the intended perlocutionary effects of an utterance can provide insight for interpretation, but such analysis occurs primarily through an examination of the illocutionary acts employed in language. Consequently, when utilizing speech act theory solely to

25. Here Buss implements with some minor clarifications the study of Ronald L. Grimes, "Infelicitous Performances and Ritual Criticism," *Semeia* 41 (1988): 103–22.

26. See, e.g., David Crystal, "Liturgical Language in a Sociolinguistic Perspective," in *Language and the Worship of the Church* (ed. David Jasper and R. D. C. Jasper; London: Macmillan, 1990), 120–46; Hilborn, "Performativity to Pedagogy"; Jean Ladrière, "The Performativity of Liturgical Language," *Concilium* 9 (1973): 50–62; A. P. Martinich, "Sacraments and Speech Act," *HeyJ* 16 (1975): 289–303, 405–17; Joseph J. Schaller, "Performative Language Theory: An Exercise in the Analysis of Ritual," *Worship* 62 (1988): 415–32; A. C. Thiselton, *Language, Liturgy and Meaning* (2d ed.; Grove Liturgical Study 2; Nottingham: Grove Books, 1986); Geoffrey Wainwright, "The Language of Worship," in *The Study of Liturgy* (ed. C. Jones, G. Wainwright, and E. Yarnold; London: SPCK, 1978), 465–73.

identify the persuasive dimension of a text the central notions of speech act theory are actually disregarded. Exploring the performative nature and specifically the various illocutionary acts within a biblical text extends well beyond identifying persuasive aspects in speech or texts.

In sum, speech act theory serves as a beneficial tool for exegesis set alongside other interpretive tools in the hermeneutical process. Although some parallel interests between speech act theory and other interpretive criticisms exist, the theory provides unique ways for understanding language. Coalescing speech act theory within or under another criticism discounts its own distinctive nature. Utilized in the exegetical process, the various ideas expressed by speech act theorists will provide vital and distinctive tools for biblical interpretation.

The Book of Isaiah and Chapters 40–55

Throughout much of the interpretive history of the book of Isaiah, the authorship was generally attributed to Isaiah ben Amoṣ. According to John Watts and others, it was most likely J. D. Döderlein in 1775[27]—possibly anticipated by the Jewish scholar Ibn Ezra (1100)[28]—who initially proposed that chs. 40–66 belong to the time of the exile and following, with the contents coming from an unknown prophet designated as Deutero-Isaiah.[29] This anonymous prophet is distinguished from Isaiah Amoṣ, whose speeches are typically restricted to chs. 1–39. About a century later, Bernhard Duhm further refined this idea by claiming that Deutero-Isaiah was limited to chs. 40–55, with chs. 56–66 constituting a third corpus ascribed to Trito-Isaiah.[30] Beginning with Duhm, critical scholars have predominantly assumed that the book of Isaiah contains the speeches of three historical prophets from three different time periods and geographical locations: Proto-/First Isaiah (chs. 1–39), Deutero-/Second Isaiah (chs. 40–55), and Trito-/Third Isaiah (chs. 56–66).

This tripartite scheme is no longer taken for granted. For example, Christopher Seitz asserts that such a view cannot be maintained because, first, the book contains only one superscription (1:1). Second, only one narrative describes the prophet's commission (6:1–13). Hence, 40:1–11

27. Watts cites Döderlein, *Esaias, ex recensione textus hebraei* (Altorfi, 1789).

28. Ibn Ezra (Abraham ben Meir), *Commentary of Ibn Ezra on Isaiah* (trans. M. Freidlander; 2d ed.; New York: Feldheim, 1966).

29. See John D. W. Watts, *Isaiah 1–33* (WBC 24; Waco, Tex.: Word, 1985), xxvi.

30. D. Bernard Duhm, *Das Buch Jesaia* (2d ed.; HKAT 3/1; Göttingen: Vandenhoeck & Ruprecht, 1902), cf. xiii–xiv, xvii–xix.

is not a prophetic commission for a Deutero-Isaiah, but must be interpreted in the light of chs. 1–39. Third, no literary boundaries can be clearly drawn between the three historical-critical Isaiahs.[31] In fact, the "whole notion of Second and Third Isaiah depends in no small part on there being a clear First Isaiah. Such an Isaiah is not to be found. Isaiah 1–39 is an extremely complex collection of material, with a diverse background."[32] Consequently, nothing of a new Second Isaiah in chs. 40–55 nor a Third Isaiah in chs. 56–66 exists.[33] Moreover, any picture of a clear-cut tripartite structure dissolves immediately with ch. 1 as it encapsulates the whole story of the book consisting of Zion's judgment and restoration.[34] In addition to all this, it is no longer possible to assume that the prophecies in chs. 40–55 have a Babylonian setting.[35]

Most likely beginning with Brevard S. Childs's canonical reading of Isaiah, the unity of the book has been a central topic of discussion among critical scholars.[36] The question though remains: What are the major divisions in Isaiah, if there are any? Dividing between chs. 1–33 and 34–66 has merit.[37] This division is supported by 1QIsa[a] with its three-line space at the end of ch 33. Further, chs. 34 and 35 summarize the concerns of the two halves as they look back and point forward to future judgment and restoration respectively. However, chs. 36–39 return to the issue of judgment and, specifically, Judah's future exile in Babylon (cf. 39:5–8). Chapters 40 and following assume that this judgment has already taken place and now has come to an end with the promise of salvation and restoration at hand. Thus, a definite break occurs between chs. 39 and 40. There is not, however, as clear a demarcation between chs. 55 and 56 as

31. Christopher R. Seitz, "Isaiah 1–66: Making Sense of the Whole," in *Reading and Preaching the Book of Isaiah* (ed. Christopher R. Seitz; Philadelphia: Fortress), 105–26 (109–10).

32. Ibid., 111.

33. Ibid., 117.

34. See ibid., 113–16.

35. See Hans M. Barstad, "On the So-Called Babylonian Literary Influence in Second Isaiah," *SJOT* 2 (1987): 90–110; idem, *A Way in the Wilderness: The "Second Exodus" in the Message of Second Isaiah* (JSSM 12; Manchester: University of Manchester, 1989); see also Ronald E. Clements, "Zion as Symbol and Political Reality: A Central Isaianic Quest," in *Studies in the Book of Isaiah* (Festschrift Willem A. M. Beuken; ed. J. van Ruiten and M. Vervenne; BETL 132; Leuven: Leuven University Press/Peeters, 1997), 3–17.

36. Brevard S. Childs, *Introduction to the Old Testament as Scripture* (Philadelphia: Fortress, 1979), 311–38.

37. E.g. Marvin Sweeney, "The Book of Isaiah as Prophetic Torah," in *New Visions of Isaiah* (ed. Roy F. Melugin and Marvin A. Sweeney; JSOTSup 214; Sheffield: Sheffield Academic Press, 1996), 50–67.

recent Isaianic scholarship has been suggesting. For instance, the first occurrence of the plural עבדים, characteristic of chs. 56–66, comes already in 54:17bα. Nevertheless, there are clear literary connections between chs. 40 and 55[38] as well as central themes running throughout chs. 40 and following that also appear in ch. 55. Most prominently, the theme of the absolute efficacy of Yahweh's word occurs throughout chs. 40–55 which begins the block (40:1–11) and comes full circle and is highlighted in ch. 55 (cf. v. 11). Further, 56:1 suggests a new beginning that also combines the central motifs of chs. 1–39 and 40–55.[39] Thus, chs. 40–55 can be understood as a major section. Yet, these chapters are integrally related to and functioning with what proceeds and follows in the whole of Isaiah.

Interpreting Isaiah 40–55

The current interpretive landscape of Isaianic studies is in a state of excitement and change.[40] This may be especially true with the study of chs. 40 and following. This shift is directly related and proportionate to the influence of more literary ways of viewing the text.[41] The appearance of James Muilenburg's and Claus Westermann's commentaries on Isa 40–66 marked a major transition point towards the contemporary trends in Isaianic research. Westermann's form-critical analysis represents the

38. See, e.g., Roy F. Melugin, *The Formation of Isaiah 40–55* (BZAW 141; Berlin: de Gruyter, 1976), 86–87.

39. Cf. Rolf Rendtorff, "Isaiah 56:1 as a Key to the Formation of the Book of Isaiah," in *Canon and Theology: Overtures to an Old Testament Theology* (trans. M. Kohl; OBT; Minneapolis: Fortress Press, 1993), 181–89.

40. For surveys of the current research conducted on Isaiah and specifically chs. 40–55, see for instance Hans-Jürgen Hermisson, "Neue Literatur zu Deuterojesaja (I/II)," *TRu* 65 (2000): 237–84, 379–430; Eugene H. Merrill, "The Literary Character of Isaiah 40–55" (Parts 1 and 2), *BSac* 144 (1987): 24–43, 144–56; Rolf Rendtorff, "The Book of Isaiah—A Complex Unity: Synchronic and Diachronic Reading," in *Prophecy and Prophets: The Diversity of Contemporary Issues in Scholarship* (ed. Yehoshua Gitay; SBLSS; Atlanta: Scholars Press, 1997), 109–28; Marvin A. Sweeney, "The Book of Isaiah in Recent Research," *CRBS* 1 (1993): 141–62; Marvin E. Tate, "The Book of Isaiah in Recent Study," in *Forming Prophetic Literature: Essays on Isaiah and the Twelve* (Festschrift John D. W. Watts; ed. James W. Watts and P. R. House; JSOTSup 235; Sheffield: Sheffield Academic Press, 1996), 22–56.

41. Seitz most recently observed that "*Isaianic interpretation is changing precisely to the degree that the role of literary context is regarded as a crucial integer in the interpretation of individual passages*" ("'You are my Servant, You are the Israel in whom I will be glorified': The Servant Songs and the Effect of Literary Context in Isaiah," *CTJ* 39 [2004]: 117–34 [124–25]).

dominant way of viewing and interpreting the biblical material since Hermann Gunkel.[42] Building on other form-critical studies and especially the work of Joachim Begrich[43] and Eberhard von Waldow,[44] Westermann identified independent small units within the corpus and analyzed each of them separately and according to the typical speech forms considered common to the prophet and his community. Westermann also understood the units in Isa 40–55 as arranged deliberately and orderly through a long redactional process. He additionally recognized that there were several longer literary poems (e.g. 49:14–26; 51:9–52:3) that extended beyond the classic form-critical assumptions.[45]

Mulienburg conceived Isa 40–66 as a lengthy literary composition.[46] The poem contains different forms, but more often than not a fusion of literary types has occurred. The blending of these forms has been intentional towards the production of a literary whole. Rather than a collection of small unrelated oracles, the poem is comprised of strophes or subordinate units that are intimately related to and building upon one another forming a coherent piece from beginning to end.[47] Further, Muilenburg rejected the form-critical assumption of typicality and thus highlighted the uniqueness and creative nature of the material. From these postulates, Muilenburg analyzed the various rhetorical and poetical devices that composed the various strophes of the poem.

Both Westermann and Muilenburg have provided much of the impetus for the current discussions on the literary unity of Isaiah as well as on the interpretation of the various units in light of one another. The recognition of the literary dimension of Isaiah and its interpretive value has only gained momentum among scholars since their work. The nature of Isa 40–55 leads the interpreter not necessarily to choose one approach over another, but rather to incorporate the insights of each with certain modifications and adjustments. In contrast to the form-critical assumptions, rhetorical critics focus on the literary cohesiveness and persuasive

42. Claus Westermann, *Isaiah 40–66* (trans. D. M. G. Stalker; OTL; Philadelphia: Westminster, 1969); trans. of *Das Buch Jesaia, 40–66* (DATD 19; Göttingen: Vandenhoeck & Ruprecht, 1966). See also idem, *Sprache und Struktur der Prophetie Deuterojesajas Mit einer Literaturübersicht "Hauptlinien der Deuterojesajaforschung von 1964–1979" zusammengestellt und kommentiert von Andreas Richter* (CThM 11; Stuttgart: Calwer, 1981).

43. Joachim Begrich, *Studien zu Deuterojesaja* (TBü 20; Munich: Kaiser, 1963).

44. Eberhard von Waldow, "Anlass und Hintergrund der Verkündigung des Deuterojesaja," (Ph.D. diss., Bonn, 1953).

45. See Westermann, *Isaiah 40–66*, 27–30.

46. J. Muilenburg, "The Book of Isaiah Chapters 40–66," *IB* 5:381–773 (391).

47. Ibid., 5:385.

strategy of a biblical text and book.[48] Rhetorical studies such as Muilenburg's, Richard J. Clifford's,[49] and Yehoshua Gitay's[50] on Isa 40–55 have provided significant perspectives towards understanding its formation and intended meaning. This reading strategy correctly focuses the exegete on the text itself to analyze the way it has been artfully composed. This is accomplished by examining the structure of the argument as well as identifying the various rhetorical strategies and literary devices employed while contemplating their function within a unit. Thus, through a careful analysis of the sequential development of the unit along with its literary devices, one can determine how the text guides the interpretive process. Nevertheless, Muilenburg's holistic composition hypothesis does not hold up against the data. John Goldingay correctly concludes that Muilenburg's literary perspective seems more impressionistic than factual while Westermann's form-critical ideas provide a certain amount of control to such impressionism.[51] Thus, rather than considering the various divisions as strophes forming a poem, the material reflects an incorporation of various oral speech forms. Similar to Roy F. Melugin's[52] and Clifford's[53] adjustments of Muilenburg, the identified strophes are rather units possessing structures and genres (as with Westermann). Yet, at the same time, they include unique and creative elements (as with Muilenburg).

Determining the relationship between these various units, however, poses a host of interpretive difficulties. The nature of the book of Isaiah is predominantly visionary (cf. 1:1) and its visionary nature reaches a climax in chs. 40–55.[54] Within these chapters different themes, images,

48. A major turning point in biblical studies was prompted by Muilenburg's presidential address at the annual Society of Biblical Literature meeting in 1968 ("Form Criticism and Beyond," *JBL* 88 [1969]: 1–18).

49. Richard J. Clifford, *Fair Spoken and Persuading: An Interpretation of Second Isaiah* (New York: Paulist, 1984); idem, "Isaiah, Book of (Second Isaiah)," *ABD* 3:490–501.

50. Cf. Yehoshua Gitay, *Prophecy and Persuasion: A Study of Isaiah 40–48* (FTL 14; Bonn: Linguistica Biblica, 1981).

51. John Goldingay, *Isaiah 40–55* (London: T. & T. Clark, 2006). (Note that the present work made use of the unpublished version of Goldingay's commentary.)

52. See Melugin, *Isaiah 40–55*, 5–10, 87–89; idem, "Deutero-Isaiah and Form Criticism," *VT* 21 (1971): 326–37; idem, "Muilenburg, Form Criticism, and Theological Exegesis," in *Encounter with the Text: Form and History in the Hebrew Bible* (ed. Martin J. Buss; SBLSS 8; Missoula, Mont.: Scholars Press, 1979), 91–99.

53. Clifford, *Fair Spoken*, 34–37; idem, "Rhetorical Criticism in the Exegesis of Hebrew Poetry," in *SBL Seminar Papers, 1980* (ed. Kent H. Richards; SBLSP 19; Chico, Calif.: Scholars Press, 1980), 17–28.

54. Scholars typically identify Isaiah as a "vision" due to the superscription in 1:1. However, it is clear that the book cannot be regarded as a vision in total (e.g.

identities, and voices appear, disappear, and reappear without much prior notice or explanation. In addition, the nature of a number of these entities is flexible and multivalent. Interpreters over the years have explored various ways to penetrate the myriad of dense and mysterious ambiguities and paradoxes that the text presents. Predominantly they have either treated each passage as separate and unrelated to its surrounding literary context (as with Westermann's form-critical emphasis) or considered the chapters as comprising a series of redactional layers (as with Westermann's redactional view). Of recent date the latter approach has found much appeal among scholars who have presented various redactional postulations. For some, the goal centers on segmenting passages one from another with the aim of identifying, clarifying, and resolving the complexities raised by the text. For example, Reinhard G. Kratz sees the "final canonical form" (*kanonische Endgestalt*) of Isa 40–55 as the interpretive problem, not the solution.[55] The juxtaposition of the various passages produces unresolved ambiguities, specifically concerning those who actually perform particular actions and/or who are being acted upon.[56] For Kratz, discovering the redactional layering and intention of this randomly selected material provides the answer for understanding Deutero-Isaiah.

Such inquiry, though, is founded on the modern presupposition that authors remain consistent in style, language, and point of view when composing a written document. Hence, evidence of another hand or author is discovered when one identifies so-called unnecessary repetitions, syntactical roughness, change in style, diversity in theological perspective, and so forth. Isolating different stages of composition and assigning corresponding dates on the basis of such negative criteria is grounded in a flawed modern optimism of consistency. It is naive to assume that a writer's or a prophet's goal was to remain consistent at all costs. Conversely, such assumptions do not allow for individual uniqueness and diversity. The criteria implemented are also subjective with no objective means available to test and verify the various proposals. Further, Childs,[57] Edgar W. Conrad,[58] Melugin,[59] among others, have

chs. 7, 36–39). Further, it is questionable whether or not 1:1 functions as the title for all of Isaiah (see John Goldingay, "Isaiah I 1 and II 1," *VT* 48 [1998]: 326–32).

55. Reinhard G. Kratz, *Kyros im Deuterojesaja-Buch: Redaktionsgeschichtliche Untersuchungen zu Entstehung und Theologie von 40–55* (FAT 1; Tübingen: J. C. B. Mohr [Paul Siebeck], 1991), 10.

56. See, e.g., Kratz, *Kyros*, 4–5.

57. See Childs, *Introduction*, 325–38; idem, *Isaiah* (OTL; Louisville, Ky.: Westminster John Knox, 2001), 3–4.

persuasively argued that the compiler(s)/redactor(s) have not left clear marks or indicators that allow for the identification of various historical layers. More problematically, such an approach dismantles the potential understanding of the central themes and message of Isa 40–55. As evidenced in the multiple redaction studies on Isaiah, identifying different stages of growth often produces a number of hypothetical historical scenarios, segmented messages, and chameleon-type identities, all of which cannot be substantiated and even generally agreed upon. For instance, according to the studies of Kratz,[60] Odil H. Steck,[61] and Henning G. Reventlow,[62] the identity of the servant of Yahweh and the accompanying message changes from layer to layer, which directly depends upon the various dates assigned to the conceived redactional process.

Despite the difficulties raised by the final form of Isa 40–55, interpreting the material as it presently stands remains more profitable and deals more concretely with the text itself. Thus, this study understands the contents of these chapters as arranged deliberately and orderly (as Westermann points out), producing an overarching intentional message. The various units within these chapters reflect oral speech forms, but they have been brought together to form artful wholes of varying lengths. Chapters 41–44 seem to contain shorter units which correspond with form-critical assumptions. However, as Goldingay has demonstrated, the units found in these chapters often form coherent literary sequences or spirals.[63] Perhaps these shorter divisions were originally independent, but as they stand now they belong to and form sizeable literary wholes

58. See specifically Edgar W. Conrad, *Reading Isaiah* (OBT; Minneapolis: Fortress, 1991), cf. 12–27; idem, "Prophet, Redactor and Audience: Reforming the Notion of Isaiah's Formation," in Melugin and Sweeney, eds., *New Visions of Isaiah*, 306–26.

59. See in particular Melugin, *Isaiah 40–55*, 82, 175; idem, "The Book of Isaiah and the Construction of Meaning," in *Writing and Reading the Scroll of Isaiah: Studies of an Interpretive Tradition* (ed. Craig C. Broyles and Craig A. Evans; VTSup 70; 2 vols.; Leiden: Brill, 1997), 1:39–51.

60. See Kratz, *Kyros*, cf. 128–47, 175–91, 209–17.

61. See Odil H. Steck, *Gottesknecht und Zion: Gesammelte Aufsätze zu Deuterojesaja* (FAT 4; Tübingen: J. C. B. Mohr [Paul Siebeck], 1992), 3–44, 149–72.

62. Henning Graf Reventlow, "Basic Issues in the Interpretation of Isaiah 53," in *Jesus and the Suffering Servant: Isaiah 53 and Christian Origins* (ed. William H. Bellinger, Jr., and William R. Farmer; Harrisburg, Pa.: Trinity, 1998), 23–38. See also Magne Saebø, "Vom Individuellen zum Kollektiven," in *Schöpfung und Befreiung* (ed. Rainer Albertz, Friedemann W. Golka, and Jürgen Kegler; Festchrift Claus Westermann; Stuttgart: Calwer, 1989), 116–25.

63. Goldingay, *Isaiah 40–55*; see, for example, idem, "The Arrangement of Isaiah XLI–XLV," *VT* 29 (1979): 289–99.

(similar to Muilenburg). The obvious arrangement and formation of these artful wholes direct the interpreter away from the improbable notion that they were composed from originally separate and unrelated shorter units.[64] In addition, Chris Franke and others have demonstrated that Isa 40–55 contains lengthier units (e.g. ch. 47) that were originally composed as they now appear (as Westermann recognized).[65] The presence of these longer poems further suggests that one should expect similar length poems throughout the corpus.[66]

In conclusion, this study approaches Isa 40–55 as an artful composition made up of poems of varying length. These larger units have been intentionally brought together in such a way as to create themes, contrasts, beginnings and endings, as well as ambiguities, tensions, peculiarities, and paradoxes. This study engages with these characteristics along with the spiral nature of the text and at the same time traces its sequential linear flow. These notions directly impact the interpretive process as the immediate and overall context are considered intentional and indispensable for understanding Isa 40–55. Further, the structure, genre, literary and rhetorical devices are all considered important guides in the interpretive process. From this methodological perspective, this study additionally explores and utilizes the central concepts of speech act theory to examine the performative nature and function of Isa 40–55.

Speech Act Theory and Isaiah 40–55

Roy Melugin asserts that the explanation of the original meaning of a passage stops short of the total interpretive procedure. In order to complete the process, he appeals to the performative use of language as a way for contemporary faith communities to participate actively in the world of the text. For Melugin, explanation of the text prepares and facilitates its performative use.[67] Descriptive explanation of the original intent or function of an ancient text is obviously important to any interpretive conclusions. However, as Melugin agrees, explanation alone does not provide the way to performative application as one must understand exactly how to conceive and determine such self-involvement. Moreover,

64. *Pace* Melugin, *Isaiah 40–55*, 81–82, 175.

65. See Chris Franke, *Isaiah 46, 47, and 48: A New Literary-Critical Reading* (Biblical and Judaic Studies 3; Winona Lake, Ind.: Eisenbrauns, 1994).

66. See, e.g., Marjo C. A. Korpel's discussion on the compositional unity of ch. 55 in "Metaphors in Isaiah LV," *VT* 46 (1996): 43–55.

67. Melugin, "Figurative Speech and the Reading of Isaiah 1 as Scripture," in Melugin and Sweeney, eds., *New Visions of Isaiah*, 282–305 (cf. 301–5).

speech act theory provides interpretive angles for identifying and understanding illocutionary acts occurring in the text itself. Performative utterances occur within the world of the text between speakers and hearers and, in other instances, the text itself addresses the reader and invites self-involvement.

Much of the language of Isa 40–55 can be seen as performative as it contains various types of illocutionary acts and elicits the self-involvement of the hearer/reader. This being so, the notions expressed within speech act theory become an important and crucial way to gain further insight into Isa 40–55. As mentioned above, the dominant use of speech act theory has focused on the perlocutionary effects or persuasive consequences of language. In contrast, speech act theorists claim that meaning is found in the illocutionary act while perlocutions derive from such utterances. I will focus on the performative dimension of chs. 40–55 and specifically on the illocutionary acts, their intended perlocutionary effects, and the self-involving nature of the text.

This study sets out to show the usefulness of speech act theory for interpreting the Old Testament material and in particular Isa 40–55. I will initially conduct this investigation by first presenting the fundamental principles of speech act theory. I will follow this in the second chapter with a survey of Old Testament studies utilizing speech act theory. In Chapters 3 and 4 I will focus on implementing the central concepts of speech act theory in the interpretation of Isa 40–55. In the third chapter, I propose a literary and prophetic strategy of this section followed by an interpretation of 41:21–29, 49:1–6, 50:4–10, and 52:13–53:12 in Chapter 4. The significance of these passages goes without saying, but they also integrally function within and succinctly express the overall prophetic strategy and performative nature of Isa 40–55.

The central illocution of Isa 40–55 is Yahweh's illocutionary act of the Cyrus event which is referred to throughout chs. 40–48. This section contains various persuasive appeals to the addressees as well as readers, but the primary focus of these arguments is grounded in and derives from Yahweh's illocution. In other words, Yahweh's speech act actually creates and substantiates his perlocutionary appeals. The central perlocutionary intention of Yahweh's illocutionary act aims at the audience's confession of Yahweh alone. Isaiah 40–55 envisions the people of God comprised of a confessional community. Individuals witnessing to Yahweh's supreme power actualize their becoming part of the people of God through their confession of him alone.

The manifold suggestions and debates over the various unidentifiable entities occurring throughout chs. 40–55 strongly suggest that they are intentionally elusive and ambiguous. Accepting and embracing the tensions, oddities, and difficulties raised by the final form of the text and reading it as it presently stands, an openness appears that naturally draws in the addressees/readers and invites them to identify with and become self-involved with it. Such openness especially arises with the servant passages and in particular the final three. These units not only contain illocutionary utterances, but also include the dimension of self-involvement. Engaging with these servant passages, the addressees/readers *involve* them*selves* and become the speaker who utters and confesses illocutionary acts that thereby commits them to certain extralinguistic entailments and obligations. In short, the Cyrus event intends to prompt the addressees to confess Yahweh alone and thereby adopt the role of his servant and become Israel, the people of God. In order to move towards these conclusions I will first begin by exploring the core notions of speech act theory all with an eye on its usefulness for biblical interpretation.

Chapter 1

SPEECH ACT THEORY AND THE HERMENEUTIC OF SELF-INVOLVEMENT

The phenomenon of language expressing action has been acknowledged, at least in a subsidiary sense, for centuries, but formal analyses of language as communicative action were not produced until the twentieth century. Inceptive notions of speech act theory are found in the work of A. Reinach (1883–1917)[1] while there are also clear antecedents in the later work of Ludwig Wittgenstein[2] among others. Nevertheless, J. L. Austin and his student John R. Searle have been identified as the principal linguistic philosophers providing the foundational understanding of speech act theory proper as it is known today. Currently, speech act theory no longer remains confined to a minor area of the philosophical inquiry of language, but embodies a vast and expanding field within linguistics. Along with Searle, linguistic philosophers such as William P. Alston, François Récanti, Daniel Vanderveken, among a host of others, continue to write on the subject. As in any area of study, speech act theory is not without controversy and disagreement; yet, linguistic philosophers universally recognize its central premises.[3] Further, even in the

1. See Barry Smith, "Towards a History of Speech Act Theory," in *Speech Acts, Meaning and Intentions: Critical Approaches to the Philosophy of John R. Searle* (ed. Armin Burkhardt; Berlin: de Gruyter, 1990), 29–61.

2. See specifically Ludwig Wittgenstein, *Philosophical Investigations* (trans. G. E. M. Anscombe; 3d ed.; Englewood Cliffs: Prentice–Hall, 1958), e.g., I §§23–25; 54; 491; II: ix, 189; II: x, 190–92.

3. Even in a more negative critique of Austin's and Searle's versions of speech act theory, Armin Burkhardt ("Speech Act Theory—The Decline of a Paradigm," in idem, ed., *Speech Acts, Meaning and Intentions*, 91–128 [92]) confesses that "it cannot seriously be denied that linguistic utterances create social facts, relations and commitments and, therefore, bring forth actions (which one may choose to call 'illocutions'). Hence, the question is not whether linguistic utterances are actions, but how linguistic (and other) actions come into being. It would, therefore, be rather silly to deny that utterances can be ascribed illocutionary forces, that they can be understood as actions of certain types and that there really are linguistic and non-linguistic actions."

midst of expansion, refinements, and disagreements, the work of Austin and Searle remain foundational in its formulation.

This chapter divides into three major sections. The first section briefly examines the basic notions of speech act theory as envisioned by Austin and Searle, respectively. The second section discusses the current issues among speech act theorists that are relative to its use in biblical interpretation. The final section will briefly examine the work of Donald Evans, Anthony C. Thiselton, and Richard S. Briggs, and concentrate on their understanding and development of a hermeneutic of self-involvement as well as their interpretive use of speech act theory.

Seminal Notions of Speech Act Theory

Speech Act Theory According to J. L. Austin

For much of his career, J. L. Austin (1911–1960) devoted himself to exploring the nature of performative utterances. Austin's most articulated development was presented in his William James Lectures at Harvard University in 1955, subsequently published in the small book *How To Do Things With Words*.[4] This work takes on the nature of an exploration in speech acts, or even a work in progress, that focuses on performative and constative utterances. In general, Austin sets out to re-focus the then-current study of language from words to sentences. He challenged the so-called "descriptive fallacy," the overarching assumption "that the business of a 'statement' can only be to 'describe' some state of affairs, or to 'state some fact,' which it must do either truly or falsely."[5] Austin acknowledged the existence of such statements, but other utterances may not be statements at all, they are "pseudo-statements." Austin, thus, distinguished two types of utterances: *constatives* and *performatives*. The former simply describe, record, or impart information whereas the latter indicate "that the issuing of the utterance is the performing of an action —it is not normally thought of as just saying something."[6] This leads Austin to formulate his thesis: "to *say* something is to *do* something; or in which *by* saying or *in* saying something we are doing something."[7] This phenomenon is illustrated in his classic example, to say "I do" during the course of a marriage ceremony does not report on a marriage, that is, "we are marrying." Rather, it is an action performed by the one

4. J. L. Austin, *How To Do Things With Words* (ed. J. O. Urmson and Marina Sbisà; 2d ed.; Cambridge, Mass.: Harvard University Press, 1975). For his other work in relation to speech act theory, see the Bibliography.

5. Austin, *Things with Words*, 1.

6. Ibid., 6–7.

7. Ibid., 12.

uttering it that indulges in the act that actually realizes the marriage relationship, that is, "marrying."

With these issues outlined, Austin immediately begins to demonstrate how the performative–constative distinction *cannot* be maintained and starts with a further analysis of performative utterances. Austin initially turns to discuss the "appropriate circumstances" of performatives. To determine such circumstances, Austin first presents several ways a performative utterance is infelicitous or unhappy. Austin classifies two main types of infelicities: *misfires* and *abuses*. With the former, a purported act or attempt is not successfully performed or is not accepted (e.g. someone who is not formally recognized conducts a marriage ceremony). With the latter, the act *is* achieved but not properly (e.g. an insincere promise). The problem, though, is that these same infelicities also apply to constatives.[8]

Regarding felicitous or happy performatives, Austin proposes a number of rules, beginning with a two-part rule regarding the necessity of *non-linguistic conventions*:

> (A.1) There *must exist an accepted conventional procedure* having a certain *conventional effect*, that procedure to include the uttering of certain words by certain persons in certain circumstances, and further, (A.2) the particular persons and circumstances in a given case must be appropriate for the invocation of the particular procedure invoked.[9]

This notion of convention leads Austin to an additional conclusion that "for a certain utterance to be happy, certain statements have *to be true*."[10] Thus, Austin identifies an inherent element of truth-value in successful performative utterances, as they correspond to facts directly related to the action of the utterance.[11] At the same time, he begins to create a blurring between the constative and performative.

From here, Austin explores ways to define more clearly what exactly constitutes a performative utterance. He begins by inquiring if grammatical or lexicographical criteria exist for distinguishing a performative. Specifically, Austin explores the verbs in the first person singular present indicative active along with verbs that explicitly mark the precise action performed in the issuing of the utterance. Additionally he discusses the insertion of the word *hereby* to elucidate a performative. However, he concludes that no such grammatical criteria or formula exists.[12] Austin, though, presses on and returns to the former criterion. He thus "reduces"

8. Ibid., 20.
9. Ibid., 14–15 (italics mine).
10. Ibid., 45.
11. See ibid., 45–47.
12. See ibid., 53–66.

performatives to these occurrences and identifies them as *explicit performatives*. Performatives, then, are such utterances as "I promise...," "I name...," "I apologize...," and so on. Austin also distinguishes this restricted performative category from *implicit* or *primary performatives*—which do not contain an explicit verb such as "I shall be there"—from statements such as "I promise that I shall be there." Even here, Austin again concludes that such a criterion ultimately fails. He further concludes that the performative–constative distinction cannot be maintained, ultimately culminating in his assertion: "whenever I 'say' anything (except perhaps a mere exclamation like 'damn' or 'ouch') I shall be performing both locutionary and illocutionary acts."[13] In other words, uttering a descriptive statement (constative) is just as much performing an act as making a marriage vow, making a promise or giving a warning (performatives). This performative–constative distinction/blurring phenomenon, then, becomes Austin's "problem" that he seeks to resolve in the second half of his book.

Austin proposes a "fresh" attempt to solve this dilemma by presenting his view of speech acts. For Austin, the total speech act consists of three kinds of stratified acts: *locutionary*, *illocutionary*, and *perlocutionary*. Austin's goal here centers on isolating and exploring the nature of illocutionary acts which corresponds to his previous notions on performatives. The *locutionary act* is the act *of* saying something as with the constative. It "is roughly equivalent to uttering a certain sentence with a certain sense and reference, which again is roughly equivalent to 'meaning' in the traditional sense."[14] Locutions also comprise three parts: *phonetic*, the act of uttering certain noises; *phatic*, the act of uttering certain vocables or words; and *rhetic*, the act of using those vocables with a certain more-or-less definite sense and reference.[15]

The *illocutionary act* is the "performance of an act *in* saying something as opposed to an act *of* saying something."[16] Illocutionary acts include "informing, ordering, warning, undertaking, etc, i.e., utterances which have a certain (conventional) force."[17] Thus, "the illocutionary act is a conventional act: an act done as conforming to a convention."[18] As with Austin's discussion on performatives, it is the uttering of a locution accompanied by a certain conventional force—for example, rules, regulations, legal provisions or settings, officially recognized customs or

13. Ibid., 133.
14. Ibid., 109.
15. Ibid., 95.
16. Ibid., 99–100.
17. Ibid., 109.
18. Ibid., 105.

practices—which allows for that saying to *count as* an illocutionary act.[19] Similarly with performatives and constatives, uncertainty permeates Austin's entire program in the distinguishing between locutions and illocutions.[20]

Perlocutions constitute the final stage of the speech act with the *perlocutionary act* consisting in "what we bring about or achieve *by* saying something, such as convincing, persuading, deterring, and even, say, surprising or misleading."[21] Such an act exists because saying "something will often, or even normally, produce certain consequential effects upon the feelings, thoughts, or actions of the audience, or of the speaker, or of other persons: and it may be done with the design, intention, or purpose of producing them."[22]

I will return to explore more of Austin's notions of speech act theory, but the above discussion presents the basis of his program. What Austin formulated in his little book essentially provides the groundwork for later linguistic philosophers further to explore and develop speech act theory.

Speech Act Theory According to John R. Searle

It has principally been Searle who has built upon, refined, and advanced Austin's understanding of speech acts. Searle's underlying thesis for his whole speech act program is: "Speaking a language is engaging in a (highly complex) rule-governed form of behavior. To learn and master a language is (*inter alia*) to learn and to have mastered these rules."[23] Thus, speaking a language consists of performing speech acts which are made possible by and performed in accordance with certain rules. Following Austin's lead, Searle further diminishes any distinction between performatives and constatives. Speaking a language, then, "is performing speech acts, acts such as making statements, giving commands, asking questions, making promises, and so on."[24] Also, meaning, as Austin proposed earlier, is not found in the word, symbol, or sentence, but in the speech act.

Searle also approves of Austin's conception of illocutionary acts, but he does not accept his distinction between locutions and illocutions.

19. For Austin's discussion on convention, see ibid., 103–4, 107, 115, 119, 121, 128.

20. See, e.g., ibid., 98–99.

21. Ibid., 109.

22. Ibid., 101.

23. John R. Searle, *Speech Acts: An Essay in the Philosophy of Language* (Cambridge: Cambridge University, 1969), 12.

24. Searle, *Speech Acts*, 16 (italics mine).

Searle's examination of Austin's notions here addresses one of his severest criticisms while at the same time begins to clarify and legitimize the notion of the illocutionary act.[25] For Searle, a distinction between locutions and illocutions only accounts for those cases where the meaning of a sentence is force-neutral. However, "no sentence is completely force-neutral," as with Austin's rhetic act, and so locutionary acts are in reality illocutionary acts of one kind or another. Thus, every "sentence has some illocutionary force-potential, if only of a very broad kind, built into its meaning."[26] Further and also in contrast to Austin, meaning and force are both inseparable and correlated. What needs distinguishing, though, is "the illocutionary act from the propositional act—that is, the act of expressing the proposition (a phrase which is neutral as to illocutionary force)."[27] The necessity for such a distinction "is that the identity conditions of the propositional act are not the same as the identity conditions of the total illocutionary act, since the same propositional act can occur in all sorts of different illocutionary acts."[28] These clarifications and adjustments lead Searle to compose an alternative conception of the total speech act:

Utterance acts:	include Austin's phonetic and phatic acts that entail uttering words and sentences.
Propositional acts:	referring and predicating.
Illocutionary acts:	statements, questions, promises, or commands.
Perlocutionary acts:	the consequences of an utterance that entail effects on the actions, feelings, attitudes, beliefs, and behavior of hearers.[29]

25. John R. Searle, "Austin on Locutionary and Illocutionary Acts," in *Essays on J. L. Austin* (ed. Isaiah Berlin et al.; Oxford: Clarendon, 1973), 141–59. Austin's distinction between locutions and illocutions has prompted a number of reactions with the more negative responses offered by L. Jonathan Cohen, "Do Illocutionary Forces Exist?," in *Symposium on J. L. Austin* (ed. K. T. Fann; London: Routledge & Kegan Paul, 1969), 420–44; Max Black, "Austin on Performatives," in Fann, ed., *Symposium on J. L. Austin*, 401–11. Others have attempted to maintain Austin's locutionary idea with certain alterations: L. W. Forguson, "Locutionary and Illocutionary Acts," in Berlin et al. eds., *Essays on J. L. Austin*, 160–85; Mats Furberg, "Meaning and Illocutionary Force," in Fann, ed., *Symposium on J. L. Austin*, 445–68; François Récanati, *Meaning and Force: The Pragmatics of Performative Utterances* (Cambridge: Cambridge University, 1987), 236–60; P. F. Strawson, "Austin and "Locutionary Meaning,'" in Berlin et al., eds., *Essays on J. L. Austin*, 46–68.

26. Searle, "Illocutionary Acts," 148.

27. Ibid., 155.

28. Ibid., 155–56.

29. See Searle, *Speech Acts*, 22–26. It is important to reiterate that the concept of a *locution* does not have any place in Searle's scheme. To use the term in an

In the formulation of his speech act theory, Searle concentrates on the nature of illocutionary acts. Correlated with his earlier discussion, "the character of the whole illocutionary act is entirely determined by the nature of its illocutionary force and propositional content."[30] Two elements comprise the syntactical structure of a sentence: *illocutionary force indicators* (typically denoted by the variable *F*) and *proposition indicators* (denoted by *p*). For instance, with the sentence "I promise that I will come," the illocutionary force indicator or prefix is "I promise" (*F*) and the propositional content is "that I will come" (*p*). The prefix "shows how the proposition is to be taken" and functions to make explicit the illocutionary force or what illocutionary act the speaker is performing with the utterance. Other indicators also include "word order, stress, intonation contour, punctuation, the mood of the verb, and the so-called performative verbs."[31]

Significant for his general understanding of speech acts, Searle distinguishes between two rules that ultimately comprise the foundation of his theory: *regulative* and *constitutive*. The former rules regulate antecendently or independently existing forms of behavior, such as rules of etiquette involving inter-personal relationships or rules for driving on a particular side of the road. The latter rules not only regulate but also create and define new forms of behavior. For instance, the rules of football or chess do not merely regulate the game, they actually create the very possibility of playing such games. The activities of these games are *constituted* by acting in accordance with the appropriate rules. Thus, such-and-such a position on a chessboard *counts as* a checkmate, or when a football team possesses the ball and during a play crosses an opponent's goal line, it *counts as* a touchdown. *Regulative rules* characteristically have the form of "Do X" or "If Y do X" whereas *constitutive*

Austinian sense when talking about Searle's view of speech acts can cause some confusion and even distortion. Briggs helpfully correlates Austin's locution and Searle's framework in a general way, as he notes that among "non-philosophers appealing to speech act theory, I judge that Searle's 'propositional act' is viewed as a kind of limiting case of an illocution, and that his 'utterance act' is what is meant by talk of a 'locutionary act.' It is probably not necessary, for our purposes, to be more precise than this" (Briggs, *Words in Action*, 47). Concerning this issue of locutions and illocutions see further Jennifer Hornsby, "Things Done with Words," in *Human Agency: Language, Duty, and Value* (Festschrift J. O. Urmson; ed. Jonathan Dancy, J. M. E. Moravcsik, and C. C. W. Taylor; Stanford: Stanford University Press, 1988), 27–46, 283–88; Récanati, *Meaning and Force*, 236–66.

30. J. R. Searle and Daniel Vanderveken, *Foundations of Illocutionary Logic* (Cambridge: Cambridge University Press, 1985), 8.

31. Searle, *Speech Acts*, 30.

rules have the form "X counts as Y," or more generally, "X counts as Y in context C." All this leads Searle to expand his thesis that "language is performing acts according to rules":

> The form this hypothesis will take is that the semantic structure of a language may be regarded as a conventional realization of a series of sets of underlying constitutive rules, and that speech acts are acts characteristically performed by uttering expressions in accordance with these sets of constitutive rules.[32]

Searle's differentiating between these rules allows him to make another distinction between *brute facts* and *institutional facts*. Brute facts derive from the natural sciences with the basis of all knowledge found in simple empirical observations.[33] Knowledge of brute facts, though, does not account for objective facts. Searle identifies these types of facts as institutional facts which in contrast to brute facts, "presupposes the existence of certain human institutions," as with marriage or the game of baseball.[34] The phenomenon of money provides the clearest illustration between these two types of facts. The existence of a piece of paper with various gray and green markings with printed words on it is a brute fact. That the piece of paper *counts as* a twenty dollar bill derives from a social, human institution that confers upon it the status of legal currency. Take away the institution and all that remains is a piece of randomly marked paper.[35] Thus, human institutions are "systems of constitutive rules" and every "institutional fact is underlain by a (system of) rule(s) of the form '*X* counts as *Y* in context *C*.' "[36] In other words, the "assignment of status function has the form 'X counts as Y in C.' "[37] Therefore, since "speaking a language is performing acts according to constitutive rules," Searle draws the consequential conclusion "that the fact that a man performed a certain speech act, e.g., made a promise, is an institutional fact."[38] Hence, the "notion of illocutionary point is the notion of what an utterance *counts as*, as determined by the constitutive rules of speech acts. Thus, performing illocutionary acts is imposing a type of status

32. Ibid., 37.

33. Here (ibid., 50–53) Searle is addressing G. E. M. Anscombe's notion of brute facts in her essay "On Brute Facts," *Analysis* 18 (1958): 69–72.

34. Searle, *Speech Acts*, 51.

35. See Searle, *The Construction of Social Reality* (New York: Free Press, 1995), 37–43; idem, *Mind, Language and Society: Philosophy in the Real World* (MasterMinds; New York: Basic Books, 1998), 126–28.

36. Searle, *Speech Acts*, 51–52.

37. Searle, *Mind, Language and Society*, 128.

38. Searle, *Speech Acts*, 52.

function."[39] Further, the ongoing use of particular performative utterances ensures the continued existence of certain institutional facts.[40] In general, then, "*where the X term is a speech act, the constitutive rule will enable the speech act to be performed as a performative declaration creating the state of affairs described by the Y term.*"[41]

To summarize, an illocution operates on the basis of and according to constitutive rules that underlay each human institution with the formulated system of X *counts as* Y in context C. This then enables the utterance to create and/or *count as* an institutional fact that brings about a new state of affairs in the world as expressed in the propositional content of the utterance. Thus, the saying "I promise to…" *counts as* a promise that obligates the speaker to fulfill the utterance. Or the saying "I order you…" *counts as* an order that attempts to get the hearer to do something. It is important to note that Searle sees institutional facts as logically dependent upon brute facts. Thus, institutional facts do not exist without brute facts and to "suppose that all facts are institutional would produce an infinite regress or circularity in the account of institutional facts. In order that some facts be institutional, there must be some other facts that are brute."[42] Searle links performative utterances with the idea of truth relating to facts in a different sense than Austin—"for a certain performative utterance to be happy, certain statements have *to be true*"—as illocutionary speech acts constitute institutional facts which presuppose brute facts.

The above presents the foundational principles of Searle's speech act theory which he expands upon in his description of the nature of illocutionary acts through an analysis of uttering a *promise*.[43] In the following section I will discuss Searle's notions on illocutionary forces and performative utterances, but for now this is adequate to engage with the various discussions offered in response to Searle as well as Austin.

Clarifications, Refinements, and Developments in Speech Act Theory

The significance of the work of Austin and Searle goes without question, but they have both left a number of issues unresolved and/or needing clarification and additional refining. At the most basic level, a problem of

39. Searle, *Mind, Language and Society*, 147 (italics mine).

40. Searle, *Social Reality*, 117–19.

41. Ibid., 54.

42. Ibid., 56; on Searle's notion of the hierarchy of facts, see further pp. 31–58, 120–26.

43. See Searle, *Speech Acts*, 54–71.

terminology permeates the current discussions on speech act theory. The terms "speech act," "illocutionary act," and "performative" are at times used to identify distinct utterances while at other times overlap. The major issues arising from both these theorists derive from their own general blurring of the performative–constative utterance. This has led to a merging of phraseology which has also impacted the conceptualization of speech act theory itself. In biblical studies there have been two typical consequences: every locution *counts as* an illocution or illocutions *count as* perlocutions. As a result, illocutionary acts have lost their distinction and significance. Additional problems arise concerning what actually constitutes a performative. As will be discussed below, Searle restricts the true performative to one type of illocution, the *declarative*. This obviously raises the issue of what exactly constitutes a performative and what comprises the relationship between performatives and illocutions. Further difficulties arise, such as determining if there is a difference between various illocutionary forces along with identifying what criteria exist for determining such distinctions. These issues are taken up by a number of speech act theorists along with Thiselton and Briggs, which will provide the substance for the following discussion.

Taxonomy of Illocutionary Acts

A major issue among speech act theoreticians concerns the illocutionary classifications offered by Austin and Searle along with a host of others in response to these two. Austin ended his book with a hesitant presentation of what he calls a "general preliminary classification" of illocutionary forces. Here, Austin discusses five classes along with particular verbs that make explicit the respective illocutionary force.[44] Searle also presents a five-fold classification,[45] now generally considered standard.[46] In contrast to Wittgenstein's notion of limitless uses of language,[47] Searle claims that we only do five things when we speak.[48] Searle discusses each of

44. See Austin, *Things With Words*, 151–64.

45. See John R. Searle, "A Taxonomy of Illocutionary Acts," in idem, *Expression and Meaning: Studies in the Theory of Speech Acts* (Cambridge: Cambridge University Press, 1979), 1–29.

46. For instance, William P. Alston in his latest work also finds problems with Austin's classifications and presents his own which virtually matches Searle's categories (see *Illocutionary Acts and Sentence Meaning* [Ithaca, N.Y.: Cornell University Press, 2000], 34).

47. Here Searle specifically refers to Wittgenstein, *Investigations*, I §23.

48. Searle asserts, "If we adopt illocutionary point as the basic notion on which to classify uses of language, then there are a rather limited number of basic things we do with language: we tell people how things are, we try to get them to do things, we commit ourselves to doing things, we express our feelings and attitudes and we

these types in terms of symbolization, illocutionary point, direction of fit, psychological state or sincerity condition, and propositional content.[49] As with Austin, he presents examples and particular verbs that identify particular illocutionary acts. Due to their similarity, it is instructive to see both taxonomies side by side:

Austin	*Searle*
Verdictive	Assertives ⊢ ↓ B(p)
Exercitives	Directives ! ↑ W (H does A)
Commissives	Commissives C ↑ I (S does A)
Behabitives	Expressives E Ø (P) (S/H + property)
Expositives	Declarations D ↕ Ø (p)

In his discussion on declarations, Searle remarks that some members of the class overlap with assertives. This is because within certain institutional situations, one not only needs to ascertain the facts but also needs an authority to decide upon those facts.[50] Thus, Searle identifies a sixth hybrid illocutionary act:

Assertive Declarations D_a ↓↕ B(p)

Searle additionally identifies twelve dimensions of variation whereby illocutionary acts differ one from another.[51] Of particular importance for Searle is the concept of *direction of fit*.[52] In his view, "direction of fit is

bring about changes through our utterances. Often, we do more than one of these at once in the same utterance" ("Taxonomy," 29).

49. See ibid., 8–12; idem, *Intentionality: An Essay in the Philosophy of the Mind* (Cambridge: Cambridge University Press, 1983), 166–76; idem, *Mind, Language and Society*, 146–52; Searle and Vanderveken, *Illocutionary Logic*, 51–62. For a graph of Searle's taxonomy, see Briggs, *Words in Action*, 51.

50. For example, when a judge says to a person on trial, "you are guilty," that judge factually assesses and simultaneously declares or designates that individual guilty.

51. See Searle, "Taxonomy," 2–8.

52. Searle confesses that it "would be very elegant if we could build our taxonomy entirely around this distinction in direction of fit, but though it will figure largely in our taxonomy, I am unable to make it the entire basis of the distinctions" ("Taxonomy," 4). According to Searle, the terminology of "direction of fit" was created by Austin which he discussed in his essay "How to Talk—Some Simple Ways," in *Philosophical Papers* (ed. J. O. Urmson and G. J. Warnock; 3d ed.; Oxford: Clarendon, 1979), 134–53. For Searle's understanding of this concept, see idem, "Taxonomy," 3–4; idem, *Intentionality*, 166–76; idem, *Mind, Language, and Society*, 100–103; Searle and Vanderveken, *Illocutionary Logic*, 52–53, 92–98; see also Daniel Vanderveken, "A Complete Formulation of a Simple Logic of Elementary Illocutionary Acts," in Tsohatzidis, ed., *Foundations of Speech Act Theory*, 99–131 (105–6).

always a consequence of illocutionary point."[53] There are four possible directional fits between language and the world:

> Words-to-world direction of fit (↓)—assertives
> World-to-words direction of fit (↑)—commissives and directives
> Double direction of fit (↕)—declaratives
> Null or empty direction of fit (Ø)—expressives[54]

Austin's and Searle's taxonomies provide paradigms for identifying certain types of illocutions, but at the same time restrict the possibility of additional illocutionary acts. Dieter Wunderlich[55] and Jerrold M. Sadock[56] have evaluated Austin's and Searle's taxonomies and have recognized this deficiency. Although Sadock and others have proposed useful alternatives taxonomies,[57] it remains more profitable to maintain both Austin's and Searle's schemes simultaneously while considering both functional and neither as definitive.[58] Adopting such a pragmatic view provides several advantageous outcomes. First, it allows the interpreter to utilize the rigorous work already accomplished on the major types of illocutionary forces accepted by most speech act theorists.[59] Yet, at the same time provision is made for identifying possible additional and unique illocutionary forces. Second, ascribing operational value to the various schemes allows one to use Searle's taxonomy without adopting wholesale his philosophical conceptions of the mind.[60] Third, as Sadock demonstrates,[61]

53. Searle, "Taxonomy," 4.

54. According to Searle, the best example illustrating the distinction between these directions of fit is presented by Elizabeth Anscombe and her portrayal of a person going shopping with a specific list of items and a detective who follows the shopper and records the purchased items. Anscombe's illustration is found in her book *Intention* (2d ed.; Oxford: Blackwell, 1963), §32. Searle's use of Anscombe's example is found in "Taxonomy," 3–4; idem, *Mind, Language and Society*, 101–2; see also Thiselton, *New Horizons*, 294–95.

55. Dieter Wunderlich, "Methodological Remarks on Speech Act Theory," in *Speech Act Theory and Pragmatics* (ed. John R. Searle, Ferenc Kiefer, and Manfred Bierwisch; Texts and Studies in Linguistics and Philosophy 10; Dordrecht, Holland: D. Reidel, 1980), 291–312.

56. Jerrold M. Sadock, "Toward a Grammatically Realistic Typology of Speech Acts," in Tsohatzidis, ed., *Foundations of Speech Act Theory*, 393–406.

57. See ibid., 395–402; see also Briggs's discussion of Sadock in *Words in Action*, 56–58.

58. So also Briggs, *Words in Action*, 57–58; Thiselton, *New Horizons*, 296.

59. Similarly Récanati, *Meaning and Force*, 152.

60. Searle's philosophy of the mind is the most complex and controversial aspect of his speech act theory. Searle's taxonomy directly derives from his philosophical conceptions of the mind and specifically his idea of Intentionality (see Searle, *Intentionality*; idem, *Mind, Language, and Society*; idem, *Social Reality*). For general

the various illocutionary forces are not independent or disassociated one from another, but rather the various dimensions of other forces are often incorporated into a single utterance with one force typically being primary. Thus, illocutions are often, if not always, multidimensional utterances. Searle's qualification to his restricted ways of speaking is quite telling as he observes that we *often combine* some of these five types "at once in the same utterance."[62] This phenomenon is evidenced in Searle's sixth overlapping illocutionary force. In addition, the utterance "I promise" combines at the least the commissive and declarative forces, which Searle himself concedes. Thus, as Briggs observes, one should "*expect* hybrids as the normal occurrence" with one of the forces being primary, and thus a "performative utterance is a certain kind of 'multiple' illocutionary act."[63]

Illocutionary Verbal Criterion

Connected with illocutionary classifications is the issue of matching verbs. The essence of the problem is accentuated by the fact that speech act theorists acknowledge no ideal set of verbs exists as exclusive indicators of illocutionary points while at the same time they ironically supply such lists.[64]

surveys of his notions, see Briggs, *Words in Action*, 53–56, 60–63. For recent critiques on Searle's notion of Intentionality, see the essays and Searle's response in E. Lepore and R. van Gulick, eds., *John Searle and His Critics* (Oxford: Blackwell), 105–92; see also Wilhelm Baumgartner and Jörg Klawitter, "Intentionality of Perception: An Inquiry Concerning J. R. Searle's Conception of Intentionality with Special Reference to Husserl," in Burkhardt, ed., *Speech Acts, Meaning and Intentions*, 210–25; Savas L. Tsohatzidis, "The Gap Between Speech Acts and Mental States," in idem, ed., *Foundations of Speech Act Theory*, 220–33. Linked to Searle's understanding of Intentionality is his notion of Background (see John R. Searle, "The Background of Meaning," in Searle, Kiefer, and Bierwisch, eds., *Speech Act Theory and Pragmatics*, 221–32; idem, *Intentionality*, 65–71, 141–59; idem, *Social Reality*, 127–47; idem, *Mind, Language and Society*, 107–9; see also idem, "Literal Meaning," in *Expression and Meaning*, 117–36). For critiques on Searle's notion of Background and his response, see Lepore and van Gulick, eds., *John Searle and His Critics*, 243–99; see also Marcelo Dascal, "Speech Act Theory and Gricean Pragmatics: Some Differences of Detail that Make a Difference," in Tsohatzidis, ed., *Foundations of Speech Act Theory*, 323–34 (cf. 330, 333).

61. See Sadock, "Typology of Speech Acts," 396–99.

62. Searle, "Taxonomy," 29; cf. Searle and Vanderveken, *Illocutionary Logic*, 52.

63. Briggs, *Words in Action*, 52, 68.

64. Thiselton confesses his own previous trouble with this issue due to the ambiguity found in Austin, Searle, and others when he presented his own list of verbs in his *New Horizons* (299), but now recognizes "that more was at issue than specific uses of specific vocabulary" ("Communicative Action," 233–34).

Subsequent to his work with Searle,[65] Vanderveken has provided possibly the most comprehensive list of English performative verbs: 70 *assertives*; 32 *commissives*; 56 *directives*; 85 *declaratives*; and 28 *expressives*.[66] Yet, he is aware of the stated problem as he prefaces his list by noting that "many speech act verbs have *several* uses and can name different illocutionary forces." For example, with the verb "swear," a speaker can swear that a proposition is true (assertive) or the speaker can also swear to a hearer that he or she will do something in the future (commissive). In addition, some performative verbs are "*systematically ambiguous* between several illocutionary points." For instance, an alert is both an assertive and directive simultaneously, as it asserts the imminence of danger and gives a directive to prepare for appropriate action.[67]

These qualitative considerations are important and necessary for the interpreter to note, but the problem of verbal criteria remains, as the more ambiguous a sentence appears or when dealing with a nominal clause, the more the axiom is true that an illocutionary act cannot be solely or at all determined by a particular verb. The answer to this dilemma lies with how such verbal lists are actually perceived and utilized. One must heed the qualifications offered by theorists and thus employ verbal criteria exclusively as functional guides for identifying particular illocutionary forces. Such lists help to provide one way to begin matching an illocutionary act with a given sentence. Further, as discussed above, such provided verbal criteria do not constitute comprehensive lists, neither for the various given categories nor to restrict the number of possible illocutionary forces.

In sum, an illocutionary force is not always identified by a corresponding verb or even by other formal indicating devices. Thus, verbal markers are limited in their scope for identifying illocutions. With this, Briggs instructively concludes that

> what we are looking for in locating and analysing illocutionary acts is not the occurrence of any particular word markers, nor even the paradigmatic cases for each type of illocutionary point, but rather *we are looking for those acts which correspond to the verbs which can be used to indicate illocutionary point*. It is in this sense that the standard lists of illocutionary verbs according to illocutionary point help us in identifying illocutionary acts in a discourse.[68]

65. Searle and Vanderveken, *Illocutionary Logic*, 179–216.

66. Daniel Vanderveken, *Meaning and Speech Acts*. Vol. 1, *Principles of Language Use* (Cambridge: Cambridge University Press, 1990), 166–219.

67. Ibid., 168.

68. Briggs, *Words in Action*, 101.

This perspective is confirmed by Thiselton's observation that most promissory acts in the New Testament do not include the term ἐπαγγελία (e.g. Matt 28:20; John 11:25; Acts 2:21) and conversely the same word may not indicate an illocution (Rom 4:13–22).[69] Even more telling, there is no actual term expressing the sole semantic domain for "promise" in the Old Testament. Only context can determine if אמר or דבר should be translated as such and further whether it is expressing an illocution or not (e.g. Exod 12:25; Num 14:40; Deut 15:6; Ps 77:9).

The Nature of Illocutions

Neither Austin nor Searle ever actually defined the nature of or what counted as an illocutionary act. Searle believed that the viability of his own analysis would provide the basis for a definition.[70] In one way or another, a consequence of this ambiguity appears in Nicholas Wolterstorff's work and his proposal of *double-agency discourse*: "one person performs some illocutionary act by way of another person performing either some locutionary or some illocutionary act." This paradigm "enables us to understand Scripture as the manifestation of God having performed illocutionary acts by way of human beings having performed locutionary and illocutionary acts."[71] In his book *Divine Discourse*, Wolterstorff presents the essence of his hermeneutical goal by stating:

> The essence of discourse lies not in the relation of *expression* holding between inner life and outer signs, but in the relation of *counting as* holding between a generat*ing* act performed in a certain situation, and the speech act generat*ed by* that act performed in that situation. *The goal of interpretation, correspondingly, is to discover what counts as what.*[72]

The core of this argument has major implications for viewing Scripture as performative for the contemporary reader; however, it also implies that any locution in Scripture can *count as* an illocution and that decision is solely based upon the subjectivity of the readers and their community.[73]

69. Thiselton, "Communicative Action," 232–33.

70. John R. Searle, "What is a Speech Act?," in *The Philosophy of Language* (ed. John R. Searle; Oxford: Oxford University Press, 1971), 39–53 (39).

71. Nicholas Wolterstorff, "The Promise of Speech-Act Theory for Biblical Interpretation," in *After Pentecost: Language and Biblical Interpretation* (ed. Craig G. Bartholomew, Colin Greene, and Karl Möller; Scripture & Hermeneutics Series 2; Carlisle: Paternoster; Grand Rapids: Zondervan, 2001), 73–90 (83); see also idem, *Divine Discourse: Philosophical Reflections on the Claim that God Speaks* (Cambridge: Cambridge University, 1995), 37–57.

72. Wolterstorff, *Divine Discourse*, 183 (italics mine on the last line).

73. This latter consequence occupies much of Briggs' attention in his *Words in Action* as he attempts to navigate through the ongoing issue of an interpretive

A related issue concerns the number of biblical interpreters appealing to speech act theory who often consider the nature of illocutions as perlocutionary. As discussed in the Introduction, applying speech act theory in order simply to identify perlocutionary effects trivializes the theory and makes it an unnecessary addition to the hermeneutical task. More problematic, such an approach misconstrues the true nature of illocutionary acts and thereby diffuses the unique significance of such utterances. Briggs correctly observes that it "seems inevitable that any attempt to subsume rhetorical interests into a speech act framework will involve some degree of distortion."[74]

Defining Illocutionary Acts. Thiselton and Briggs have suggested a way to address these issues by viewing illocutionary forces ranging from weak to strong along a spectrum of strengths. Although not proposing such a paradigm, they derive this notion from G. L. Warnock's analysis of Austin's thoughts on performative utterances. In order to evaluate this concept it is important briefly to summarize Warnock's essay.

Warnock begins by stating that his co-worker's basic thought—"to *say* something is to *do* something"—was originally "that *sometimes* saying is doing."[75] Thus, Austin's initial theory concerning performative utterances conceived of them as a *special* case. The question, then, is *how* are certain utterances sometimes operative? For Austin, *conventions* "provide that saying something or other is to be, is to constitute or count as, doing whatever it may be."[76] Here, Warnock, along with P. F. Strawson,[77] recognize the supreme importance Austin places on extralinguistic convention as the defining feature for demarcating performatives. With this, he identifies in Austin's work a special class of utterances that, by virtue of non-linguistic conventions, *count as* doing.

Evidenced in his later work, Austin took for granted that speech acts in general were "conventional or conventional-constituted acts." For Warnock, this assumption is exactly where Austin went astray due to its indefensibility. For instance, there is no convention involved when saying, "The train leaves at three" in order for the hearer to hurry and finish

community's role in interpretation and in answer provides ways speech act theory can help in determining legitimate illocutions in the biblical text (see *Words in Action*, cf. 105–43).

74. Ibid., 96.

75. G. J. Warnock, "Some Types of Performative Utterance," in Berlin et al., eds., *Essays on J. L. Austin*, 69–89 (69).

76. Ibid., 70–71.

77. P. F. Strawson, "Intention and Convention in Speech Acts," in Searle, ed., *The Philosophy of Language*, 23–38.

his/her lunch. Warnock thus concludes that "illocutionary forces…are not in general convention-constituted." According to Warnock, the "idea that linguistic doings are somehow *all* "conventional" is an improper hangover" of Austin's original thoughts on convention-dependent performative utterances.[78]

Warnock also notices in Austin's work a second special type of utterance, the *explicit performative*. Sayings like "I promise…" or "I advise you to…" are not utterances involving convention, but are performatives simply due to the standard meaning of the utterance. For Warnock,

> explicit performatives, for the most part anyway, are not by *convention* operative utterances, to issue which conventionally counts as doing this or that; there are no special conventions; they are indeed utterances in issuing which (happily) this or that is done, but *what* is done is done simply in virtue of what they mean.[79]

From these observations, Warnock concludes that Austin introduced two sub-classes of performatives simultaneously: *conventionally "operative" utterances* and *explicit performative utterances*. These types of utterances are both performatives, but they remain distinct, as the former type of utterances count as doing by virtue of *non-linguistic convention* whereas the latter are all by definition of a certain verbal form—first person present indicative active—and count as doing solely on the level of *linguistic convention*. Thus, although all utterances can rightly be categorized as speech acts, there still remains "a legitimate *sub-class* of utterances called 'performative'" and, in fact, there are "at least two such special sub-classes."[80]

Warnock's analysis finds parallels with Searle's most recent re-examination of his understanding of performative utterances.[81] Searle's primary goal is to demonstrate how performatives do not derive from assertives, but rather vice versa. While addressing his main goal Searle describes his understanding of performative utterances and begins by rehearsing Austin's failure to distinguish them from other types of utterances. Searle believes that the correct way to situate the notion of performatives within a general theory of speech acts is that

78. Warnock, "Performative Utterance," 76.

79. Ibid., 86.

80. Ibid., 87.

81. John R. Searle, "How Performatives Work," in *Essays in Speech Act Theory* (ed. Daniel Vanderveken and Susumu Kubo; P&BNS 77; Amsterdam: John Benjamins, 2002), 85–107, 288–89.

> some illocutionary acts can be performed by uttering a sentence containing an expression that names the type of speech act, as in for example, "I order you to leave the room." These utterances, and only these, are correctly described as performative utterances. On my usage, the only performatives are what Austin called "explicit performatives." Thus, though every utterance is indeed a *performance*, only a very restricted class are *performatives*.[82]

This restricted class is Searle's *declarative* force. In fact, "all performatives are declarations"; however, not "all declarations are performatives."[83] For Searle, the important distinction is not between which declarations are peformatives and which are not, but between declarations that create a linguistic entity and ones that create a non-linguistic entity.

Non-linguistic declarations are utterances such as adjourning a meeting, pronouncing a couple man and wife, and declaring war that require extralinguistic conventions to operate successfully.[84] In contrast, *linguistic performatives* are sayings expressing a promise, order, or statement by way of declaration. Both types are speech acts and so they are both linguistic and have their point in creating new institutional facts corresponding to the propositional content. Sometimes these new facts are themselves speech acts (*linguistic declarations*), other times the new facts are not further speech acts (*extralinguistic declarations*). For example, the linguistic saying "I promise" creates the institutional fact of a promise whereas the non-linguistic saying "The meeting is adjourned" creates the institutional fact of an adjournment. Both these types of utterances are performative and conventionally operative. The non-linguistic declaratives are operative through extralinguistic conventions and linguistic declaratives through social communicative conventions or rules.

Searle here isolates a performative class of utterances in contrast to constatives. He essentially distinguishes the same two types of performatives as Warnock discovered in Austin's work; yet, for Searle, these are both explicit performatives. Throughout his discussion on speech act theory, Searle has consistently emphasized extralinguistic convention as the defining and operative feature of performatives.[85] For instance, even in this recent essay Searle asserts that the "most prominent exceptions to

82. Ibid., 86–87.

83. Ibid., 91. This conclusion corroborates with his earlier suggestion with Vanderveken that performative utterances are in each instance declarations (Searle and Vanderveken, *Illocutionary Logic*, 3).

84. For Searle's four conventional features, see his "Performatives," 98; see also idem, "Taxonomy," 18.

85. See, e.g., Searle, *Speech Acts*, 38–40; idem, "Taxonomy," 18; idem, "Performatives," 100.

the claim that *declarations require extra-linguistic institution* are supernatural declarations," for example, when God says, "Let there be light!"[86] This emphasis has been a typical criticism of Searle and thus one could deduce from his work two different classes of performatives: a special performative (conventionally operative) and a quasi-performative (non-conventionally operative). Yet, Searle's prototype illocutionary utterance is the linguistic declarative/performative of promising.[87] In fact, Searle early on asserted that "'I promise" and 'I hereby promise' are among the *strongest* illocutionary force indicating devices for *commitment* provided by the English language."[88] Despite his longstanding emphasis on convention and specifically non-linguistic convention, Searle identifies here both the non-linguistic and linguistic declaratives as performatives.[89] Thus, Searle's and Warnock's theses demonstrate that there are at least two types of performatives.

Turning back to Thiselton's and Briggs's suggestion, a spectrum of strengths allows for the typical view among speech act theorists that all utterances constitute speech acts but differ in strength. This distinction between strong and weak illocutions provides a way to steer clear of the current state of biblical studies that sees all texts as speech acts.[90] The issue still remaining, though, concerns what actually is a strong or the strongest illocution. Briggs summarizes his conception as follows:

> I shall call *a strong illocution* one which *relies on* a *non-linguistic convention*. This class, following Warnock, *overlaps* with but is not identical to Austin's explicit performative, and will include the Queen's saying "I name this ship…" not because it is an explicit performative, although it is, but because the conventions in place are not simply linguistic ones. I shall call *a weak illocution* one where the *linguistic meaning itself is the only or only significant convention in view*. "The lamp is on the table" is a weak illocution, as is the explicit "I state that the lamp is on the table." Austin's performative–constative distinction is thus retained on one level (strong against weak illocutions) while collapsed in Austin's own manner on another level (both are illocutions).[91]

86. Searle, "Performatives," 99 (italics mine).
87. See Searle, *Speech Acts*, 54–64.
88. Ibid., 58.
89. In my dissertation I focused on Searle's stress on non-linguistic convention along with its accompanied criticisms and consequently overemphasized his distinction between these two types of performatives (Jim W. Adams, "Speech Act Theory, Biblical Interpretation, and Isaiah 40–55" [Ph.D. diss., Fuller Theological Seminary, 2004], 92, 102).
90. Thiselton, "Communicative Action," 237.
91. Briggs, *Words in Action*, 64–65 (italics mine).

Warnock's analysis concerns the legitimacy of the existence of performative utterances in contrast to constatives; thus, Briggs is correct that lying at either end of the spectrum should be Austin's constative (weak) and performative (strong). Yet, although he sees strong illocutions *overlapping* with performatives, he still makes a clear and definite distinction between non-linguistic and linguistic illocutions as strong and weak respectively. The implication of this demarcation is that utterances such as "I promise" would thus constitute a weak illocution and be placed on the same or similar level as constatives. Warnock and Searle, however, have established that such an utterance *counts as* a performative. In all fairness, the example Briggs gives for a weak illocution falls within the category of a true constative. Moreover, he asserts that Warnock has demonstrated that Austin's and Searle's emphasis on convention is insufficient for defining the characteristics of illocutions.[92] Further, he later considers the utterance, "I promise to be there" as an explicit strong illocution.[93] However, the language he uses *here* potentially restricts the strong illocution category.

Based on all of the above, I consider the conceptual framework of illocutions operating along a spectrum of strengths as insightful and valuable. This paradigm, though, does not necessarily derive uniquely from Warnock's analysis, but reflects the nature of the various illocutionary forces as understood by Searle as well as other theorists. Strong illocutionary acts are either non-linguistically conventional, as when the Queen says, "I name this ship…" or linguistically conventional, as in "I promise…" Both are strong illocutions or performatives. Admittedly, though, the *strongest* illocution is one that clearly involves extralinguistic action and has its operating force in non-linguistic conventions. This weak/strong spectrum additionally helps to acknowledge other forces operating with a degree of strength besides the declarative/performative. Rather than completely dismissing all other illocutions as potentially performative, incorporating such a framework allows other types of illocutionary forces to be considered functioning performatively or as strong illocutions.

Illocutionary Acts and Perlocutionary Effects. In general, linguistic philosophers base their theory of meaning in either psychological effects or illocutionary acts. According to William P. Alston, "communication theorists have concentrated exclusively on the production of psychological effects on hearers (perlocutionary acts) as the semantically crucial

92. Ibid., 67.
93. Ibid., 127.

category of communicative acts."[94] Paul Grice is most often identified as the foundational theorist of this understanding of communication.[95] In contrast, most speech act theorists base meaning in the illocutionary act.[96] Despite this, biblical interpreters applying speech act theory often use it in perlocutionary terms which may be, in part, due to Austin's imprecision.

Austin confessed that "it is the distinction between illocutions and perlocutions which seems likeliest to give trouble."[97] It is clear that Austin considered locutions bringing about perlocutionary effects.[98] Although not as explicit, Austin seems to consider perlocutions deriving from illocutions.[99] Thus, both locutions and illocutions produce perlocutionary effects.[100] Austin does identify certain criteria for distinguishing the illocution and perlocution. To start, illocutions have a certain force *in* saying something whereas perlocutions achieve certain effects *by* saying something. This is Austin's "in/by" test which he confesses, and actually demonstrates, is "at best very slippery."[101] Austin also asserted that "illocutionary acts are conventional acts" whereas "perlocutionary acts are not conventional."[102] Steven Davis and Alston demonstrate, though, that Austin's notion of convention fails to distinguish in every instance the illocution from the perlocution.[103]

Austin suggests three additional distinctions between the two acts. First, *securing uptake*, which "amounts to bringing about the understanding of the meaning and of the force of the locution." Second, *taking effect*, which entails the "brining about states of affairs in the 'normal' way, i.e., changes in the natural course of events" in contrast to 'producing consequences.'" Finally, inviting *a response* or *sequel* such as "an order invites the response of obedience and a promise that of fulfilment."[104] Austin's additional criteria also fail to distinguish the two

94. Alston, *Illocutionary Acts*, 163.

95. See in particular Grice's essays "Meaning" (213–23), "Logic and Conversation" (22–40), "Utterer's Meaning and Intentions" (86–116), and "Utterer's Meaning, Sentence-Meaning, and Word-Meaning" (117–37), repr. in H. P. Grice, *Studies in the Way of Words* (Cambridge, Mass.: Harvard University Press, 1989).

96. See, e.g., J. R. Searle, F. Kiefer, and M. Bierwisch, "Introduction," in idem, eds., *Speech Act Theory and Pragmatics*, vii.

97. Austin, *Things with Words*, 110.

98. See ibid., 130–31.

99. See ibid., 110–11.

100. See further Steven Davis, "Perlocutions," in Searle, Kiefer, and Bierwisch, eds., *Speech Act Theory and Pragmatics*, 37–55 (37–39).

101. Austin, *Things with Words*, 131.

102. Ibid., 121.

103. Davis, "Perlocutions," 46–47; Alston, *Sentence Meaning*, 25.

104. Austin, *Things with Words*, 117.

concepts as Davis exposes.[105] Austin's examples of his speech act account are also troublesome, such as:

> Locution: He said to me, "Shoot her!" meaning by "shoot" shoot and referring by "her" to her.
> Illocution: He urged (or advised, ordered, etc.) me to shoot her.
> Perlocution: He persuaded me to shoot her.[106]

Here "urging" and "persuading" express virtually identical ideas and thus Austin's illocution is essentially a perlocution.[107]

Searle only briefly touches on the distinction between illocutions and perlocutions. He originally augments Austin's ideas in response to Grice's view of meaning.[108] For Searle, perlocutionary acts are the consequences or subsequent effects of illocutionary acts.[109] Meaning is derived from a combination of intention and convention and the characteristic intended effect of meaning is understanding. The effect of understanding is not a perlocutionary effect, but an illocutionary one.[110] Illocutionary acts typically require intentionality whereas perlocutionary acts do not. For instance, in order to promise something you must intend to do so, but a speaker may persuade someone unintentionally. Thus, the "fact that illocutionary acts are essentially intentional, whereas perlocutionary acts may or may not be intentional, is a consequence of the fact that the illocutionary act is the unit of *meaning* in communication."[111] Consequently, perlocutionary acts are not linguistic in nature, but are subsequent psychological effects of linguistically conventional illocutions. This distinction is clear due to the fact that in order for a speaker to persuade he must utter a statement that conventionally *counts as* a speech act. Hence, one cannot persuade someone by uttering, "I hereby persuade you." A speaker must include the illocution of a warning, request, or informing in order for the utterance to *count as* a performative.[112] In light of Searle's distinctions, one can readily see how Austin's illocution example above is not linguistically conventional.[113]

105. Davis, "Perlocutions," 44–45.
106. Austin, *Things with Words*, 101–2.
107. See Briggs, *Words in Action*, 41.
108. Searle specifically responds to Grice's essay "Meaning"; see Searle, *Speech Acts*, 42–50, 71.
109. Ibid., 25.
110. Searle and Vanderveken, *Illocutionary Logic*, 11.
111. Searle, *Mind, Language and Society*, 137.
112. See Searle, *Speech Acts*, 25; Searle and Vanderveken, *Illocutionary Logic*, 12.
113. See Davis, "Perlocutions," 46.

In Alston's latest and most mature articulation of his speech act account, he concentrates on demonstrating that meaning derives from the illocutionary act and not the perlocution.[114] Like Searle, Alston defines the nature of illocutions through an analysis of *promising*.[115] In his discussion, Alston follows Searle's notion of the *speaker's obligation* in promising;[116] but he goes beyond Searle by identifying it as the *key* characteristic of the illocution. The speaker *taking responsibility* for an utterance is not only necessary but also functions as the sufficient dimension of the utterance to *count as* an illocutionary act.[117]

Alston's notion of *taking responsibility* is in direct response to those proposing a Griceian type perlocutionary act theory to linguistic meaning.[118] As with Searle, such an account does not work because one can in fact utter a sentence without intending to affect the hearer. Other utterances do not involve persuasive aspects at all. For instance, the utterance, "I pronounce you man and wife" does not persuade the couple that they are married; rather, the utterance creates the fact that they are married.[119] Sentence meaning, then, is found in the illocutionary act alone. It is the illocution that comprises the linguistic component of communication, not the perlocution. Nevertheless, "typical linguistic communication involves both illocutionary acts and perlocutionary intentions."[120] Somewhat agreeing with Austin, Alston also sees certain perlocutions deriving from "sentential acts" (Alston's reduction of Austin's locution to his simple phatic act classified as a "sentential act").[121] Yet, concurring with most speech act theorists, perlocutionary acts derive from illocutionary acts, not vice versa.[122] A "sentence has a distinctive perlocutionary act potential *only by virtue* of having a distinctive illocutionary act potential."[123]

Sentence meaning for Alston is *illocutionary act potential*. Determining meaning transpires by matching the content of an illocutionary act

114. See Alston, *Sentence Meaning*, cf. 147–73.

115. See ibid., 51–80. For Alston's earlier analysis of promising and critique of Searle's understanding of promising, see "Searle on Illocutionary Acts," in Lepore and van Gulick, eds., *John Searle and His Critics*, 57–80.

116. See Searle, *Speech Acts*, 62.

117. See William P. Alston, "Illocutionary Acts and Linguistic Meaning," in Tsohatzidis, ed., *Foundations of Speech Act Theory*, 29–49 (40–45); idem, *Sentence Meaning*, cf. 54–65.

118. See Alston, *Sentence Meaning*, 33–50, 162–73; idem, "Linguistic Meaning," 39–45.

119. See, Alston, *Sentence Meaning*, 166–67.

120. Ibid., 169.

121. See ibid., 25–26, 31–32.

122. See, e.g., ibid., 31.

123. Alston, "Linguistic Meaning," 35.

type with the content of a sentence meaning. Thus, one identifies "a sentence meaning with its *matching illocutionary act potential*, that is, with the potential to perform illocutionary acts of the type that exactly matches that meaning. That potential exactly mirrors the meaning; it must, for it was specifically selected to do so."[124] To "construct a matching illocutionary act type" one needs "to find just the degree of specificity that is embodied in the sentence meaning in question—with respect to identity of referents, predicative aspects of the propositional content, illocutionary force, and so on."[125]

What distinguishes or classifies an utterance to count as an illocutionary act is "a speaker's *taking responsibility* for the obtaining of a state of affairs or the satisfaction of a condition." This means that "asserting, presupposing, or implying that p are all ways of *taking responsibility* for its being the case that p."[126] Thus, an utterance places the speaker under obligation to take responsibility for the truthfulness or the performance of an utterance. Such obligation is monitored by socially entrenched rules of communication determined and implemented by the community to which the speaker belongs.[127] The notion of taking responsibility, then, demarcates the illocutionary act from the perlocutionary act. Moreover, an utterance *counts as* an illocutionary act of a certain type by virtue of the speaker *taking* the stance of *responsibility* for the utterance.

Alston's concept of taking responsibility sharpens the nature of illocutionary acts as they clearly include the dimension of the speaker's total *involvement* of the *self*. Further, without dismissing proper conventions with certain utterances, the linguistic content of an utterance expressing self-involvement in the sense of Alston's taking responsibility *counts as* a strong illocution. This notion leads to the fact that illocutionary acts are not the same as perlocutions and that the latter depend upon and derive from the former.

124. Alston, *Sentence Meaning*, 180.

125. Alston, "Linguistic Meaning," 37–38.

126. Ibid., 40.

127. Alston describes the essence of taking responsibility as follows: "The utterance is made the illocutionary act it is, apart from any conventional effect production that is essentially involved, not by any 'natural' facts about the speaker—his beliefs, perlocutionary intentions, or whatever—but by a 'normative' fact about the speaker —the fact that he has changed his normative position in a certain way by laying himself open to the possibility of censure, correction, or the like in case the conditions in question are not satisfied. What the speaker does, again apart from conventional effect production, to make his utterance a token of a certain illocutionary act type, is to 'stick his neck out' in this way, making himself the one who is to 'respond' if the conditions in question are not satisfied" (*Sentence Meaning*, 70–71).

Jennifer Hornsby adds an important element to the above discussion as she attempts to "provide an account of an idea of *illocution* which reveals the use of words to be *communicative* action."[128] Hornsby's thesis is that the "true significance of *illocution* is shown when speech act theory is located in a broader, social context."[129] Agreeing with Warnock and Strawson, Hornsby criticizes Austin, as well as Searle and Vanderveken, that illocutions are solely marked by non-linguistic convention.[130] For Hornsby, although "illocutionary acts require consequences of a sort," "they require no specific conventions beyond the locutionary ones which (arguably) are presupposed to them."[131] Thus, the only element Hornsby sees as necessary for successful illocutions is what she calls "reciprocity," which replaces convention as the key to illocution. As a result, no response is necessary for an illocutionary act to obtain success, only reciprocity. The "speaker relies only on a certain receptiveness on her audience's part for her utterance to work for her as illocutionarily meant: the audience takes her to have done what she meant to." For example, a particular utterance is taken as a warning simply on the basis of "normal linguistic exchange."[132] Reciprocity also provides Hornsby with making a clear distinction between illocutions and perlocutions, as the former need only reciprocity to have their proper consequences whereas the latter invoke either more than reciprocity or something quite else. Thus, perlocutionary acts should be thought to be outside of the province of a study of language.[133]

What is significant about Hornsby's essay is the fact that regardless of the response a particular utterance produces, only the proper linguistic conventions operating within reciprocity constitute the necessary factor for the performance of a successful illocutionary act. Applying Hornsby's analysis, Briggs states that

128. Jennifer Hornsby, "Illocution and Its Significance," in Tsohatzidis, ed., *Foundations of Speech Act Theory*, 187–207 (187).

129. Ibid., 187.

130. See ibid., 191–92, 202.

131. Ibid., 192.

132. Ibid., 192. Hornsby illustrates her thesis with the case of a woman responding to a man's sexual advances with "No." The judge in the process of acquitting the man of rape claims that "it is not just a question of saying no." Here, the judge wants the jury to believe that the woman meant "Yes" by saying "No." The judge's interpretation of the woman's "No" as "Yes" demonstrates that to "do a perfect illocutionary act of refusing, an utterance of the word 'no' is not enough: a woman may mean to refuse, but a condition of her having fully successfully refused—that she be recognized as attempting to refuse—may not be fulfilled" (p. 199).

133. See ibid., 195.

> the notion of reciprocity underlies the type of convention which is invoked when weak illocutions are in view. To put the point the other way around: where the non-linguistic conventions are in place (e.g. it is in fact the Queen naming the ship and not me), then the further convention required for a successful illocution simply is that of reciprocity.[134]

If understood correctly, in the first part of his conclusion Briggs brings out an important point by emphasizing the necessity of reciprocity when dealing with weak illocutions, as the linguistic exchange between a speaker and hearer within a particular society determines which utterances *count as* illocutions. In the second part—reciprocity is the only additional component necessary for a successful, conventionally oriented illocution—and with the adjustments discussed above, this would also be true of other types of *linguistic* illocutions.

Yueguo Gu recently re-evaluated Austin's work and the small number of essays to date devoted to the notion of perlocutionary acts within speech act theory.[135] For Gu, the conception of the perlocutionary act expressed in the literature is fundamentally misguided.[136] This is primarily based on the assumption that the speaker's speech act *causes* the perlocutionary effect within the hearer. For Gu, the hearer is ultimately the one responsible for the effects of an illocutionary act uttered by the speaker.[137] Thus, there are only a few marginal cases where a speaker performed a perlocutionary act causing an incontrollable response. Communication between a speaker and hearer is more of a "transaction." The speaker's illocutionary act plays a triggering role while the hearer's response is her/his contribution to the transaction. Thus, the "successful performance of the illocutionary act involves the utterance...and illocutionary intention on S's part, and the understanding of illocutionary force or recognition of illocutionary intention on H's part." For Gu, this linguistic and communicative transaction model allows the perlocution

134. Briggs, *Words in Action*, 67.

135. Yueguo Gu, "The Impasse of Perlocution," *JP* 20 (1993): 405–32.

136. Apart from Austin, Gu identifies four essays devoted to the subject: Ted Cohen, "Illocutions and Perlocutions," *FL* 9 (1973), 492–503; P. N. Campbell, "A Rhetorical View of Locutionary, Illocutionary, and Perlocutionary Acts," *QJS* 59 (1973): 284–96; R. N. Gaines, "Doing by Saying: Toward a Theory of Perlocution," *QJS* 65 (1979): 207–17; Davis, "Perlocutions."

137. Gu claims that "the so-called perlocutionary effects are not in fact caused by S[peaker], but actively produced by H[earer], who has the claim to the agency of the effects. Thus, the perlocutionary act cannot be said to be performed by S alone. It is a joint endeavour between S and H. It involves S's performance of speech acts and H's performance of response-acts. The relation between S's speech acts and H's response-acts is anything but causal" ("Perlocution," 422).

concept to come under the domain of linguistic pragmatics or linguistic communication.[138]

Gu's study underscores Austin's blurry distinction between illocutions and perlocutions while also exposing a lack of precision among other theorists. Briggs, though, correctly balances Gu's analysis by asserting that these particular theorists are clarifying "the importance of context for perlocution, but do not suggest that this can really be incorporated into illocutionary aspects of speech act theory."[139] Important for this study, though, is Gu's notion that speech acts *trigger* rather than *cause* the hearer's response. As Alston and others have purported, a speaker can utter illocutionary acts with intended perlocutionary effects which are dependent upon and prompted by those utterances; however, these effects are ultimately caused by the hearer as Gu describes. Mutual understanding, in line with Hornsby's reciprocity thesis, makes an utterance a successful illocutionary act. Therefore, when an illocution is uttered with desired perlocutionary effects it seems best to describe these effects as *triggered* or *intended* by the illocution. The effect lies outside language proper and is left up to the decision making processes within the hearer whether or not to respond appropriately.

Steven Davis adds a final aspect to the above discussion with his notion that certain utterances are in essence anti-individualistic.[140] Davis applies the studies of T. Burge on individualism and observes that illocutionary acts depend on the existence of both the speaker and the hearer. With this, Davis's thesis is that "illocutionary acts like promising, begging and betting cannot be individuated individualistically, since for there to be such acts there must be others with whom a speaker interacts."[141] Further, "an act of promising depends on the linguistic practices of a speaker's linguistic community." As Searle demonstrates, "an utterance of 'I promise to do A' will place him under an obligation to do A."[142] Davis's ideas here add to the concept of illocutionary acts, as they presuppose a mutual self-involvement between the speaker and hearer which, in turn, keeps the speaker accountable to fulfill his speech act. Thus, illocutionary acts operate within an intersubjective, public, and extralinguistic world that imposes ethical demands upon the speaker to perform his utterances.[143]

138. Ibid., 427–28.

139. Briggs, *Words in Action*, 96 n 72.

140. Steven Davis, "Anti-Individualism and Speech Act Theory," in Tsohatzidis, ed., *Foundations of Speech Act Theory*, 208–19.

141. Ibid., 215.

142. Ibid., 216.

143. See further Thiselton, "Communicative Action," 224–25.

Conclusion

The term "speech act" properly functions as the governing concept that every utterance to one degree or another constitutes the performance of an action. As Thiselton, Briggs, and others have adopted, perhaps the best term describing the function of particular utterances and texts is "communicative action," as it conveys simultaneously the linguistic exchange between speaker and hearer that *counts as* doing. This larger category also applies in general to "performatives"; yet, a special type of utterance exists that *counts as* doing, which is properly identified as a performative—a linguistic utterance that may or may not involve non-linguistic conventions. Within the larger category of speech acts lie illocutionary forces that operate along a spectrum of strengths with constatives and performatives or strong illocutions lying at each end respectively. Also at the weak end of the spectrum lies the simple utterance of a sentence which generally corresponds with Austin's locution (phonetic and phatic aspects), Searle's utterance act, or Alston's sentential act. Degrees of strength are assigned to various illocutionary forces on a case-by-case basis, but a declarative type force or some type of a multidimensional illocution most consistently constitutes a strong or the strongest type of performative utterance. Degrees of strength among the various illocutionary forces depend upon the non-linguistic and/or linguistic conventions involved. The self-involvement of the speaker comprises the central characteristic of illocutionary acts as utterances place to one degree or another the speaker under certain public and social obligations and commitments.

Hermeneutic of Self-Involvement: Donald D. Evans, Anthony C. Thiselton, and Richard S. Briggs

One of the earliest and perhaps most important studies on speech act theory was produced by another of Austin's students, Donald D. Evans, in his book *The Logic of Self-Involvement*.[144] Evans's book was published in 1963 directly on the heels of *How To Do Things With Words*, wherein he presents his own views on the nature of performative utterances and their relation to religious language. It should be noted that his study does not represent the more sophisticated articulations of speech act theory. Still, Evans's notions are seminal and thus provide important insights for understanding speech act theory proper along with its hermeneutical

144. Donald. D. Evans, *The Logic of Self-Involvement: A Philosophical Study of Everyday Language with Special Reference to the Christian Use of Language About God as Creator* (London: SCM Press, 1963).

significance for biblical interpretation. Above all, Evans demonstrates ways to explore the aspect of the self-involvement of the reader within a speech act account that focuses on language as performative. Only a few biblical interpreters have acknowledged the significance of Evans's original work apart from Thiselton and Briggs. When it comes to speech act theory and biblical interpretation, Thiselton is without a doubt the principal biblical scholar who comprehensively understands the theory in all its complexities and developments. He has been explicating, utilizing, and demonstrating its interpretive significance since 1970. In his work, *Words in Action*, Briggs follows Thiselton's lead and ventures beyond his teacher while demonstrating breadth and unique insight in dealing with the various discussions and applications of speech act theory. Briggs's work is especially significant as it comprises the only study since Evans with the sole purpose of utilizing the concepts of speech act theory to develop a hermeneutic for interpreting performative types of biblical texts.

Donald D. Evans and The Logic of Self-Involvement

Evans examines how certain types of language are self-involving, in other words, the logical connections between a person's utterances and their practical commitments, attitudes, and feelings.[145] Evans centers his investigation on the language of creation and presents the parameters of his study by posing the question:

> In saying, "The Creator made the world," does a man commit himself to any future conduct, or imply that he has a particular attitude or intention, or express a feeling or attitude? Or is the utterance a neutral, impersonal statement of fact, like saying, "Jones built the house"?[146]

As expected, Evans understands the language of creation as self-involving, and so the rest of his book sets out to demonstrate his thesis.

In Part I, Evans analyzes self-involving aspects of everyday language and begins his investigation by utilizing Austin's notion of performatives. He essentially adopts his teacher's illocutionary classifications but chooses to categorize them all as *performatives*. In addition, he replaces Austin's *expositives* with *constatives*. Evans claims that the reason for this surprising inclusion of constatives derives from one of Austin's own

145. It is important to note that Evans followed *The Logic of Self-Involvement* with a number of essays that reveal some modifications to his initial suggestions about performative language. However, Briggs has demonstrated that Evans's "work on self-involvement can still be pursued with profit today, independently of his own later modifications and changes in emphasis" (*Words in Action*, 166; for Briggs's excellent evaluation of Evans's earlier and later work, see pp. 152–66).

146. Evans, *Self-Involvement*, 11.

criteria for distinguishing the performative and constative—the latter are true or false.[147] However, the performative/constative distinction again becomes blurred by the fact that Evans identifies constatives as performatives within his own classification. Further, he concludes with Austin that "*all* utterances are deeds, all utterances have performative force."[148] What Evans actually distinguishes, then, is between *performatives* and what he calls *flat constatives*. This distinction centers on utterances that have *evaluative* or *value-judgment* aspects and those that do not. Flat constatives are statements, assertions, reports, and the like which do not entail a value-judgment whereas utterances that have evaluative elements constitute self-involving performatives.

Among Evans's five categories, he identifies *Behabitives* and *Commissives* as the two primary performatives expressing self-involvement. With this, Evans presents his fundamental idea:

> Behabitives are utterances in which the speaker implies various mental states (intentions, attitudes) other than, or in addition to, belief; Commissives are utterances in which the speaker commits himself to future patterns of more-than-verbal behaviour; flat Constatives are utterances which have a factual content, and which are neither Behabitive nor Commissive. Thus, *no flat Constative entails a Behabitive or Commissive*; that is, *no flat Constative entails a self-involving utterance.*[149]

"Self-involving performative force," then, "is what makes 'evaluative' language differ from other language in such a way that there is an 'autonomy of value.' "[150] Extending this analysis, Evans notes that no *flat exercitive* or *verdictive* entails a behabitive or commissive. All of this provides introductory support for Evans's thesis that based on "the *logical* character of the 'autonomy of value,' " the utterance, "God is my Creator," is not a flat constative.[151]

Evans further clarifies his distinction between performatives and flat constatives by discussing his notions of *performative* and *causal forces*, terms he uses instead of Austin's *illocution* and *perlocution*, respectively.[152] Evans relates these two forces to institutional-relation words which "include as part of their meaning some indication of conduct which is thought to be appropriate."[153] Further, "when words are used

147. For Evans's full discussion, see ibid., 38 n. 1.
148. Evans, ibid., 75; see Evans's discussion on pp. 44–46.
149. Ibid., 57.
150. Ibid., 58.
151. Ibid., 66.
152. Ibid., 71.
153. Ibid., 67.

performatively, institutional relations are sometimes established and sometimes invoked."[154] Evans distinguishes the two forces by claiming that the performative force forms part of an utterance's meaning whereas the causal force does not, and both are usually used independent of each other. For example, a speaker may say, "Jones is treacherous" *performatively* in order to warn the hearer or *causally* in order to alarm the hearer. Like his teacher, Evans here does not make a clear distinction between illocutions and perlocutions.

In his second and third chapters, Evans explores expressions of feeling and attitude. He describes two related ideas that prove important for his larger thesis: *rapportive language* and *onlooks*. Evans only touches on his notion of rapportive language, which is not a classification of use, but rather a *condition of understanding*.[155] Evans defines such language: "Where an utterance referring to an agent's action is *understood* only to the extent that one has an affinity and a rapport with the agent, the utterance is 'rapportive.'"[156] This type of language is typically self-*revealing* and does not need to be linguistically self-*involving*.

Onlooks involve the disposition of a person's attitude towards someone or something. When one states, "I'm for *x*," or "I regard *x* as important," that person *takes up "a position* in relation to *x*."[157] Thus, Evans coins the term "'onlook' as a substantive for what it is to 'look on *x* as *y*.'"[158] Obviously no flat constative entails "an expression of onlook" or "an utterance which implies an onlook."[159] According to Evans, onlooks can occur in a variety of ways. Certain performatives have a commissive element, which entails a personal involvement with *x* that naturally leads to one seeing *x* as *y*. Onlooks may also involve feelings as with expressives. Verdictives entail looking on *x* as *y*, which involves placing *x* within a structure, organization, or scheme. Further, the verdictive element in onlooks gives the behabitive element particularity. Furthermore, the utterance combining commissive and verdictive aspects combines an undertaking with a judgment.

Evans sets onlooks into two main classifications: *literal* and *non-literal*; and the latter includes *mere-metaphors*, *parabolic*, and *analogical onlooks*. Evans focuses his analysis on parabolic and analogical onlooks, which he identifies as the two main kinds of non-literal onlooks. The

154. Ibid., 68.
155. Ibid., 110–13.
156. Ibid., 110–11.
157. Ibid., 123.
158. Ibid., 125.
159. Ibid., 135.

former is exemplified by the sentence, "I look on Henry as a brother," where the similarity between *x* and *y* is the appropriate feelings and behavior. The latter is like the sentence, "I look on alcoholism as a disease," where the similarity also involves the appropriate response but additionally conveys an independent similarity as the basis of that response. From here, Evans extends his parabolic onlook notion to religious language and specifically *divine onlooks*, which constitute biblical assertions concerning God, humanity, and creation. "Religious belief is the conviction (or hope) that one's onlook conforms to an authoritative onlook, a divine onlook."[160] All this leads to the heart of Evans's argument "that the biblical conception of world-Creation is a 'vision for working purposes in the world.' It is a complex onlook-attitude which, the Christian believes, is 'prescribed by God'; that is, the divine onlook is authoritative."[161]

In Part II, Evans begins his analysis on creation as a performative action by presenting his working assumption: the Exodus events, which consisted of the miraculous deliverance from slavery and the institution of the covenant along with the giving of the land, "provided the paradigm case or norm for the rest of religious thought."[162] For Evans, "all Israelite thought about God tended to combine the ideas of miraculous power and society-producing authority."[163] Hence, creation of both the world and the nation Israel involves the dual concepts of "supernatural causal power" and "institutional authority." Regarding the creation of Israel, causal power is evidenced in the miracle of Israel's deliverance accomplished by Yahweh while institutional authority occurred through the establishment of the covenant between the two. The establishment of the covenant provides Israel with a subordinate status, an appointed role, a divinely bestowed value, and Yahweh's ongoing self-commitment and operative authority.

160. Ibid., 140.

161. Ibid., 141.

162. Ibid., 145–46. Evans appears to operate under the then-dominant view that Israel's conception of creation derived from its own historical creation. Until fairly recently, Old Testament interpreters simply assumed that Israel's creation theology was secondary at best (cf. Gerhard von Rad, "The Theological Problem of the Old Testament Doctrine of Creation," in *The Problem of the Hexateuch* (London: SCM Press, 1984), 131–43 [cf. 142]). This presupposition, however, can no longer be maintained (see, e.g., Rolf Knierim, "Cosmos and History in Israel's Theology," *HBT* 3 [1981]: 59–123). Despite Evans's presuppositions, his basic thesis does not rise or fall on this assumption and so it remains intact.

163. Evans, *Self-Involvement*, 145.

World-creation corresponds to the Exodus tradition as God's "word" has both causal power that brought about the existence of the world and institutional authority. The same four institutional ideas related to Israel also correlate with world-creation. Thus, God's word has exercitive force that establishes the subordinate status and role of the creature. His word further carries verdictive force that determines the value of the creature and, finally, commissive force, as God commits himself through his word of promise to maintain the order in creation. Evans elaborates on this last idea by stating:

> The efficacious word of God in Creation has not only supernatural causal power but also Exercitive, Verdictive and Commissive force; and man's word concerning the Creator who is Lord, Appointer, Evaluator and Guarantor is self-involving acknowledgment. In the biblical context, if I say, "God is my Creator," I acknowledge my status as God's obedient servant and possession, I acknowledge my role as God's steward and worshipper, I acknowledge God's gift of existence, and I acknowledge God's self-commitment to me. This act of acknowledgment includes both Behabitive and Commissive elements.[164]

Evans's thesis is that in the acknowledgment of God as creator, an exchange of self-involving performative utterances between the human being and God occurs that includes various implications and commitments. Evans does not draw a clear distinction between illocutionary acts and perlocutionary effects, as he earlier identifies the latter with causal forces. This breakdown obviously originates from Austin's work but may also derive from Evans's attempt to locate the hearer's self-involvement in God's creative utterances.[165] Evans goes on to say:

> In his utterance concerning Creation, biblical man implies that he takes the divine action to be a performative; that is, he *looks on* Creation *as* a performative action. This is a parabolic onlook, the basis for other parabolic onlooks… Thus, in various ways, the Creative "word" of God is correlated with the self-involving word of man. The correlation occurs because of a basic onlook: in the biblical context, a man looks on Creation as an action which has various performative forces and which is correlated with various performative replies… In the biblical context, world-Creation is understood in terms of a parabolic onlook. Thus, in the biblical context, the utterance "God is my Creator" is profoundly self-involving.[166]

164. Ibid., 158.

165. See further Briggs' assessment in light of Evans's later work (*Words in Action*, 165).

166. Evans, *Self-Involvement*, 159–60. It is important here briefly to comment on Evans's notion of "the biblical context," which ends up as a condition for successful self-involvement. For Evans, the biblical context constitutes what he calls

Importantly, such a self-involving utterance includes a *stance* towards a state of affairs expressed in the propositional content that then *entails* certain obligations and benefits.

The above presentation is sufficient to understand the essence of Evans's hermeneutic of self-involvement and how it impacts biblical interpretation. Evans's blurring of illocutionary acts and perlocutionary effects does not preclude the value of his notion of self-involvement. In fact, both Thiselton and Briggs demonstrate the significance of his work while at the same time maintaining a clear distinction between these two concepts.

Anthony C. Thiselton

Throughout much of his career, Thiselton has focused on developing and articulating a hermeneutic that incorporates speech act theory and comes under the larger concept of self-involvement. Thiselton expresses the essence of his hermeneutic of self-involvement by stating that

> the speaker "stands behind" the words giving *a pledge and personal backing* that he or she is prepared to undertake commitments and responsibilities that are entailed in extra-linguistic terms by the proposition which is asserted.[167]

"traditional-contextual": "the words have the meaning which is built up in the Bible as a whole, as the Bible is interpreted according to some theological tradition" (see further Briggs's assessment in light of Evans's later work [*Words in Action*, 165]). Evans acknowledges two aspects to his biblical context: the content of the biblical canon and various theological interpretative-traditions. Briggs correctly concludes that Evans is actually speaking of an *ideal* biblical context here. Briggs qualifies Evans's first context by putting the point as a conditional: "*if* one uses the word 'Creator' in an utterance like 'God is my Creator' in such a way that all the biblical connotations are intended, *then* one is actually doing much more than making a statement (uttering a flat constative) because one is thereby involved in a whole series of attitudinal and other self-involving speech acts" (*Words in Action*, 159). This context is obviously the most important, but one cannot deny that the interpretation of the Bible lies in the hands of various believing communities. Because various theological traditions exist, Evans acknowledges that perhaps a better phrase is "*a* biblical context"; yet, he chooses to continue to use "*the* biblical context" meaning "the biblical context which *I* am expounding" (*Self-Involvement*, 161). Here Evans explicitly divulges that he is talking in terms of an ideal biblical context. Thus one must include the additional condition of interpretive communities who determine what comprises and constitutes a self-involving utterance along with its implications and commitments.

167. Thiselton, *New Horizons*, 617. Briggs comments that Thiselton's observation here stands at the heart of self-involvement as a hermeneutical tool (*Words in Action*, 149).

For Thiselton, such a hermeneutic is not self-imposed upon the text, but rather reflects the very nature and intent of much of the biblical text. Thiselton asserts:

> In the biblical texts themselves, biblical authors are concerned to address the hearer or the reader, and in particular both Jesus and Paul, as well as the author of Luke–Acts, allow their material, vocabulary, and mode of communication to take account of the nature of the audience whom they are addressing.[168]

Towards the development of this interpretive strategy and early in his career, Thiselton first implemented Austin's notions along with the work of Wittgenstein and Evans in an essay concerning the parables of Jesus.[169] Thiselton specifically addresses Ernst Fuchs's emphatic contrast between functions of language in "language-event" (*Sprachereignis*) and propositions and assertions. For Thiselton, Fuchs's contrast eliminates the performative force of assertions, as they "may function in various ways and with various effects," which Wittgenstein and others have demonstrated.[170] Thus, Fuchs's sweeping generalization concerning assertions poses problems; however, in light of Austin and Wittgenstein, his notion of the parables as language-event, or as performative and self-involving, points in the right direction for interpreting the parables of Jesus. Thiselton has most recently revisited the parables in both the Old Testament and New Testament.[171] For Thiselton, the very use of parables demonstrates the fact that they purposefully draw in the hearer/reader "into the process of working out meaning, force and application." Thus, as "Wittgenstein, once again, urged, it is in the *application* of a piece of language in which meaning and understanding, as a communicative act or process, reside."[172]

Thiselton claims that his most creative use of Austin's work is found in his essay concerning the power of words.[173] Specifically he addresses those who appeal to a "Hebraic mind" that viewed language in a primitive

168. Thiselton, *New Horizons*, 273.

169. Thiselton, "The Parables as Language-Event: Some Comments on Fuch's Hermeneutics in the Light of Linguistic Philosophy," *SJT* 23 (1970): 437–68.

170. Thiselton, "Language-Event," 439; see Wittgenstein, *Investigations*, I §§21, 23, 24, 79.

171. See Thiselton, "Communicative Action," 164–72.

172. Thiselton, "'Behind' and 'In Front of' the Text: Language, Reference and Indeterminacy," in Bartholomew, Greene, and Möller, eds., *After Pentecost*, 97–120 (104).

173. Thiselton, "The Supposed Power of Words in the Biblical Writings," *JTS* 25 (1974): 283–99; see also idem, *New Horizons*, 292–93.

and simplistic sense and thus thought words possessed an innate, irresistible power.[174] In order to test the validity of such claims, Thiselton focuses on the words "curse" and "blessing" while contrasting the causal force of perlocutionary effects with the institutional force of illocutionary acts. Thiselton utilizes two aspects of Austin's work. First, blessing and cursing fall under his category of behabitives, which means that the words uttered by a person have power because they constitute a performative act. Thus, in general, "word and event are indeed one," but not because of *word-magic* which supposes words *do* things, but because blessing or cursing is a speech act. Second, blessing and cursing operate according to non-linguistic conventions. Hence, acts of blessing rest "on procedures or institutions accepted within Israelite society, and usually involving conventionally accepted formulae. They are effective, in most cases, only when performed by the appropriate person in the appropriate situation." Significantly, as in the case of Jacob's blessing upon Isaac, a "convention for withdrawing the performative utterance did not exist; hence the original performative utterance remains effectively in force."[175] Thiselton recognizes that blessing and cursing can be power-laden based on its divine origin. However, he distinguishes between supernatural utterances and performatives "which *do* things on the basis of conventional procedures in which the appropriate persons take part."[176] Here, Thiselton defines performatives as non-linguistic conventional utterances which corresponds to Austin's assumptions.

Thiselton's use of speech act theory has primarily centered on its interpretive value for Christology. Looking at the Synoptic Gospels, Thiselton explores Matthew's interest in the authority of Jesus' words and teaching that also elicit self-involvement. For instance, the speech act of Matt 28:18–20 contains three different types of illocutions. "Go therefore and make disciples" constitutes an *exercitive*, which appoints, commands, and assigns an institutional role. "Teaching them to observe all that I have commanded you" combines the *exercitive* and *behabitive* dimensions of authorization. "Lo, I am with you always, to the close of the age" represents a *commissive* that embodies the self-commitment of a promise or pledge. In relation to self-involvement, if "a present-day

174. Thiselton cites in particular Lorenz Dürr, *Die Wertung des göttlichen Wortes im Alten Testament und im antiken Orient* (Leipzig: Hinrichs, 1938), 52, 61, 71; Gerhard von Rad, *Old Testament Theology* (trans. D. M. G. Stalker; 2 vols.; New York: Harper & Row, 1962–65), 2:85.

175. Thiselton, "Power of Words," 294.

176. Ibid., 296. William J. Urbrock follows Thiselton's suggestions here in his essay "Blessings and Curses," *ABD* 1:755–61.

reader feels any sense of identification with the addressees, the effect of the language transcends information, or narrative report. A commission assigns a task and a role; an authorization confers a status, a pledge or a promise invites trust, and also action which takes the promise for its basis."[177]

Thiselton also looks at the implicit Christology lying hidden behind the overt speech acts of Jesus.[178] In particular, Thiselton investigates how the speech of Jesus in Luke often presupposes that he acted and spoke as Messiah. Thus, the *operative effectiveness* of particular utterances such as "My son, your sins are forgiven you" (Mark 2:5//Matt 9:2//Luke 5:20), "Be silent; come out of him" (Mark 1:25), and "Peace! Be still!" (Mark 4:35–41//Matt 8:23//Luke 8:22–25), "depends on *a state of affairs about the identity, role, and authority of Jesus*."[179] In other words, the operative nature of Jesus' speech acts depends upon the presupposition "that outside language Jesus possesses a particular institutional role and status."[180]

This leads Thiselton to address the problem of dualism in christological research by looking at the distinction between *institutional authority* and *perlocutionary causal force*. For Thiselton, this distinction is absolutely crucial for interpreting the Christology of the Synoptic Gospels:

> Explicit rhetoric urging christological claims risks subordinating illocutionary to perlocutionary force. On the other hand, operative illocutions raise the christological question (which may result in the inquirer's reaching a christological confession): "Who has the right, status, and institutionally validated role to 'acquit,' to 'judge,' to 'justify,' or to 'reckon as'?"[181]

A classic example distinguishing institutional authority and causal power occurs in the conversation between Jesus and the centurion whose slave needed healing (Luke 7:1–10). The centurion understood what it meant to stand in a chain of command and thus he could say, "only *say the word* and my servant will be *healed*" (vv. 7–8). With this in mind, distinguishing between these two concepts is key, as "the performing of acts on the basis of *causal force* constitutes in essence an *act of power through*

177. Thiselton, *New Horizons*, 286–87.

178. A. C. Thiselton, "Christology in Luke, Speech-Act Theory, and the Problem of Dualism in Christology after Kant," in *Jesus of Nazareth, Lord and Christ: Essays on the Historical Jesus and New Testament Christology* (ed. Joel B. Green and Max Turner; Grand Rapids: Eerdmans; Carlisle: Paternoster, 1994), 453–72 (466).

179. Ibid., 461.

180. Ibid., 454.

181. Ibid., 462–63.

self-assertion. On the other hand, illocutionary acts which rest on institutional roles serve their purpose as *acts which point by implication away from the self to some source of authority which lies beyond the self alone*."[182]

Thiselton also examines Searle's notion of direction of fit and notes that the language of biblical texts and of Christian theology operates in both directions. For Thiselton:

> The important direction of fit in terms of *cash value for the process of salvation is that the promissory language of Jesus can transform states of affairs to fit the messianic word of promise*. Here the promissory *word* is primary and life-changing. But this can be so...only because certain *truths about the status, authority, and role* of Jesus can in principle be asserted—that is, that the word fits the state of affairs which it portrays.

Accordingly, "christology has to do with an interplay between assertions which 'fit' states of affairs and changes in states of affairs to make them 'fit' a promissory word." With all this, Thiselton concludes that Searle's notion of "world-to-word" direction of fit touches a central nerve of Christology and helps to soften the problem of dualism in modern Christology, as the "many utterances...of what Jesus came to do carry presuppositions about his authorization and authority to put verbal promises, especially promises of God, into operative effect, where prophets, wise people, and others had failed to do so."[183]

Thiselton has most recently produced a commentary on 1 Corinthians and incorporates speech act theory in his interpretation.[184] Without dismissing the value of rhetorical analysis, Thiselton convincingly identifies illocutionary acts in Paul's writings which have been typically understood as instances of persuasive speech. In fact, he sets the whole letter of 1 Corinthians within the larger framework of contrasting Paul the *apostle* of Jesus Christ with the typical *rhetoricians* of the Greco-Roman world. Hence, to "write as *apostle* is to point away from the self and to disengage from the *causal* power of rhetoric in order to allow the *kerygma* of the gospel of the cross to perform the *illocutionary act* of transformation and promise in which both divine agent and apostolic agent pledge themselves to constraints that make possible its operative performance."[185] His conclusions provide for a more accurate

182. Ibid., 463.
183. Ibid., 466.
184. A. C. Thiselton, *The First Epistle to the Corinthians* (NIGTC; Grand Rapids: Eerdmans, 2000).
185. Thiselton, "Communicative Action," 225–26; see further idem, *Corinthians*, 41–52.

interpretation as well as a self-involving reading of the letter that goes beyond rhetorical analysis.

In his work with speech act theory, Thiselton demonstrates its interpretive value and at the same time its restricted application to certain types of texts. His work also displays that speech act theory constitutes one aspect of his hermeneutical approach. Thiselton shows tendencies in his earlier work of locating the operative force of performatives in non-linguistic convention; however, his later suggestion of the weak/strong spectrum adjusts this somewhat as he identifies Searle's prototype linguistic performative of promise as "a *very strong illocutionary act*."[186] Thiselton also highlights the fact that much of the language used in the biblical text is self-involving and not merely descriptive. Further, he exemplifies the importance of a comprehensive understanding of speech act theory, particularly focusing on the distinction between illocutionary acts and perlocutionary effects. This important point in speech act theory is insightfully used in both the interpretation of speech acts in the world of the text as well as speech acts addressing the reader.

Richard S. Briggs and Words in Action

In his book *Words in Action*, Briggs presents his hermeneutic of self-involvement in two main parts: (1) Speech Acts, Texts and Construal: The Problem of Criteria; and (2) Aspects of Self-Involvement in Interpreting New Testament Speech Acts. Briggs's essential understanding and adaptation of speech act theory proper has been presented throughout the previous section, which much of his hermeneutic assumes.

Following his preliminary analysis of speech act theory, Briggs concludes his first part with his idea of *construal* as an interpretive strategy. Briggs directly derives this notion from Searle's constitutive rule formula: X *counts as* Y in context C. To navigate between the *minimalist/objectivist* position—representational view of language—and the *constructivist/pragmatist* position—every locution *counts as* an illocution—Briggs suggests seeing construal operating across a spectrum of strengths. For Briggs, a weak construal is appropriate when construing *X* as *Y* is minimal or non-existent whereas stronger construal involves a more deliberate interpretive move.[187] This suggestion constitutes Briggs's *mediating position* that allows for both extreme types of construal along with others that range in-between them.[188] This paradigm is an additional,

186. Thiselton, "Communicative Action," 236–38.

187. Briggs, *Words in Action*, 122; for Briggs characterization of his spectrum of strengths, see p. 124.

188. For Briggs' ranges of possible formulations of construal, see ibid., 122.

but not correlated, variable to his weak/strong spectrum of illocutions. Hence, an explicit *strong* illocution requires a *weak* or minimal construal. Conversely, a *weak* illocution, such as "John sat down," may be read in a *strong* construal sense as an assertion, taken as an indication of John's protest, counted as the end of his speech and so on.[189]

In Part II Briggs begins by presenting his hermeneutic of self-involvement that draws substantially from Evans's original ideas. For Briggs, Evans's work demonstrates "that the reader of the biblical text is neither independent of that text, nor constituted entirely in the reading process, but is involved with the text by virtue of the irreducibly communicative dynamic of the text."[190] Briggs, agreeing with Thiselton, asserts that the basic point about self-involvement is that

> the speaking subject invests him or herself in a state of affairs by adopting a *stance* towards that state of affairs. Where self-involvement is most interesting and significant is in cases where the stance is logically (or "grammatically") *entailed* by the utterance itself.[191]

Such self-involvement is most noticeable in present tense first person language. Since many biblical expressions are functionally equivalent to first person utterance, self-involvement suggests itself as a useful hermeneutical option.

An important aspect of Briggs's thesis is his view that self-involvement is a *speech act category* which also operates across a spectrum of strengths as with illocutions. Distinction between strengths is not based in some property of language "but the felicity or otherwise of this distinction in clarifying points of interest." Following Evans, while the utterances "I am six feet four inches tall" and "I am a Christian" are grammatically similar; the former is weak whereas the latter is strong. The difference between the two utterances centers entirely upon the matter of the scope of the entailments. Thus in uttering the above strong utterance, "I take a *stance* in the public domain which *commits* me to certain forms of (positive and negative) behavior," which is in fact "strongly self-involving" language.[192] According to Briggs, although these utterances have identical surface grammar, their logical grammar is very different.

With his hermeneutic outlined, Briggs demonstrates how the language of confessing, forgiving, and teaching are self-involving in nature.

189. Ibid., 126–27.
190. Briggs, "Speech-Act Theory," 240.
191. Briggs, *Words in Action*, 148 (italics mine).
192. Ibid., 151 (italics mine).

Towards this end, Briggs adopts Terrence W. Tilley's understanding that these three types of utterances are "'*institutionally free*' declarative speech acts."[193] Yet, Briggs also recognizes the commissive and assertive forces included in such utterances. In Tilley's terms, "an institutionally free speech act is one which 'can be performed without regard to the person's institutional status or role,' in contrast to some status or role requirement within an institution which is necessary for the performance of institutionally bound speech acts."[194] In other words, the acts of confession, forgiveness, and teaching can generally be performed by anyone. These types of utterances are *institutionally free, self-involved speech acts*. With these preliminary thoughts in place, Briggs sets forth his thesis: "While the self may not be *constituted* by the performance of declarative speech acts, I shall endeavor to show how the self (the speaking subject) is, to use Ricoeur's word, *refigured* in the process of performing such acts."[195]

Briggs considers the *confession of faith* to be a strong illocution by virtue of its self-involving commissive and declarative forces. Briggs focuses his discussion on the earliest Christian confession, "Jesus is Lord." To "confess Jesus is therefore to stake one's claim in the public domain as a follower of Jesus. Its criteria are public: 'Jesus is Lord' said by someone who never makes reference to Jesus in any other instance is an infelicitous confession."[196] In contrast to the typical conclusion concerning this confession, Briggs emphasizes that "at issue are the non-linguistic states of affairs which underwrite the strong illocutionary act of confession. The self is *involved* with states of affairs, and not simply *constituted* by the adoption of some particular attitude."[197] This example displays the *dual focus* of a hermeneutic of self-involvement as identified by Evans: *stance* and *entailment*. The former concerns the states of affairs asserted in the propositional content of an utterance while the latter involves the lifestyle implications that normatively accompany the uttering of such a statement. It is self-involvement, rather than some other criteria such as the verb ὁμολογέω ("I confess"), that marks a confession as a strong speech act.

Briggs next looks at the *forgiveness of sin*. He initially remarks that the utterance, "I forgive you" performs a speech act, yet not all aspects of

193. Ibid., 179 (italics mine); Terrence W. Tilley, *The Evils of Theodicy* (Washington: Georgetown University Press, 1991), 72.

194. Briggs, *Words in Action*, 180; Tilley, *Theodicy*, 33.

195. Briggs, *Words in Action*, 179; for his full discussion, see pp. 180–82.

196. Ibid., 186.

197. Ibid., 187.

forgiveness can be analyzed from a speech act perspective. With this qualification, Briggs discusses the theological problem of forgiveness and concludes, following Joram G. Haber's performative account, that it is the "overcoming of resentment."[198] Briggs finds additional benefits from Haber's model, which allows him to focus on the nature of institutional facts involved in forgiveness. Using Haber's sixth condition of forgiveness—"S has overcome his resentment for X's doing A, or is at least willing to try to overcome it"—coupled with Searle's formula of constitutive rules, Briggs expresses forgiveness as:

> (6a) S is willing to count X as X' who did not perform A but this cannot be cashed out as a statement such as (6b) The offensive results of A are removed or destroyed precisely because of the distinction between brute and institutional facts.

In general, "in forgiving we may say that the forgiver adjusts his or her stances towards the various brute facts involved, and thus changes the institutional facts involved."[199]

For Briggs, a key question to ask is not is such and such an attitude or action or disposition a sin but which of these *count as* sin. Briggs argues that "sin is an institutional fact created out of the act of counting acts or dispositions as evils." Evil is "the mysterious brute fact" and, in "a certain sense, evil impinges on the creation as brute facts which are the chaos from which we fashion our institutional facts, which are the sins."[200] Briggs follows the general theological understanding of sin as a *dispositional* phenomenon—human beings are inherently sinful—and concludes that in forgiving, "the forgiver's *disposition* is refigured through an act of self-involvement. At the same time, a new stance is taken toward brute facts, which is in accord with Haber's condition (6) on overcoming resentment." Hence, forgiveness represents a *refiguring* of dispositions, but more importantly the speech act itself *refigures* the institutional realities concerned through an act of self-involvement.[201] The speech act of forgiveness is felicitous when the stance of resentment is overcome and the institutional fact of sin is successfully removed.

198. Briggs cites here J. G. Haber, *Forgiveness* (Savage: Rowman & Littlefield, 1991). For Briggs summary and critiques of Haber's ideas, see *Words in Action*, 220–28.

199. Briggs, *Words in Action*, 224. Briggs offers the example that "if you burned down my house, and the house no longer stands, this is a brute fact unaffected by my forgiveness, whereas the institutional fact that you owe me £50,000 to rebuild the house may be forgiven, and, indeed, 'removed' from our social reality" (ibid.).

200. Ibid., 229.

201. Ibid., 234 (italics mine).

From this perspective Briggs explores forgiveness in the New Testament and focuses his study around the uses of ἀφίημι and ἄφεσις organized around the self-involved speech act categories of *stance* and *entailment*. Briggs's thesis is that "forgiveness in the New Testament is concerned above all with issues of *reciprocity* (stance) and *membership* (entailment)."[202] Briggs first examines *reciprocity* and isolates Matt 6:14–15 as a representative formulation. Here, the speech act "I forgive your debt (to me)" overcomes resentment with the expectation of repayment abandoned. This in turn alters the institutional fact. The logical grammar of this passage is not that God's forgiveness is offered only after the human act of forgiveness; rather "the human person involved is *re-constituted* (or refigured, to use Ricoeur's word) through performing the act of human forgiveness in such a way that he or she becomes a recipient of God's forgiveness."[203] The refigured *stance* realized through forgiveness leads to the *entailment* of restored relationship.

The speech act of *teaching* is Briggs's final topic, which he suggests is of particular interest for exploring the relationship between brute and institutional facts. Briggs identifies teaching as a speech act that combines various illocutionary forces and is thus a multidimensional speech act: "*assert* and *tell* as assertives; *assure* and *certify* as commissives; *tell*, *instruct* and *prescribe* as directives; *declare*, *approve*, *stipulate*, *define* and so forth as declaratives; and perhaps even *acclaim* and *disapprove* as expressives."[204] Due to this range of illocutions, Briggs sees the speech act of teaching operating across the spectrum of strengths. Hence, "the speech act of teaching can rarely be reduced to simply informing someone that something is the case."[205]

Briggs's work provides an essential and important contribution for understanding speech act theory itself and how aspects of it can be applied interpretively to the biblical text. Still, there are several issues that need addressing before concluding this section. First, Briggs disagrees with his teacher by arguing that speech act theory is not an answer to the hermeneutical problem.[206] Yet, the very notion of self-involvement points to a *fusion of horizons* between the reader and the text, as both Evans and Thiselton demonstrate. Further, Briggs's own arguments concerning self-involvement do not seem to correspond to his stated position. For example, Briggs asserts that "illocutionary acts are simply

202. Ibid., 240.
203. Ibid., 242 (italics mine).
204. Ibid., 257–58.
205. Ibid., 262.
206. Ibid., 6–9.

incomprehensible if they are abstracted from the on-going commitments and public stances required of a speaker (or interpreter)."[207] Thus, in strongly self-involving cases the speaking subject is "an irreducible aspect of the *process of understanding*."[208] Briggs correctly asserts that speech act theory is not a comprehensive interpretive tool, but a hermeneutic of self-involvement, especially as envisioned by Briggs himself, which directs the reader to *involve* one*self* with the text whereby meaning is determined.

Second, Briggs's expansion on Evans's notion of self-involvement as a speech act category needs further clarification. In the language utilized by speech act theorists, the term "category" is generally synonymous with "classification" in regards to illocutionary typologies. Briggs also considers stance and entailment as speech act categories and self-involvement as a force. In his larger program, Briggs summarizes the scope of the interpretive relevance of speech act theory to three *strong* categories: strong illocutions, strong construal, and strong self-involvement;[209] thus, separating strong illocutions from strong self-involvement. Self-involvement, though, does not express force alone in every instance, as Briggs, along with Evans, continually acknowledges illocutionary forces expressing strong self-involvement. Although he sees self-involvement ranging from strong to weak, his work often reflects that this is based more on accompanied illocutionary forces rather than self-involvement alone, which generally corresponds to the very nature of illocutionary acts as observed above.

Before drawing any conclusions on this issue, the related concept of institutionally free speech acts needs examining. The question arises, "Is self-involvement considered a speech act category in order to allow for non-conventional utterances to *count as* strong illocutionary acts?" On the one hand, Briggs affirms this question, as "institutionally free" for him essentially means that anyone, and specifically those *not* occupying an authorized position, can perform utterances that *count as* strong speech acts.[210] On the other hand, Briggs discusses the implications of self-involving utterances operating because of formal institutions. In other instances, Briggs identifies the notion of *institutionally free utterances* with *self-involved non-conventional utterances*. Thus, Briggs's notion of self-involvement as a speech act category may be a way to maintain the basic speech act principles of Austin and Searle and their

207. Briggs, "Speech-Act Theory," 264 (italics mine).
208. Briggs, *Words in Action*, 152 (italics mine).
209. Ibid., 295.
210. This is exactly Tilley's point (see *Theodicy*, 55).

emphasis on non-linguistic convention along with his own stated concept of strong illocutions, while, at the same time, allowing for certain non-conventional utterances to *count as* strong speech acts that contain the sole dimension of self-involvement providing the sufficient and legitimate force necessary for such categorization.

To conclude, in addition to his theoretical discussions on speech act theory proper Briggs's use of speech act theory and advancement of Evans's original work exhibit three main contributions. First, Briggs provides an insightful expansion upon Evans and Thiselton in the development of a hermeneutic of self-involvement that focuses on the personal involvement of the reader in the performative language expressed in the biblical text. Second, Briggs raises the real possibility of identifying additional illocutions that are not clearly distinguished by illocutionary markers. Through a Searlean form of construal, one can *count* certain locutions *as* illocutions. Searle's constitutive rule formula provides a speech act criterion for determining illocutionary acts which would not otherwise be conceived as such. Finally, he more fully develops the important notion of self-involvement as a speech act category that allows for certain utterances that solely express self-involvement to *count as* strong speech acts. As I have discussed above, self-involvement is a central component to the entire framework of speech act theory, especially as stressed by Alston. The nature of illocutionary acts contains to one degree or another the dimension of self-involvement. Yet, as Briggs claims, certain self-involving utterances that do not necessarily contain any other illocutionary markers or non-linguistic conventions can *count as* strong communicative action. This correlates with the above conclusions that certain utterances can be classified as performatives or as strong illocutionary acts because of clear extralinguistic, self-involved stances or actions expressed or assumed in the linguistic content. Hence, such strong self-involving utterances are speech acts and a speech act category set alongside strong illocutionary acts.

Conclusion

Correlated with the concepts espoused by speech act theorists, Evans, Thiselton, and Briggs provide a sound framework for understanding the interpretive relevance of speech act theory. More specifically, with some slight adjustments and clarifications, these three interpreters demonstrate the more significant uses of speech act theory in biblical exegesis; specifically, the illocutionary/perlocutionary distinction along with the overarching hermeneutic and speech act category of self-involvement. These discussions along with the previous sections form a grid for applying speech act theory in biblical interpretation along with analyzing the various attempts at incorporating it in Old Testament interpretation, which will be examined in the following chapter.

Chapter 2

UTILIZATIONS OF SPEECH ACT THEORY IN OLD TESTAMENT INTERPRETATION

Since the inception of speech act theory not many Old Testament interpreters have explored its use for biblical exegesis; however, in the last decade or so a few studies have incorporated the discipline ranging from simple identification of performative utterances to developing speech act type criticisms.

Performative Verbs and Utterances in Old Testament Translation and Interpretation

Semitic Performative Verbs

Semitic specialists have been identifying performative type verbs and expressions in Akkadian, Ugartic, and Classical Hebrew. Such analysis has become an accepted and important component in Semitic syntactic description.[1] For instance, the Assyriologist Werner Mayer presents a list of "performative" (*Koinzidenzfall*) verbs for a number of Semitic languages.[2] In their analysis of Hebrew syntax, Bruce K. Waltke and M. O'Connor designate a verbal category as the "instantaneous perfect" which "represents a situation occurring at the very instant the expression is being uttered," which chiefly occurs with *verba dicendi* (verbs of speaking, swearing, declaring, advising, etc.).[3] In line with these studies, Dilbert R. Hillers also offers a list of Hebrew performative verbs.[4] Some of the verbs suggested by these specialists, however, are not

1. Dilbert R. Hillers, "Some Performative Utterances in the Bible," in *Pomegranates and Golden Bells* (Festschrift Jacob Milgrom; ed. David P. Wright, David N. Freedman, and Avi Hurvitz; Winona Lake, Ind.: Eisenbrauns, 1995), 757–66 (757).

2. Werner Mayer, *Untersuchungen zur Formensprache der babylonischen "Gebetsbesch-wörungen"* (Studia Pohl: Series Major 5; Rome: Pontifical Biblical Institute Press, 1976), 183–201.

3. *IBHS* §30.5.1d.

4. Hillers, "Performative Utterances," 761–64.

performatives as speech act theorists describe. For instance, Hillers identifies the phrase שלחתי לך שחד, "*I am sending* you a present" (2 Kgs 15:19//2 Chr 16:3), as a performative. Similarly, Waltke and O'Connor propose פרשתי ידי אליך, "*I spread out* my hands to you" (Ps 143:6a), as an example of their instantaneous perfective. The criterion employed in these instances appears to be that the action is either reported or accomplished *while* speaking, not necessarily speaking *counting as* doing. Such verb lists can provide help towards identifying illocutionary acts, but in certain instances the verbs classified as performatives do not match the nature of performative utterances.

In a similar way, Dennis Pardee and Robert Whiting have examined the relationship between epistolary perfects and performatives and conclude that such verbs are not performatives.[5] Thus, and as concluded above, writing, sending, requesting and the like are all reporting an action rather than effecting one.[6] They do identify the prostration formula—for example, "seven (times) and seven (times) do I fall"—as "a pure performative," an "epistolary-performative." This is true because the utterance "effects the act of obeisance without necessarily performing the act to which the formula makes reference" as with Austin's behabitive, "I salute you."[7] Extending this analysis and from a self-involvement perspective, the behabitive expresses a particular *stance* or posture the person takes in relation to the addressee and at the same time the commissive dimension *entails* that the speaker/writer acts in certain ways in relation to the addressee. Pardee and Whiting also see the blessing formula "I (hereby) bless you," particularly in later West Semitic letters, as a performative ("the declaration of the blessing effects the blessing = *benedictio*");[8] however, they do not explain how the action transpires in speech act terminology. Pardee and Whiting show more caution when identifying performatives and when doing so their analysis essentially corresponds to the criteria established by speech act theorists.

Performative Verbs and Utterances in Old Testament Translation

In a short essay, Norbert Lohfink limitedly uses speech act theory in order to examine covenant as a "contract" (*Vertrag*) in Deut 26–29.[9] Although

5. Dennis Pardee and Robert M. Whiting, "Aspects of Epistolary Verbal Usage in Ugaritic and Akkadian," *BSO(A)S* 50 (1987): 1–31 (cf. esp. 23–28). Pardee briefly discussed this relationship in "The 'Epistolary Perfect' in Hebrew Letters," *BN* 22 (1983): 34–40.

6. Pardee and Whiting, "Epistolary Verbal Usage," 30.

7. Ibid., 29–30; Austin, *Things with Words*, 81, 85.

8. Pardee and Whiting, "Epistolary Verbal Usage," 4, 30–31.

9. N. Lohfink, "Bund als Vertrag im Deuteronomium," *ZAW* 107 (1995): 215–39.

he is aware of Searle's work, Lohfink primarily refers to Austin, and specifically his criterion for explicit performatives. Lohfink identifies 28:69 and 26:17–19 as instances expressing a "report" (*Protokoll*) of a performative.[10] He specifically identifies 27:1, 9 and 29:9–14 as performatives.[11] Lohfink's speech act analysis begins and ends with simple performative identification and thus he only provides an entry point for utilizing the discipline for interpretation.

On a much larger scale, Andreas Wagner has recently produced a manual for interpreters to identify illocutionary acts within the biblical text.[12] Wagner's discussion on the philosophical understanding of speech act theory is informed by both Austin and Searle, as well as other earlier theorists. The overall presentation of his book primarily operates along the different classifications of illocutionary acts. Although he is aware of other taxonomies, Wagner chooses to use Searle's categories.[13] He identifies the five classifications by four Hebrew verb lists[14] and additional grammatical criteria such as volitional expressions,[15] interjections,[16] and confessions.[17] Another important illocutionary marker for Wagner is Austin's explicit performative criterion.[18]

Wagner has followed this work with two essays that explore specific texts in order to demonstrate the importance of speech act theory in biblical exegesis, and specifically, in relation to identifying illocutionary forces for translating.[19] For instance, he examines Gen 1:29 and identifies the verbal clause as a declarative and a first person performative. To indicate its performative function, he follows Austin's notion by inserting "hereby" (*hiermit*) into his translation: ויאמר אלהים הנה נתתי לכם...,

10. Ibid., 224–25.

11. Ibid., 224–26.

12. Andreas Wagner, *Sprechakte und Sprechaktanalyse im Alten Testament: Untersuchungen im biblischen Hebräisch an der Nahstelle zwischen Handlungsebene und Grammatik* (BZAW 253; Berlin: de Gruyter, 1997).

13. For Wagner's discussion and examples, see ibid., 20–27, 220–43.

14. Ibid., 98–132.

15. Ibid., 133–38.

16. Ibid., 161–210.

17. Ibid., 210–20.

18. Ibid., 93–98, 155–57.

19. Andreas Wagner, "Die Bedeutung der Sprechakttheorie für Bibelübersetzungen, Aufgezeigt an Gen 1,29, Ps 2,7 und Dtn 26,17–19," in *The Interpretation of the Bible* (ed. Jože Krašovec; JSOTSup 289; Sheffield: Sheffield Academic Press, 1998), 1575–88; idem, "Die Stellung der Sprechakttheorie in Hebraistik und Exegese," in *Congress Volume: Basel, 2001* (ed. A. Lemaire; VTSup 92; Leiden: Brill, 2002), 55–83.

"*Da sprach Gott: 'Hiermit gebe ich euch... '.*"[20] He similarly designates as declaratives the nominal clauses in Job 2:6, הנו בידך אך את־נפשו שמר, "*Hiermit ist er in deiner Hand. Aber schone sein Leben,*" and 1:12, הנה כל־אשר־לו בידך רק אליו אל־תשלח ידך, "*Hiermit ist alles, was ihm gehört, in deiner Hand. Nur gegen ihn sollst du deine Hand nicht ausstrecken.*"[21] Wagner analyzes Ps 2 in a more extensive manner. In general, he sees the psalm comprised of "directive questions" and "assertive responses" (*Repräsentative Aussagen*).[22] Within this four-strophe psalm, Wagner focuses on v. 7 and identifies the nominal clause in v. 7aβ, בני אתה, and the verbal clause in v. 7b, אני היום ילדתיך, as declaratives. He indicates their performative nature by again inserting *hiermit* in each clause, "*Du bist (hiermit) mein Sohn. Ich "gebäre" dich hiermit.*" In connection with this type of utterance, Wagner has explored the existence of explicit performatives uttered in the second and third persons.[23] He specifically identifies 2 Sam 12:13 and 1 Sam 10:1 as clear examples. The former text does contain a declarative/performative which is introduced by the narrator. The second example begins with a narrative description of Samuel's actions followed by Wagner's declarative which is a rhetorical question. This utterance is essentially an indirect speech act, which I will discuss in Chapter 4, and in this instance it operates through non-linguistic conventions (Samuel pouring oil on Saul's head followed by a kiss); but it is not a declarative/performative in the sense of how Austin and Searle describe. Regarding the utterance in Ps 2:7, it is actually the king repeating or giving voice to Yahweh's speech—somewhat like a confession—that would most likely operate through non-linguistic conventions. I will reserve any further comments until Chapter 4 where I will additionally discuss this type of utterance in relation to Isa 49:3.

Wagner critiques Lohfink's suggestion that Deut 26:17–19 constitutes a *Protokoll*. According to Wagner, these verses express a declarative explicit performative speech act in the same way as 2 Sam 12:13 along with the declarative nature of אמר in the Hiphil.[24] Thus he begins both vv. 17 and 18 with *hiermit* and translates אמר as "declare" (*erklären*).[25] In line with the above discussion, Wagner does not appear to take into account that Moses here is rehearsing what Israel and Yahweh "declared" earlier; the actual declarative utterance does not occur in these verses.

20. See Wagner, "Bibelübersetzungen," 1576–78; idem, "Hebraistik und Exegese," 70.

21. Wagner, "Hebraistik und Exegese," 71.

22. Ibid., 72–79; see also idem, "Bibelübersetzungen," 1577–78.

23. Wagner, *Sprechaktanalyse*, 155–57.

24. See Wagner, "Bibelübersetzungen," 1580–84.

25. Ibid., 1584.

Wagner's work, especially his monograph, provides a significant contribution to the Old Testament interpreter for incorporating speech act theory into biblical exegesis. He does not enter into much interpretive discussion, but as a manual it offers examples of Hebrew illocutionary markers and verbal and nonverbal utterances for the interpreter to begin identifying illocutionary speech acts. Wagner demonstrates sophistication in his speech act analysis, though, as he astutely recognizes, the verb ברך can express different illocutionary forces and hybrids depending upon grammatical and contextual factors.[26] His translations are not necessarily unique, but he introduces illocutionary analysis into the equation in a manner which ultimately impacts interpretation. Still, in order to properly and critically utilize his suggestions, one must have a basic working knowledge of speech act theory which includes the more recent discussions. Wagner provides an extensive Hebrew verb list and as with other such lists it must be utilized with the qualifications discussed above. Further, his confining illocutions to Searle's taxonomy can potentially mislead as well as restrict illocutionary analysis. In the final analysis, Wagner's speech act guide can be used fruitfully for exploring the usefulness of speech act theory in biblical exegesis.

Performative Verbs and Utterances and Interpretation

Tryggve N. D. Mettinger employs a source and redactional approach to the historical development of the monarchy in Israel while incorporating Austin's speech act theory in a few instances.[27] Regarding performatives, he analyzes the divine first person language used in the actualization of a chosen individual becoming king and the son of God. For instance, in the Succession Narrative, Solomon's designation as נגיד (1 Kgs 1:35) "is a performative utterance and is to be understood as meaning 'and I hereby appoint him *nagîd*…' "[28] Thus, these words are not reflecting an earlier designation, as often thought, but rather "David's words instantly bring about the state of things that they speak of."[29] Similarly, following the casting of lots, the people appointed Saul as king through their acclamation (1 Sam 10:24) which "had the character of a performative utterance."[30] Divine performative utterances also determine the nature of royal charisma: martial for Saul and judicial wisdom for Solomon.[31]

26. See Wagner, *Sprechaktanalyse*, 253–85.

27. Tryggve N. D. Mettinger, *King and Messiah: The Civil and Sacral Legitimation of the Israelite Kings* (ConBOT 8; Lund: Gleerup, 1976).

28. Ibid., 23.

29. Ibid., 161–62.

30. Ibid., 135.

31. Ibid., 240–41.

Mettinger also suggests that the Servant of Yahweh in Isa 40–55 displays royal features and particularly in the first Servant Song. He understands the verb נתתי in 42:1bα as a performative that actualizes the reception of "the charisma of the Spirit."[32] Mettinger additionally looks at the divine sonship of the king. Similar to Wagner, he concludes that the phrase in Ps 2:7aβ–b constitutes a divine solemn, performative utterance that "initiates the king's status as son of God at the same moment that it is pronounced."[33] After examining Pss 89 and 110, Mettinger concludes that the king's "divine sonship commenced at a definite point in time and was brought about by a performative utterance of God," a divine act of will and not by descent.[34] Mettinger's work is insightful and demonstrates a sound implementation of Austin's theory. His study exemplifies the value that speech act theory can have on exegesis and also historical inquiry in the examination of certain types of texts. Yet, as with Wagner's observations, his discussion on Ps 2 needs some modification.

Perlocutionary Effect Criticism

Old Testament interpreters have often fused speech act theory with rhetorical and/or literary analysis.[35] Further, they typically employ this eclectic type method primarily to locate perlocutionary effects in the biblical text.[36] The most significant work among those utilizing speech act theory to this end has been conducted by Dale Patrick.

Patrick has appealed to speech act theory on a number of occasions with the culmination of his work expressed in his most recent book exploring the rhetoric of revelation.[37] Patrick recognizes Wolterstorff and

32. Ibid., 249.

33. Ibid., 261.

34. Ibid., 265, 266.

35. E.g. Donald K. Berry, *The Psalms and Their Readers: Interpretive Strategies for Psalm 18* (JSOTSup 153; Sheffield: Sheffield Academic Press, 1993).

36. Those who coalesce speech act theory with literary and/or rhetorical criticisms often appeal to Stanley Fish ("Austin and Searle," 197–245) along with Mary L. Pratt (*Toward a Speech Act Theory of Literary Discourse* [Bloomington: Indiana University Press, 1977]). It is important to note that in Fish's subsequent Preface to his essay he concluded that his speech act analysis of Shakespeare's *Coriolanus* was a series of large mistakes (pp. 197–200). See further Briggs's rigorous analysis of the early and later Fish where he turns his early argument on its head as Fish himself distinguishes between "trivial" and "significant" illocutions, which ends up supporting the notion of strong and weak illocutions (*Words in Action*, 86–91). See also Briggs's balanced assessment of Pratt's use of speech act theory (ibid., 91–95).

37. Dale Patrick, *The Rhetoric of Revelation in the Hebrew Bible* (OBT; Minneapolis: Fortress, 1999); cf. the Bibliography for the articles on which this work builds.

his work *Divine Discourse* as "an ideal dialog partner";[38] yet more often than not he contrasts his ideas with the philosopher's. He sees Evans's original work, though, as providing more support for his suggestions.[39] Despite these affinities, he makes it quite clear that his method extends beyond the philosophical concerns of speech act theory.

Patrick focuses on what he calls a *transaction* between text and audience, that is, how the biblical text *performs* in relation to a reading audience. He conceives this transaction through rhetorical criticism along with literary criticism in combination with speech act theory. Patrick confesses that in a previous work with Allen Scult, "I began to *synthesize* rhetorical analysis with J. L. Austin's speech-act theory.[40] Discourse not only persuades by what it says, but by what happens between speaker and addressee in the saying."[41] Patrick asserts that the rhetorical dimension of performatives has not been of much concern among speech act theorists. Further, speech acts are pragmatic and as "interpreters of discourse, we are justified in regarding *performative utterances*, as well as other categories of discourse, as *rhetorical phenomenon*."[42]

In general, Patrick's method involves tracing the performative rhetorical and literary strategies of the text. To locate the rhetorical dimension of performative utterances, Patrick suggests that one must "move from viewing the illocutionary act as performance of a speaker to a *transaction* between speaker and addressee." This transaction is found in Austin's notion of perlocutionary effect. Certain types of speaking do not cause effects as the addressee "may refuse to respond appropriately." Consequently, rhetoric becomes a necessary dimension in language use and thus "a speaker will choose an *illocutionary act* and wording that promises to *strike* the addressee favorably."[43]

Patrick's overall thesis is: "God's utterances are—at least in significant cases—linguistic acts that put in force the knowledge they communicate."[44] Patrick elaborates on his thesis by suggesting that

> the performative utterances of God require responses from the addressee, which differ in kind from those that do not. The performative creates the knowledge it communicates and constructs a relationship between

38. Ibid., 183.

39. Patrick compares and contrasts with these two authors, see ibid., 183–96.

40. Dale Patrick and Alan Scult, *Rhetoric and Biblical Interpretation* (JSOTSup 82; Sheffield: Almond Press, 1990).

41. Patrick, *Rhetoric of Revelation*, xvii–xviii (italics mine).

42. Ibid., 12 (italics mine).

43. Ibid., 10 (italics mine).

44. Ibid., 8; for Patrick's idea of performative utterances creating revelation, see ibid., 52, 119, 184–88.

> speaker and addressee. To know the truth of the utterance, the addressee must enter into the relationship and play the role specified by the illocutionary force of the utterance.[45]

Patrick sees performative utterances such as promises creating revelation or knowledge. This type of utterance provides *potential* relationship with all its benefits, but the utterance is only truly operative when the hearer ventures out and trusts that promise. The promise has been rhetorically designed in such a way to persuade the addressees of its truth. If the hearer responds, a *transaction* between the speaker and addressee transpires that actualizes the promise and thus creates the constructed relationship. This transaction occurs on two levels: (1) between the personae within the textual world, which provides a grid for (2) a transaction between the narrative world and the reader.

To demonstrate his thesis, Patrick's "classic example" is the call of Moses (Exod 3–4).[46] Throughout the text, Patrick identifies several performative utterances: the revelation of the name Yahweh, God's commission to Moses to act as his agent, God's promise of deliverance to the enslaved Israelites, and the command to celebrate the Passover meal. The giving of the name (3:14) creates a new reality that "is a gracious act toward Moses and the people, for it grants accessibility to God in prayer."[47] The institution of the name in 3:15 expresses exercitive force of a command that establishes the framework for all future commerce between God and people. The giving of the name also makes God's previous promise of deliverance (3:8) more believable, as the promise alone cannot be confirmed by reason or experience. Although Yahweh has obligated himself to fulfill his promise through his utterance, Moses and the people must initiate its actualization by first trusting in order to experience the reality of the promised deliverance. Persuasion to trust is also conveyed through God's *expression of feelings* that has motivated him to liberate Israel (3:7, 9, 16). Performatively, it gives access to God's mind as well as it implicates him in the truth of the utterance. Rhetorically, God's motive provides the basis for trusting in the promise.[48]

Moses' commission is also a performative act which expresses an exercise of authority related to the power of command. In order to realize the illocutionary force of the commission, "Moses must accept God's

45. Ibid., 193.

46. Patrick originally explored this text in his book *The Rendering of God in the Old Testament* (OBT; Philadelphia: Fortress, 1981), 94–96. The basic notions of this analysis are found in idem, "The Rhetoric of Revelation," *HBT* 16 (1994): 20–40.

47. Patrick, *Rhetoric of Revelation*, 24.

48. Ibid., 26.

authority in the utterance and respond by taking responsibility for the role assigned him. Moses must obey, confident in the commission, to discover in the course of events whether it is true."[49] Thus:

> To know is not to do, and without the doing the knowledge—which consists of performative utterances—is empty. Moses can know the truth of the promise and the supporting utterances only if he embarks on the journey. Revelation becomes knowledge of God only when it is received in faith and obedience.[50]

In fact, the objections of Moses demonstrate that he is not within the relationship provided by the performative utterance. Following Moses' initial objection, God assures him with what Patrick calls "language of prediction," something which is not performative in character (3:18–20). These utterances are contingent on the promise and commission. Here, Patrick's assessment may work for vv. 18 and 19, but v. 20 is an example of Searle's linguistic declarative/performative utterance. Patrick concludes his exegesis with a brief examination of Exod 6:2–13, which he also classifies as a call of Moses. The difference between the two calls is that in ch. 6 "the performatives now 're-create' a relationship and promise already in force."[51] This recreation is based on Yahweh's promises of the past and not on the groaning of his people as in Exod 3. It remains unclear, though, how such recreation comes about and how the mention of groaning in v. 5a fits with this conclusion. Unfortunately, Patrick also passes over the various declarative/performative utterances expressed in vv. 6–8.

Patrick next turns to his main concern of the transaction between text and audience. "The rhetoric of the narrative seeks to elicit the kind of faith in YHWH's promises and commands that they originally called for."[52] In order for a "fusion of the horizons" to occur, the reading audience must not be passive, rather "it must construe and apply the communication." Patrick also notes that transaction between text and reader cannot occur when readers "adopt the *stance* of impartial observers."[53]

According to Patrick, the revelation and institution of the name reaches beyond the narrative horizon to include the audience. The giving of the name "is both a command and promise, for it instructs the audience in how it can gain access to YHWH; obviously it applies to the reading

49. Ibid., 28.
50. Patrick, "Rhetoric of Revelation," 30.
51. Patrick, *Rhetoric of Revelation*, 31.
52. Patrick, "Rhetoric of Revelation," 32.
53. Patrick, *Rhetoric of Revelation*, 32; see further p. xix.

audience just as much as to the personages of the narrative world."[54] Most importantly, the reading audience is included among the textual addressees through "ritual reenactment" of the Passover meal. The command to perform the Passover directly addresses the reader (Exod 13:3, 8–9). By obeying the command, the reader becomes the recipient of the promise of deliverance the command implements. Patrick claims:

> The promise of deliverance from slavery becomes the inauguration of a continuing relationship between YHWH and Israel, a relationship that continues into the Passover present. The people become the recipients of this promise by identifying themselves with Israel in the performance of God's commandment. Thus…the text enters into a performative transaction with the audience not by promises that apply to the audience, but by commandments that incorporate individuals into the people whose Lord is a God of promise.[55]

The design of the entire exodus narrative rhetorically aims at highlighting the demonstration of Yahweh's power (cf. Exod 10:1–2), which produces a "monotheistic" rendering of the exodus event. Thus, the narrative presentation of Yahweh's monopoly of power becomes the persuasive means for the audience to obey the command of performing the Passover, which in turn provides ways to witness and confirm this power in the re-enactment of the event.

Patrick displays how one can utilize several reading criticisms with speech act theory. Patrick also discloses knowledge of Austin's view of illocutionary acts and performatives,[56] but his rhetorical program seems to compel him to describe illocutions and performatives in terms of perlocutions. This is further exemplified in Patrick's conclusion as he contrasts his work with Wolterstorff's. He reflects again on the promise in Exod 3:8 and asserts that in order for Moses to experience the promise, he must first trust God. He goes on to say that the "promise must, to use Austin's terms, have the proper perlocutionary effect *to have its* illocutionary force. Many promises and agreements are performative *transactions*—all parties must play their assigned role for the action to succeed."[57] Quite possibly due to his sole appeal to Austin, Patrick suggests that performative utterances simultaneously *count as* illocutionary acts and perlocutionary effects. Further, perlocutionary effects comprise the operating force for illocutions. Clearly such an understanding is erroneous from a speech act perspective, as illocutions do not depend upon

54. Ibid., 35.
55. Ibid., 39–40.
56. See ibid., 7–10.
57. Ibid., 187 (italics mine).

perlocutions, rather vice versa. Patrick's speech act imprecision is additionally seen in his assertion that an expression of feeling *counts as* a performative. Following his dialogue with Wolterstorff, Patrick presents Evans's notion of behabitives and self-involvement, but he does not use this analysis in his own interpretation.[58] Although Patrick's ideas on feelings have merit, an illocutionary analysis coupled with notion of self-involvement would provide ways properly to elucidate such expressions within a speech act account. As mentioned above, Patrick also at times overlooks certain illocutionary acts within the text, which may be due to his focus on what he recognizes as *transactional* utterances. Despite these issues, Patrick's main speech act error stems from his inexact language concerning performatives and illocutions as established by theorists. Many of the persuasive aspects Patrick identifies can be located in the design of the text alone rather than with various speech acts. Nevertheless, his lack of speech act precision produces a kind of literary perlocutionary effect type criticism.

Patrick's proposal for following the rhetorical and literary scheme of the text for the reader to construe its transactional aspects has much to endorse. That biblical utterances such as a promise are transactional is perceptive and provides another angle that correlates nicely with the notion of self-involvement. That is, the addressee/reader must actively engage through self-involvement with an utterance in order to experience its illocutionary force. Yet, it is important to note that not all of Yahweh's performative utterances require the addressee's transactional response in order to be actualized. In addition, Patrick's idea of *transaction* is not the same as Gu's theory of communication, but there are certain parallels while at the same time Gu provides a corrective that situates illocutions and perlocutions in their proper relationship. Patrick's point is well taken that in order to adopt a particular stance, one must have a predisposition to become a self-involved reader in order to participate in various communicative actions. Patrick also adds a unique perspective for validating truth which connects well with Searle's idea that institutional facts presuppose brute facts. Thus, when readers trust in a promise through self-involvement with the text, they test the truthfulness of both the utterance and the one promising. All in all, Patrick points to significant ways for exploring the self-involvement of the addressee and reader with particular utterances expressed in the text, but his blurring of speech act theory with rhetoric clouds its uniqueness, which ends up distorting the nature of illocutionary speech acts as Briggs forewarned.

58. See ibid., 194.

Illocutions Count as Perlocutions

Related to the above approach, but far less complex, is the identification of illocutions and interpreting them in a perlocutionary sense.[59] Of particular interest in this category is Robert P. Carroll's use of Austin in his exploring the apparent failure of prophecy.[60]

Robert P. Carroll

According to Carroll, performative language consists of illocutionary acts and perlocutionary acts. Applying this understanding to prophecy, Carroll sets forth his thesis:

> Taking language as having a performative dimension it is necessary to read prophecy as not only saying things but also doing and achieving things. Such a performative element in prophetic language would make it less prone to analysis in terms of *true–false categories* and more appropriately open to being considered in terms of *happy–unhappy possibilities*. The success or failure of various prophetic performatives would then be related to their ability to *persuade* the community to follow them rather than to a capacity for seeing the future before it came into being. It would provide a more adequate account of the complexities of prophecy than the traditional foreteller of the future approach.[61]

Hence, the nature of the prophet's task was to penetrate the community's consciousness and create a response to his message. "The prophet attempted to create the future, not to predict it! The future does not exist, so the task of the prophets is to put it across in such a way that what will come into existence will be a community conforming to their understanding of reality."[62] By preaching, the prophet is *doing* something, which means that his language constitutes *performative*. Unlike the king of Israel whose utterances operated according to the convention of his institutional authority, prophetic proclamation had little conventional force, except for within a cultic community. The failure of the prophets

59. E.g. Stephen B. Reid, "Psalm 50: Prophetic Speech and God's Performative Utterances," in *Prophets and Paradigms* (Festschrift Gene M. Tucker; ed. S. B. Reid; JSOTSup 229; Sheffield: Sheffield Academic Press, 1996), 217–30; D. Brent Sandy, *Plowshares and Pruning Hooks: Rethinking the Language of Biblical Prophecy and Apocalyptic* (Downers Grove, Ill.: InterVarsity, 2002), cf. 80–102.

60. Robert P. Carroll, "Second Isaiah and the Failure of Prophecy," *ST* 32 (1978): 119–31; idem, *When Prophecy Failed: Reactions and Responses to Failure in the Old Testament Prophetic Traditions* (London: SCM Press, 1979).

61. Carroll, *When Prophecy Failed*, 71 (italics mine).

62. Carroll, "Second Isaiah," 128.

was due to the facts that they were not recognized as holding legitimate, institutional authority along with their own inability to convince their addressees. Hence, the power or authority of the prophets was based on persuasion rather than any institution.[63]

Carroll applies his thesis to Second Isaiah and identifies him as a cult prophet who employed rhetoric in his preaching. "Viewing him as a cult prophet would account for the gap between proclamations of salvation (a motif strongly associated with the cult) and their realizations in reality because the world of the cult had its own values and to relate them to the real world would be category confusion."[64] However, Carroll admits that the biblical notion of prophecy as the proclamation of the word which accomplishes its purposes (cf. Isa 55:11) runs counter to this suggestion. He thus combines the nature of cultic language with his understanding that performative language *count as* perlocutions. If Second Isaiah's prophecy is understood as prediction, then he would be categorized as a false prophet because of his failed vision of a permanent salvation. In contrast, Second Isaiah's performative language viewed as rhetorical reduces "his message to a conventional statement that 'the future belongs to God' and the exiles should return home when the opportunity arises."[65] Consequently, his preaching does not fail because of its lack of fulfillment (true/false categories), but because he did not persuade the people to respond and thus create his vision of the future (happy/unhappy categories). The community is therefore to blame. In the final analysis, Second Isaiah presented a serious dilemma when he claimed that a god who cannot foretell the future is no god (cf. Isa 41:21–29). In response, the oracles in Isa 56–66 confirm the community's culpability as they accuse and vilify them, whereas the narrative of Ezra 1–4 attempts to show how Second Isaiah's great expectations of the return were in fact realized.

Carroll's overall goal in dealing with unfulfilled prophecy is important, but he does not need speech act theory to substantiate his claims. Ironically, his appeal to performative language actually subverts his thesis. As will be discussed in greater detail, the texts that Carroll conceives as solely rhetorical and not predictive clearly involve strong illocutionary acts that include intended perlocutionary effects.

63. Patrick similarly views the authority of the prophet depending solely upon the power of rhetoric (*Rhetoric of Revelation*, 122, 148).

64. Carroll, *When Prophecy Failed*, 152.

65. Carroll, "Second Isaiah," 131.

Terry Eagleton

The literary theorist Terry Eagleton examines the book of Jonah and briefly incorporates Austin's speech act theory in his analysis.[66] His analysis is not necessarily perlocutionary in orientation, but it fits well with the issues raised by Carroll as well as those addressed by Walter Houston below. Eagleton's conclusion concerning his application of Austin is as follows:

> The only successful prophet is an ineffectual one, one whose warnings fail to materialize. All good prophets are false prophets, undoing their own utterances in the very act of producing them. In the terms of J. L. Austin's *How to Do Things With Words*, prophetic utterances of Jonah's sort are "constative" (descriptive of some real or possible states of affairs) only in what one might call their surface grammar; as far as their "deep structure" goes they actually belong to Austin's class of "performatives," linguistic acts which get something done. What they get done is to produce a state of affairs in which the state of affairs they describe won't be the case. Effective declarations of imminent catastrophe cancel themselves out, containing as they do a contradiction between what they say and what they do.[67]

What Carroll attempts to resolve through speech act theory, Eagleton does not hesitate to exploit. Eagleton's understanding of declaratives, however, is solely based on Austin's non-linguistic conventional assumptions. Thus, judgment speeches categorized as such become false or unhappy when not fulfilled. As with Carroll, unfulfilled prophecy equals infelicitous performatives. Before drawing any conclusions, Houston's essay needs examining.

Illocutionary Acts with Perlocutionary Effects

Houston dialogues with the work of both Carroll and Eagleton in order to answer whether prophecies of judgment are intended to evoke repentance or simply to announce inexorable doom.[68] Houston's appeal to speech act theory is larger in scope than those above, in that he cites Austin, Searle, and Vanderveken along with Thiselton's study on words. In his assessment of Carroll and Eagleton, Houston correctly concludes that both

66. Terry Eagleton, "J. L. Austin and the Book of Jonah," in *The Book and the Text: The Bible and Literary Theory* (ed. Regina M. Schwartz; Oxford: Blackwell, 1990), 231–36.

67. Ibid., 233.

68. Walter Houston, "What Did the Prophets Think They Were Doing? Speech Acts and Prophetic Discourse in the Old Testament," *BibInt* 1 (1993): 167–88.

confuse the nature of illocutions and perlocutions. In response to Carroll, Houston states that the success of a performative utterance does not depend upon the hearers' response, but on the institutional character of illocutionary acts. Illocutionary force, for Houston, consists of the addressees simple recognition that a prophet was among them coupled with the "shared understanding of what the prophet was doing."[69] In addition, the prophet was authorized to speak the word of Yahweh, often evidenced by the messenger formula.[70] With this perspective, Houston sets forth his thesis that the proclamation of judgment "is to be understood as *declarative*" that "brings the hearers (or a third party) *under judgment*. It initiates an objective state of condemnation." As in a court of law, this *state* constitutes a verdict of guilt upon the people "regardless of whether the sentence has yet been carried out, or ever will be."[71]

Concerning evidence of a state of affairs brought about by the declarative speech act, Houston appeals to Austin's claim: "The total speech act in the total situation is the *only actual* phenomenon which...we are engaged in elucidating."[72] For Houston, "the total situation" in relation to judgment speeches "must include evidence of the appropriate or expected response to the words we are studying."[73] Houston examines such responses in the Deuteronomistic History, Jeremiah, and the book of Jonah, and first identifies the repentant response of the people, which in turn causes Yahweh's revoking of his judgment. Here, Houston addresses Eagleton's thesis and initially concludes that "while the response of mourning-repentance is treated as appropriate, it does not always secure a remission of the threatened penalty." Further, the only successful prophetic oracle is not one that only achieves the effect or remission of doom, but "is communicatively successful purely and simply if it is *understood* as a divinely guaranteed announcement of judgment." Houston consents to Eagleton's view that judgment speeches are successful because of their realized perlocutionary effects rather than the actualization of destructtion. The consequence of this, though, is that the speech "neither asserts a future state of affairs (assertive) nor commits its ultimate author, God, to future action (commissive)," which such utterances characteristically express.[74] Yet, Houston claims that oracles of judgment understood as *declaring a state of judgment* provides a better alternative solution.

69. Ibid., 178.

70. For Houston's full discussion on illocutionary force and authority, see ibid., 175–79.

71. Ibid., 180.

72. Austin, *Things with Words*, 148.

73. Houston, "Prophetic Discourse," 182.

74. Ibid., 183–84.

In his select survey of the biblical material, Houston identifies an ambiguity between prayer to avert judgment and mourning over an accomplished act of destruction.[75] Yet, in principle, the declaration is absolute. "The state of condemnation it creates is a fact, not a mere expectation. But it is *not* in principle *unalterable*." Consequently, an appeal can be made to the highest court ruled by the Sovereign Lord, Yahweh. Thus, there is nothing inappropriate about these two different responses set alongside each other.[76] In sum, the prophecy of judgment pronounces a state of judgment that contains two possible perlocutionary effects of either repentance in lieu of mercy or mourning caused by judgment. The prophet has successfully accomplished his assignment by uttering the illocutionary act of judgment that is not contingent upon either subsequent perlocutionary effect.

There is much to commend about Houston's study, and especially his distinction and the proper relation between illocutionary acts and perlocutionary effects.[77] Houston's proposals concerning judgment speeches as *declarations*, however, could be sharpened. Houston accurately considers the declarative illocution of judgment as pronouncing condemnation. Also, his conclusion that judgment speeches simultaneously possess the perlocutionary effects of awakening repentance and absolute doom seems quite clear. For Houston, the question of which effect is intended is transcended by locating the prophetic word in the institutional nature of the illocutionary force: the public recognition of a prophet authorized by Yahweh. Houston's overall assumption here is that the prophetic word's operative force lies in non-linguistic convention. Moreover, he downplays the supernatural dimension of judgment speeches. These interpretive decisions appear to be directly dependant upon Thiselton's early understanding that performative blessings and curses operate through extralinguistic force.[78] Defining judgment speeches as *non-linguistic* declarative/performatives, however, does not answer the issue raised by both Carroll and Eagleton. In actuality, such a description supports their thesis that when such illocutions do not transpire, the conditions of success dictate that the utterance is infelicitous. Also, Houston's institutional fact of "shared understanding" finds more correlation with Hornsby's notion of reciprocity as the conventional force rather than a

75. See ibid., 184–86.

76. Ibid., 186–87 (italics mine).

77. Briggs highlights Houston's work here as one of the few examples of properly utilizing the illocutionary/perlocutionary distinction ("Speech-Act Theory," 253).

78. See Houston, "Prophetic Discourse," 175.

formal extralinguistic convention. Further, most prophetic utterances are supernatural if understood as the word of Yahweh and thus they are *linguistic* declarative/performatives, as Searle recognizes as the prominent exception among this classification.

Taking all of the above into account, judgment speeches should be considered strong linguistic performatives involving several illocutionary forces. In one sense, the illocution is an *assertive–declaration* hybrid that assesses the addressees as guilty and simultaneously categorizes them as such. Thus, as Houston asserts, judgment oracles place the addressees under judgment. The declarative point has two aspects here: the declaring of the state of guilt and the accompanying penalties of that assessment. These types of utterances also express the *directive* point. Judgment type speeches typically have the directive point as primary, but this does not mean that in certain instances the declarative dimension may dominate. Houston agrees with this in principle as he understands that the decision of executing judgment is alterable. The biblical material, however, seems to assume that these utterances typically come with an inherent offer of mercy which is actualized through the desired response of humble repentance (cf. Jer 18:1–12). This is evidenced by, first, the very fact that judgment is announced before any disaster actually occurs which implicitly indicates that its realization can possibly be avoided. Second, Yahweh can and does change his course of action—most often seen in his turning from judgment to mercy—(e.g. Exod 32:7–14; Jer 18:1–12; 26:1–3; Hos 11:8–9; Amos 7:1–6; Jonah 3:4–10), which Eagleton does not apparently take into account.

The directive force often functions with the *assertive* force. As Searle and Vanderveken have shown, "if I warn you (assertive) that the bull is about to charge, the aim of issuing a warning would normally be to get you to take some evasive action (directive)." Yet, on the other hand, "when I warn you to do something, I would normally be asking you to do it (directive) while implying that if you do not do it, it would be bad for you (assertive)."[79] Warnings *count as* strong illocutionary acts as they direct the hearer to future or potential threatening occurrences that will directly have an impact on him if not responded to appropriately, for example, a charging bull, a soon arriving train, or impending judgment. Thus, legitimate warnings are not weak or empty speech acts, since they point to real consequences if not heeded. Thus, as directives, they find success simply because a warning has been uttered and not due to any perlocutionary effect as Eagleton asserts and Houston concedes.

79. Searle and Vanderveken, *Illocutionary Logic*, 203.

Judgment speeches, then, are multidimensional illocutions expressing both directive and declarative points.[80] Similar to Houston, judgment speeches typically assess the state of affairs of the addressee as forensically guilty (assertive), which in turn designates them as condemned (declaration) while at the same time warning them (assertive–directive) of impending doom (declaration) to be executed at a subsequent point in time. If the warning is not heeded, then the future implied consequences (assertive) will be realized through the actualization of disaster (declaration). These utterances are also linguistic supernatural performatives in a Searlean sense. Their operative force lies in their supernatural nature coupled with the convention of reciprocity. Oracles of judgment typically have the directive point as primary, but this does not mean that in certain instances the declarative dimension may dominate.

It is important to mention how form critics tend to avoid the term "threat" or "warn" when defining the genre of judgment speeches. For Westermann, the term "threat" (*Drohwort*) does not clearly describe the nature of an *announcement of judgment*, as the genre "has the character of something settled: God has decided upon doom. The announcement itself is already a part of the sentence that has been decided upon by God. It is something essentially different from a threat."[81] The reason for such a conclusion is based in the semantic domain of the term "threat," as it implies a conditional aspect. Further, the term does not relate to the semantic property of "promise," which describes the essence of the correlating genre, *announcement of salvation*. The criteria for viewing judgment oracles in this manner are not necessarily derived from any single genre or from the biblical context but lies in the interpreter's understanding of the nature of the prophetic word. For example, Tucker asserts:

> The basic distinction between predictions and prophetic announcements lies in the conception of the power of the prophetic word. As the prophets

80. Houston talks in terms of the prophets warning or calling for repentance, but he does not explore the directive force with judgment speeches. This is most likely due to his sole focus on conventional authority for successful illocutionary acts. For instance, Houston criticizes Carroll and his view of illocutionary force of prophecy as "proclamation, threat and warning" which for Houston are "types of illocutionary force which certainly do not depend on authority" ("Prophetic Discourse," 178).

81. Claus Westermann, *Basic Forms of Prophetic Speech* (trans. H. C. White; Louisville, Ky.: Westminster John Knox, 1991), 66; for Westermann's full discussion, see pp. 64–70. See further Tucker's similar conclusions in *Form Criticism*, 61–64.

> see it, their words are not speculations about coming events, but the very word of God about the future. That word—the word of God spoken through the mouth of the prophet—has the power to create history.[82]

Tucker, along with Westermann, points to the general performative nature of supernatural declarations. Still, both these interpreters come close to characterizing prophetic announcements as power-laden, irrevocable utterances as Thiselton addresses.[83] In an earlier essay, Houston presents a more accurate perspective while appealing to the linguistic type of performative:

> There is plenty of evidence (for example Isa 55:10f) to suggest that the prophets frequently thought of their words as *creating* the realities of which they spoke. This may be seen as a magical idea, but it makes more sense to understand it performatively. Prophecy is presented as the word of God and is concerned primarily with God's own actions, often explicitly and always by implication. When a person speaks of his own actions in the future we do not usually call it prediction: we may call it proposal, promise, undertaking, warning, threat, vow: all names of illocutionary acts which may be seen as guaranteeing to the hearer the reality of which they speak in advance.[84]

Thus, prophetic announcements are surely not predictive, but as supernatural linguistic performatives they require the subsequent performance of the utterance. In the case of judgment speeches, disaster may be revoked, which neither Tucker nor Westermann seem to take into account, unless explicitly stated; and even then "perhaps" God may turn (cf. Jonah 3:1–10).

In an attempt to sharpen Houston's observations, I conclude that oracles of judgment are multidimensional strong linguistic performatives that most often have the directive dimension functioning as the primary force that warns the addressees of impending doom accompanied with the intended perlocutionary effect of repentance. Multidimensional judgment speeches find success in the fact that a warning has been issued or disaster has been realized. The declarative dimension disallows the utterances to be conceived as predictive in nature, which Tucker and Westermann correctly emphasize. The directive dimension provides for the utterance to be felicitous despite a revoked declarative point.

82. Tucker, *Form Criticism*, 61–62.

83. Carroll also understands biblical prophecy in this sense; see his *When Prophecy Failed*, 58–61.

84. Walter Houston, "'Today, in Your Very Hearing': Some Comments on the Christological Use of the Old Testament," in *The Glory of Christ in the New Testament: Studies in Christology* (ed. L. D. Hurst and N. T. Wright; Oxford: Clarendon, 1987), 37–47 (41).

Speech Act Theory and Self-Involvement

Not many have explored the notion of self-involvement in Old Testament interpretation. Briggs isolates Timothy Polk's analysis of Jeremiah as the single book-length Old Testament work that has made significant use of the concept.[85] Although not using such terminology, David Clines's study on the Suffering Servant has significant parallels with the notion of self-involvement. Because his work more directly relates to my thesis in the following chapter, I will wait to discuss it there. Since Polk's study, I am only aware of Patrick's work that displays certain correspondences to the concept of self-involvement.

Before the publication of his work on Jeremiah, Polk briefly used speech act theory in the study of the term משל in Ezekiel. Polk's thesis is that "the speech-acts designated *mĕšālîm* are aptly suited for religious discourse (and Scripture) by virtue of a heightened performative and reader-involving quality." Polk describes this quality as "paradigmatic-parabolic."[86] The משל as a paradigm performs an operation on the audience, it is behavior-affecting while as a parable it is reader-involving; readers participate in the משל and identify their place in its world and hence their relationship to its truth. Thus, in the reader's judgments toward the משל, the משל judges the reader.[87] Of particular interest is Polk's analysis of Ezek 14:7–8 and the addressees identified as משל which finds parallels in Isa 14:16. In these texts, the addressee become a משל-byword and as such they typically "find themselves as objects of horror and astonishment, being spat at, ridiculed, taunted, and abhorred."[88] The addressees identify themselves parabolically through the משל and thereby acknowledge their status as byword and paradigmatically assess their condition accordingly, while at the same time they have become a משל and a אות and thus a "speech-act, a metaphor, a parable" with the intention that the "addressees address others. They are not just the thing signified but the signifier itself." The addressees "are to be the living testimony to his sovereign lordship and the text in which other potential apostates can read their fate."[89]

Significant for this study is Polk's notion that people actually become a speech act. It is quite clear that God here transforms the addressees into bywords through his *declarative* illocution and as such function as living

85. Briggs, *Words in Action*, 167–71.

86. Timothy Polk, "Paradigms, Parables, and *Mĕšālîm*: On Reading the *Māšāl* in Scripture," *CBQ* 45 (1983): 564–83 (564–65).

87. Ibid., 573.

88. Ibid., 577.

89. Ibid., 578.

witnesses for others. Polk, however, does not explain how these idolaters actually become an additional speech act in the sense of the performative utterance expressed in v. 8, if that is what he is suggesting. But by using such language it seems that this is the only logical speech act conclusion. In any case and following Polk's lead, upon the performance of God's utterance the human bywords would become a living *directive* illocutionary act that warns others to avoid their fate (cf. v. 6). They would not, however, become declaratives in the sense of creating other bywords through themselves (as Polk's language seems to indicate), but as directive speech acts they would warn others to adhere to Yahweh and thus avoid experiencing and becoming his משל illocutionary act.

Turning to Polk's study on Jeremiah, recent prophetic research has been focusing on the literary characterization of the prophets. The question currently raised concerns whether the prophet is a historical person and/or a literary character.[90] Polk follows this line of thinking and focuses on "the prophet *as depicted in the text*." From this point of view, he considers the prophet in terms of a "literary-theological construct," a "prophetic 'persona.'"[91] Polk also identifies within the text "a high degree of functional, or deliberate ambiguity." For Polk, *ambiguity* does not mean "hopeless obscurity or the absence of sense but rather a superfluity of sense, multiplicity of meaning, polysemousness." By *functional* he means "that the polysemous condition fits into a larger pattern; the multiple meanings are related, and there is a point to their relatedness."[92] These literary functional ambiguities ultimately contribute "to the book's depiction of the prophet as a theological paradigm."[93] The intended point of the book "is a depiction of the prophet that evokes a set of insights into God's purpose and a set of responses to his call."[94] In his study, Polk focuses on the first person language of the prophet, which is performative in character, since the prophet does not talk so much *about* God as *to* him. In his speech, the prophet utters various types of action language, as Polk identifies it, such as confession, praise, anguish, sorrow, contrition, hope, and joy.[95] Through this language the prophet is characterized as

90. For a recent collection of essays devoted to this subject, see Johannes C. de Moor (ed.), *The Elusive Prophet: The Prophet as Historical Person, Literary Character and Anonymous Artist* (OTS 45; Leiden: Brill, 2001).

91. Timothy Polk, *The Prophetic Persona: Jeremiah and the Language of Self* (JSOTSup 32; Sheffield: JSOT Press, 1984), 10.

92. Ibid., 165.

93. Ibid., 166.

94. Ibid., 18.

95. Polk (ibid., 179 n. 28) only in passing refers to Austin and Evans in relation to performative speech, but he does discuss the notion throughout his study.

wise, obedient, trusting, and also faint-hearted and in need of admonishment. By this "Jeremiah is depicted in, and defined by, struggle."[96] This first person speech of the literary persona, then, constructs "a self" for the reader to identify with.

Polk supports his thesis by first examining the language of self, and specifically, the metaphor of the heart in Jer 4. He suggests that the lament the people are exhorted to make in v. 8, Jeremiah expresses for them in his own grief in v. 19. Polk goes on to say:

> He *makes* lamentation. His words do not only *say*, they *do*. They do not describe a condition so much as enact one. They do not refer to, render an account of, offer a theory on, or speak discursively about (among other things) a physical human heart or the historical personage who owned it. Rather, the words are *of* and belong to a man's lamentation. Actualizing the human capacity for grief and *being* the grief behavior itself, the words actualize the self who speaks them. They constitute the speaker as a grieving self.

With these words of lament, the text is "at once rendering an identity description (that is, characterizing the persona of Jeremiah) while showing how identity happens, how a self comes to be, achieves form and definition, indeed constitutes itself. Specifically, it shows the self to be the achievement of the responsible, first-person use of the language of the heart."[97] Thus, while the "biblical text does not as a rule speak discursively or theoretically about the concept of 'self,' by delineating a range of behavior regarded as essential to a proper relation to God, it illustrates what it means to have a self."[98] Polk turns from here to examine other texts concerning the prophetic "I" and the confessions in Jeremiah. Overall, the book of Jeremiah "intends its representation of the prophetic self 'be used as an indirect route of insight for others' and that it eventuates in the rendering of a persona 'molded by God.'"[99]

This is not the place, nor is it necessary for this study, to enter into the question of the historicity of the prophets.[100] Nor does one have to accept

96. Ibid., 170.

97. Ibid., 46–47.

98. Ibid., 57.

99. Ibid., 169. Polk here is utilizing and quoting from the work of Sallie McFague TeSelle, *Speaking in Parables: A Study in Metaphor and Theology* (Philadelphia: Fortress Press, 1975), 169.

100. For critiques on the practice of reducing the prophets simply to literary personae see Hans M. Barstad, "No Prophets? Recent Developments in Biblical Prophetic Research and Ancient Near Eastern Prophecy," *JSOT* 57 (1993): 39–60; R. P. Gordon, "Where Have All the Prophets Gone? The 'Disappearing' Israelite Prophet Against the Background of Ancient Near Eastern Prophecy," *BBR* 5 (1995):

Polk's view that Jeremiah is a theological construct in order to utilize his work. Briggs insightfully suggests that "Polk's work of self-*constitution* may profitably be transposed to the speech-act key of self-*involvement* and taken as a particularly clear example of the possibilities inherent in such a hermeneutic."[101] Understood this way, Polk's focus on the "non-referential 'I' of self-involvement," as Briggs calls it, makes a significant contribution to the notion of self-involvement.[102]

Conclusion

One of the obvious problems arising from the majority of Old Testament interpreters surveyed above is their sole dependence upon Austin. As evidenced throughout, this has often led to a severe blurring of illocutionary acts with perlocutionary effects, with the result of distorting the central notions of speech act theory. Yet, the blame is not solely Austin's imprecision, since Thiselton, Mettinger, and others have successfully used the philosopher's views. Houston's research extends beyond Austin and he properly distinguishes between illocutionary acts and perlocutionary effects. Despite the refinements offered above, his work is an important study for understanding the hermeneutical value of speech act theory. One of the most useful Old Testament studies has been produced by Wagner, but extensive knowledge of speech act theory is required in order properly to employ his manual. Polk's study also demonstrates ways to explore the self-involving language within the prophetic material, which I will return to in greater detail below. In the first chapter I attempted to present the central notions of speech act theory. Coupled with this discussion and in light of Evans, Thiselton, and Briggs, along with the above analysis, the way is prepared to explore the performative nature and function of Isa 40–55.

67–86; see also Terry L. Fenton, "Israelite Prophecy: Characteristics of the First Protest Movement," in de Moor (ed.), *The Elusive Prophet*, 129–41.

101. Briggs, *Words in Action*, 170.

102. See ibid., 168–70.

Chapter 3

A PROPOSAL FOR THE PERFORMATIVE NATURE AND PROPHETIC FUNCTION OF ISAIAH 40–55

This chapter seeks to set out the basic concerns of Isa 40–55 in order to locate the four passages selected for this study within their larger prophetic context. The subjects of deliverance and servanthood, found in Isa 41:21–29; 49:1–6; 50:4–11; and 52:13–53:12, represent two dominant themes running throughout chs. 40–55. Isaiah 41:21–29 primarily constitutes a speech act challenge for those claiming divinity and directly relates to the overthrow of Babylon and the provision of deliverance for the people of God. The other texts are the three final so-called "Servant Songs," which obviously relate to servanthood, but are also more complex with a long, storied interpretive history.

Preliminary Issues

An original speaker/writer, addressee, and occasion lies behind these chapters, but recovering the actual, real events is extremely difficult. In fact, as Melugin warns, such an endeavor ultimately ends up as a creation of the interpreter that is shaped by his own culture and personal history.[1] On the other hand, determining the function of a text lies on surer ground. Goldingay correctly asserts that we cannot say how Isa 40–55 functioned historically, but we can say how the prophetic hermeneutic designs it to function.[2] Thus, the concern here centers on the prophetic function or

1. Roy F. Melugin, "Prophetic Books and the Problem of Historical Reconstructions," in *Prophets and Paradigms* (Festschrift Gene M. Tucker; ed. Stephen B. Reid; JSOTSup 229; Sheffield: Sheffield Academic Press, 1996), 63–78 (cf. 74–77).

2. Goldingay, "Isaiah 40–55 in the 1990s: Among Other Things, Deconstructing, Mystifying, Intertextual, Socio-Critical, and Hearer-Involving," *BibInt* 5 (1997): 225–46 (244–45). The concept of prophetic hermeneutic comes from James A. Sanders, "Adaptable for Life: The Nature and Function of Canon," in *From Sacred Story to Sacred Text* (Philadelphia: Fortress, 1987), 9–39; see also idem, *Canon and Community: A Guide to Canonical Criticism* (GBS; Philadelphia: Fortress, 1984).

strategy of these chapters and how they call the addressee/reader to adopt particular stances and entailments.

The literary addressee provides one of the more significant aspects for determining the function of this block of text. Distinct from much of Isa 1–39, chs. 40–55 address a community who has experienced, in one way or another, the destruction of Jerusalem and the deportation of large numbers of Israelites to Babylon. The text specifically addresses the people of God located in Jerusalem (e.g. 40:1–2) and Babylon (e.g. 47:3). This group can be identified as Jacob–Israel, Zion–Jerusalem, and Yahweh's servant; yet, these designations do not always have clear referents. The text also addresses the nations (e.g. 41:1–4) as well as other gods (e.g. 41:21–29). Linked to each of these entities, except the idol-gods, is a second masculine plural addressee who occupies a predominant place within these chapters.[3] Apart from Yahweh, various voices also appear with the first person singular and plural voice playing a significant role. These identities, addressees, and voices are at times identifiable; at other times, they are unidentifiable and thus elusive, suggesting intentional ambiguity. Consequently, an *openness* within the text occurs that draws in the reader, invites, and, in fact, implores self-involvement with it. Goldingay points to this phenomenon with his notion of "hearer-involving" and his observation that a "feature of Isa 40–55 is a running ambiguity regarding its audience."[4]

What enhances this openness are the dynamic and dramatic visionary qualities of this section. The text presents possibilities, what could be and happen if the addressee/reder embraces them. Isaiah 40–55 does concern itself with the past,[5] but it primarily focuses on the future. Still, this is not necessarily a distant future, but a future ready to be realized through and by the addressee/reader. Since, though, the text continues to live in time, the future in certain instances has become the past, but the completed past does not close off additional future possibilities. For Annemarike van der Woude, it is the text itself that provides readers with the entrance into its message. "The very stuff and structure of these chapters has been designed to invite, to urge the readers to become involved personally in

3. Patricia T. Willey observes that this addressee runs throughout chs. 40–55 and is directly related to those designated as the people of God. Thus, the second masculine plural audience "seems to correspond most closely to the prophet's actual audience" (*Remember the Former Things: The Recollection of Previous Texts in Second Isaiah* [SBLDS 161; Atlanta: Scholars Press, 1997], 180). However, this addressee does not always refer to Israel, but also points to other identities such as the nations (45:20–25). Consequently, Willey's conclusion does not work out in each instance.

4. See Goldingay, "Isaiah 40–55," 241; see further pp. 241–46.

5. *Pace*, Conrad, *Reading Isaiah*, cf. 158–62.

the history of the LORD and his people."[6] More exacting, the text envisions the people of God comprised of a *community* who *confess* Yahweh alone, not simply those possessing some genealogical criterion. Thus, the text dramatically invites and leads its addressees/readers to *involve* them*selves* with itself and thereby become the people of God.

David Clines also anticipates this idea of openness in his important study on Isa 52:13–53:12, whose implications have not been fully considered.[7] Utilizing Austin's work and Thiselton's early study on parables, Clines highlights the enigmatic nature of the passage and its consequential openness. According to Clines, "The impasse of historical-critical scholarship in the face of the enigmas of the poem can function heuristically in directing our attention away from a sense of 'the poem as problem' to the poem as language-event."[8] For Clines, the text creates a world, but it cannot "be viewed objectively, from the outside, as a spectator. One needs to be a *participant* in it, to *experience* it, in order to *understand* it."[9] Thus, "the reader is bidden to give assent to—or rather, to *enter*" this world. "The means by which the reader of the poem is able to enter the world of the poem is by *identification* with the *personae* of the poem, that is, by an *assumption* of one of the roles presented in the poem."[10] As mentioned above, Clines expresses some of the basic tenets of a hermeneutic of self-involvement. It is my contention that Clines's overall thesis should not be restricted to Isa 52:13–53:12, since the majority of chs. 40–55 bear similar ambiguous characteristics which translate into salient features for exploring self-involvement within a speech act account. In particular, intentional anonymity is a prominent feature in the final three servant passages. Where I differ from Clines is in his idea of identification and his literary tendencies to grant complete autonomy to the text and the reader.[11] Regarding identification, the notion of self-involvement nuances Clines's concept as the addressee/reader *involves* the *self* in the text by uttering speech acts and thereby adopting prescribed stances and entailments, not simply identifying with personae. Concerning the openness of the text, a hermeneutic of self-involvement,

6. Van der Woude, "Can Zion Do Without the Servant in Isaiah 40–55?," *CTJ* 39 (2004): 109–16 (110).

7. David J. A. Clines, *I, He, We, and They: A Literary Approach to Isaiah 53* (JSOTSup 1; Sheffield: JSOT Press, 1976).

8. Ibid., 59.

9. Ibid., 54 (italics mine).

10. Ibid., 62 (italics mine except for *personae*).

11. Ibid., 61; see further pp. 59–61. The latter point is exactly Melugin's problem with Clines's approach ("On Reading Isaiah 53 as Christian Scripture," in Bellinger and Farmer, eds., *Jesus and the Suffering Servant*, 55–69 (cf. 57–59, 64–65).

as conceived by Evans and more fully articulated by Thiselton and Briggs, seriously takes into account the overall context of the passage so that the text intentionally guides the addressee/reader.[12]

Polk's suggestions regarding the language of self in Jeremiah correlate well with those of Clines. The phrase "non-referential," as Briggs coins it, though, may be too strong for the "I" in Isa 40–55 and specifically the first person singular in the second and third servant passages. An "I/me" occurs in the testimonies of Isa 6:1–13 and Jer 1:4–10, but in these cases the first person voice is explicitly identified with a name. Isaiah 49:1–6 and 50:4–9 also contain an "I/me" and are similar in form to Isa 6 and Jer 1; however, these passages are significantly different from the testimonies of these two prophets due to the fact that they do not provide the name of the speaker. For a number of different reasons and from a representational perspective, interpreters do not hesitate to designate a speaker who has uttered or will utter them, for example, Isaiah of Jerusalem, Israel, a remnant of Israel, Second Isaiah, Jeremiah, Cyrus, Moses, David, a Davidic Messiah, Jesus Christ, and so on. Yet, no one agrees who this first person singular voice belongs to. In fact, it is not even clear if this voice is male or female.[13] This controversy demonstrates that the voice in the second and third servant passages is in the strict sense actually anonymous, unlike the "I/me" in Isa 6 and Jer 1. Thus, the nature of these passages makes them open to being approached as anonymous and dynamic, something that the notion of self-involvement within a speech act account can access and illuminate. There is no denying that "behind" the text is a prophet who is naturally the antecedent of the "I/me," but this voice ultimately remains elusive. Thus, rather than considering the first person voice as non-referential, it is best to consider the "I/me" as intentionally and functionally ambiguous. This functionally ambiguous "I/me," "we," and "servant" openly await to identify antecedents who self-involvingly engage with the text and thereby confess their commitment to Yahweh alone and adopt the open role and responsibilities of his people, his servant.

12. For an example of reading the final three servant passages based on Clines's suggestions and without taking much consideration of their larger literary context, see the study of Francis Landy, "The Construction of the Subject and the Symbolic Order: A Reading of the Last Three Suffering Servant Songs," in *Among the Prophets: Language, Image and Structure in the Prophetic Writings* (ed. P. R. Davies and D. J. A. Clines JSOTSup 144; Sheffield: Sheffield Academic Press, 1993), 60–71.

13. For those seeing this voice as a female Second Isaiah, see, for example, Sean McEvenue, "Who Was Second Isaiah?," in van Ruiten and Vervene, eds., *Studies in the Book of Isaiah*, 213–22; Bebb Wheeler Stone, "Second Isaiah: Prophet to Patriarchy," *JSOT* 56 (1992): 85–99.

One last issue before moving on concerns how contemporary readers can be addressed by the same ancient material as the intended addressee? Willem A. M. Beuken provides a way to navigate through this dilemma.[14] In his analysis of Isa 45:18–25, Beuken highlights the question raised by the passage: "how can Yhwh address the nations if the particular reasoning which supports his claims seems to presuppose an audience that has gone a long way with him?" Beuken's answer is that while God addresses the nations, "*Israel is listening*" so that God's claim "has a message for her too." Thus, there is a twofold audience simultaneously addressed in this text: "one on the stage, the nations, and one in the house, Israel."[15] Following Beuken's trajectories, the audience in these chapters is sometimes in Jerusalem and at other times in Babylon. Sometimes it is Jacob–Israel, and/or a servant, and/or Zion–Jerusalem. Sometimes it is the nations and sometimes the idol-gods. So, while the prophet and the text address these various entities on stage, the "*reader is listening*" in the house. The various messages addressed to specific audiences become the means whereby the reader is also addressed.[16] The reader, however, is not simply listening to monologues and dialogues, but the text leads the reader to become self-involved with them and at times is invited to become the speaker. Following the text's strategy, the reader is implored to identify with the addressee and embrace the prescribed stances and entailments through self-involvement. The different addressees and readers in various times and settings converge when they engage in the overarching prophetic function of the chapters.

Performative Nature and Prophetic Function of Isaiah 40–55

My basic thesis is that much of the language of Isa 40–55 is performative and that it functions as such within this section's overarching prophetic strategy. The central message of these chapters is a *call to return or turn to Yahweh*. The way the text describes the nature of this return is for the addressee *to forsake sin, acknowledge and confess Yahweh as God alone*, and *embrace the role of his servant*. In order to defend my thesis I will turn to the text itself.

The first section of this block comprises chs. 40–48, which focus on Jacob–Israel and the fall of Babylon, whereas chs. 49–55 center on Zion–

14. W. A. M. Beuken, "The Confession of God's Exclusivity by All Mankind: A Reappraisal of Isa 45,18–25," *Bijdragen* 35 (1974): 335–56.

15. Ibid., 346; Goldingay also follows Beuken's suggestions here (*Isaiah 40–55*).

16. Similarly Peter D. Quinn-Miscall, *Reading Isaiah: Poetry and Vision* (Louisville, Ky.: Westminster John Knox, 2001), 118–20.

Jerusalem and its restoration. Two primary concerns occupy the first section: (1) the overthrow of Babylon and provided deliverance for Jacob–Israel and (2) the manufacture and worshiping of idol-gods. These two motifs intertwine, as the ultimate purpose of the provided deliverance from Babylon aims at Jacob–Israel's forsaking all other idol-gods as well as returning wholeheartedly back to Yahweh. Yahweh initiates the return of the addressee by first announcing his own return to Jerusalem. The block opens with a type of prologue for the whole:

> 40:1 Comfort, comfort my people
>   says your God!
> 2 Speak unto the heart of Jerusalem
>   and call out to her!
> for she has finished her service,
>   for her iniquity has been paid for,
> for she has received from Yahweh's hand
>   double for all her sins.
> 3 A voice calls out:
>   "Prepare in the wilderness
>   a way for Yahweh.
>   Make straight in the desert
>   a highway for our God.
> 4 Every valley will rise up
>   and every mountain and hill will sink down.
> The uneven ground will become smooth,
>   and the rough places leveled.
> 5 And the glory of Yahweh will be revealed
>   and all flesh will see it at once,
>   for the mouth of Yahweh has spoken."
> 6 A voice says, "Call out!"
>   And I respond, "What shall I call out?"
> All flesh is grass
>   and all its loyalty like a wild flower;
> 7 grass withers, a flower fades
>   when Yahweh's breath blows on it—
>   surely the people are grass;
> 8 grass withers, a flower fades,
>   but the word of our God will stand forever.
> 9 Get yourself up onto a high mountain,
>   messenger Zion!
> Raise up your voice with strength,
>   messenger Jerusalem!
> Raise it up! Do not be afraid!
> Say to the cities in Judah,
>   "There, your God!"
> 10 There, Lord Yahweh comes in strength
>   and his arm ruling for him.

There, his payment is with him
    and his wages before him.
11Like a shepherd he pastures his flock,
    he gathers together with his arm.
He carries them in his bosom,
    gently leads those with young.

The significance of this opening section lies in its placement and role within the book of Isaiah. It recalls themes presented in chs. 1–39 and also introduces some of the motifs, addressees, and voices that occur throughout the rest of the subsequent chapters.[17] In fact, Melugin has observed that 40:1–8 forms a microcosm of chs. 41–48 and 40:9–11 corresponds to 49:14–55:13.[18] Thus, this passage sets the stage and tone for what follows.

Right from the start, the addressee/reader enters a world of ambiguity and paradox with sudden and unexplained appearances of various voices and addressees.[19] The prevailing consensus among Isaianic scholars has been that this section was composed in light of and is literarily dependent upon Isaiah's vision of Yahweh in ch. 6.[20] Hence, these verses present a dialogue between Yahweh and his heavenly council.[21] In addition, some

17. See in particular Hans M. Barstad, "Isa 40,1–11. Another Reading," in *Congress Volume: Basel, 2001* (ed. A. Lemaire; VTSup 92; Leiden: Brill, 2002), 225–40; see also Reinhard G. Kratz, "Der Anfang des Zweiten Jesaja in Jes 40,1f. und seine literarischen Horizonte," *ZAW* 105 (1993): 400–419.

18. Melugin, *Isaiah 40–55*, 85–86.

19. John Goldingay observes that one could locate as many as seven mostly unidentified entities in v. 1 alone (*Isaiah 40–55*). See further Stephen A. Geller, "A Poetic Analysis of Isaiah 40:1–2," *HTR* 77 (1984): 413–20.

20. For general studies on the relationship between Isa 6 and 40, see Peter Ackroyd, "Isaiah 36–39: Structure and Function," in *Von Kanaan bis Kerala Kerala* (Festschrift J. P. M. van der Ploeg; ed. W. C. Delsman et al.; AOAT 211; Neukirchen–Vluyn: Neukirchener Verlag, 1982), 3–21 (4–9); Knut Holter, "Zur Funktion der Städte Judas in Jesaja XL 9," *VT* 46 (1996): 119–21; Rolf Rendtorff, "Isaiah 6 in the Framework of the Composition of the Book of Isaiah," in *Canon and Theology: Overtures to an Old Testament Theology* (trans. M. Kohl; OBT; Minneapolis: Fortress, 1993), 170–80; Archibald van Wieringen, "Jesaja 40,1–11: eine drama-linguistische Lesung von Jesaja 6 her," *BN* 49 (1989): 82–93; see also Bernard Gosse, "Isaïe VI et la Tradition Isaïenne," *VT* 42 (1992): 340–49.

21. Along with those cited above, see specifically Frank M. Cross, "The Council of Yahweh in Second Isaiah," *JNES* 12 (1953): 274–77; Christopher R. Seitz, "The Divine Council: Temporal Transition and New Prophecy in the Book of Isaiah," *JBL* 109 (1990): 229–47; idem, "The Book of Isaiah 40–66: Introduction, Commentary, and Reflections," *NIB* 6:307–502 (327–39); see also Melugin, *Isaiah 40–55*, 82–84; idem, "The Servant, God's Call, and the Structure of Isaiah 40–48," in *SBL Seminar*

see the prophetic call of Second Isaiah during this gathering of the council.[22] Interpreters typically identify 1 Kgs 22 as a clear parallel text for understanding 40:1–11. In the former passage, the prophet Micaiah describes Yahweh before his council (v. 19). Following this gathering, Yahweh asks who will go to deceive Ahab, with unidentified council members deliberating over the request (v. 20). Among these, one spirit comes before Yahweh and says, "I will deceive him" (v. 21). However, this is where any parallels begin and end.

In 40:1, Yahweh, or a speaker on his behalf, issues a call to a second masculine plural addressee to comfort עמי followed by the speech formula יאמר אלהיכם. The phrases "my people" and "your God" are expressions explicitly related to the covenant language—"You will be my people and I will be your God" (e.g. Exod 6:7; Lev 26:12; Deut 26:17–18; 29:13).[23] As the text progresses, an unidentified voice calls out to the same addressee to clear the way in the wilderness for Yahweh (vv. 3–5). Connected with v. 1, Yahweh is referred to as אלהינו in v. 3bβ. Following this, a dialogue ensues between two additional unidentified voices. One issues a call to a masculine singular addressee who responds by asking, "What shall I call out?" (v. 6aβ).[24] Without ascribing to either

Papers, 1991 (ed. E. H. Lovering, Jr.; SBLSP 30; Atlanta: Scholars Press, 1991), 21–30 (21–24).

22. See, e.g., Clifford, *Fair Spoken*, 71–76; Karl Elliger, *Deuterojesaja* (BKAT 11/1; Neukirchen–Vluyn: Neukirchener, 1978), 10–12; Norman C. Habel, "The Form and Significance of the Call Narratives," *ZAW* 77 (1965): 297–323 (314–16); Jan L. Koole, *Isaiah*. Part 3. Vol. 1, *Isaiah 40–48* (trans. A. P. Runia; HCOT; Kampen: Kok Pharos, 1997), 63–67; J. L. McKenzie, *Second Isaiah* (AB 20; Garden City, N.Y.: Doubleday, 1968), 16–18; Muilenburg, "Chapters 40–66," 424–31; R. N. Whybray, *Isaiah 40–66* (NCB; Grand Rapids: Eerdmans, 1975), 48–51.

23. So also, e.g., Klaus Baltzer, *Deutero-Isaiah: A Commentary on Isaiah 40–55* (trans. M. Kohl; Hermeneia; Minneapolis: Fortress, 2001), 49–50; W. A. M. Beuken, *Jesaja deel II A* (POT; Nijkerk: G. F. Callenbach, 1979), 18–19; Childs, *Isaiah*, 297; Jan P. Fokkelman, "Stylistic Analysis of Isaiah 40:1–11," in *Remembering All the Way...* (ed. A. S. van der Woude; OTS 21; Leiden: Brill, 1981), 68–90 (73); John Goldingay, *Isaiah* (NIBC 13; Peabody: Hendrickson, 2001), 223; Geller, "40:1–2," 415; Koole, *Isaiah 3/1*, 50–51; Marjo C. A. Korpel, "Second Isaiah's Coping with the Religious Crisis: Reading Isaiah 40 and 55," in *The Crisis of Israelite Religion: Transformation of Religious Tradition in Exilic and Post-Exilic Times* (ed. J. C. de Moor; OTS 42; Leiden: Brill, 1999), 90–113 (92); Christopher R. North, *The Second Isaiah: Introduction, Translation and Commentary to Chapters XL–LV* (Oxford: Clarendon, 1964), 72–73; John N. Oswalt, *The Book of Isaiah, Chapters 40–66* (NICOT; Grand Rapids: Eerdmans, 1998), 49.

24. In v. 6aβ^1 the MT has ואמר, "and one/he responds." This reading is challenged by 1QIsa[a] ואומרה, LXX καὶ εἶπα, and Vg *et dixi*, "and I say/respond," which

voice, a confession and/or protest appears describing the instability and transiency of humanity in contrast to the permanence and stability of the word of אלהינו (vv. 6b–8).[25] The expression, "our God" also corresponds to covenant language. Although the antecedents of "your," "our," and "I" are not explicitly identified, they must refer to those who belong to Yahweh's people in one way or another.[26] With this in mind, the phrase אלהינו never occurs in texts involving Yahweh's council (Isa 6:1–13; Jer 23:16–22; Zech 3:1–7; Pss 82; 89:5–8; 103:19–22; Job 1:6–12; 2:1–6; 15:8; 38:4–7; Dan 7:9–14).[27] In fact, such an expression rarely, if ever, occurs in the divine assemblies in other ancient Near Eastern literature.[28]

the consonantal MT allows for a repointing to a Qal Impf 1cs אֹמַר. Either rendering works within the context of vv. 1–11. The Versions are read here due to their textual significance and because of its correlation with the functionally ambiguous "I" scattered throughout these chapters.

25. Interpreters are divided on whether vv. 6b–8 is a protest or a confession. Either option is possible with the phrase possibly conveying both ideas.

26. In his earlier essay Seitz claimed that the voice in vv. 6b–7 "belongs to an anonymous member of the heavenly council" ("Divine Council," 245). However, he concedes in a later essay that it is not clear if the voice in v. 6 "is a celestial voice or a representative voice more generally"; see "How is the Prophet Isaiah Present in the Latter Half of the Book? The Logic of Chapters 40–66 within the Book of Isaiah," *JBL* 115 (1996): 219–40 (232).

27. For general discussions concerning the council of Yahweh, see Gerald Cooke, "The Sons of (the) God(s)," *ZAW* 76 (1974): 22–47; Frank M. Cross, *Canaanite Myth and Hebrew Epic: Essays in the History of the Religion of Israel* (Cambridge, Mass.: Harvard University Press, 1973), 186–90; Edwin C. Kingsbury, "The Prophets and the Council of Yahweh," *JBL* 83 (1964): 279–86; Patrick D. Miller, "The Divine Council and the Prophetic Call to War," *VT* 18 (1968): 100–107; idem, "Cosmology and World Order in the Old Testament: The Divine Council as Cosmic-Political Symbol," *HBT* 9 (1987): 53–87; E. Theodore Mullen, Jr., *The Divine Council in Canaanite and Early Hebrew Literature* (HSM 24; Chico, Calif.: Scholars Press, 1980); idem, "Divine Assembly," *ABD* 2:214–17; H. Wheeler Robinson, "The Council of Yahweh," *JTS* 45 (1944): 151–57.

28. Within the divine assembly one god typically oversees the meeting. In the case of El in the Canaanite pantheon and Marduk in the Mesopotamian pantheon, they are considered the chief gods, "king and lord of the gods," but are not typically described by the other council members as "our god." For discussions on the divine assembly in Mesopotamian literature, see Geoffrey Evans, "Ancient Mesopotamian Assemblies," *JAOS* 78 (1958): 1–11; idem, "Ancient Mesopotamian Assemblies: An Addendum," *JAOS* 78 (1958): 114–15; Thorkild Jacobsen, "Primitive Democracy in Ancient Mesopotamia," in *Toward the Image of Tammuz and Other Essays on Mesopotamian History and Culture* (Cambridge, Mass.: Harvard University Press, 1970), 157–70; idem, *The Treasures of Darkness: A History of Mesopotamian Religion* (New Haven: Yale University Press, 1976), 86–91. For Ugaritic material, see Cross, *Canaanite Myth*, 177–86; John Macdonald, "An Assembly at Ugarit?," *UF* 11

This type of language would typically be reserved for human devotees (cf. Isa 42:17b). Moreover, in 40:1–11 there is no typical gathering of the council around Yahweh nor any deliberation, only commands.[29]

Rather than issuing the call among Yahweh's council, it is instead directed to the people of God using the language of a prophetic commission.[30] In typical paradoxical fashion, the ones called to comfort and the ones to be comforted are one in the same—Yahweh's people.[31] As just introduced, other voices appear within this general call. One issues a call to a second masculine addressee among the people of God which is responded to by an unidentified individual. What will become clearer as the chapters unfold is that while Yahweh exhorts the collective people of God to return to him, the call is individualized and each person within the community is left to make their own personal decision. Taking this into account, the individual call given here does not clearly indicate that one single person is addressed. The ambiguous "I" draws the addressee/reader into the text and invites self-involvement with it right from the beginning. The passage ends with a series of second feminine singular imperatives directed towards messenger Zion–Jerusalem (v. 9a–bβ^1)[32]

(1979): 515–26; Mullen, *Assembly of the Gods*; idem, *ABD* 2:214–17; Mark S. Smith, *The Origins of Biblical Monotheism: Israel's Polytheistic Background and the Ugaritic Texts* (Oxford: Oxford University Press, 2001), 41–53, 217–25; see also Cristoph Uehlinger, "Audienz in der Götterwelt: Anthropomorphismus und Soziomorphismus in der Ikonographie eines altsyrichen Zylindersiegels," *UF* 24 (1992): 339–59.

29. So Joseph Blenkinsopp, *Isaiah 40–55* (AB 19A; New York: Doubleday, 2002), 179–80; see also Oswalt, *Chapters 40–66*, 50.

30. Goldingay (*Isaiah 40–55*) observes that since in ch. 41 the position of king belongs to the whole people, ch. 40 perhaps already points to a parallel democratizing of the call of prophet.

31. Blenkinsopp states that the prologue begins "with a summons to prophets in general, or to a specific prophetic group, to proclaim a message of comfort and hope to Yahveh's people" (*Isaiah 40–55*, 180). However, it is impossible to isolate such a group from within this second masculine plural addressee. Similarly, but pointing in the right direction, Fokkelman concludes that the "first verse creates at once a difference between a small group, those who hear the speaker/poet, and the larger collective of the people of God. The difference is above all that the small group must offer comfort and that the large group must receive comfort" ("Stylistic Analysis," 72).

32. The addressee is identified as מבשרת ציון...מבשרת ירושלם. The syntax of these phrases can be understood in a number of ways. As with the majority of translators, it seems best to understand מבשרת in apposition to the names (GKC §128k). This is based upon the fact that מבשרת is feminine singular, the accompanying imperatives are also feminine singular, and "the cities of Judah" are explicitly identified as the addressee of the message (v. 9bβ1). Further, this is the typical syntactical

followed by the actual message she is to proclaim (vv. 9bβ^{2}–11). In the same manner as vv. 1–2, these verses are not prefaced; they are simply voiced. Presumably they comprise the contents of the proclamation asked for in v. 6a.[33] Thus, the message consists of a call to messenger Zion–Jerusalem to prepare herself and to announce the return of Yahweh and his people to herself.

These verses provide the transition of the addressee/reader from inevitable judgment (chs. 1–39) to promised deliverance. Specifically, an individual call is proclaimed to all those among the people of God. The message itself announces the end of punishment for the people of Jerusalem and the return of Yahweh and his people to his city. The face-less voices and addressees highlight the message above all else, and thus it is the message that is introduced here, not any one messenger.[34] As Melugin concludes, "A prophetic message is without doubt commissioned here."[35] The remainder of chs. 40–55 expands upon this general call and appeals to the addressee/reader to reciprocate Yahweh's act and return to Jerusalem with him. Those who respond to this call will participate in this message of good news and simultaneously announce to Zion to prepare herself for Yahweh's and their return.

According to the remainder of the first section, Jacob–Israel is spiritually far away from Yahweh, expressed concretely by the geographical location of the exiles along with the desert, mountainous span lying between them and their home. In the first appearance of Jacob–Israel, the people express that Yahweh is, in fact, far from them:

> [40:27b]My way is hidden from Yahweh
> and my cause is disregarded by my God?

Jacob–Israel seriously questions Yahweh's sovereign power in light of the current desolation of Jerusalem (44:26–28). The city's destruction demonstrates for them that he is no match to the Babylonians and their gods (40:12–31). Consequently, Jacob–Israel has grown weary of Yahweh and thus no longer calls upon him (43:22).

Yahweh makes it clear, though, that Jacob–Israel's sin has caused their present circumstances (42:23–25). Yet, the people still have not turned from their unrighteousness. In particular, and like their ancestors before them, Jacob–Israel is deeply entrenched in the making and worshiping of

construction in Isaiah when these names are preceded by another noun or participle (e.g. 1:8aα; 37:22b; 41:14aα; 52:2; 62:11aβ^{1}; see also 47:1a).

33. So, e.g., Goldingay, *Isaiah 40–55*; Koole, *Isaiah 3/1*, 70.
34. Cf. Westermann, *Isaiah 40–66*, 32.
35. Melugin, "Servant," 24; similarly Seitz, "Prophet Isaiah," 228–32.

other gods (e.g. 40:18–20; 42:17; 44:9–17; 45:20; 46:1–7).[36] In fact, their ongoing wicked ways have caused Yahweh to become a weary servant, thus reversing the master–servant role (43:24b).[37] Moreover, Jacob–Israel would readily attribute any demonstration of power to any other god besides Yahweh. The beginning of ch. 48 expresses this explicitly:

> 48:1 Hear this, house of Jacob,
> the ones called by the name Israel
> and those who came forth from the loins of Judah,
> the ones who swear by the name Yahweh
> and those who invoke the God of Israel—
> not in truth nor in righteousness.
> 2 Indeed, they call themselves after the holy city
> and they rely upon the God of Israel,
> Yahweh of Hosts is his name.
> 3 The former things from long before I declared
> and they went out from my mouth
> and I proclaimed them;
> suddenly I acted and then they came about.
> 4 Because I know that you are stubborn
> and your neck is an iron sinew
> and your forehead is bronze.
> 5 Thus I declared to you long before;
> before it came about I proclaimed it to you.
> Lest you say, "My idol did them"
> or "My image and my cast image commanded them."

36. In contrast to the typical assumption among some redaction critics and other interpreters, the idol passages in chs. 40–48 are considered integral to the message of Isa 40–55. See especially Richard J. Clifford, "The Function of Idol Passages in Second Isaiah," *CBQ* 42 (1980): 450–64; Franke, *Isaiah 46, 47, and 48*; Jacques Guillet, "La Polemique Contre les Idoles et le Serviteur de Yahve," *Bib* 40 (1959): 428–34; Knut Holter, *Second Isaiah's Idol-Fabrication Passages* (BBET 28; Frankfurt: Peter Lang, 1995); Hendrik C. Spykerboer, *The Structure and Composition of Deutero-Isaiah with Special Reference to the Polemics Against Idolatry* (Meppel: Krips, 1976); Rikki E. Watts, "Consolation or Confrontation? Isaiah 40–55 and the Delay of the New Exodus," *TynBul* 41 (1990): 31–59; Westermann, *Isaiah 40–66*, 15–17; Andrew Wilson, *The Nations in Deutero-Isaiah: A Study on Composition and Structure* (ANETS 1; Lewiston: Edwin Mellen Press, 1986), 129–92; see also W. M. W. Roth, "For Life, He Appeals to Death (Wis. 123:18): A Study of Old Testament Idol Parodies," *CBQ* 37 (1975): 21–47.

37. Goldingay, *Isaiah*, 252. Verse 24b literally reads: אך העבדתני בחטאותיך הוגעתני בעונתיך, "Instead you have made me serve because of your sins, you made me weary because of your iniquities." See further John Goldingay, "Isaiah 43,22–28," *ZAW* 110 (1998): 173–91; see also Michael Rosenbaum, *Word-Order Variation in Isaiah 40–55: A Functional Perspective* (SSN 35; Assen: Van Gorcum, 1997), 78–82.

Rikki Watts correctly concludes, "Nothing has changed. The old sins persist. They are Israel in *name* and *lineage only*, no longer worthy of being true Israel."[38] Just as idol-gods cannot see, hear, or understand, idolatrous Jacob–Israel is blind, foolish, and deceived (44:18–20). Thus, these defective imperfections are self-imposed as Jacob–Israel refuses to acknowledge Yahweh's supremacy and to fear him alone (42:20, 25). Consequently, Jacob–Israel is not merely depressed and in need of comfort, but is rebellious and in need of confrontation.

In the face of such continued rebellion and rejection, Yahweh undauntedly comes as the nation's holy one, kinsman-redeemer, creator, king, and savior to deliver them (e.g. 41:14; 43:1, 3, 15; 44:6, 24; 47:4; 48:17). Yahweh will thus provide a way for Jacob–Israel to leave Babylon and return to Jerusalem. In order to accomplish this, Yahweh designates the Persian king Cyrus as רעי and משיחו whom he will take by the hand and for whom he will provide military success, climaxed with the overthrow of Babylon and restoration of Jerusalem. The captives, though, feel insignificant and afraid. Yahweh thus reassures Jacob–Israel by asserting that he has not rejected (41:9bβ^2) nor forgotten them (44:21bβ). The people should not fear, for he will uphold and help them (41:10). Even more significantly, Yahweh reaffirms their position as his chosen servant (e.g. 41:10–14). Yahweh also ascribes kingly status to his servant Jacob–Israel. As Edgar W. Conrad demonstrates, the "fear not" oracles in this section (e.g. 41:8–13, 14–16; 43:1–7; 44:1–5) parallel the oracles addressed to King Ahaz (7:4–9) and Hezekiah (37:6) along with those proclaimed to Babylonian kings.[39] Thus, Yahweh links the ideas of servant and king, which also recall the titles applied to king David (e.g.

38. Watts, "Consolation or Confrontation?," 48 (italics mine). Philip R. Davies claims that the polemics in Isa 40–55 are not attacking the worship of other deities, "but the iconic worship *of the god Yahweh*"; see his "God of Cyrus, God of Israel: Some Religio-Historical Reflections on Isaiah 40–55," in *Words Remembered, Texts Renewed* (Festschrift John F. A. Sawyer; ed. J. Davies, G. Harvey, and W. G. E. Watson; JSOTSup 195; Sheffield: Sheffield Academic Press, 1995), 207–25 (222). There is no doubt that throughout its history Israel practiced iconic worship of Yahweh, but in the polemics of Isa 40–48 Yahweh explicitly contrasts himself with other idol-gods who Jacob–Israel is invoking (46:1–7; cf. 48:4–8).

39. Edgar W. Conrad, "Community as King in Second Isaiah," in *Understanding the Word* (Festschrift Bernhard W. Anderson; ed. J. T. Butler, E. W. Conrad, and B. C. Ollenburger; JSOTSup 37; Sheffield: Sheffield Academic Press, 1985), 99–111; idem, *Fear Not Warrior: A Study of 'al tîrā' Pericopes in the Hebrew Scriptures* (BJS 75; Chico, Calif.: Scholars Press, 1985), 52–62, 79–107; see also Hugh G. M. Williamson, *Variations on a Theme: King, Messiah and Servant in the Book of Isaiah* (Carlisle: Paternoster, 1998), 116–29.

2 Sam 3:18; 1 Kgs 11:34; Ps 89:3, 20).[40] Yahweh confronts the sinfulness of Jacob–Israel and exhorts his people to return to him (44:22) and prepare to leave Babylon, for their redemption has been set in motion:

> [48:20]Go forth from Babylon!
> Flee from the Chaldeans!
> Declare with a sound of jubilation!
> Proclaim this!
> Send it out to the ends of the earth!
> Say, "Yahweh has redeemed his servant Jacob!"

Although redemption is secured, the fact that Yahweh exhorts Jacob–Israel to leave Babylon implies that the people retain the option to remain in Babylon or return to Zion. Hence, to stay constitutes a rejection of Yahweh, whereas leaving entails forsaking their fear and sin while at the same time entrusting themselves to Yahweh alone and embracing their original role as his servant.

To persuade the addressees to turn to Yahweh, an array of arguments are put forward such as the historic relationship between Yahweh and Jacob–Israel (e.g. 41:8–9; 48:17–19), Yahweh's faithfulness and the sureness of his word (e.g. 40:6–8; 45:23; 46:8–11), his pre-eminence over all of creation (e.g. 40:15–20; 44:6–8; 45:20–25), his promise of deliverance (e.g. 40:29–30; 41:10–21; 42:10–16; 43:1–7, 14–21; 46:12–13), his superior knowledge (e.g. 40:13–14; 44:25), his former and ongoing creative activity (e.g. 40:12, 28; 42:5, 9; 44:24; 45:7, 11–13, 18; 48:12–16), and so on. Yet, the primary grounds for prompting Jacob–Israel to return are the overthrow of Babylon and the future provision of deliverance. These acts exhibit Yahweh's sovereign power and simultaneously prove his sole claim to deity. Throughout this section, Yahweh repeatedly asserts his incomparability with any other being. In certain key instances, Yahweh claims his uniqueness through the rhetorical question, "Whom will you compare me to?" (40:18, 25; 46:5; see also 44:7, 8).[41]

40. See Walther Zimmerli and Joachim Jeremias, *The Servant of God* (rev ed.; SBT 20; London: SCM Press, 1965), 22–23. Hans Wildberger suggests that the election language in these chapters directly relates to the traditions concerning the Davidic king (cf. Pss 78:67–72; 89:1–4, 19–29; 132; see his "Die Neuinterpretation des Erwählungsglaubens Israels in der Krise der Exilszeit," in *Wort–Gebot–Glaube: Beiträge zur Theologie des Alten Testaments* (ed. H.-J. Stoebe; Feschrift Walther Eichrodt; ATANT 59; Zürich: Zwingli, 1970), 307–24.

41. The terms דמה and משל are used in these verses to indicate Yahweh's absolute distinctiveness. C. J. Labuschagne remarks that the verb דמה "which means '*to resemble, to be like in outward appearance, to look like*,' is used in connection with Yahweh only to express His incomparability" (*The Incomparability of Yahweh in the Old Testament* [POS 5; Leiden: Brill, 1966], 29).

The comparison is specifically directed to the idol-gods which Jacob–Israel has been invoking. The way Yahweh chooses to demonstrate his incomparability consists in the successful performance of a speech act. An important passage within this section is found in ch. 43:

[43:8]Bring out the people who are blind, though having eyes,
and the deaf, though having ears.
[9]All the nations have gathered themselves together,
and the peoples assemble.
Who among them can declare this?
Or the former things proclaim to us?
Let them present their witnesses so that they may verify,
that they may hear and respond, "It is true!"
[10]You are my witnesses, declaration of Yahweh,
and my servant whom I have chosen
in order that you may know and believe me
and understand that I am he.
Before me no God was formed
nor will there be one after me.
[11]I, I am Yahweh
and apart from me there is no savior.
[12]I myself declared, then I saved, then I proclaimed
and there is no strange god among you
and you are my witnesses, declaration of Yahweh,
that I am God!
[13]Even from the first I am he
and no one can deliver from my hand.
I act and who can reverse it?

This passage expands upon earlier texts that describe Yahweh's challenge to the idol-gods to demonstrate their power (cf. 41:21–29). Here, Yahweh assigns his idolatrous blind and deaf servant to be his witnesses. The idol-gods also have their witnesses ready to testify to their power, but they too cannot *see* and do not *know* true deity (44:9b). Ironically, Jacob–Israel has already been testifying to the power of these idol-gods and could easily fall within this group. However, Yahweh has reaffirmed Jacob–Israel as his chosen servant and here appoints his people to a new task. The parallel designations עדי and עבדי in v. 10a indicated that when Jacob–Israel fulfills the role as Yahweh's witness, they thereby participate in the responsibilities of Yahweh's servant.[42] The term עדה

42. Following the Syriac, *BHS* suggests that the singular עבדי should be pointed as a plural עֲבָדַי to create a grammatical parallel. Duhm also repoints the noun to the plural as Israel is the servant here, not the servant of the Songs (*Jesaia*, 289–90). However, the LXX, Tg, Vg and possibly 1QIsa[a] all support the MT (see Dominique Barthélemy, *Critique Textuelle de L'Ancien Testament* [OBO 50/2; Göttingen: Vandenhoeck & Ruprecht, 1986], 313–14).

functions here in a legal sense[43] and thus the witnesses representing each are carefully to weigh and test the evidence for the claim of deity. The successful performance of a speech act will definitively prove divinity.

The self-presentation or identification formula concerning "knowing Yahweh" (vv. 10b–11) is expressed in a number of ways throughout the book of Isaiah and predominantly occurs in chs. 40–55 (19:21; 37:20; 41:20; 43:10–11; 45:3, 6; 49:23, 26; 52:6; 60:16).[44] In a recent comprehensive and rigorous analysis of the phraseology of "knowing Yahweh," Marc Vervenne demonstrates that " 'knowing YHWH' is closely associated with the description of divine *actions* in the history of Israel, and in particular with the *announcement* of those *actions* which are going to take place."[45] Here, the reason for Yahweh's appointing Jacob–Israel as his witness, and the intended perlocutionary effect of Yahweh's declaration of the Cyrus event, is for the people themselves to *know* that Yahweh has actualized the event and that they will acknowledge that he alone is God.[46] Jacob–Israel's call to be a witness, then, has its own aim of convincing the witnesses themselves. As the people of God are to announce to themselves the return of Yahweh (40:1–11), similarly they

43. See D. Levy and J. Milgrom, "עדה," *TDOT* 10:468–80 (472–73).

44. See Marc Vervenne, "The Phraseology of 'Knowing YHWH' in the Hebrew Bible," in van Ruiten and Vervenne, eds., *Studies in the Book of Isaiah*, 467–92 (467–68).

45. Ibid., 468 (italics mine). For further analysis of the formula see the now classic work of Walther Zimmerli, *I Am Yahweh* (ed. W. Brueggemann; trans. D. W. Stott; Atlanta: John Knox, 1982); see also Beuken, "God's Exclusivity," 350–55; Sheldon H. Blank, "Studies in Deutero-Isaiah," *HUCA* 15 (1940): 1–46 (13–14, 34–46).

46. Concerning the function of למען beginning in v. 10bα, Vervenne concludes that the phraseology of knowing Yahweh "expresses clearly purpose when it is constructed with a final particle (cf. 41,20; 43,10; 45,3.6)." In these instances, Vervenne claims that "YHWH's intervention is 'degraded,' as it were, to mere 'material knowledge' which in itself possesses little value." In contrast, the function of the formula expressing consequence of an event has value (e.g. Isa 49:23, 26; 60:16). "If YHWH lets himself be known *in what he does*...then his intervention has actual value in itself. The recognition of YHWH *takes place* in what he does." In other words, the phraseology "indicates that an intervention of YHWH is in fact an intervention of YHWH" ("Phraseology," 491–92). Vervenne is correct in understanding the phraseology in the above texts as expressing purpose, but his distinctions between purpose and consequence need qualification since he apparently does not take the larger context of the phrase into consideration. Specifically, the function of the formula expressing purpose in 43:10–11 is intimately related to the consequence of the Cyrus event. Thus, the purpose of Yahweh's declaration is realized upon the actualization of the event which consequently demonstrates that Yahweh has in fact intervened.

are to witness to themselves about his incomparability. Thus, the way to return to Yahweh and embrace the role of his servant is to acknowledge Yahweh as the one and only God. Further, to confess allegiance to Yahweh alone and to testify to his supremacy places one in the tradition of Yahweh's prophets, who were also identified individually as עבדי (e.g. Isa 20:3) and collectively as עבדי הנביאים (e.g. 2 Kgs 9:7; 17:13, 23; Jer 7:25; Ezek 38:17).[47] Just a few lines earlier in this unit, Yahweh reminds his servant Jacob–Israel that this prophetic role has been their assignment all along. Yahweh makes this explicitly clear by using conventional prophetic terminology, the noun מלאך with the verb שלח, to identify them as "my messenger whom I send" (42:19aβ; see Isa 6:8; 44:26a; see also 1 Sam 19:20–21).[48]

Chapters 49–55 begin a new focus, as the section now turns to the restoration of Jerusalem while the names Jacob and Israel begin to disappear. At the same time, Zion–Jerusalem reappears and thus recalls her appearance in the opening chapter (40:2, 9). As ch. 40 starts abruptly announcing the end of judgment and time of salvation, chs. 49–55 presuppose the overthrow of Babylon and the deliverance home secured. In this second section there will be no more talk about Cyrus, Babylon's fall, former and new things, idol-gods, and the incomparability of Yahweh. The second section builds upon these themes and specifically looks for a response. The consistent subject remains, though, the issue of sin and the call to return to Jerusalem (51:17; 52:1–2, 11–12). As the first section closes with a command to leave Babylon, towards the close of the second a similar call is issued:

> 55:6Seek Yahweh while he can be found!
> Call on him while he is near!
> 7May the wicked one forsake his way
> and the guilty one his thoughts.
> May he return to Yahweh that he may have compassion on him
> and to our God for he will abundantly forgive.

A call is directed to the addressee that exhorts each individual person to forsake sin and return to Yahweh.

In chs. 49–55 the key *leitmotif* of servanthood becomes even more central. It is beyond the scope of this study to present the vast amount of different views and suggestions concerning the so-called "Servant Songs"

47. See Zimmerli and Jeremias, *Servant of God*, 23–25.

48. On the term מלאך designating prophets, see D. N. Freedman and B. E. Willoughby, "מלאך," *TDOT* 8:308–24 (315–16). On שלח and the commissioning/sending of prophets, see M. Delcor and E. Jenni, "שלח," *TLOT* 3:1330–34 (1333).

and the identity of the servant portrayed in them.[49] In short, the ongoing debate concerning the servant arises from the final form as it presents a complex figure that is identified and anonymous, apparent and ambiguous, understandable and paradoxical. Specifically, the text depicts the servant as a king who will establish justice, while at the same time, the servant rejects Yahweh's commands. The servant is a prophet and also the recipient of that message. The servant is blind, deaf, and imprisoned in certain instances and righteous, obedient, and insightful in others. The servant is clearly collective Jacob–Israel and yet at times the servant appears more as an individual. Perhaps the most paradoxical aspect is how servant Jacob–Israel has the task of restoring servant Jacob–Israel.

Recognizing some of these issues, Bernhard Duhm identified four Servant Songs within chs. 40–55 (42:1–4; 49:1–6; 50:4–9 [10, 11]; 52:13–53:12). Duhm claimed that these Songs exhibited a difference in language and style, a loose connection with their surrounding context, and a different servant in distinction from servant Jacob–Israel in other passages.[50] Thus, Duhm concludes that the Servant Songs originally existed as an independent corpus that was subsequently inserted into Second Isaiah. This being so, these four Songs must be extricated from their literary contexts and interpreted exclusively in light of one another. Although Duhm's hypothesis was the dominant paradigm for interpreters from every tradition throughout the twentieth century, it has caused more perplexities than answers.[51] Christopher R. North has convincingly

49. For analyses of the four servant passages and the various suggestions concerning the identity of the servant, see especially Christopher R. North, *The Suffering Servant in Deutero-Isaiah: An Historical and Critical Study* (2d ed.; Oxford: Oxford University Press, 1956); H. Haag, *Der Gottesknecht bei Deuterojesaja* (EdF 233; Darmstadt: Wissenschaftliche Buchgesellschaft, 1985); C. G. Kruse, "The Servant Songs: Interpretive Trends Since C. R. North," *SBibT* 8 (1978): 3–27; H. H. Rowley, "The Servant of the Lord in the Light of Three Decades of Criticism," in idem, *The Servant of the Lord* (2d ed.; Oxford: Blackwell, 1965), 3–60; Harry M. Orlinsky, "The So-Called 'Servant of the Lord,' and 'Suffering Servant' in Second Isaiah," in *Studies in the Second Part of the Book of Isaiah* (ed. H. M. Orlinsky and Norman H. Snaith; VTSup 14; Leiden: Brill, 1967), 1–133 (23–51). For a more recent survey, see Hermisson, "Literatur zu Deuterojesaja," 414–30.

50. See Duhm, *Jesaia*, xviii, 277–80, 330–34, 341–44, 355–68.

51. For discussions on the failure of Duhm's paradigm, see in particular Tryggve N. D. Mettinger, *A Farewell to the Servant Songs: A Critical Examination of an Exegetical Axiom* (SM 1982–1983: 3; Lund: Gleerup, 1983); idem, "In Search of the Hidden Structure: YHWH as King in Isaiah 40–55," in Broyles and Evans (eds.), *Writing and Reading the Scroll of Isaiah*, 1:143–54 (152–54); Hans M. Barstad, "The Future of the 'Servant Songs': Some Reflections on the Relationship of Biblical

demonstrated that Duhm's literary and content criteria have no basis.[52] Further, Duhm has not evaluated the nature of the passages accurately; Goldingay correctly observes that these

> four passages are no more "songs" than other parts of Isaiah 40–55 (certainly less so than a passage such as 42:10–12) and no more lyrical and heightened in tone and expression than other parts of Isaiah (such as 43:1–7; 49:15–21; 54:1–17). As poetry, these four passages are thus not distinctive from other parts of chapters 40–55, though they are on the whole more lyrical and heightened than the other passages about Yahweh's servant.[53]

Thus, although four servant passages clearly distinguish themselves in content from the other texts discussing the servant, their poetical style resembles that of the rest of chs. 40–55, and they do not display a separate, unique genre.[54]

An additional problem with Duhm's hypothesis is that these servant passages are clearly embedded within their present literary context[55] and are, in fact, integral to the prophetic function of chs. 40–55. Thus, as Hans Barstad asserts, "Any attempt to remove the so-called classic 'servant songs' from their context, any attempt to make of them a separate corpus within Isa 40–55, is bound to fail."[56] Just as problematic, Duhm's theory has created a hegemonic tradition standing over and above these texts as the sole, authoritative grid that dictates how interpretation must proceed. Thus, the necessary interpretive conclusions have already taken place even before the reader begins surveying the material. Consequently, the reader is closed off from the text, thus suppressing interpretation and, most grievously, self-involvement. In the final analysis, the Duhmian model does not hold any promise for a way forward and thus should be forever abandoned.

Scholarship to its Own Tradition," in *Language, Theology, and the Bible* (Festschrift James Barr; ed. S. E. Balentine and J. Barton; Oxford: Clarendon, 1994), 261–70.

52. North, *Suffering Servant*, 156–91.

53. Goldingay, *Isaiah*, 238; see further Melugin, *Isaiah 40–55*, 64–74; Westermann, *Isaiah 40–66*, 20–21.

54. Klaus Baltzer has attempted to establish a single *Gattung* for the four Songs by identifying elements of an ideal biography in each (see "Zur formgeschichtlichen Bestimmung der Texte vom Gottesknecht im Deuterojesaja-Buch," in *Probleme biblischer Theologie* [Festschrift Gerhard von Rad; ed. H. W. Wolff; Munich: Kaiser, 1971], 27–43; idem, *Deutero-Isaiah*, 19–20). See Mettinger's critique of Baltzer's suggestion (*Servant Songs*, 16–17).

55. See specifically Mettinger, *Servant Songs*, 18–28.

56. Barstad, "Future of the 'Servant Songs,'" 267.

Approaching the servant passages from within their literary context provides a more fruitful framework for interpretation to transpire. To begin, the term עבד occurs thirteen times in chs. 40–48 and always in the singular (41:8aα, 9bα; 42:1aα, 19 [2×]; 43:10aβ; 44:1a, 2bα, 21 [2×], 26aα; 45:4aα; 48:20bβ).[57] In seven of these instances, Jacob–Israel is explicitly identified as עבד (41:8; 44:1, 2, 21 [2×]; 45:4; 48:20). In four of the remaining occurrences, עבד refers to the nation without much scrutiny required (41:9; 42:19 [2×]; 43:10). The identities of the two remaining instances of עבד are not as easily determined; however, the dominant use of the term inferentially points to Jacob–Israel. One of these two instances occurs in the first servant passage. Within this text royal terminology and imagery is expressed that has also been applied to Jacob–Israel in other passages.[58] Yahweh speaks thus about his servant:

> 42:1 There, my servant whom I uphold,
>   my chosen one in whom my soul delights.
> I have placed my spirit upon him,
>   he will bring forth justice to the nations.
> 2 He will not cry out nor lift up,
>   he will not make his voice heard in the street.
> 3 He will not break a bruised reed
>   nor snuff out a smoldering wick.
> In truth he will bring forth justice.
> 4 He will not fail nor be discouraged
>   until he establishes justice in the earth
>   and for his teaching the coastlands will wait.

Here Yahweh says that he "upholds" (תמך) his servant as he does servant Jacob–Israel in a previous statement (41:10bβ). Yahweh refers to the servant as בחירי and just prior to this he reminds his servant Jacob–Israel that he has "chosen" (בחר) them (41:8aβ, 9bβ). The singular noun form בחירי only occurs two other times with both denoting Jacob–Israel (43:20bβ[3]; 45:4aβ). It is also worth noting that the LXX assumes the

57. On the occurrences of עבד in Isa 40–66, see Ingrid Riesener, *Der Stamm* עבד *im Alten Testament: Eine Wortuntersuchung unter Berücksichtigung neuerer sprachwissenschaftlicher Methoden* (BZAW 149; Berlin: de Gruyter, 1979), 235–51.

58. Regarding the royal depiction of the servant in 42:1–4, see especially Otto Kaiser, *Der Königliche Knecht: Eine Traditionsgeschichtlich-exegetische Studie über die Ebed–Jahwe–Lieder bei Deuterojesaja* (FRLANT 70; Göttingen: Vandenhoeck & Ruprecht, 1962), 14–39; Antti Laato, *Servant of YHWH and Cyrus: A Reinterpretation of the Exilic Messianic Programme in Isaiah 40–55* (ConBOT 35; Stockholm: Almqvist & Wiksell, 1992), 74–87; Shalom M. Paul, "Deutero-Isaiah and Cuneiform Royal Inscriptions," *JAOS* 88 (1968): 180–86 (181–82); Williamson, *Variations on a Theme*, 130–48.

servant in 42:1–4 is Jacob–Israel, as the first line reads: Ιακωβ ὁ παῖς μου, ἀντιλήμψομαι αὐτου· Ισραηλ ὁ ἐκλεκτός μου (v. 1a).[59] In addition to all this, Goldingay has unquestionably identified 41:1–20 and 41:21–42:17 as parallel sequences or spiral sections.[60] Each section opens with a courtroom scene that involves a challenge to determine divinity (41:1–7//41:21–29), followed by a passage concerning Yahweh's servant (41:8–16//42:1–9), and concluding with a vision of Yahweh's transforming provision for Jacob–Israel in the wilderness (41:17–20//42:14–17). This structural patterning clearly suggests that the servant figure in both sequences is one and the same—Jacob–Israel. As Goldingay asserts, "One would need some explicit contrary indication if one were not to make this inference from the structural parallel."[61] From all of this, there can be no doubt that Jacob–Israel is the עבד referred to in this first servant passage.[62]

The problem with Jacob–Israel lies with the nation's inability to fulfill such an assignment. In 42:1–4, the servant is to bring "justice" (משפט) to the nations through Yahweh's Torah. Yet, Jacob–Israel complains that their "cause" (משפט) is being ignored by him (40:27), while the nation has completely rejected Yahweh's commands (48:18a). The servant is to heal the broken and oppressed, but Jacob–Israel is broken and weak (42:22). In the immediate verses following the first servant passage, which must also refer to servant Jacob–Israel, Yahweh appoints his people to be a covenant, a light to the nations, to open blind eyes, and to bring people out of dark places (vv. 6b–7). Yet, Jacob–Israel is blind, deaf, in darkness, and imprisoned (vv. 19, 20). As discussed above, Yahweh faithfully loves Jacob–Israel despite these fatal flaws and graciously continues to consider the nation as his servant. Moreover, Yahweh assigns his servant a new task: to witness to his demonstration of power. Jacob–Israel should have been testifying to Yahweh's supreme power since the exodus event and fulfilling its role as a kingdom of priests (cf.

59. N. L. Tidwell goes so far as to claim that the MT is corrupt and the LXX preserves the original reading; see his "My Servant Jacob, Is. XLII 1: A Suggestion," in *Studies on Prophecy: A Collection of Twelve Papers* (ed. G. W. in Anderson et al.; VTSup 26; Leiden: Brill, 1974), 84–91). All the other Versions support the MT.

60. Goldingay, "Arrangement of Isaiah," 289–99.

61. Ibid., 292.

62. On this conclusion, see further Childs, *Isaiah*, 323–25; Knud Jeppesen, "From 'You, My Servant' to 'The Hand of the Lord is with My Servants,' " *SJOT* 1 (1990): 113–29 (119–20); Ulrika Lindblad, "A Note on the Nameless Servant in Isaiah XLII 1–4," *VT* 43 (1993): 115–19; Peter Wilcox and David Paton-Williams, "The Servant Songs in Deutero-Isaiah," *JSOT* 42 (1988): 79–102 (85–88); Williamson, *Variations on a Theme*, 132–48.

Exod 19:6). However, like their ancestors before them, the people have failed miserably, as they continue to look to other gods for help and consequently testify to their power. Yahweh responds by exhorting Jacob–Israel to forget the former things because he is going to do something new (43:18–19a). Yahweh promises a new or second exodus (vv. 19b–21) that will be proclaimed through a new song (v. 21; cf. 42:10).[63] As a witness to the actualization of this new promise, Jacob–Israel has the opportunity to fulfill the role of the servant prescribed in ch. 42 by first acknowledging and then testifying to Yahweh's incomparability as the one and only God. The only way to fail in this opportunity is to reject Yahweh as God alone and instead entrust themselves to idol-gods (v. 17).

Chapter 49 begins with the servant *leitmotif* with the focus quickly shifting to Zion–Jerusalem. Patricia T. Willey has observed that the two figures alternate between sections while never appearing together nor being discussed in relation to one another:

49:1–13	Servant
49:14–50:3	Zion–Jerusalem
50:4–11	Servant
51:1–8	Masculine plural addressee
51:9–52:12	Zion–Jerusalem
52:13–53:12	Servant
54:1–17	Zion–Jerusalem[64]

The block ends with a second masculine singular and plural addressee (55:1–13). Despite this alteration between these two entities, and as John Sawyer points out, the experiences of the servant and Zion–Jerusalem spanning across chs. 40–55 parallel one another, as both progress "from abandonment, loneliness and fear to fulfillment and joy."[65]

Regarding the servant, the noun עבד occurs seven more times in the singular (49:3a, 5aα^2, 6aα^1, 7aβ^2; 50:10aβ; 52:13a; 53:11aβ). The second

63. Interpreters have long since recognized the exodus motif in chs. 40–55. In contrast, Barstad confines the Exodus texts to those specifically referring to Israel's original release from Egypt (43:14–17; 48:20–22; 51:9–11); see his *Way in the Wilderness*; idem, "Isa 40,1–11," 237–40. Bradley J. Spencer also follows this line of thought in his "The 'New Deal' for Post-exilic Judah in Isaiah 41,17–20," *ZAW* 112 (2000): 583–97.

64. Patricia T. Willey, "The Servant of YHWH and Daughter Zion: Alternating Visions of YHWH's Community," in *SBL Seminar Papers, 1995* (ed. E. H. Lovering, Jr.; SBLSP 34; Atlanta: Scholars Press, 1995), 267–303 (273); idem, *Former Things*, 105.

65. John F. A. Sawyer, "Daughter Zion and Servant of the Lord in Isaiah: A Comparison," *JSOT* 44 (1989): 89–107 (99).

section opens with an unidentified first person singular voice who Yahweh declares as עבדי and ישראל (49:3). Coupled with this explicit parallel with servant Jacob–Israel, the voice in this passage confesses that he has *also* been appointed to be a light to the nations (49:6bα). In addition, Yahweh speaks earlier about Jacob–Israel:

> 43:1 And now thus said Yahweh,
> your creator, Jacob and your former, Israel.
> "Do not fear for I have redeemed you!
> I called you by your name, you are mine."

Yahweh similarly asserts that he formed servant Jacob–Israel from the womb (44:2aβ^1). The voice here reverberates the same terminology about himself:

> 49:1b Yahweh called me from the womb,
> from the insides of my mother he pronounced my name.

Further, the literary structures of 42:1–9 and 49:1–13 correspond to each other: a discussion about the servant (42:1–4; 49:1–6) followed by additional comments given by Yahweh introduced by similar speech formulas (42:5–9; 49:7–13). From these parallels, the logical conclusion is that this servant passage also speaks of Jacob–Israel (cf. 49:3). However, as the second servant passage progresses, the speaker is given the additional assignment of restoring Jacob–Israel (49:5). Given this task, the fact that Jacob–Israel is blind and deaf, and here a first person singular "I" speaks, this servant figure now becomes somewhat distinguished from servant Jacob–Israel referred to in chs. 40–48.

Isaiah 49:1–6 highlights the age-old crux of the interpretation of the servant passages and their portrayal of the servant. Jewish and Christian interpreters throughout the centuries have offered numerous suggestions concerning the identity of the servant and whether the figure is either an individual or collective group. Even when viewing the servant passages within their literary context, scholars remain divided between these two options. Regarding the latter position, P. A. H. de Boer's assessment still reflects a large number of interpreters as he concludes, "The word Israel [in v 3] is certainly fatal to any individualistic theory."[66] More recently, Mettinger has made a strong case for identifying the servant throughout the chapters as the nation Israel.[67] Scholars typically oppose this view by questioning the reasonableness of Israel given an assigned task to Israel.

66. P. A. H. de Boer, *Second-Isaiah's Message* (OTS 11; Leiden: Brill, 1956), 53.

67. Mettinger, *Servant Songs*, 29–43.

Maintaining the Servant Songs paradigm, Hans-Jürgen Hermisson has suggested that the Songs reveal a historic ideal group of prophets who have the assignment of restoring disloyal Israel back to Yahweh.[68] Laato follows Hermisson closely and identifies "two different 'servant-Israels.'" The disloyal Israel is criticized and exhorted to trust in Yahweh's plan of salvation in 42:14–44:8 and 46:3–48:21 while 48:20–52:12 as well as 42:1–9 and 52:13–53:12 describe the ideal Israel.[69] Hermisson and Laato offer a seemingly plausible suggestion, but despite their rigorous exegesis, with or without the Duhmian model it is virtually impossible to locate two such historical groups within Isa 40–55.[70]

Because of the difficulties associated with the collective interpretation, a large number of interpreters claim that the figure must be an individual. A few scholars hold to a purely messianic interpretation of the servant passages.[71] These interpreters generally follow the Duhmian approach and are thus susceptible to the same problems as discussed above. Because 49:1–6 and 50:4–9 are analogous testimonies to Isa 6 and Jer 1, a large number of interpreters understand this "I/me" to be a Second Isaiah.[72] Seitz slightly differs from this and suggests that throughout chs. 40–48 "the question is, 'Who will accept the call God has issued in 40:1–11?' Will Israel be the servant God commissions her to be?" Not until 48:16 does a historical individual step forward who Seitz identifies as the "servant-author."[73] Further, this "servant carries Israel's history with

68. Hans-Jürgen Hermisson, "Israel und der Gottesknecht bei Deuterojesaja," *ZTK* 79 (1982): 1–24.

69. Laato, *Servant of YHWH*, 35.

70. Laato follows Hermisson in retaining the Servant Songs model and at the same time he finds much affinity with Mettinger's study and thus he considers them as integral parts of the composition of Isa 40–55 (see Laato, *Servant of YHWH*, 16–21; idem, "The Composition of Isaiah 40–55," *JBL* 109 [1990]: 207–28). Thus, Laato attempts to hold onto the Duhmian model while at the same time following Mettinger's literary approach that ultimately condemns that same paradigm. Hans-Jürgen Hermisson, on the other hand, takes to task Mettinger's suggestion in a review article and maintains the traditional approach to the Servant Songs; see his "Voreiliger Abschied von den Gottesknechtsliedern," *TRu* 49 (1984): 209–22.

71. E.g. Koole, *Isaiah 3/1*, 210, idem, *Isaiah*. Part 3, Vol. 2, *Isaiah 49–55* (trans. A. P. Runia; HCOT; Leuven: Peeters, 1998), 6–7; F. Duane Lindsey, "The Call of the Servant in Isaiah 42:1–9," *BSac* 139 (1982): 12–31 (12); J. Alec Motyer, *The Prophecies of Isaiah: An Introduction and Commentary* (Downers Grove, Ill.: InterVarsity, 1993), 13–16, 318–19, 384; Oswalt, *Chapters 40–66*, 107–9.

72. E.g. Blenkinsopp, *Isaiah 40–55*, 78, 300; Whybray, *Isaiah 40–66*, 135; Wilcox and Paton-Williams, "Servant Songs," 88–100.

73. Seitz, "Divine Council," 246; idem, "Prophet Isaiah," 237–38; idem, "Isaiah 40–66," 318, 321.

prophecy in him and, in so doing, is 'Israel' in a very specific sense."[74] Similarly to Seitz, Childs argues that historical speculation suggesting that a prophetic figure such as Second Isaiah has replaced collective Israel misses the point of the text. "The identity of the first person singular voice in 48:16 and 49:1–6 remains fully concealed." This person has not replaced Israel, but is "a faithful embodiment of the nation Israel who has not performed its chosen role (48:1–2)."[75]

H. G. M. Williamson claims that the figure in 42:1–4 is an ideal held out before Israel as vision and aspiration.[76] But due to the failure of his people, Yahweh changes his plan and turns to one, Deutero-Isaiah, who will now take on the role of the servant.[77] Yet, Williamson concedes that because of the parallel descriptions and assignment of the figure here and Jacob–Israel, we "have no way of telling, so far as I can see, whether the servant of 49:1–6 is an individual or a group."[78] Melugin also recognizes the ambiguity of the first person voice throughout chs. 40–55. For Melugin, though, the ambiguity is intentional, and thus the "I" is at once prophet and people, individual and Israel.[79] Melugin, and to some degree Childs, aligns himself with the suggestions of Otto Eissfeldt[80] and H. Wheeler Robinson.[81] These two interpreters suggest that the servant is

74. Seitz, "Prophet Isaiah," 236.

75. Childs, *Isaiah*, 385; see further pp. 383–86.

76. Williamson, *Variations on a Theme*, 142.

77. Ibid., 148–52. Somewhat similar, Tod Linafelt claims that the speech of Yahweh beginning in 48:17 continues to 49:3. Thus, in vv. 1–3 it is "YHWH describing what the speech of Israel should be!" In v. 4 the prophet laments over the failure of Yahweh's word and in v. 5 the prophet is then identified as the servant. "Because Israel has failed to assume the role of servant and speak rightly, as called to do in 48:17–49:4, the prophet is 'now' given the task of witnessing to 'the nations' (49:6) in addition to his previous task of bringing back Israel (49:5–6)"; see Tod Linafelt, "Speech and Silence in the Servant Passages: Towards a Final-Form Reading of the Book of Isaiah," in *The Theological Interpretation of Scripture* [ed. S. E. Fowl; Blackwell Readings in Modern Theology; Cambridge: Blackwell, 1997], 199–209 [204–5]).

78. Williamson, *Variations on a Theme*, 152.

79. See Melugin, *Isaiah 40–55*, 84, 152–55; idem, "Servant," 29–30.

80. Otto Eissfeldt, "The Ebed-Jahwe in Isaiah xl.–lv in the Light of Israelite Conceptions of Community and the Individual, the Ideal and the Real," *ExpTim* 44 (1932–33): 261–68; idem, *The Old Testament: An Introduction* (trans. P. R. Ackroyd; New York: Harper & Row, 1965), 340–41.

81. Melugin cites here H. W. Robinson, "The Hebrew Conception of Corporate Personality," in *Werden und Wesen des Alten Testaments* (ed. P. Volz, F. Stummer, and J. Hempel; BZAW 66; Berlin: de Gruyter, 1936), 48–62. Robinson's essay was reprinted with minor corrections and updating in his *Corporate Personality in Ancient Israel* (rev. ed.; Philadelphia: Fortress, 1980), 25–44.

Israel, understood as a "corporate personality or individual." This conclusion is based on the hypothesis that Israel viewed itself as "a unity, an individual."[82] According to Robinson, the prophet "*is* Israel created to be the Servant; he is Israel, though working alone to make Israel what she ought to be; he is Israel finally become a light of nations to the end of the earth."[83] Along similar lines, Ronald E. Clements critically combines the suggestions of Mettinger, along with J. Lindblom[84] and Robinson, and claims that the four Servant Songs within their literary context point strongly to a collective group of exilic Israelites who suffered individually and also representatively for the nation.[85]

All of these proposals clearly demonstrate the paradoxical and elusive portrayal of the servant in Isa 40–55 and the consequential impossibility of definitively identifying the servant in each instance. The final form of the text presents a servant figure who is simultaneously collective Jacob–Israel and some other ambiguous voice identified with the same imagery and terminology as servant Jacob–Israel. In distinction from those above, Goldingay recognizes and attempts to maintain this tension.[86] Jacob–Israel is Yahweh's servant, but because of the nation's condition they are in no position to fulfill the servant responsibilities. Thus, "the identity of the servant which was explicit in chapter xli is open in chapter xlii. The picture of the servant has become a role seeking for someone to fulfil it."[87] Second Isaiah answers this call and is identified by the "I" in the second and third servant passages. As with those above, the prophet becomes Jacob–Israel's representative who will fulfill their servant role. However, Jacob–Israel retains their servant status and the prophet becomes a model or example for the people to imitate and thereby embrace the stance of Yahweh's servant (cf. 50:10). The final servant passage functions in the same way as the first, as each describes rather than identifies the servant. Overall, 52:13–53:12 is a vision that implores the self-involvement of the reader and at the same time functions as another description of what it means to be Yahweh's servant.

The approach I take in this study situates the servant passages within the proposed prophetic strategy of Isa 40–55. This includes "embracing"

82. Eissfeldt, "Ebed-Jahwe," 264–65.

83. Robinson, *Corporate Personality*, 41.

84. J. Lindblom, *The Servant Songs in Deutero-Isaiah: A New Attempt to Solve an Old Problem* (LUÅ 47.5; Lund: Gleerup, 1951).

85. R. E. Clements, "Isaiah 53 and the Restoration of Israel," in Bellinger and Farmer, eds., *Jesus and the Suffering Servant*, 39–54 (cf. 53).

86. For Goldingay's discussions on the servant and the servant passages, see *Isaiah*, 237–42, 280–85, 189–91, 301–9.

87. Goldingay, "Arrangement of Isaiah," 292.

the passages' intentional ambiguity, which characterizes the entire corpus, and viewing the language as performative and not simply representational. Within this conceptual framework, one can explore how the servant passages function in conjunction with their overall literary context as they invite the self-involvement of the addressees/readers. In short, Yahweh identifies Jacob–Israel as עבדי, but the people are not his servant in truth. Those who embrace the open role through self-involvement will constitute the true people of God. Addressees/speakers who adopt the position of Yahweh's servant have the task of calling and being examples to Jacob–Israel in order to prompt them also to embrace their servant status.

Similar to the servant figure, the symbol Zion–Jerusalem is flexible, multivalent, and paradoxical, but even more so.[88] In general, the symbol refers to the geographical city of Jerusalem (44:26, 28; 46:13; 51:3, 11), and in other instances, the people inhabiting the city (40:1–2; cf. 51:16; 52:7–9). Zion–Jerusalem is also depicted as a woman who often parallels the descriptions of Jacob–Israel in the first section.[89] As already displayed,

88. Recent attention has been paid to the role Zion–Jerusalem plays in Isa 40–55 and in particular chs. 49–55. See in particular Richtsje Abma, "Traveling from Babylon to Zion: Location and its Function in Isaiah 49–55," *JSOT* 74 (1997): 3–28; Ulrich Berges, "Personifications and Prophetic Voices of Zion in Isaiah and Beyond," in de Moor, ed., *The Elusive Prophet*, 54–82 (cf. 64–72); Hans-Jürgen Hermisson, "Die Frau Zion," in van Ruiten and Vervenne, eds., *Studies in the Book of Isaiah*, 19–39; Knud Jeppesen, "Mother Zion, Father Servant: A Reading of Isaiah 49–55," in *Of Prophets' Visions and the Wisdom of Sages* (Festschrift R. Norman Whybray; ed. H. A. McKay and D. J. A. Clines; JSOTSup 162; Sheffield: JSOT Press, 1993), 109–25; Normon W. Porteous, "Jerusalem-Zion: The Growth of a Symbol," in *Verbannung und Heimkehr: Beiträge zur Geschichte und Theologie Israels im 6. und 5. Jahrhundert v. Chr* (Festschrift Wilhelm Rudolph; ed. A. Kuschke; Tübingen: J. C. B. Mohr [Paul Siebeck], 1961), 235–52; Sawyer, "Daughter of Zion"; Odil H. Steck, *Gottesknecht und Zion*, 126–46; Willey, "Daughter Zion"; idem, *Former Things*.

89. In these chapters and elsewhere in the Old Testament, the personification of the city Zion–Jerusalem in feminine imagery follows, but not completely, the typical portrayal of cities in other ancient writings. Along with the above, see also Klaus Baltzer, "Stadt-Tyche oder Zion–Jerusalem: Die Auseinandersetzung mit den Göttern der Zeit bei Deuterojesaja," in *Alttestamentlicher Glaube und Biblischer Theologie* (Festschrift Horst D. Preuss; ed. J. Hausmann and H.-J. Zöbel; Stuttgart: Kohlhammer, 1992), 114–20; Mark E. Biddle, "The Figure of Lady Jerusalem: Identification, Deification and Personification of Cities in the Ancient Near East," in (eds.), *The Biblical Canon in Comparative Perspective* (ed. K. L. Younger, W. H. Hallo, and B. F. Batto; ANETS 11; Lewiston: Edwin Mellen, 1991), 172–94; Aloysius Fitzgerald, "The Mythological Background for the Presentation of Jerusalem as a Queen and False Worship as Adultery in the Old Testament," *CBQ* 34 (1972): 403–16; idem,

both figures are referred to by two parallel names and are presented in collective and individual terms. Further, Zion–Jerusalem is the messenger of the good news of promised deliverance (40:9–11) and the recipient of the good news of her restoration (52:1–10). Similar to Jacob–Israel's first words, Zion–Jerusalem's only utterance is a complaint:

> 49:14 Yahweh has forsaken me,
> and my Lord has forgotten me.

Zion–Jerusalem is the child of Yahweh's womb (49:15a). She is also a wife and mother sent into slavery because of her sins, along with her children (50:1; 54:7–8a). Yet, this childless mother and abandoned wife will soon be restored and see children (49:14–23; 50:1–3; 54:1–17). Yahweh promises Zion–Jerusalem a second exodus (51:9–11; 52:3) and exhorts her to arouse and prepare herself to leave (51:17a; 52:11–12). Whereas secure daughter Babylon-Chaldea will soon fall, lie in dust and darkness, and will become a widow without children (47:1–15), daughter Zion–Jerusalem is called to shake off the dust from her captor's demise and return to Yahweh (52:1–2).[90] She is in darkness, but Yahweh has not forgotten (49:15) nor rejected her (54:7–8). Thus, she should not fear, for Yahweh will deliver her home (51:12–16). As will soon be disclosed, though, the city remains unfaithful to Yahweh and unrighteous (e.g. 57:6–13). Although never explicitly stated, these parallels point to a blending between the servant and Zion–Jerusalem figures, as in certain instances the city functions as the counterpart to Jacob–Israel. Still, such interaction does not lead to complete identification since the servant and Zion–Jerusalem also remain distinct.[91]

"*BTWLT* and *BT* as Titles for Capital Cities," *CBQ* 37 (1975): 167–83; Elaine R. Follis, "The Holy City as Daughter," in *Directions in Biblical Hebrew Poetry* (ed. E. R. Follis; JSOTSup 40; Sheffield: JSOT Press, 1987), 173–84; John J. Schmitt, "The Gender of Ancient Israel," *JSOT* 26 (1983): 115–25; idem, "The Motherhood of God and Zion as Mother," *RB* 92–94 (1985): 557–69.

90. For a comparison between Lady Babylon and Zion–Jerusalem, see Mark E. Biddle, "Lady Zion's Alter Egos: Isaiah 47:1–15 and 57:6–13 as Structural Counterparts," in Melugin and Sweeney, eds., *New Visions of Isaiah*, 124–39.

91. The majority of the interpreters noted above see clear distinctions between the servant and Jacob–Israel and Zion–Jerusalem. In contrast, Leland E. Wilshire argues that the two figures are inseparably fused; see his "The Servant-City: A New Interpretation of the "Servant of the Lord" in the Servant Songs of Deutero-Isaiah," *JBL* 94 (1975): 356–67; idem, "Jerusalem as the 'Servant City' in Isaiah 40–66: Reflections in the Light of Further Study of the Cuneiform Tradition," in *The Bible in the Light of Cuneiform Literature: Scripture in Context III* (ed. W. W. Hallo, B. W. Jones, and G. L. Mattingly; ANETS 8; Lewiston: Edwin Mellen, 1990), 231–51.

Another important link between Jacob–Israel, Zion–Jerusalem, and the servant is found in the concept of posterity expressed in the terms זרע ("seed, descendents"), צאצאים ("offspring"), בנים ("sons"), and בנות ("daughters").[92] Servant Jacob–Israel is the descendent of Abraham (41:8) who has descendents in captivity (45:19aβ). Yahweh promises deliverance to Jacob–Israel's descendents (43:5bα) whom he calls his sons and daughters (v. 6b). At the close of ch. 48, Yahweh laments over the failure of Jacob–Israel and how their descendents could have been like the sand and its offspring like grain, if only the nation would have obeyed his commands (vv. 18–19). 44:1–5 presents an important description of the descendents of Jacob–Israel who will become Yahweh's future community:

> 44:1 But now listen Jacob my servant
> and Israel whom I have chosen.
> 2 Thus said Yahweh,
> who made you and who formed you from the womb,
> he will help you.
> Do nor fear my servant Jacob
> and Jeshurun whom I have chosen.
> 3 For I will pour out water on thirsty land
> and streams upon dry ground.
> I will pour out my spirit upon your descendents
> and my blessing upon your offspring.
> 4 And they will spring up in the midst of the grass
> like willows by streams of water.
> 5 This one will say, "I belong to Yahweh"
> and this one will call himself by the name "Jacob."
> And this one will write with his hand, "belongs to Yahweh"
> and with the name "Israel" he will entitle himself.

Here these descendents are directly associated with Jacob–Israel, but they freely choose to belong to Yahweh and thus comprise his people. The people identified as Jacob–Israel will constitute a *confessional community* realized through personal, individual decisions.[93] Significantly, this passage is followed by another challenge to the idol-gods that reiterates Jacob–Israel's appointment as Yahweh's witness (vv. 6–8). Those who form collective Jacob–Israel are Yahweh's witnesses, but the weighing of the evidence is an individual endeavor. Those who witness to themselves

92. W. A. M. Beuken has pointed the importance of this concept in relation to righteousness and the composition of Isa 55–66; see his "The Main Theme of Trito-Isaiah: 'The Servants of YHWH'," *JSOT* 47 (1990): 67–87.

93. Cf. Joseph Blenkinsopp, "Second Isaiah—Prophet of Universalism," *JSOT* 41 (1988): 83–103 (86); Motyer, *Prophecy of Isaiah*, 342–43; Westermann, *Isaiah 40–66*, 137–38.

and confess Yahweh alone will embrace becoming his people, servant Jacob–Israel.

In similar terms to Jacob–Israel, Zion–Jerusalem is described as a bereaved mother who will surprisingly see children again (49:20–21). Zion–Jerusalem's sons and daughters will be carried back to her (vv. 22b, 25). As noted above, mother and her children were sent away because of sin (50:1b). Presently, none of her sons have the ability to guide her (51:18). In fact, they are helpless like their mother due to Yahweh's judgment (v. 20). Yet, Yahweh promises that barren Zion–Jerusalem will see numerous sons (54:1). Her descendents will dispossess the nations and inhabit desolate places (v. 3) and her sons will be disciples of Yahweh and will experience great peace (v. 13).

All these descriptions brought together highlight another paradox: mother Zion–Jerusalem has children, but they are dead; she is currently barren and, in fact, has not been with a man (49:21). Further, she is in exile with her children and at the same time home in Jerusalem waiting for her children to return. The notion of posterity becomes even more complex in the final servant passage as Yahweh and his servant will also see descendents (53:10aβ). Chapter 54 ends by additionally linking Zion–Jerusalem's children with the idea of the servant. The singular form עבד never occurs again in the book of Isaiah after 53:11aβ, and following this verse Yahweh's people are no longer identified by the singular noun (54:17bα; 56:6aβ; 63:17bα; 65:8bα, 9bβ, 13 [3×], 14a, 15aα; 66:14bα). Thus, it is the descendents/children of Zion who are now designated as עבדי יהוה (54:17bα). Willey sees a connection between these descendents with Jacob–Israel, Zion–Jerusalem, and the servant by observing that the addressee referred to in the masculine plural "you" appears from the beginning to the end of Isa 40–55. In the Zion sections the masculine plural addressees are distinct from her. Further, this "plural audience is identified with 'the offspring of Israel,' and with 'my witnesses, my servant,' and thus doubly aligned with the figure 'Israel/Jacob my servant/my chosen.' In addition, they are identified with the 'children' of Zion who are soon to return."[94] These identities further come together within the overarching call to return to Yahweh. Thus, Yahweh calls to the addressee to embrace the status of being his servant and thus become the true children of Zion–Jerusalem. Later, Yahweh will designate these descendents as עבדי and בחירי (65:9, 13).

94. Willey, *Former Things*, 180. Willey additionally claims that when "Zion enters in Isa 49:14, YHWH ceases speaking to the masculine singular addressee" (ibid., 179). However, 51:16 reads ולאמר לציון עמי־אתה, "and saying to Zion, you (masculine singular) are my people."

One final concern arises from Isa 40–55: Yahweh's call to the nations. A key passage is found at the close of ch. 45:

> 45:20 Gather yourselves and come!
> Come forward together, fugitives of the nations!
> They do not know, those who carry around their wooden images
> and those who pray to a god who cannot save.
> 21 Declare and put forward,
> let them even consult together.
> Who has proclaimed this beforehand,
> declared it long before?
> Was it not I, Yahweh?
> There is no other god apart from me!
> A righteous God and savior,
> there is none except me.
> 22 Turn to me and be saved all the ends of the earth!
> For I am God and there is no other.
> 23 I swear by myself,
> from my mouth righteousness has gone forth,
> a word and it will not return
> that to me every knee will bend,
> every tongue will swear.
> 24 Only in Yahweh, it is said about me,
> are righteousness and power.
> All who have raged against him
> will come before him and be ashamed,
> 25 but by Yahweh all the descendents of Israel
> will be justified and exult.

As with idolatrous Jacob–Israel, the nations also become witnesses to Yahweh's demonstration of power. The nations do not *know* true deity due to the nature of their gods. To address this, Yahweh's exclusive claim to divinity centers on the fact that he alone is God because he is the only savior.[95] In a similar way to the first exodus, Yahweh's choosing of Cyrus is for Jacob–Israel's deliverance (45:4–5) with the accompanied purpose of demonstrating his power so that both his chosen people and the nations will *know* that he alone is God (cf. 45:6). Further, in the same manner as Yahweh calls his chosen nation to return to him, he issues a call to all those on the earth to recognize the futility of idolatry and to turn to him.[96] Yahweh invites individuals among the nations to acknowledge that

95. See Beuken, "God's Exclusivity," 335–56.

96. The "universalistic" ideas expressed here along with those found in the servant passages conflict with the "nationalistic" notions found elsewhere (e.g. 41:15–16; 45:14; 49:22–26). The tension between these two ideas throughout the Old Testament is a complex issue and it is beyond the scope of this study to deal with at

he alone can save[97] and to confess that "only in Yahweh is righteousness and power."[98] Expanding upon 44:5, this passage ends by further identifying the descendents of Jacob–Israel to include any from among the nations who confess Yahweh alone.[99] This would include contemporary readers as well. "We ourselves must turn to the LORD and acknowledge his kingship. Thus, we become Zion's still-missing offspring, and, by having her children back, she will be able to act as a herald of good tidings."[100]

Drawing all of the above together, the prophetic function of Isa 40–55 revolves around the explicit call issued by Yahweh to return to him with an uncompromising allegiance and by embracing the role of his servant. This call runs throughout these chapters while servant Jacob–Israel disappears, a servant figure continues throughout, and Zion–Jerusalem appears, disappears, and reappears. The overall prophetic strategy of

any length. In short, these two diverse ideas must be held together as they complement one another (see Goldingay, *Isaiah*, 143–44, 264). On the one hand, the nation Israel is Yahweh's own special people while on the other he is concerned for all the peoples of the earth. Here in Isa 40–55, Yahweh issues a call to Israel as well as the nations, but only those who turn and confess him alone will constitute his people. For various interpretations on the universalistic/nationalistic perspective in Isa 40–55, see Blenkinsopp, "Second Isaiah," 83–103; Robert Davidson, "Universalism in Second Isaiah," *STJ* 16 (1963): 166–85; Paul-Eugène Dion, "L'universalisme religieux dans les différentes couches rédactionneles d'Isaïe 40–55," *Bib* 51 (1970): 161–82; A. Gelston, "The Missionary Message of Second Isaiah," *SJT* 18 (1965): 308–18; Roman Halas, "The Universalism of Isaias," *CBQ* 12 (1950): 162–70; D. E. Hollenberg, "Nationalism and 'The Nations' in Isaiah XL–LV," *VT* 19 (1969): 23–36; Orlinsky, "So-Called 'Servant of the Lord,'" 97–117; D. W. van Winkle, "The Relationship of the Nations to Yahweh and to Israel in Isaiah XL–LV," *VT* 35 (1985): 446–58; idem, "Proselytes in Isaiah XL–LV? A Study of Isaiah XLIV 1–5," *VT* 47 (1997): 341–59; Williamson, *Variations on a Theme*, 116–29.

97. On the wordplay of אל in vv. 20–21 that contrasts the two occurrences of אל in question, see Knut Holter, "The Wordplay on אֵל ('God') in Isaiah 45,20–21," *SJOT* 7 (1993): 88–98.

98. Yahweh's declaration that he alone is God and no other deity exists additionally points to the universalistic concerns in Isa 40–55; see further Ronald E. Clements, "Isaiah 45:20–25: The Goal of Faith," *Int* 40 (1986): 392–97; Herbert G. May, "Theological Universalism in the Old Testament," *JBR* 16 (1948): 100–107; Westermann, *Isaiah 40–66*, 176; Wilson, *Nations in Deutero-Isaiah*, 129–92; see also Hans Wildberger, "Der Monotheismus Deuterojesajas," in *Beiträge zur Alttestamentlichen Theologie* (Festschrift Walther Zimmerli; ed. H. Donner, R. Hanhart, and R. Smend; Göttingen: Vandenhoeck & Ruprecht, 1977), 506–30.

99. So Beuken, "God's Exclusivity," 349–50; Childs, *Isaiah*, 356; Motyer, *Prophecies of Isaiah*, 367; see further Blenkinsopp, "Second Isaiah," 85–92.

100. Van der Woude, "Zion Without the Servant," 116.

these chapters points to one goal, which was spoken of at the start: Yahweh returning to Zion–Jerusalem with his people, his servants. It is the functionally ambiguous "I/me" in 49:1–6 that transports the self-involved addressee/reader from Babylon to Zion, from the collective servant Jacob–Israel to the confessional servants of Yahweh.[101] Yahweh's people are self-inflicted with blindness and deafness due to their own idolatry, and thus unable to fulfill their servant responsibilities. Israel is Israel in name only. Consequently, 42:1 and following function as a visionary call of a servant to execute justice and be a light to the nations. At the same time, Yahweh gives Jacob–Israel another assignment to witness to themselves about his sovereign power. By embracing this appointment Jacob–Israel will carry out their responsibilities as Yahweh's servant. This assignment, though, is extended to each individual person among Jacob–Israel and the nations for the purpose of acknowledging and confessing Yahweh alone. Thus, the witness task is an open call to any and all to adopt the role of Yahweh's servant. Those who acknowledge Yahweh's speech act of the Cyrus event and voluntarily embrace the call to confess Yahweh alone will not only display what it means to be true Israel, they will actually constitute the people of God. Corresponding to the fact that when an individual testifies to Yahweh's sole claim to deity that person accepts the role of Yahweh's servant, becoming the people of God is likewise realized through personal confession. Those who return to Yahweh will be identified as his servants and the children of Zion. The servants of Yahweh will form a confessional community realized by personal choice, not national lineage, who will return and dwell with the king in his city.

The above discussion has attempted to set out the basic concerns and emphases of Isa 40–55 in order to locate the four passages selected for closer examination within the literary and prophetic function of these chapters. Much of Isa 40–55 operates along the same lines as what speech act theorists have identified as performative language. Thus, speech act theory, along with its overarching concept of self-involvement, offers particularly appropriate hermeneutical tools for interpreting this block. In fact, such an approach is fundamental when dealing with the four passages selected as Isa 40–55 issues a call to the ancient and contemporary addressee to become self-involved with them.

101. Jeppesen, following Eduard Nielsen ("Deuterojesaja: Erwägungen zur Formkritik, Traditions-undRedaktionsgeschichte," *VT* 20 [1970]: 190–205 [199]), similarly suggests that 49:1–6 functions as a bridge between chs. 40–48 and 49–55 ("My Servant," 122).

Chapter 4

ANALYSIS OF ISAIAH 41:21–29; 49:1–6; 50:4–11; 52:13–53:12

With the suggested performative and prophetic purpose for Isa 40–55 presented, this chapter will focus on the four selected passages from a speech act perspective and their integral function within chs. 40–55. The analysis of each passage will follow the basic format of translation, an examination of structure and genre, and an interpretive analysis. The translation sections will comprise a large part of the exegetical task. The analysis sections will address some interpretive issues, but will primarily concentrate on the communicative action within the texts.

Isaiah 41:21–29

Translation

21Present[a] your case, says Yahweh!
  Produce your strong evidence,[b] says the King of Jacob!
22Let them produce[c] and declare[d] to us
  what is going to occur.
The previous events, what were they?
Explain them so that we can make up our minds
  and recognize their outcome.[e]
Or proclaim to us the things to come,[f]
23declare the events to come
  so that we may know that you are gods.
Indeed, do good and do evil[g]
  so that we may be in fearful awe[h] all at once.
24As expected,[i] you are less than nothing
  and your action less than non-existent.[j]
It is an abomination for whoever chooses you.[k]
25I have aroused one from the north
  and he has come from the rising sun,
  he will proclaim my name.[l]
And when he comes,[m] officials are as fresh mortar
  and he is as a potter who tramples clay.

26Who declared this from the beginning
so that we could recognize it?
And from beforehand so that we could say,
"He was right"?
No, there was no one who declared it.
No, there was no one who proclaimed it.
No, there was no one who heard your words.
27First to Zion, there, there they are[n]
and to Jerusalem I appoint a messenger.[o]
28But when I look,[p] there is no one
and from among these,[q] there is no counselor
that I could ask them and they reply with even a single word.
29Thus, all of them are sinful deception.[r]
Their works are non-existent.
Their images are open air.[s]

a) The verb קרבו is a Qal pf. 3cp. Although an anomaly, the verb can be pointed as a Piel impv., which nicely parallels the Hiphil impv. in the second line. The LXX translates both verbs in this verse with the same term in the indicative, ἐγγίζει and ἤγγισαν ("draw near, approach"). Watts concludes that the MT may be sustained "if the addressees of the verbs are the idols or their devotees, and the 3d pers references are to their proofs" (*Isaiah 34–66* [WBC 25; Waco, Tex.: Word, 1987], 112 n. 21.a). With some variation, a few interpreters understand vv. 21–22a as addressing the nations or the idols' devotees (e.g. Motyer, *Prophecies of Isaiah*, 315; L. G. Rignell, *A Study of Isaiah Ch. 40–55* [LUÅ 52/5; Lund: Gleerup, 1956], 28; Charles C. Torrey, *The Second Isaiah* [New York: Scribner's, 1928], 230; Wilson, *The Nations in Deutero-Isaiah*, 52). The MT corresponds to other degrading remarks that the nations must carry their gods from place to place (cf. 46:1–7); however, the MT is awkward in light of the following verbs as most translators concede. Further, the overall context clearly indicates that the primary addressees of this unit are the idol-gods rather than their devotees and so the Piel impv. is preferred. The 2mp impv. is confirmed by α′ θ′ ἐγγίσατε ("draw near!") and σ′ προσαγάγετε ("come near!").

b) עצמותיכם is a fp noun + 2mp suffix which only occurs in this form here and is from עצום ("strong"; e.g. Isa 40:29; see BDB, 783; *HALOT*, 867–68). The term literally means "your strong things" and here refers to forensic proofs or evidence (cf. N. Lohfink, "עצם," *TDOT* 11:289–303 [290]; see further Koole, *Isaiah 3/1*, 189–90). Following the LXX's αἱ βουλαὶ ὑμῶν and Syr's *trʿytkwn*, Begrich emends the MT to מועצותיכם ("your counsels"); see his *Deuterojesaja*, 44 n. 148. R. R. Ottley, though, notes that for "strong arguments, strengths" Gk uses ἰσχυρίζομαι or διισχυρίζομαι and thus the LXX may have paraphrased or hastily read עצמותיכם as מועצתיכם; see *The Book of Isaiah According to the Septuagint* (Cambridge: Cambridge University Press, 1906), 303–4. Torrey suggests that the prophet originally wrote עצביכם ("your idols") while the MT is the product of a scribal error for עצבותיכם ("your pains/woes"), which is a punning substitute for "idol" as in 45:16 (*Second Isaiah*, 318). This emendation does not correspond to the parallel ריבכם ("your case/argument") in the previous colon nor does it fit the overall context. The MT finds support among the Versions: α′ ὀστεώσεις ὑμῶν; θ′ τὰ κραταιώματα ὑμῶν; σ′ τὰ ἰσχυρὰ ὑμῶν; Vg *si quid forte habetis*; Tg חזיתכון.

c) The verb יגישו is a Hiphil juss. 3mp which 1QIsa[a] confirms יגישו. Most of the Versions understand the verb as a simple Qal juss. 3mp יגשו ("let them draw near/ approach"): LXX ἐγγισάτωσαν; σʹ προελθέτωσαν; Vg *accedant*; Tg יתקרבון; Syr *nqrbwn*. This is followed by a large number of scholars, but it seems best to maintain the MT as the Hiphil corresponds to the following verb יגידו and recalls the Hiphil impv. הגישו in v. 21b (so also cf. Barthélemy, *Critique Textuelle*, 290–91; Jan de Waard, *A Handbook on Isaiah* [ed. H. P. Scanlin; TCT 1; Winona Lake, Ind.: Eisenbrauns, 1997], 158; Marjo C. A. Korpel and Johannes C. de Moor, *The Structure of Classical Hebrew Poetry: Isaiah 40–55* [ed. J. C. de Moor; OTS 41; Leiden: Brill, 1998], 73). Further, the placement of the four verbs in vv. 21b–22bα display a semantic AA'BB' pattern along with a morphological ABB'A' pattern: הגישו יגישו יגידו הגידו. Moreover, these two verbs summarize the essence of the request to the gods: to announce and produce an event. Further, as de Waard notes, it is interesting that the same two terms occur together in 45:21aα, הגידו והגישו, which no correction of the MT "has ever been proposed in spite of the same behavior of the ancient versions" (*Handbook on Isaiah*, 158). The object of the verb יגישו, then, could either be עצמותיכם from v. 21bα (NRSV) or את אשר תקרינה from v. 22aβ which is also the direct object of יגידו (NASB). The latter object is preferred due to the change from the previous impvs. to the juss. here and, as noted, presents the essence of the request.

d) יגידו is a Hiphil juss. 3mp from נגד. As with above, this term here is addressing the gods to announce a future event which corresponds to its typical usage throughout Isa 40–55 (see cf. F. García-López, "נגד," *TDOT* 9:174–86 [181–82]). Thus, it is not likely that the verb here addresses the nations to call upon or "to divine, contact" their gods as Samuel Iwry suggests ("New Evidence for Belomancy in Ancient Palestine and Phoenicia," *JAOS* 81 [1961]: 27–34 [33–34]).

e) The cohors. here are expressing purpose. The cohor. typically expresses purpose/result especially when following another volitional form (see IBHS §34.5.2b; *GBH* §116b; GKC §108d).

f) The MT here contains an atypical pair of tricola found in v. $22b\alpha^1$–$22b\beta^1$and vv. $22b\beta^2$–23a. Due to this and an apparent lack of logical sequencing, some translators transpose the final bicolon of v. 22bβ (e.g. *BHS*; Beuken, *Jesaja II/A*, 96–98; Blenkinsopp, *Isaiah 40–55*, 203; Duhm, *Jesaia*, 274–75; J. Morgenstern, *The Message of Deutero-Isaiah in its Sequential Unfolding* [Cincinnati: Hebrew Union College Press, 1961], 154; Antoon Schoors, *I Am God Your Savior: A Form-Critical Study of the Main Genres in Is. XL–LV* (VTSup 24; Leiden: Brill, 1973), 214; Westermann, *Isaiah 40–66*, 81; Whybray, *Isaiah 40–66*, 68). 1QIsa[a] follows similarly to the MT but has אחרונות without the 2mp suffix and inserts an additional או before the noun which syntactically links ונדעה with v. 22bα. The LXX follows closely to the MT, but also does not include the suffix, καὶ γνωσόμεθα τί τὰ ἔσχατα, and reads a ו with καὶ instead of the MT או in v. $22b\beta^2$, as does the Vg with *et*. Both the Tg and Syr support the MT. Applying John T. Willis' analysis ("The Juxtaposition of Synonymous and Chiastic Parallelism in Tricola in Old Testament Hebrew Psalm Poetry," *VT* 29 [1979]: 465–80), Goldingay sees each tricola possessing the parallel pattern of ABB' and CC'D respectively. Thus, they exemplify two standard forms of interrelationships within the tricola whereby the middle colon stands in chiastic relationship with one colon and in synonymous relationship with the other. Goldingay (*Isaiah 40–55*) further identifies within the each tricola a degree of mutual ABC–A'B'C' parallelism.

The initial pair of cola, הבאות...הראשנות present the distinctive themes of each. The middle pair hold each tricola together and begin with the key impv. הגידו. The third pair both begin with ונדעה which also expresses the recurrent climactic theme of chs. 40–55. Thus, reversing the last bicolon of v. 22b does not find support from the Versions and additionally violates the poetic patterns inherent within these lines (see also North, *The Second Isaiah*, 103).

g) This is a lit. translation of אף־תיטיבו ותרעו. It is important to note that the two verbs are connected by a ו and not או, which is how the majority of translators understand the ו to function here. Nevertheless, although או is the explicit particle Hebrew uses to express the disjunctive "or," the ו can be used in this same way (see *GBH* §175a; *IBHS* §39.2a). The LXX follows closely to the MT, εὖ ποιήσατε καὶ κακώσατε ("do good and do harm"), as does the Tg אם יכלן אינון לאיטבא ולאבאשא ("if they are able to do good and evil"). The Vg explicitly reads a disjunctive particle with *aut* while the Syr repeats אף instead of ו with *ʾp…ʾp* producing "both—and, and—also" (see J. Payne Smith, ed., *A Compendious Syriac Dictionary Founded Upon the Thesaurus Syriacus of R. Payne Smith* [Winona Lake, Ind.: Eisenbrauns, 1998], 25). M. J. Mulder follows the Syr and translates "*zowel goed als kwaad*" ("Filologische Kanttekeningen Bij Jes. 41:23b; 42:19b en 43:14b," in *De Knecht: Studies rondom Deutero-Jesaja* [Festschrift J. L. Koole; ed. H. H. Grosheide et al.; Kampen: Kok, 1978], 141–49 [141–42]).

h) Lit. ונשתעה ונרא ("terrified and see"). The first verb is a Qal cohor. 1cp from שתע (see *HALOT*, 1671). For the second verb נרא, Q suggests ונראה from ראה ("that we may see"). However, K is also from ראה, but in an unusual cohor. form (see GKC §§48g; 109d). *BHS* suggests that K should be understood from ירא and pointed as וְנִרָא ("and we will be afraid"). Thus, the typical translation of the two verbs in v. 23bβ has been adopted by a majority of translators: "that we may be terrified and afraid" (e.g. RSV; NRSV; NIV). Many translators have also assumed that K is from ירא, but rather it is simply a conjectural reading apparently first proposed by Robert Lowth (see de Waard, *Handbook on Isaiah*, 159; see further Barthélemy, *Critique Textuelle*, 292–93). The verb ראה is confirmed by 1QIsa[a] ונשמעה ונראה ("so that we may hear and see"); LXX καὶ θαυμασόμεθα καὶ ὀψόμεθα ("and we will be amazed and see"); Vg *et loquamur et videamus* ("and let us speak and see"). The Tg renders ונסתכל ונדין ("that we may consider and judge"). No real problem arises from the conjectural reading of ירא, which finds support in 41:10 where the verbs occur in parallel (so Goldingay, *Isaiah 40–55*). Nevertheless, the verbs שתע and ירא are virtually synonymous and produce an unnecessary redundancy, unless understood as a hendiadys. Further, the MT text makes sense and finds clear support with the Versions.

i) Rather than הן, 1QIsa[a] uses הנה here. There is no real distinction between these two particles, which can both function as conjunctions and adversatively; see C. J. Labuschagne, "The Particles הֵן and הִנֵּה," in *Syntax and Meaning: Studies in Hebrew Syntax and Biblical Exegesis* (ed. A. S. van der Woude; OTS 18; Leiden: Brill, 1973), 1–14; Dennis J. McCarthy, "The Uses of *w*^{e}*hinnēh* in Biblical Hebrew," *Bib* 61 (1980): 330–42.

j) The two prep. phrases מאין and מאפע could be the result of dittography (so, e.g., Elliger, *Deuterojesaja*, 172; H. L. Ginsberg, "Some Emendations in Isaiah," *JBL* 69 [1950]: 51–60 [58]; Morgenstern, *Deutero-Isaiah*, 154–55; Westermann, *Isaiah*

40–66, 82; Whybray, *Isaiah 40–66*, 69). 1QIsa[a] has the first prep. phrase מאין, but does not include the second (see further Barthélemy, *Critique Textuelle*, 294). The Tg has לא מדעם...למא without the prep. on either. Syr does not have a מ for the first phrase, but includes it on the second: *lʾmdm…mnḥrbʾ*. The LXX translates the first prep. phrase with πόθεν ("from where/what place?") and the second with ἐκ γῆς ("from earth"). πόθεν suggests that the LXX read מאין but as the interrogative particle אין (see BDB, 32; *HALOT*, 42). The second phrase also supposes that the מ was in view. Elliger (*Deuterojesaja*, 172) postulates that the LXX understood מאפע as either מארץ ("from earth") or מעפר ("from dust"). The Vg also reads the מ with both phrases *ex nihilo* ("from nothing")…*ex eo quod non est* ("from nothing that is nothing"). אפע is a *hapax* and so a number of translators emend to the noun אפס (so *BHS*). However, אפע is most likely related to אפס (cf. v. 29aβ) that also expresses non-existence (see BDB, 67; *DCH* 1:359; *HALOT*, 79), which both the Tg and Vg confirm (see cf. Barthélemy, *Critique Textuelle*, 294–95; Goldingay, *Isaiah 40–55*; see also F. Delitzsch, *Biblical Commentary on the Prophecies of Isaiah* [4th ed.; Edinburgh: T. & T. Clark, 1892], 2:161–62; Koole, *Isaiah 3/1*, 196; Watts, *Isaiah 34–66*, 112 n. 24c). Moreover, Lawrence Boadt suggests that the poet may have chosen אפע, which meant the same as אפס due to the lack of ס in this line coupled with the line's strong ע alliteration potential ("Intentional Alliteration in Second Isaiah," *CBQ* 45 [1983]: 353–63 [360]). Thus, it is unnecessary to emend מאפע to מאפס and, with most recent translators, keep the מ in both instances and see it as functioning as a comparative marker (see GKC §133a–b; *IBHS* §11.2.11e).

k) This final clause תועבה יבחר בכם is confirmed by 1QIsa[a] and the other Versions and so there are no grounds for considering it a gloss (so Duhm, *Jesaia*, 275) or needing emendation (so Ginsberg, "Emendations," 58; Torrey, *Second Isaiah*, 318–19, followed by Morgenstern, *Deutero-Isaiah*, 155). The phrase is lit. "an abomination he chooses in you." It is possible to take תועבה as the predicate of the one who chooses, "he who chooses you is an abomination" (see Deut 22:5; 25:16), which is how the Vg translates *abominatio est qui elegit vos* (so also, e.g., GKC §155n; *GBH* §157a; similarly RSV; NRSV; NASB; NIV; Blenkinsopp, *Isaiah 40–55*, 204; Childs, *Isaiah*, 313; Korpel and de Moor, *Hebrew Poetry*, 73; Watts, *Isaiah 34–66*, 110). The LXX βδέλυγμα ἐξελέξαντο ὑμᾶς (while switching to the 3pl.), Tg תועיבא דאתרעיתון לכון, and Syr *wṭspwtʾ hy ʿbytʿwn* understand תועבה as the object of the clause: "in you one chooses an abomination" (cf. v. 29b; 44:19; so also, e.g., Baltzer, *Deutero-Isaiah*, 115, 120; Beuken, *Jesaja II/A*, 100; Goldingay, *Isaiah 40–55*; Koole, *Isaiah 3/1*, 196; Muilenburg, "Chapters 40–66," 461; Rignell, *Study of Isaiah*, 29; Westermann, *Isaiah 40–66*, 82). North translates the colon both ways: "who chooses you is loathsome as you are!" (*Second Isaiah*, 37; so also NEB). Understanding תועבה as the object corresponds to Isa 44:19 wherein an idol is explicitly identified as a תועבה, but it is possible that the colon is ambiguous, allowing for both readings (see Deut 18:12; Ps 115:8).

l) Instead of the 1cs suffix with בשמי, 1QIsa[a] has a 3ms בשמו, which suggests that קרא should be understood as a Niphal יִקָּרֵא ("he was called by his name"; cf. *BHS*; similarly, e.g., NRSV; Blenkinsopp, *Isaiah 40–55*, 204; Morgenstern, *Deutero-Isaiah*, 151, 155; Schoors, *I am God*, 213, 219; Watts, *Isaiah 34–66*, 110, 112 n. 25.e, f). This pass. nuance is supported by the LXX, although in the pl., κληθήσονται ("they will be called"). The Tg confirms the 1cs suffix, but the line conveys a different idea from the MT אגברניה בשמי ("I will make him strong by my name"). Both the Vg *vocabit nomen meum* and Syr *wyqrʾ bšmy* confirm the MT. Beginning with Duhm (*Jesaia*, 275–76) and based chiefly on 45:4–5, some translators follow 1QIsa[a] and additionally emend the verb to either a pf. קראתי or impf. אקרא (e.g. Baltzer, *Deutero-Isaiah*, 115; Beuken, *Jesaja II/A*, 100–101; Westermann, *Isaiah 40–66*, 82; Whybray, *Isaiah 40–66*, 69–70). Following A. B. Ehrlich (*Randglossen zur hebräischen Bibel*, vol. 5 [Leipzig: Hinrich, 1912], 151), Koole (*Isaiah 3/1*, 198) emends the verb to יקרב ("who approaches") based on either haplography or the shared ב intentionally written only once (see Wilfred G. E. Watson, "Shared Consonants in Northwest Semitic," *Bib* 50 [1969]: 525–33). This is a plausible suggestion, but it does not have any support from the Versions. A large number of translators maintain the MT (cf. Barthélemy, *Critique Textuelle*, 295–97; Childs, *Isaiah*, 314; de Waard, *Handbook on Isaiah*, 160; Korpel and de Moor, *Hebrew Poetry*, 73). The notion of Cyrus calling on Yahweh's name can be sustained as Goldingay (*Isaiah 40–55*) points out that this corresponds to Old Testament expectations regarding foreign peoples as well as fitting the attitude expressed about Cyrus in Isa 41. However, as those who emend the MT, Isa 45:5 does not corroborate with this conclusion nor does the Old Testament ever indicate that Cyrus called upon Yahweh's name. The formulaic phrase קרא בשם can be used in several different ways: calling/invoking the name of someone (e.g. Gen 4:26; 12:8; Ps 116:4, 13, 17), setting apart a person for a specific task (e.g. Exod 31:2; 35:30), as election language (e.g. Isa 43:1bβ), or proclaiming a name or person (cf. Exod 33:19). The latter is a conceivable way of understanding this clause with the ב functioning as an indicator of the direct object of the verb (see *IBHS* §11.2.5f; *GBH* §125m). Thus, due to Yahweh's announcement of Cyrus and his corresponding actions he will proclaim the name Yahweh (so also Motyer, *Prophecies of Isaiah*, 317).

m) Due to supposed haplography, *BHS* suggests that the Tg read ויבס ("and he treads") for the MT ויבא which is followed by a large number of translators. However, the Tg essentially contains both verbs וייתי וידוש ("and he will come and will trample"). Goldingay (*Isaiah 40–55*) correctly concludes that this is hardly evidence that the MT read a form of the verb בוס rather than בוא, particularly in this especially paraphrastic Tg verse. Because of a supposed scribal error, de Boer (*Second-Isaiah's Message*, 8, 44) redivides and emends the MT ויבא סגנים to read ויבס גנים ("he tramples down enclosures") while Ginsberg ("Emendations," 59) emends to ויבס גוים ("and he has trampled nations"). 1QIsa[a] supports the MT, but uses the plural ויבואו סגנים כמו חמר ("and officials came as fresh mortar"). Similar to 1QIsa[a] along with supplementing an additional clause, the LXX renders ἐρχέσθωσαν ἄρχοντες, καὶ ὡς πηλὸς κεραμέως...οὕτως καταπατηθήσεσθε ("and let rulers come, and as potter's clay...in this manner you will be trampled"). Emending the MT is unnecessary as the previous cola speak of Cyrus' arousing and this elliptical bicolon speaks of his future arrival while assuming the verbal idea of trampling/treading in the following bicolon (see Goldingay, *Isaiah 40–55*; Korpel and de Moor, *Hebrew Poetry*, 74 n. 16, 102). While maintaining the MT, another viable alternative has been proposed by Barthélemy (*Critique Textuelle*, 297–98) who assumes the general semantic meaning of בוס for בוא here "*fouler, piétiner*" based on the use of בוא in Isa 41:3 and Ps 36:12 along with the verb paralleled with רמס in Isa 28:15, 18.

n) The translation is a literal rendering of the MT ראשון לציון הנה הנם. The problem here is the phrase הנה הנם which the Versions seem unsure about: 1QIsa[a] רישון לציון הנה הנומה ("first to Zion, there the speaker"[?]); LXX ἀρχὴν Σιων δώσω ("I will give a beginning/ruler to Zion"); Tg פתגמי נחמתא דאתנביאו נבייא מלקדמין על ציון הא אתו ("The words of comfort that the prophets prophesied from the first concerning Zion, there, they have come"). The Vg renders closely to the MT *primus ad Sion dicet ecce adsunt* ("the first to Zion will say, behold, they are here") as does the Syr *ršyt*ʾ *dṣhywn hlyn* ʾ*nyn*. The phrase in the MT has also produced many different conjectures and emendations (see *BHS*; Elliger, *Deuterojesaja*, 174–75; Koole, *Isaiah 3/1*, 200–203; Antoon Schoors, "Les choses antérieures et les choses nouvelles dans les oracles Deutéro-Isaïens," *ETL* 40 [1964]: 19–47 [28–31]). Godfrey R. Driver initially proposed that ראשון is a term used in a court of law meaning "leading counsel." Driver also proposes that within הנה הנם lies the verb הֲכִנוֹתִי or הֵנַחְתִּי ("I have put up, provided") which is parallel to אתן and translates the first colon as "I put up a first speaker for Zion"; see his "Problems of the Hebrew Text and Language," in *Alttestamentliche Studien* (ed. H. Junker and J. Botterweck; Bonn: Hanstein, 1950), 46–61 (46–47); followed by Morgenstern, *Deutero-Isaiah*, 153. C. F. Whitley correctly rejects Driver's suggestion for understanding ראשון, but emends הנה הנם based on Isa 43:8–13 and in particular the phrase אנכי הגדתי in v. 12aα[1]. Thus, the MT was originally הנה הגדתי ("behold I declared"); see Whitley's "A Note on Isa XLI. 27," *JSS* 2 (1957): 327–28; similarly also, e.g., RSV; NRSV; Blenkinsopp, *Isaiah 40–55*, 204 n. m; Schoors, *I am God*, 220–21; Westermann, *Isaiah 40–66*, 82; Whybray, *Isaiah 40–66*, 70. Elliger completely reworks the colon אמרי לציון הנני נתנם, "*'Meine Sprüche' für Zion, 'die gab ich dauernd von mir'*" (*Deuterojesaja*, 171, 175). D. Winton Thomas proposes that הנם derives from מָנָה and in the Piel means "appoint, ordain." The original reading of the term parallels אתן in the following colon and was אֲמַנֶּה and originally meaning "A forerunner for Zion, I appoint"; see Thomas's "A Note on the Hebrew Text of Isaiah XLI. 27," *JTS* 18 (1967): 127–28. Goldingay (*Isaiah 40–55*) follows Thomas' subsequent suggestion and emends הנם to a Hophal הֻמְנָה and translates the first colon: "the first was appointed for Sion." Alfred Guillaume understands 1QIsa[a] הנומה also as a ptc. from נמה derived from the Arab *namā* ("he brought tidings"); see Guillame, "Some Readings in the Dead Sea Scroll of Isaiah," *JBL* 76 (1957): 40–43 (40). The problem is that this term does not occur elsewhere in Hebrew and apparently not outside of Arab (see further E. Y. Kutscher, *The Language and Linguistic Background of the Isaiah Scroll [I Q Isa[a]]* [STDJ 6; Leiden: Brill, 1974], 450–51). Following North (*Second Isaiah*, 104), Anthony Gelston suggests that 1QIsa[a] הנומה provides a clue to the revocalization of הנה הנם with the final translation, "Behold the speaker." Gelston re-points הנם as הַנָּם, consisting of the definite article and a Qal ptc. from נום which in Post-Biblical Hebrew means "to speak" and relates to נאם ("utterance, oracle"), but is a *hapax* as a verb (Jer 23:31; see Kutscher, *Isaiah Scroll*, 450–51). Gelston acknowledges the syntactical difficulties and improbable incorporation of this translation and so he suggests that the phrase be considered an "aside" like "yours truly" or a gloss identifying the messenger of good tidings with the prophet himself ("'Behold the Speaker': A Note on Isaiah XLI 27," *VT* [1993]: 405–8). Beuken, following 1QIsa[a], may best summarize the frustrations this colon causes by concluding that one can only offer a paraphrase of the verse: "*Zie Hem die van oudsher voor Sion aanwezig tot haar gesproken heeft; ja, aan Jeruzalem gaf Ik een vreugdebode*" (*Jesaja II/A*, 103). As demonstrated, the difficulties of understanding the phrase הנה הנם are clear. Many of the emendations have merit, but no conjecture has proven convincing while the MT obviously remains the more difficult reading and finds some support from the Vg (so, e.g., NASB; NIV; Childs, *Isaiah*, 315 n. e).

o) The LXX renders this last colon quite differently from the MT: καὶ Ιερουσαλημ παρακαλέσω εἰς ὁδόν ("and I will encourage Jerusalem on the way"). However, the other Versions confirm the MT: 1QIsa[a] ולירושלים מבשר אתן; Tg ולירושלם מבשר אתן; Vg *et Hierusalem evangelistam dabo*; Syr *wlʾ wršlm msbrnʾ ʾtl*.

p) ואראה is a rare form and so based on the Vg *et vidi* ("and I looked"), Tg וגלי קדמי ("and it was revealed before me"), and Syr *ḥrt*, *BHS* repoints the verb as a converted future, which is followed by a number of scholars (cf. Isa 50:2; 59:16). 1QIsa[a] has the impf. ואראה. Although uncommon, וארא can be a Qal juss. 1cs in a conditional clause (Isa 42:6; see GKC §109h; *GBH* notes that this form is rare and suspect §114g). The LXX may support the MT as v. 27 ends with εἰς ὁδόν, which is a possible corruption of εἰ εἶδον for וארא (see Torrey, *Second Isaiah*, 321). Duhm (*Jesaia*, 277) unnecessarily emends the verb to ואלה (so also Elliger, *Deuterojesaja*, 175–76).

q) The LXX begins the v. with ἀπὸ γὰρ τῶν ἐθνῶν ("for from the nations") and for ומאלה in v. 28aβ it translates καὶ ἀπὸ τῶν εἰδώλων αὐτῶν ("and from their images"). The initial bicolon may be due to the influence of Isa 63:3 (Goldingay, *Isaiah 40–55*) while North postulates that ומאלה was originally ומאלהיהם ("and among their gods"). For North (*Second Isaiah*, 104), this is due to reverential grounds as *ex hypothesi* heathen gods were not gods as in 2 Sam 5:21 and 1 Chr 14:12. Begrich (*Deuterojesaja*, 46 n. 152) followed by Westermann (*Isaiah 40–66*, 82) emend ומאלה to ואמלל ("I would speak"). However, the majority of translators maintain the MT, although the LXX's and North's interpretations are certainly correct.

r) The MT און is confirmed by θ′ and σ′ with ἄδικοι ("wickedness, wrongdoing") along with the Vg *iniusti* ("wrongful, unrighteous"). The LXX condenses the MT with apparent ellipsis while referencing those who manufacture the images: εἰσὶν γὰρ οἱ ποιοῦντες ὑμας, καὶ μάτην οἱ πλανῶντες ὑμᾶς ("for the ones making you are *nothing* and empty are the ones who deceive you"). 1QIsa[a], Syr, and Tg read אין ("nothingness") instead of און. Yet, 1QIsa[a] derives from an archetype which makes it extremely difficult to distinguish between the י and ו (see Barthélemy, *Critique Textuelle*, 301; de Waard, *Handbook on Isaiah*, 162). Due to the latter manuscript support and the parallels found in 40:17 and 41:12, 24, translators often emend the MT to אַיִן as *BHS* suggests. Similarly, Duhm emends to מאין (*Jesaia*, 277). However, the MT has support from some of the Versions and constitutes the more difficult reading (so also, e.g., RSV; NRSV; NASB; NIV; Barthélemy, *Critique Textuelle*, 300–301; Childs, *Isaiah*, 314; Delitzsch, *Isaiah* 2:164; Goldingay, *Isaiah 40–55*; Koole, *Isaiah 3/1*, 204–5; Korpel and de Moor, *Hebrew Poetry*, 74). This colon, then, reflects the accusation of v. 24b since both speak of the sinfulness of idolatry and also corresponds to v. 24aα (see Goldingay, *Isaiah 40–55*) with the final terms of each colon possibly displaying a polysemantic pun (for this poetical device, see Wilfred G. E. Watson, *Classical Hebrew Poetry: A Guide to its Techniques*

[JSOTSup 26; Sheffield: JSOT Press, 1995], 241–42) since און can also convey the idea of "deception, nothingness" (see Karl H. Bernhardt, "און," *TDOT* 1:140–47 [142–43]; *HALOT*, 22; see also Baltzer, *Deutero-Isaiah*, 122).

s) Lit. רוח ותהו ("breath and emptiness").

Structure and Genre

As Goldingay has demonstrated, this unit begins the major section comprising of 41:21–42:7.[1] The vast majority of interpreters recognize vv. 21–29 forming a literary unit.[2] In addition to the structural pattern surrounding these verses, a number of other factors within and outside these verses also indicate that they form a single unit. For instance, the passage opens with two parallel speech formulas, יאמר יהוה...יאמר מלך יעקב. Also, 42:1 begins with הן that often alerts the reader of Isaiah that a new unit or section is beginning. The MT distinguishes vv. 21–29 as a unit with a caesura and a פ after v. 20 and v. 29. 1QIsa[a] also has a space after v. 20 and begins a new line after v. 29. Verses 24 and 29 arrive at parallel conclusions that bring to a close their respective section. Further, both verses begin with הן and also contain paronomasia involving the terms מאין/און and מאפע/אפס. In addition, running throughout the unit is the *leitmotif* term נגד (vv. 22aα^2, 22bα, 23aα, 26aα^1, 26bα^1). Goldingay has also noted a chiastic structure between vv. 21–24 and 25–29: a movement from word to deed (vv. 21–24) and from deed to word (vv. 25–29).[3]

Regarding the internal structure of the passage, the MT has an additional caesura between v. 24 and v. 25 while 1QIsa[a] has a small space between the two verses. Verses 25–29 do not include another legal summons corresponding to v. 21. Thus, the passage contains two main sub-units: (I) Yahweh's summons to the gods (v. 21) and (II) Yahweh's challenge and demonstration of divinity (vv. 22–29).[4] Within the second section there are two sub-units: (A) Yahweh's challenge to the idol-gods to prove their divinity (vv. 22–24) and (B) Yahweh's response and claim of divinity (vv. 25–29). A detailed structure can be seen as follows:

1. Goldingay, "Arrangement of Isaiah," 289–92; see further Jerome T. Walsh, "The Case for the Prosecution: Isaiah 41.21–42.17," in Follis, ed., *Directions in Biblical Hebrew Poetry*, 101–18. For similar proposals, see further W. A. M. Beuken, "Mišpāt: The First Servant Song and Its Context," *VT* 22 (1972): 11–23; Clifford, *Fair Spoken*, 89–93; Motyer, *Prophecy of Isaiah*, 314–25.

2. See especially Goldingay, *Isaiah 40–55*; Koole, *Isaiah 3/1*, 187–88; Korpel and de Moor, *Hebrew Poetry*, 87–92; Melugin, *Isaiah 40–55*, 98; Schoors, *I am God*, 213–16; Westermann, *Isaiah 40–66*, 82–83.

3. Goldingay, *Isaiah 40–55*.

4. Most interpreters also divide this section into two units, but divide between vv. 24 and 25 (so, e.g., Gitay, *Prophecy and Persuasion*, 104–5; Muilenburg, "Chapters 40–66," 460–63; Walsh, "Case for the Prosecution," 108–10).

I. Yahweh summons the idol-gods to court (v. 21)
II. Yahweh's challenge of demonstrating divinity (vv. 22–29)
A. Challenge proper and verdict (vv. 22–24)
1. Yahweh's series of challenges with evaluative purposes (vv. 22–23)
a. First challenge concerning future and past events (vv. 22a–bβ^{1})
1) Challenge concerning future events (v. 22a)
2) Challenge concerning past events (v. 22bα^{1}–bβ^{1})
a) Challenge proper (v. 22bα^{1})
b) Evaluative purpose (v. 22bα^{2}–bβ^{1})
b. Second challenge concerning future events (vv. 22bβ^{2}–23aβ)
1) Challenge proper (vv. 22bβ^{2}–23aα)
2) Evaluative purpose (v. 23aβ)
c. Third challenge concerning future events (vv. 23b)
1) Challenge proper (v. 23bα)
2) Evaluative purpose (v. 23bβ)
2. Yahweh's evidentiary verdict (v. 24)
a. Concerning the idol-gods (v. 24a)
b. Concerning those who choose idol-gods (v. 24b)
B. Yahweh's response and evidence for his claim to divinity (vv. 25–29)
1. Evidence proper (v. 25)
a. Descriptive announcement of future event (v. 25a)
b. Descriptive action of future event (v. 25b)
2. Yahweh's personal claim of the event (vv. 26–28)
a. First denouncement of other claims of the event (v. 26)
1) Rhetorical questions concerning announced event (v. 26a)
2) Denouncement proper (v. 26b)
b. Second denouncement of other claims of the event (vv. 27–28)
1) Announcement of the event (v. 27)
2) Denouncement proper (v. 28)
3. Yahweh's evidentiary verdict (v. 29)

Most form critics identify this passage as a trial speech.[5] This is specifically based on the presence of ריב ("legal dispute, case, lawsuit")[6] and the basic structure and content of the so-called trial speech between Yahweh and the nations and/or their gods.[7] In his assessment of the trial

5. On the trial speeches in Isa 40–55, see Begrich, *Deuterojesaja*, 26–48; Melugin, *Isaiah 40–55*, 45–63, 98; Horst D. Preuss, *Deuterojesaja: Eine Einführung in seine Botschaft* (Neukirchen–Vluyn: Neukirchener, 1976), 21–22; Schoors, *I am God*, 181–245; Westermann, *Sprache und Struktur*, 51–61; idem, *Isaiah 40–66*, 63–64, 82–83.

6. *HALOT*, 1225–26.

7. For various form-critical suggestions on the structure of trial speeches, see Melugin, *Formation of Isaiah 40–55*, 45–63; Schoors, *I am God*, 181–88; Marvin A. Sweeney, *Isaiah 1–39, with an Introduction to Prophetic Literature* (FOTL 16; Grand Rapids: Eerdmans, 1996), 27–28; Westermann, *Sprache und Struktur*, 52–61.

speeches in Isa 40–55, Antoon Schoors concludes that they primarily function as a defense of Yahweh's claim of sole supreme sovereign power in distinction from the idol-gods.[8] Yahweh's summons to the gods here is not a "real" trial, but is a taunt which sarcastically mocks the idol-gods Jacob–Israel and the nations are appealing to.[9] Yet, at the same time, Yahweh uses this speech in order to assert his sole responsibility for the Cyrus event which in turn demonstrates his own claim of deity.[10]

The case here concerns the claim of divinity. A request for evidence is issued and witnesses are assigned to weigh the arguments. Within this imaginary court Yahweh occupies the positions of plaintiff, judge, and jury. In speech act terms, this taunt includes a number of the illocutions and specifically the assertive, expressive, and declarative/verdictive forces that are directly related to this taunt type genre. Yahweh makes assertions and expresses his opinion about the idol-gods and their devotees while rendering a declarative/verdictive decision about their existence and claim to deity. In conjunction with these forces, Yahweh implicitly utters directives to the addressees. In this simulated court case, Jacob–Israel, the nations, and readers comprise the additional members of the jury as they *listen in* and are indirectly and directly challenged by Yahweh's assertions and claims.

Interpretive Analysis

Verse 21: Yahweh here summons the idol-gods to court in order for them to demonstrate clear evidence of their divinity. In speech act terminology, Yahweh utters a directive illocution to the idol-gods to substantiate the claim of divinity.

Verse 22a–bβ ^{1}: Yahweh presents his challenge to the idol-gods that involves both future (v. 22a) and past events (v. 22b–bβ^{1}). Before discussing the challenge of future events, the past events challenge will be briefly examined. A number of suggestions have been offered toward understanding the idea of former/previous events (ראשׁ) and last/new events (אחר).[11] Most interpreters correctly link the meaning of the phrase

8. Schoors, *I am God*, 239–40; so also Beuken, "God's Exclusivity," 345–46.

9. I am grateful to Roy Melugin for his valuable suggestions on this section, which took a different form in the dissertation version of the present study.

10. So also Conrad, *Fear Not Warrior*, 106.

11. For discussions on this concept, see Aage Bentzen, "On the Ideas of 'the Old' and 'the New' in Deutero-Isaiah," *ST* 1 (1947–48): 183–87; Henk Leene, "History and Eschatology in Deutero-Isaiah," in van Ruiten and Vervenne, eds., *Studies in the Book of Isaiah*, 223–49; Christopher R. North, "The 'Former Things' and the 'New Things' in Deutero-Isaiah," in *Studies in Old Testament Prophecy*

with Yahweh's self-title (e.g. אני ראשון ואני אחרון),[12] which, as Rosario P. Merendino observes, is strategically located in the beginning, middle, and the end of the first section (41:4b; 44:6bα; 48:12b).[13] In connection with the first and last events, Yahweh's sovereignty relates to the first events because he is the first and Yahweh's sovereignty relates to the last events because he is the last.[14] Within chs. 40–48, the former events cannot be reduced to one single concept, but rather encompass several acts performed by Yahweh: creation (40:21–26), the original exodus of Jacob–Israel (43:16–18), the call of Abraham, functioning as a type of Cyrus,[15] with the accompanied election of Israel (41:1–4), the Cyrus event (48:3), and implicitly the prophecies in chs. 1–39 concerning the fall of Jerusalem. The challenge here summons the idol-gods to interpret history by connecting together the beginning with the end in such a way that it satisfactorily explains the present.[16] The exact antecedent of the former events is unclear. The described events in 41:2–3 are the closest and most plausible reference which are also directly linked to Yahweh's self-title (v. 4). If this is correct, then the challenge consists of the idol-gods making sense of the imminent arrival of Cyrus in light of Israel's beginnings and future.[17]

Verses $22b\beta^2$*–23a:* The key term נגד occurs in the first colon (v. 22aα) and here. As already pointed out, this verb occurs five times in this unit and always in the Hiphil. As other interpreters have observed, נגד is also the *leitmotif* term of chs. 40–48. The verb occurs seventeen other times in the first section (40:21aβ; 42:9bα, 12b; 43:$9a\beta^1$, 12aα; 44:$7a\alpha^2$, 7b, $8a\alpha^3$; 45:19bβ, 21aα, $21b\alpha^2$; 46:10aα; 48:3aα, 5aα, 6aβ, 14aβ, $20a\beta^1$).

(Festschrift Theodore H. Robinson; ed. H. H. Rowley; New York: Scribner's, 1950), 11–26; Antoon Schoors, "Choses antérieures," 19–47; Carroll Stuhlmueller, "First and Last and Yahweh—Creator in Deutero-Isaiah," *CBQ* 29 (1967): 495–511.

12. H. G. M. Williamson sees 8:23 (9:1) as the background of this phrase; see his "First and Last in Isaiah," in McKay and Clines, eds., *Of Prophets' Visions and the Wisdom of Sages*, 95–108 (98–99).

13. Rosario P. Merendino, *Der Erste und der Letzte: Eine Untersuchung von Jes 40–48* (VTSup 31; Leiden: Brill, 1981), cf. 7–8.

14. Goldingay, *Isaiah 40–55*.

15. Gwilym H. Jones, "Abraham and Cyrus: Type and Anti-Type?," *VT* 22 (1972): 304–19; Rignell, *Study of Isaiah*, 21–23; *pace* Charles C. Torrey, "Isaiah 41," *HTR* 44 (1951): 121–36.

16. So, e.g., Baltzer, *Deutero-Isaiah*, 118–19; Goldingay, *Isaiah*, 236; Motyer, *Prophecy of Isaiah*, 315–16; Oswalt, *Chapters 40–66*, 100–2; Westermann, *Isaiah 40–66*, 84–85.

17. So also Jones, "Abraham and Cyrus," 318.

Significantly, נגד does not appear at all in chs. 49–55 and only three times following this block (57:12a; 58:1bα; 66:19bβ²), and seven times in chs. 1–39 (3:9aβ; 7:2aα; 19:12aβ; 21:2aβ, 6bβ, 10bβ²; 36:22b). In chs. 40–48, נגד predominantly occurs in the Hiphil and often in parallel with שמע in the same stem. Further, the term is used in the same general sense and contextual concerns as 41:21–29. Significantly, two of the three occurrences that do not function in this way are used to command that praise be נגד unto Yahweh in response for what he has נגד (42:12b; 48:20aβ¹).

In the translations of this study I define נגד with the English verb "declare" due to its context and illocutionary function.[18] נגד in v. 22bα², however, is used in a different sense. As translated, the term conveys the meaning of "to explain, interpret"[19] in relation to making sense of the past. The remaining uses of נגד concern the performance of an utterance, and specifically, the declarative illocution. In these cases, most interpreters translate נגד with either "declare," "announce," or "tell." The former two verbs are preferred over the less expressive "tell." Still, in light of speech act linguistics, the verb "declare" properly indicates the illocutionary act conveyed by נגד.

Concerning the future events challenge, the illocutionary act that Yahweh requests from the idol-gods is specifically a declarative/performative. Further, the type of utterance is a strong linguistic supernatural performative. To recall, performatives are either linguistic or non-linguistic. Searle's exception to the former condition is a supernatural declaration. The challenge here constitutes a linguistic supernatural declarative/performative that does not operate through extralinguistic conventions in the same way Yahweh commands things into existence (e.g. Isa 40:21–26; Gen 1:1–2:4a).

In relation to the words-to-world concept, the declarative expresses both directions of fit (↕). Yahweh requests the idol-gods successfully to declare a future event that transforms reality whereby the world fits the propositional content (↑ world-to-words) by saying that the propositional content matches the world (↓ words-to-world). The illocutionary act is satisfied when the gods bring about the propositional content of their utterance. The purpose of the speech act request is expressed with the phrase ונדעה כי אלהים אתם (v. 23aβ), which is a play on Yahweh's typical self-identification formula, for example, ידע כי אני יהוה.[20] Thus, the

18. Wagner only briefly examines נגד in the Hiphil from a speech act perspective, but he does not examine its use in Isa 40–55 (see *Sprechaktanalyse*, 108).

19. See Claus Westermann, "נגד," *TLOT* 2:714–18 (715–16).

20. So also Blank, "Deutero-Isaiah," 13.

perlocutionary effect of the successful speech act challenge consists in providing clear evidence that the idol-gods are indeed divine.

Interpreters have generally understood the essence of this challenge as described above. Yet, at the same time, these same scholars discuss this challenge in terms of predicting, foretelling, and foreknowing the future. For instance, form critics identify this type of challenge as a *Weissagungsbeweis* typically translated in English as "prediction proof." Relatedly, Koole sees a close semantic connection between the parallel terms נגד and שמע in this context (v. 26), but he translates the latter term with "to predict" (*voorspellen*).[21] Similarly, Sheldon Blank follows his examination of 41:21–29 and questions, "How does foreknowledge serve as a test of divinity?"[22] These representative examples present two contradictory ideas, since the notions of "predict" and "foreknowing" do not convey the same concept as declaring or actualizing the future. To predict the future is to describe events that will inevitably transpire through natural or scientific observation or by supernaturally foreseeing and/or foreknowing the future course of history. Again, although interpreters typically understand the essence of this challenge, such language misconstrues it. The challenge here consists of the successful performance of a declarative illocutionary act: declaring a future event that brings about a transformation of the states of affairs in the world.

Verse 23b: These lines directly link speech with action. The phrase תיטיבו ותרעו may be a merism—separate components that represent a totality or global idea.[23] Understood this way, Yahweh requests that the idol-gods "do everything" or "do at least something, anything."[24] More likely, the idol-gods are called upon to prove that they are capable of doing good for their adherents or evil against their enemies.[25] This

21. Koole, *Isaiah 3/1*, 192–93; for Koole's original Dutch commentary, see *Jesaja II deel I: Jesaja 40 tot en met 48* (CHOT; Kampen: Kok, 1985), 130–31.

22. Blank, "Deutero-Isaiah," 3. For similar descriptions of the challenge, see also Beuken, *Jesaja II/A*, 97–98; Blenkinsopp, *Isaiah 40–55*, 205–6; Childs, *Isaiah*, 321; Delitzsch, *Isaiah*, 2:160; Motyer, *Prophecy of Isaiah*, 315–16; Muilenburg, "Chapters 40–66," 460–61; Schoors, *I am God*, 240; Smith, *The Origins of Biblical Monotheism*, 190–93; Oswalt, *Chapters 40–66*, 99–100; Watts, *Isaiah 34–66*, 118.

23. See Luis A. Schökel, *A Manual of Hebrew Poetics* (Subsidia Biblica 11; Rome: Pontificio Istituto Biblico, 1988), 83–84; Watson, *Hebrew Poetry*, 321–24.

24. E.g. Baltzer, *Deutero-Isaiah*, 119; Motyer, *Prophecy of Isaiah*, 316; Oswalt, *Chapters 40–66*, 102; Rignell, *Study of Isaiah*, 29; Watts, *Isaiah 34–66*, 118; Westermann, *Isaiah 40–66*, 85; Whybray, *Isaiah 40–66*, 69.

25. So Goldingay, *Isaiah 40–55*; Koole, *Isaiah 3/1*, 194. Mulder ("Filologische Kanttekeningen," 141–42) suggests that the gods also know good and evil.

interpretation is more in line with Yahweh's history of acts (cf. Lam 3:37–38) and his speech act described in these chapters. Yahweh's challenge, then, includes a measure of specificity as he requests the idol-gods to utter a particular future act that benefits their devotees in one way or another.

Verse 24: As expected in a taunt, the idol-gods offer no evidence for divinity. This is also expressed and elaborated upon in the arguments set forth in Isa 40–48 that they cannot speak or act, and that, in fact, they must be carried from place to place (46:6–7). Yahweh weighs the argument of silence and concludes that the idol-gods do not exist. In the first two clauses, Yahweh utters another illocution, but with nominal clauses and without any explicit illocutionary markers. These utterances are both hybrid assertive–verdictive/declaratives. Yahweh assesses the evidence and simultaneously declares the idol-gods as non-existent. In the final clause, Yahweh utters an assertive–expressive–directive. Yahweh asserts that one who chooses idol-gods *count as* a תועבה, which is incompatible with Yahweh's character.[26] With the expressive dimension Yahweh divulges his attitude towards idols and those who worship them. The concern here is not so much focused on attacking the system of polytheism, but on the incongruity of Yahweh and the worship of other gods. Yahweh is a jealous God (Exod 20:5; 34:14) and for those who consider themselves his people, they must acknowledge and worship him alone. As creator of the world and of Israel, Yahweh's assertive represents accurately a state of affairs which confronts the readers' point of view concerning truth. To choose and confess allegiance to the idol-gods *counts as* sin against Yahweh (cf. Exod 20:3–5), which expresses the directive dimension of the utterance. Thus, this utterance also warns against the sinfulness of idolatry. This final clause challenges the listener to become self-involved with the text, and adopt the stance of Yahweh's assertive–expressive and heed the warning or suffer the consequences.

The final clause of v. 24 makes it clear that Yahweh's verdict is not a definitive conclusion for all those who are included in the "we/us/our" group. This entity has not appeared in the previous chapters until now and it does not refer to the council of Yahweh.[27] As discussed in the previous chapter, Yahweh's demonstration of power is specifically directed at the human witnesses Jacob–Israel and the nations. Through self-involvement, the readers include themselves in this open first person

26. See E. Gerstenberger, "תעב," *TLOT* 3:1428–31; Michael A. Grisanti, "תעב," *NIDOTTE* 4:314–18.

27. *Pace* Seitz, "Isaiah 40–66," 352, 356.

plural group of witnesses. The listener is invited to either affirm or disagree with Yahweh's verdict. To choose either Yahweh or the idol-gods is a speech act. Specifically, the speaker utters a confession that involves the expressive and commissive illocutions. With the expressive dimension the listener/confessor takes a stance concerning either Yahweh or the idol-gods. To confess one or the others entails the rejection of the one not confessed. With the commissive dimension listeners/speakers commit themselves to the demands of either. However, to confess allegiance to the idol-gods constitutes choosing unreality, nonexistence. Such a decision does not correspond to Yahweh's assessment concerning these idol-gods and thus the person remains in a deceived state.

Verse 25: Yahweh responds to the silence of the idol-gods by describing a specific future event which takes up again the rhetorical questions and assertions raised in 41:2–4. These verses refer to Yahweh's speech act that describes an anonymous conqueror who will eventually be identified as Cyrus (44:28; 45:1). Combining all of the texts in chs. 40–48 that express Yahweh's performative utterance, it includes Cyrus' military campaign leading to the overthrow of Babylon, the provision of deliverance for Jacob–Israel, and the restoration of Jerusalem (e.g. 40:10–11; 41:2–3, 14–20; 43:1–21; 44:6–8, 26–28; 45:1–25; 47:1–15; 48:1–22). Yahweh's Cyrus speech act is a strong linguistic declarative–commissive performative. Regarding the first dimension, Yahweh has declared the Cyrus event. The successful performance of this illocution will be achieved when Yahweh brings about a new state of affairs in the extralinguistic world that matches his utterance (↑) by declaring that the propositional content fits reality (↓). With the commissive dimension, Yahweh also commits himself to the extralinguistic action of delivering Jacob–Israel safely from Babylon unto Zion–Jerusalem and restoring his city, which he has spoken of in 40:1–11.

It is important to draw attention to the fact that Yahweh's actual declarative of the Cyrus event is not explicitly expressed in chs. 40–48. In v. 25 and throughout this section, Yahweh's illocutionary act is presented as already beginning to take place, but not yet fully realized. In this first section, Yahweh claims that he declared it from the beginning, in former times, from beforehand, from old. This language corresponds to the fact that Yahweh declared the overthrow of Babylon through other prophets, and specifically, Isaiah ben Amoṣ declared earlier that the Medes would conquer the city (13:17–22). For this reason, Yahweh considers the Cyrus event as his *former* declared event (cf. 48:3). Yet, at the same time, Yahweh claims that his illocutionary act is a *new* event (48:6–8; see also 43:14–21). What is new here is the specificity of Cyrus named as the conqueror of Babylon and that he will restore Jerusalem (cf. 45:13). In light of 41:2–3, Yahweh answers the dual challenge extended to the idol-gods with his former/new declarative. Upon the actualization of the event, Yahweh will tie together and coherently make sense of Jacob–Israel's past, present, and future.

Verse 26a: Yahweh turns to the illocutionary aspect of the Cyrus event. In these lines Yahweh issues a double rhetorical question to identify the one responsible for this event.[28] Regarding the rhetorical questions found throughout chs. 40–48, J. Kenneth Kuntz has demonstrated that they play an important role for asserting Yahweh's incomparability.[29] In these lines, Yahweh is not asking who declared this event, but who apart from him declared it, as he is now included in the "we/us/our" group that recalls the challenge issued in vv. 22–23. The self-evident answer is, "No one," which is made explicit in v. 26b. This answer distinguishes Yahweh from the idol-gods as the sole, incomparable God responsible for the Cyrus event.

Questions by their very nature are dialogical and self-involving. According to Wallace L. Chafe, imperatives generally "request some form of *non-linguistic* behavior or action" whereas "questions are concerned primarily with *linguistic* responses."[30] However, speech act theorists demonstrate that questions are illocutionary acts, since they directly or indirectly request from the listener some type of linguistic

28. Rhetorical questions are questions with implied unstated, direct, and obvious answers, but as Watson (*Hebrew Poetry*, 338–40) observes, in Hebrew poetry a reply is often given. Watson further observes that such questions are largely composed of parallel couplets, but also extend into a series. For further analyses of rhetorical questions in the Old Testament, see, e.g., Walter Brueggemann, "Jeremiah's Use of Rhetorical Questions," *JBL* 92 (1973): 358–74; Robert Gordis, "A Rhetorical Use of Interrogative Sentences in Biblical Hebrew," *AJSL* 49 (1932/33): 212–17; Moshe Held, "Rhetorical Questions in Ugaritic and Biblical Hebrew," *Eretz-Israel* 9 (1969): 71–79; Schökel, *Hebrew Poetics*, 150–51, 162; L. J. de Regt, "Implications of Rhetorical Questions in Strophes in Job 11 and 15," in *The Book of Job* (ed. W. A. M. Beuken; BETL 114; Leuven: Leuven University Press, 1994), 321–28; idem, "Discourse Implications of Rhetorical Questions in Job, Deuteronomy and the Minor Prophets," in *Literary Structure and Rhetorical Strategies in the Hebrew Bible* (ed. L. J. de Regt, J. de Waard, and J. P. Fokkelman; Assen: Van Gorcum, 1996), 51–78.

29. Kenneth J. Kuntz, "The Form, Location, and Function of Rhetorical Questions in Deutero-Isaiah," in Broyles and Evans, eds., *Writing and Reading the Scroll of Isaiah*, 1:121–41.

30. Wallace L. Chafe, *Meaning and the Structure of Language* (Chicago: University of Chicago, 1970), 309 (italics mine). Kuntz is apparently in agreement with this observation ("Rhetorical Questions," 121).

or non-linguistic action. All real questions are generally categorized as directives. In addition to correctly recognizing this type of illocution, it is profitable to view the force of the question along the suggested spectrum of strengths.[31] In other words, questions range from weak to strong depending upon the force of the directive.[32] Thus, questions are illocutionary acts that range from asking a hearer to provide some information (weak) to requesting the hearer to perform some type of action (strong). In addition, direct questions may possess more strength than indirect ones due to the latter's inherent vagueness. For example, the indirect directive, "Can you reach the salt?" could be uttered in order for someone to pass the salt, or "It is hot in here" to request that someone turn on the air-conditioner. For Searle, indirect utterances are speech acts, but because they communicate more than is expressed within the propositional content, they rely on "mutually shared background information, both linguistic and non-linguistic, together with the general powers of rationality and inference on the part of the hearer."[33] However, indirect speech acts are not explicit declarative/performatives.[34]

Rhetorical questions, as opposed to real or genuine questions, can also express illocutionary force. In speech act terms, they are generally indirect speech acts that inferentially request the hearer to respond in some way.[35] These types of questions are also hybrid in nature as they contain an assertive and interrogative dimension. Jürgen Schmidt-Radefeldt observes:

31. Vanderveken discusses degree of strength in relation to questions and the directive force; see his *Meaning and Speech Acts*, 127–28, 149.

32. Searle confesses that he originally thought that every question simply requests information; see his *Speech Acts*, 66–67, 69. However, he later adjusted his conclusion to include questions requesting a promise to be made or to perform speech acts; see his "Conversation," in *(On) Searle on Conversation* (Searle et al.; P&BNS 21; Amsterdam: Benjamins, 1992), 7–29 (8–9).

33. John R. Searle, "Indirect Speech Acts," in *Expression and Meaning*, 30–57 (31–31); see also Searle and Vanderveken, *Illocutionary Logic*, 10–11.

34. Searle, "Performatives," 90, 92–93. Searle's notions on indirect speech acts are far more complex than what appears here. Beyond Searle's own discussion, see further, for example, Rod Bertolet, "Are There Indirect Speech Acts?," and David Holdcroft, "Indirect Speech Acts and Propositional Content," both in Tsohatzidis, ed., *Foundations of Speech Act Theory*, 335–49, 350–64, respectively.

35. Categorizing rhetorical questions as indirect speech acts is not without some debate: see, for example, see Gloria I. Anzilotti, "The Rhetorical Question as an Indirect Speech Device in English and Italian," *Canadian Modern Language Review* 38 (1982): 290–302; Ferenc Kiefer, "Yes–No Questions as Wh–Questions," in Searle, Kiefer, Bierwisch, eds., *Speech Act Theory and Pragmatics*, 97–119 (98–99); Jürgen Schmidt-Radefeldt, "On So-Called 'Rhetorical' Questions," *JP* 1 (1977): 375–92 (390–91).

> Because of the somewhat undefinable nature of rhetorical questions with regard to their classification as questions and/or statements, the other dialogue-partner can "answer the question" and/or "contradict the statement"—in as much as opportunity is given him. Thus pragmatically it can be up to the addressee whether he accepts a rhetorical question as an assertion (as it is intended by the speaker) or, contrary to the speaker's expectation, takes up the interrogative element in the rhetorical question as an opportunity for intervention.[36]

From an illocutionary perspective, the assertive dimension expresses an assertive–expressive force while the interrogative dimension is an indirect directive. Yet, such questions possess a self-involving dimension, which speech act theorists have not explored in any great detail. The self-involving force of these types of questions is further conveyed by their inherent ambiguous nature. Through this question a speaker makes value assessments and simultaneously asks a question that forces the listener to answer by adopting or rejecting the assertion. In other words, a speaker utters a belief concerning a particular state of affairs and expresses a stance about that belief (assertive–expressive). The interrogative aspect, then, requires a response from the listener (directive). Through self-involvement the hearer either adopts or rejects the assumed answer. By incorporating this dimension, rhetorical questions can be understood as strong self-involving speech acts.

C. J. Labuschagne, in his classic work on the incomparability of Yahweh, discusses the importance of rhetorical questions in the Old Testament that bears similar language to the concept of self-involvement:

> The rhetorical question is one of the most forceful and effectual ways employed in speech for driving home some idea or conviction. Because of its impressive and persuasive effect the hearer is not merely [a] listener: he is forced to frame the expected answer in his mind, and by doing so he actually becomes a *co-expressor* of the speaker's conviction.[37]

Similarly, Watson remarks that rhetorical questions are generally "used *for dramatic effect*: it *involves* the audience directly, if they are addressed, or it creates tension which then requires resolution."[38] Rhetorical critics have typically emphasized the assertive dimension and thus the persuasive function of *rhetorical* questions,[39] but Labuschagne and Watson also

36. Schmidt-Radefeldt, "'Rhetorical' Questions," 381.

37. Labuschagne, *Incomparability*, 23 (italics mine).

38. Watson, *Hebrew Poetry*, 341 (italics mine with "*involves*").

39. Kuntz ("Rhetorical Questions," 123) and Yehoshua Gitay ("A Study of Amos's Art of Speech: A Rhetorical Analysis of Amos 3:1–15," *CBQ* 42 [1980]: 293–309 [302]) also cite the above quote, but both naturally emphasize the rhetorical aspect of Labuschagne's observations.

point to their self-involving nature. With the above observations, rather than viewing rhetorical questions as solely persuasive in orientation, they are linguistic and self-involving utterances that require a response. In short, rhetorical questions are indirect self-involving speech acts that are accompanied with perlocutionary intentions. The intended effects are for the listener to confessionally assent to the implied biased assertion and thereby adopt particular non-linguistic stances and entailments. Within this text, the rhetorical questions force the "we/us/our" witnesses to assess the evidence concerning the Cyrus event while retaining the option either to agree with Yahweh's assertive or suggest another answer that counters his claim.

Verse 26b: Yahweh emphatically denies any other claim to the Cyrus speech act. Yahweh asserts that he alone declared the event and no other deity can claim such responsibility. By stating the implied answer this reinforces Yahweh's claim to the Cyrus event and invites the reader to *co-express* Yahweh's assertion.[40] To agree with Yahweh's assertion confesses him as God alone whereas to question Yahweh's claim confesses allegiance to other gods. As discussed in v. 24, this confession also consists of the expressive–commissive illocutions. To co-express Yahweh's assertion speakers adopt a stance towards Yahweh and the idol-gods and simultaneously commits themselves to Yahweh alone.

Verse 27: As demonstrated in the note above, this bicolon is difficult to make sense of. Reading the MT, the issue lies with the first colon and the antecedent of the third masculine plural suffix. Some suggest that this refers to the imminent events,[41] the arriving armies of Cyrus to Babylon,[42] or the returning exiles to Zion as depicted in 40:9–11.[43] While all of these are reasonable proposals, from a grammatical standpoint, the immediate antecedent of the suffix is אמריכם in v. 26bβ. Neil J. McEleney follows this line of thinking and concludes that "the verse should be understood as the quotation of what the gods' 'words' referred to in the previous verse should be." He translates v. 27 as the content of v. 26bβ, "No one to hear your words: 'The first news for Sion: Behold, here they

40. Similarly Kuntz, "'Rhetorical' Questions," 138.

41. E.g. Delitzsch, *Isaiah*, 2:163–64; Motyer, *Prophecy of Isaiah*, 317; Oswalt, *Chapters 40–66*, 104–5; Rignell, *Study of Isaiah*, 30; Torrey, *Second Isaiah*, 320.

42. E.g. Koole, *Isaiah 3/1*, 202.

43. E.g. Barthélemy, *Critique Textuelle*, 300; J. Gerald Janzen, "Isaiah 41:27: Reading הנה הנומה in 1QIsa[a] and הנה הנם in the Masoretic Text," *JBL* 113 (1994): 597–607 (cf. 602); Muilenburg, "Chapters 40–66," 463; de Waard, *Handbook on Isaiah*, 161.

are!' Or 'To Jerusalem I am sending a messenger.' "[44] This points in the right direction, as the issue throughout this unit and chs. 40–48 centers on who declared the Cyrus event. However, these lines are not concerned with what the idol-gods words *should be*; rather, they make explicit that the *words* concerning Zion–Jerusalem were only spoken by Yahweh. Yahweh asserts that no one else declared the coming of Cyrus, and specifically, the announcement and call to Zion–Jerusalem in 40:1–11.[45]

Verse 28: Yahweh reiterates his earlier taunting denouncement in v. 26 that no other god has declared the Cyrus event. In fact, he cannot find any among these idol-gods to even reply with a single word to his questions. According to Yahweh, no idol-god has provided any evidence to refute his claim that he alone declared this event.

Verse 29: As in v. 24a, Yahweh concludes with similar assertive–expressive–declarative illocutions and thus reaffirms the evidence and declares the idol-gods as non-existent. The reader is left to evaluate the evidence and either agree or disagree with Yahweh's assertion.

Conclusion

As a whole, this passage integrally functions with the overarching prophetic strategy of chs. 40–55. In particular, the passage works in close connection with the other idol passages that polemically satirize the practice of idolatry. Specifically, it addresses the main thematic arguments expressed in chs. 40–48: idols cannot speak or act and thus possess no ability whatsoever to deliver (see also Ps 115). Conversely, Yahweh is the only one who declared the Cyrus event because he is the only deity who actually speaks and acts. However, this passage is not merely a rhetorical device to denounce the existence of idol-gods,[46] but it asserts that Yahweh is solely responsible for the Cyrus event. Throughout these chapters, idolatry is taken seriously, as Jacob–Israel is comparing Yahweh with other gods and choosing them over him. This is the very reason for Yahweh's speech act: to demonstrate his incomparability and sole claim to deity. Yahweh's declarative brings about the overthrow of Babylon and provides for Jacob–Israel's return to Jerusalem. With this speech act Yahweh does not attempt to persuade the reader, but he demonstrates his divinity that in turn offers convincing evidence for his sole claim to deity. Corresponding to the purpose of the challenge extended to

44. Neil J. McEleney, "The Translation of Isaias 41,27," *CBQ* 19 (1957): 441–43 (442).

45. Similarly Watts, *Isaiah 34–66*, 119.

46. *Pace* Childs, *Isaiah*, 321.

the idol-gods, the intended perlocutionary effect of Yahweh's successful illocution is that the human witnesses Jacob–Israel and the nations would acknowledge the evidence and testify that he alone is God.[47] While Yahweh addresses and taunts the idol-gods, Jacob–Israel, the nations, and the readers are *listening*. Every listener includes him/herself among the ambiguous and open "we/us/our" witnesses and becomes challenged by Yahweh's claim that he declared the Cyrus event. The perlocutionary effect, though, remains contingent upon each witness' evaluation of Yahweh's assertion.

Without explanation or identification, a single voice begins the second section of Isa 40–55.[48] Chapters 49–55 are no longer concerned with Cyrus, old and new events, idol-gods—only Yahweh and his future community. Chapters 40–48 point to this community who will confess Yahweh alone. The first section looks ahead to the overthrow of Babylon and now Yahweh's call and the intended perlocutionary effect of his declarative/performative look for a response. It is this singular voice who responds. Typical language expressed by Yahweh to his servant Jacob–Israel is found throughout 49:1–6; however, the language here functions as a personal confession. The functionally ambiguous "I/me" implores each addressee/reader to identify with the voice and adopt the role of the servant through this confession. The voice is not a self-constructed persona, as Polk might suggest, but a means for the addressee/reader to *involve* the *self* and utter speech acts. Correlating with the prophetic function of chs. 40–48, this passage along with the other servant texts provides concrete ways for the addressee/reader to accept Yahweh's call, to express allegiance to him alone, embrace the status of being his servant, confess sin, and to function as his witness to his sovereign power.

47. Similarly Laato, *Servant of YHWH*, 208.

48. In 48:16b an individual voice appears and states: "And now Lord Yahweh has sent me and his spirit." Interpreters have disputed the authenticity of this colon (see Schoors, *I am God*, 281–83). However, the Versions support the MT. Those who accept the colon typically understand the first person to be the servant (e.g. Baltzer, *Deutero-Isaiah*, 293; Blenkinsopp, *Isaiah 40–55*, 294; Childs, *Isaiah*, 377–78; Koole, *Isaiah 3/2*, 4; Motyer, *Isaiah*, 381; Seitz, "Divine Council," 246; Westermann, *Isaiah 40–66*, 203). For some (e.g. Melugin, *Isaiah 40–55*, 138–39; Oswalt, *Chapters 40–66*, 278), the voice is the prophet responsible for chs. 40–48. Within the context of ch. 48 and specifically vv. 12–16 the addressee is clearly Jacob–Israel. The nation has previously spoken in similar first person terms (40:27b). Further, Jacob–Israel has been *sent* as Yahweh's messenger (42:19a) and with the first servant passage has been endowed with Yahweh's spirit (42:1bα). With this, the voice seems to belong to Jacob–Israel, but due to the openness of Jacob–Israel's servant role, the self-involved addressees/readers would identify themselves with the voice.

Isaiah 49:1–6

Translation

[1]Listen to me, islands
and listen attentively, peoples from far away!
Yahweh called me from the womb,[a]
from the insides of my mother he pronounced my name.
[2]And he has made my mouth like a sharp sword,
in the shadow of his hand[b] he has hidden me.
He has made me a polished arrow,
in his quiver he has concealed me.
[3]And he said to me, "You are my servant,
you are Israel,[c] through whom I will glorify myself."
[4]And I thought to myself, I have labored in vain
and for entirely no reason[d] I have exhausted my strength.
Unexpectedly though,[e] my judgment is with Yahweh
and my reward is with my God.
[5]Now Yahweh said,
who formed me from the womb to be his servant,
for the purpose of restoring Jacob to himself
and so Israel will not withdraw.[f]
And I am honored[g] in the eyes of Yahweh
and my God has become my strength.[h]
[6]And so he said, "It is easy, because[i] you are my servant,[j]
simply to raise up the tribes of Jacob
and to return the preserved ones[k] of Israel.[l]
Thus I will make you a light to the nations,
to be my salvation to the end of the earth."

a) LXX translates this bicolon as ἐκ κοιλίας μητρός μου ἐκάλεσεν τὸ ὄνομά μου ("from my mother's womb he called my name").

b) 1QIsa[a] has here ידיו ("his hands").

c) ישראל is missing from the Hebrew Manuscript Kennicott 96. Consequently, translators are divided upon the authenticity of ישראל here with the majority of early translators considering the term as a later insertion (e.g. Duhm, *Jesaia*, 331–32; Karl Elliger, *Deuterojesaja in seinem Verhältnis zu Tritojesaja* [BWANT 63; Stuttgart: Kohlhammer, 1933], 38; Westermann, *Isaiah 40–66*, 209; Whybray, *Isaiah 40–66*, 137–38) followed by a smaller group of contemporary interpreters (e.g. Blenkinsopp, *Isaiah 40–55*, 297 n. c; Gillis Gerleman, "Der Gottesknecht bei Deuterojesaja," in idem, *Studien zur alttestamentilichen Theologie* [FDVNF; Heidelberg: Schneider, 1980], 38–60 [54–55]; B. J. Oosterhoff, "Tot een Licht der Volken," in Grosheide et al., eds., *De Knecht: Studies rondom Deutero-Jesaja*, 157–72 [159]). As discussed above, the main issue here revolves around the question of how this servant figure can be identified as Israel and at the same time have a mission to the nation Israel. North observed that the name Israel "has commonly been deleted by those who favoured an individual, and retained by those who supported a collective interpretation, though there are exceptions on both sides" (*Suffering Servant*, 118;

see also idem, *Second Isaiah*, 187–88). Julius A. Bewer examined the text-critical value of Kenn 96 and concluded that the manuscript contained a number of careless errors and omissions of which 49:3 is no exception ("Two Notes on Isaiah 49:1–6," in *Jewish Studies* [Festschrift George A. Kohut; ed. S. W. Baron and A. Marx; New York: Alexander Kohut Memorial Foundation, 1935], 86–90). Harry Orlinsky challenges Bewer's conclusions and claims that ישראל is a gloss and so it has no place in v. 3 ("So-Called 'Servant,'" 81–89; see also idem, "'Israel' in Isa. XLIX: A Problem in the Methodology of Textual Criticism," *Eretz-Israel* 8 [1967]: 42–45). A. Gelston recently took up Bewer's claims about Kenn 96 by re-examining the scribal nature of the manuscript and confirmed Bewer's assessment and concludes that little weight can be placed on the omission of ישראל in 49:3 ("Isaiah 52:13–53:12: An Eclectic Text and a Supplementary Note on the Hebrew Manuscript Kennicott 96," *JSS* 35 [1990]: 187–211 [204–10]). Examining the MT, Norbert Lohfink has convincingly demonstrated that there is no textual or literary basis for the omission of ישראל in v. 3; however, Lohfink considers vv. 5–6, which repeats the name, a secondary addition ("'Israel' in Jes 49,3," in *Wort, Lied und Gottesspruch: Beiträge zu Psalmen und Propheten* [Festschrift Joseph Ziegler; ed. J. Schreiner; FzB 2; Stuttgart: Katholisches Bibelwerk, 1972], 217–29 [cf. 226–28]). In the final analysis, Kenn 96 cannot provide textual support for the omission of the name while 1QIsa[a], LXX, Tg, Vg, and Syr all confirm the MT. Moreover, the presence of ישראל constitutes a more difficult reading as evidenced by most modern interpreters (for further discussions see especially W. A. M. Beuken, "De Vergeefse Moeite van de Knecht: Gadachten over de Plaats van Jesaja 49:1–6 in de Context" in Grosheide et al., eds., *De Knecht: Studies rondom Deutero-Jesaja*, 23–40 [36–39]; idem, *Jesaja deel II B* [POT; Nijkerk: Callenback, 1979], 17–18; Koole, *Isaiah 3/2*, 11–13; Julian Morgenstern, "The Suffering Servant—A New Solution," *VT* 11 [1961]: 292–320, 406–31 [306–8]; Wilcox and Paton-Williams, "Servant Songs," 88–93).

d) Lit. לתהו והבל ("for nothing and no purpose"). 1QIsa[a] repeats the prep. לתהו ולהבל.

e) אכן expresses emphatic–assertive–contrastive force that emphasizes the unexpected, a decisive turning point in thought (see *DCH* 1:248–49; *HALOT*, 47; *IBHS* §39.3.5d; Israel Eitan, "Hebrew and Semitic Particles: Comparative Studies in Semitic Philology," *AJSL* 45 [1929]: 48–63, 130–45, 197–211 [197–98]; Fredric J. Goldbaum, "Two Hebrew Quasi-Adverbs: לכן and אכן," *JNES* 23 [1964]: 132–35; William L. Holladay, *Jeremiah 1* [Hermeneia; Philadelphia: Fortress, 1986], 124; Takamitsu Muraoka, *Emphatic Words and Structures in Biblical Hebrew* [Leiden: Brill, 1985], 132–33).

f) Followed by a large number of translators, Q suggests לו for לא which 1QIsa[a], LXX, α′, Tg, and Syr follow with the generally proposed translation of "and so Israel might be gathered to him." Although this suggestion has textual support and it nicely parallels the previous colon, K remains the more difficult reading and is supported by 4QIsa[d], σ′, θ′, and Vg. Wilson emends the MT to a Qal inf. לאסוף ("to gather") to parallel the previous colon (*Nations in Deutero-Isaiah*, 267); but this is unnecessary. Duhm reads the MT and translates the colon: "and so that Israel may not be snatched up" (*Jesaia*, 333: "*Und dass Israel nicht hingerafft werde*"). Similarly, de Boer translates "so that Israel be not swept away" (*Second-Isaiah's Message*, 26, 53), Gerleman suggests "and so that Israel may not be snatched away" ("Gottesknecht," 55: "*und damit Israel nicht weggerafft werde*"), and Rignell proposes "and Israel will not perish" (*Study of Isaiah*, 61). The verb יאסף is a Niphal impf. 3mp and understood passively means "be carried off, removed" as Duhm et al. translate (cf. Isa 16:10; see BDB, 62; *DCH* 1:347–48; *HALOT*, 74; see also Oswalt, *Chapters 40–66*, 285 n. 4; *pace* Geo Widengren, "Yahweh's Gathering of the Dispersed," in *In the Shelter of Elyon: Essays on Ancient Palestinian Life and Literature* [Festschrift G. W. Ahlström; ed. W. B. Barrick and J. R. Spencer; JSOTSup 31; Sheffield: JSOT Press, 1984], 227–45 [cf. 232–33]). However, the verbal stem can also convey a reflexive nuance meaning "to withdraw itself" (Isa 60:20; see BDB, 62; *HALOT*, 74). Understood this way, the purpose of the servant's task involves restoring Israel to Yahweh instead of withdrawing from him (so also Goldingay, *Isaiah 40–55*).

g) Tg ויקירנא and Syr *ʾštbḥt* suggest reading as *waw* consecutive, "so that I may be honored" (so also Goldingay, *Isaiah 40–55*; Watts, *Isaiah 34–66*, 184 n. 5.d).

h) Duhm claims that v. 5b originally belonged at the end of v. 3 (*Jesaia*, 331–32; so also, e.g., Kaiser, *Königliche Knecht*, 59–60; North, *Second Isaiah*, 55; Whybray, *Isaiah 40–66*, 139; Wilson, *Nations in Deutero-Isaiah*, 266–67). *BHS* suggests that v. 5b should be placed at the end of v. 4 (so also, e.g., Blenkinsopp, *Isaiah 40–55*, 297). These transposition proposals attempt to smooth out a more difficult reading which ends up as unnecessary and do not find any support from the Versions. On the poetic coherence of vv. 5–6, see Beuken, "Vergeefse Moeite," 27–33; idem, *Jesaja II/B*, 20–27.

i) The LXX completely changes the meaning of נקל by rendering Μέγα σοί ἐστιν ("it is great for you"). In a similar way, both the Vg and Tg translate the line as a question which may be supported by 1QIsa[b] הנקל. The majority of translators understand the מ prefix here as expressing comparison, that is, "it is too small," which suggests that the task here is less important than the work for the nations (see, e.g., Childs, *Isaiah*, 385). In contrast, the מ, here is understood as causative (so Goldingay, *Isaiah 40–55*; according to Beuken ["Vergeefse Moeite," 31] so also J. Bachmann, *Praeparation und Commentar zum Deutero-Jesaja, Heft 2: Jesaja Kap. 49–58* [Berlin, 1891], 81; on the causative use of מ see Deut 7:7aα; 2 Sam 3:11b; Nah 1:5aα; Hab 2:8bα, 17bα; *IBHS* §11.2:11d). Thus, because the speaker is identified as Yahweh's servant the task is not limited to the nation Israel alone.

j) In the Tg the addressee is referenced in the plural throughout v. 6a, but returns to the sg. in v. 6b (see Bruce D. Chilton, *The Isaiah Targum: Introduction, Translation, Apparatus and Notes* [The Aramaic Bible 11; Wilmington, Del.: Glazier, 1987], 96).

k) The K, 1QIsa[a], and 1QIsa[b] נציירי and the Q Qal pass. ptc. נצורי appear to have the same meaning "protected/preserved ones." Whybray (*Isaiah 40–66*, 139) feels that the sense of these terms is not appropriate and so emends to נצרי ("offshoots, descendants"); so also, e.g., de Boer, *Second-Isaiah's Message*, 26; North, *Second Isaiah*, 55). *BHS* (666) suggests the Syr rendering ונצרי ("and the green shoots of"). This corresponds with "tribes," but the MT and 1QIsa[a] remain the more difficult reading and is followed by most translators. Further, the text seems to be referencing the return of a remnant of Israel as confirmed in both the LXX τὴν διασπορὰν τοῦ Ισραηλ ἐπιστρέψαι ("to return the diaspora of Israel") and the Tg וגלות ישראל לאתבא ("and to return the exiles of Israel").

l) 1QIsa[a] reverses יעקוב and ישראל (followed by Wilson, *Nations in Deutero-Isaiah*, 267). 1QIsa[b] along with the other Versions support the MT.

Structure and Genre

The boundaries of this passage have long been accepted since Duhm's identification of the Servant Songs. The MT concurs by placing a caesura and a ס after 48:22 and 49:6. 1QIsa^a also recognizes this by beginning new lines after these same verses.[49] As noted above, although a definite similarity exists between 42:1–9 and 49:1–13, a break occurs at the end of v. 6. This is chiefly indicated by the speech formula in v. $7a\alpha^1$ that introduces a change of speaker from an anonymous first person to Yahweh. Internally, a division occurs between vv. 4 and 5 which is essentially indicated by עתה and the speech formula אמר יהוה in v. $5a\alpha^1$. 1QIsa^a also sees a break between vv. 1–4 and vv. 5–6 by placing a space between the verses. Thus, there are two sub-units: (I) an individual confession concerning Yahweh's call (vv. 1–4) and (II) a confessional rehearsal of the call with additional comments on the assignment (vv. 5–6). A detailed structure can be seen as follows:

I. Confession to the foreign nations of Yahweh's call (vv. 1–4)
    A. Summons to the foreign nations to listen (v. 1a)
    B. Confessional call (vv. 1b–3)
        1. Call proper (v. 1b)
        2. Yahweh's provision and protection (v. 2)
        3. Yahweh's declarative (v. 3)
            a. Introductory speech formula (v. 3aα)
            b. Declarative proper (v. 3aβ–b)
                1) Declared as Yahweh's servant and Israel (v. 3aβ–bα)
                2) Purpose (v. 3bβ)
    C. Confession and testimony (v. 4)
        1. Introductory formula (v. $4a\alpha^1$)
        2. Confession and testimony proper (v. $4a\alpha^2$–b)
            a. Confession of struggle (v. $4a\alpha^2$–aβ)
            b. Testimony of response of Yahweh (v. 4b)
II. Rehearsal of confession of Yahweh's call (vv. 5–6)
    A. Introductory formula (v. $5a\alpha^1$)
    B. Digression concerning Yahweh's call and sustenance (v. $5a\alpha^2$–b)
        1. Call proper (v. $5a\alpha^2$)
        2. Purpose of call (v. 5aβ)
        3. Sustenance proper (v. 5b)
    C. Return to Yahweh's call (v. 6)
        1. Introductory formula (v. $6a\alpha^1$)
        2. Call proper (v. $6a\alpha^2$–b)
            a. Concerning the nation Israel (v. $6a\alpha^2$–aβ)
            b. Concerning the foreign nations (v. 6b)

49. See further Korpel and de Moor, *Hebrew Poetry*, 406–9.

Based on the discussion in the previous chapter, neither this passage nor the final two servant passages are songs. Rather, this unit primarily exhibits the language and imagery of the commissioning of a prophet and king.[50] Verses 1b–2 and 4aα^2 resemble the call of a prophet and in particular the call of Jeremiah. Verse 3 points to the installation of a king that resembles Isa 42:1–4 and Ps 2:7–9.[51] At the same time, the call to the nations in v. 1b and the military language in v. 2 also expresses royal motifs (Isa 1:4; Ps 2:7–9). The reference to פה in v. 2aα combines both aspects of the king and prophet.[52] Further, the call from the womb mirrors the language in Jeremiah's call (Jer 1:5) and also recalls the royal motif found in both Babylonian[53] and Egyptian texts.[54] Thus, this passage draws together the two roles that have been previously applied to Jacob–Israel in chs. 40–48. Verses 5–6 display aspects of a thanksgiving psalm (cf. Pss 30; 116). Begrich categorizes the entire unit as such a psalm (*Danklied*).[55] However, these psalms typically describe or assume a response of action by Yahweh whereas here the speaker responds with a word (see, e.g., Pss 30; 34; 116).[56]

Recognizing both the prophetic and kingly motifs, Melugin concludes that this passage simply imitates "in general the style of the report of a commissioning."[57] Specifically, most interpreters see clear parallels between this passage and the report of Jeremiah's call (Jer 1:4–10).[58]

50. So, e.g., Goldingay, *Isaiah 40–55*; Koole, *Isaiah 3/2*, 4–5; Laato, *Servant of YHWH*, 111–13; Melugin, *Isaiah 40–55*, 70; Williamson, *Variations on a Theme*, 152–54. Some interpreters acknowledge the royal motifs in this passage, but emphasize the prophetic over the kingly aspects (e.g. Elliger, *Verhältnis*, 51; Westermann, *Isaiah 40–66*, 207–8; Whybray, *Isaiah 40–66*, 135–37; Zimmerli and Jeremias, *Servant of God*, 27–28).

51. See Kaiser, *Königliche Knecht*, 53–65; Laato, *Servant of YHWH*, 112–13.

52. Melugin, *Isaiah 40–55*, 70. Kaiser (*Königliche Knecht*, 58) sees the reference to the mouth typical of the activity of the king. In contrast, Muilenburg ("Chapters 40–66," 566–67) emphasizes the prophetic aspect of the mouth.

53. See Paul, "Deutero-Isaiah," 184–86.

54. See Walter Beyerlin, ed., *Near Eastern Religious Texts Relating to the Old Testament* (trans. J. Bowden; OTL; Philadelphia: Westminster, 1978), 27–30.

55. Begrich, *Deuterojesaja*, 55–56, 140–41.

56. See Melugin, *Isaiah 40–55*, 69–70; see also Hans-Jürgen Hermisson, "Der Lohn des Knechts," in *Die Botschaft und die Boten* (Festschrift Hans Walter Wolff; ed. J. Jeremias and L. Perlitt; Neukirchen–Vluyn: Neukirchener, 1981), 270–76.

57. Melugin, *Isaiah 40–55*, 70. Much of what follows was prompted by Roy Melugin's critique and suggestions of my earlier proposal that 49:1–6 is "more of a confessin than a report" ("Speech Act Theory," 222–23).

58. See in particular Willey, *Former Things*, 193–97; for an analysis of the literary links between Jeremiah and the servant passages, see Blank, "Deutero-Isaiah," 28.

Definite similarities between these two passages exist, but there are also significant distinctions. Following N. Habel's genre analysis of a typical prophetic call narrative, Jeremiah's call begins with one of the book's formulaic introductory phrases (e.g. Jer 2:1; 4:11aα, 13aα) and here it functions as the *divine confrontation* (1:4). This is followed by a dialogue that begins with Yahweh's *introductory word* (v. 5a) and then *commission* (v. 5b). Jeremiah, then, reports his *objection* to Yahweh's commission (v. 6) which Yahweh responds to with a *reassurance* of his presence (vv. 7–8) and confirming *sign* (vv. 9–10).[59] In connection with this type of genre, Isa 49:1–6 contains a commission (vv. 1b–3, 5–6), but is missing the other elements which I will discuss in a moment.

Another important aspect of 49:1–6 is the opening lines and specifically the call to the foreign nations. Yahweh has issued a very similar call to the same addressees in 41:1a:

> Listen to me (החרישו אלי) in silence, islands (איים)
> and let the peoples (לאמים) renew strength.

Significantly, these lines are the first summons to "listen" as well as the first description of the Cyrus event (vv. 2–4). In 46:3 Yahweh has also issued a call to Jacob–Israel that is not only reminiscent of the above lines, but it also resembles 49:1:

> Listen to me (שמעו אלי) house of Jacob
> and the whole remnant of the house of Israel!
> Who has been carried since you were born,
> who has been upheld since leaving the womb.

This summons precedes another speech about Yahweh's uniqueness and supremacy in comparison to the idol-gods (see also 46:12–13). Towards the end of the first section, Yahweh calls for Jacob–Israel to "listen to me" (שמע אלי) and again his claim of the Cyrus event (48:12–16). What ties these texts together is the summons and its typical form as well as its placement and the reason for the call.

As touched on above, the summons in 49:1a also has parallels with Ps 2. The psalm speaks of the "nations" (גוים) and the "peoples" (לאמים) (v. 1). The psalm contains various voices speaking with v. 7 uttered by the king. The second colon also resembles 49:3 as the king repeats Yahweh's declarative illocution: אמר אלי בני אתה. Melugin has also observed that the summoning of the nations is common in Israel's hymns (e.g. Pss 96:7–9; 97:1; 117:1). The nations are also summoned in connection with judgment against Israel (e.g. Amos 3:9) and to hear a song (Judg 5:3) or

59. Habel, "Call Narratives," 305–9.

a wisdom teaching (Ps 49:2). Yet, a summoning of the nations in a report of a commissioning only occurs in 49:1–6. Thus, Melugin concludes that Deutero-Isaiah transformed the traditional language of commissioning reports for his own purposes and with v. 1a "he wanted to emphasize that the servant's mission is directed to the nations."[60] Yet, the phrase also directly links the speaker with Yahweh's call to the nations and Jacob–Israel to acknowledge his Cyrus speech act.

Drawing all of this together, in the first servant passage Jacob–Israel is directed to bring justice to the nations (גוים) while the coastlands (איים) wait for its law (42:1b, 4b). Due to the nation's self-imposed inability to fulfill this commission, the servant role becomes open to any and all. In chs. 40–48 Yahweh calls for witnesses and confessors of him alone and by doing so they become his servant. In 49:1–6 such a confession occurs. The fact that the servant role is open, along with the appearance of the ambiguous "I/me" here, strongly suggests that these lines function as a confession. What further supports this claim is that this text does not contain the expected elements of a typical call narrative. Apart from the commission, this passage does not have a divine encounter, an introductory word, an objection, a reassurance, or a confirming sign. Perhaps v. 4a could be seen as an objection, but this is not based in a lack of qualification for the task as with Jeremiah or Moses, or uncleanness with Isaiah ben Amoṣ.[61] Servant Jacob–Israel has uttered its objections to Yahweh (40:27), but the speaker here willingly embraces the open role of Yahweh's servant. Verse 4b is not a reassurance offered by Yahweh, but is rather the speaker's own confession of confident hope in Yahweh. There is no dialogue here, the exchange between Yahweh and the speaker is ultimately expressed solely through the speaker (vv. 3, 6). The absence of the specificity accompanied with the typical divine encounter designating particular individuals for special tasks is especially significant. For Seitz, the one feature that seems inconsistent with "this nearly classic call narrative," "is the lack of a serious, *present* encounter with the divine." "What was said to Jeremiah in direct speech (Jer 1:5) is recollected by this figure using indirect speech (49:1)." Thus, this "unit is not so much the account of a call as a report of one who had been called."[62] Seitz, as well as Melugin, are correct that this text is a report of a commission, but what commission is being reported? The only explicit commission is that which has been issued to Jacob–Israel and the

60. Melugin, *Isaiah 40–55*, 70–71.

61. So also Seitz, "Prophet Isaiah," 234; similarly Melugin, *Isaiah 40–55*, 71.

62. Seitz, "Prophet Isaiah," 233–34.

nations. Yahweh has called these two people groups to be his witnesses to his supremacy as demonstrated in the Cyrus event and thereby embrace the open servant role (43:8–13). As discussed in the previous chapter and in connection with this, Yahweh has addressed Jacob–Israel as a king throughout the first section (cf. 41:8–13). Yahweh has also addressed the people of God as a prophet and commissioned them as well as a prophetic message (40:1–11; 42:19). Further, Yahweh has spoken to Jacob–Israel while mixing both kingly and prophetic phraseology and motifs (e.g. 44:1–5).[63]

In sum, 49:1–6 is a report of a commissioning offered previously, but now embraced afresh by confessors of Yahweh alone. In other words, it is a report of an *open* commission that functions as a confession as the speaker commands the nations to "listen to me"—in the same way Yahweh did earlier to the nations and Jacob–Israel—"as I announce my embracing of the call and commission of Yahweh's servant." Through this utterance the speaker utilizes the conventional language found in chs. 40–48 and other Israelite literature as well as recalls language Yahweh has used for his servant Jacob–Israel. Obviously the one ultimately responsible for this unit would naturally be identified as the speaker/author, but this figure is unnamed and elusive while at the same time the addressee/reader is implored to identify with the servant and self-involvingly become the "I/me." Thus, as Isa 40–55 envisions the people of God comprised of those who confess Yahweh alone, this passage functions as a means whereby that confession is uttered. Thus, this passage is a report of a commissioning offered throughout chs. 40–48, but it dynamically and performatively functions as a confessional acceptance of the open call for the position of Yahweh's servant.[64]

Interpretive Analysis

Verse 1: In the first bicolon, the addressee/speaker calls to those on the islands and coasts of the Mediterranean Sea[65] and exhorts them to listen to *me*. As discussed in the previous chapter, the second bicolon resembles Yahweh's election language for servant Jacob–Israel expressed in terms of יצר, ברא, and בחר (41:8–9; 43:1aβ, 7, 21; 44:2a, 21, 24a; 45:11aβ). Here, the utterers implicitly align themselves with Jacob–Israel through self-involvement by proclaiming that Yahweh has called "*me*." This is explicitly seen in the beginning of ch. 44:

63. On 44:1–5, see Conrad, *Fear Not Warrior*, 90–107.

64. Lindblom (*Servant Songs*, 24) calls this passage "a prophetic confession."

65. *HALOT*, 38.

[1]But now listen Jacob my servant
and Israel whom I have chosen.
[2]Thus said Yahweh,
who made you and who formed you from the womb,
he will help you.
Do nor fear my servant Jacob
and Jeshurun whom I have chosen.

Along with these directive–expressive–commissive illocutions and as discussed above, Yahweh has uttered a number of directive illocutions throughout chs. 40–48 to Jacob–Israel to accept their prophetic and kingly roles (e.g. 40:1–11; 42:1–4, 19; cf. 43:8–13). Here, the speakers embrace Yahweh's directive by confessing the typical language of such roles. The speakers fully identify themselves with Jacob–Israel by confessing Yahweh's expressions about his special relationship with the nation and inferentially the directives as well. Through this self-involved confession, the speakers additionally express a commissive illocution. This dimension is not explicitly expressed in the text, but if this unit is in fact a confession, then, as Evans and Briggs have shown, the commissive force is inherently part of the confessionary utterance. Thus, the confessors adopt the stance and attitude of Yahweh's servant and commit to the extralinguistic obligations and responsibilities assigned to servant Jacob–Israel, which assume the commission issued throughout chs. 40–48 and will be reiterated as well as expanded upon in the following lines. As Briggs discusses, with the strong illocutionary act of confession, the *self* is *involved* in the non-linguistic states of affairs that underwrite the content of the utterance; it is not merely the espousal of an attitude.[66]

The phrase הזכיר שמי has prompted a number of suggestions of the actual name given that typically corresponds to the interpreter's identification of the servant figure, including, "Isaiah," "Moses," "David," etc.[67] The phrase somewhat parallels Yahweh's calling of Cyrus' name in 45:4bα and also Marduk's pronouncing the name of Cyrus found in the Cyrus Cylinder.[68] Most modern interpreters do not identify the person here as "Cyrus." This is primarily based on the fact that Cyrus is clearly distinguished from servant Jacob–Israel in 45:4 and because the Persian king completely disappears from chs. 49–55.[69] The parallel terms קרא

66. Briggs, *Words in Action*, 187.

67. Duhm (*Jesaja*, 331) understands the name as עבד יהוה. However, the term עבד is never used as a name in the Old Testament, only a title.

68. See *ANET*, 315; *COS* 2:315. For the general phrase *zakār šumi*, see *AHw*, 1503–4; *CAD* 21:19–20; *CDA*, 443; Paul, "Deutero-Isaiah," 181–82.

69. Even Blenkinsopp (*Isaiah 40–55*, 299–300), who sees Cyrus as the servant in 42:1–4, does not identify him with the voice in chs. 49–55.

and זכר used here also occur in 48:1. The verbs are employed in the latter verse in a negative way to critique Jacob–Israel's designation as "Israel" because of their idolatry. Thus, the nation is Israel in name only. A similar expression to v. 1b is found in 43:1:

> And now thus said Yahweh,
> your creator, Jacob and your former, Israel.
> "Do not fear for I have redeemed you!
> I called you by your name, you are mine."

In light of all this, the most reasonable name referred to here is "Israel," which becomes explicit in 49:3.

Verse 2: With these lines, the utterer continues to confess his self-involved adoption of the prophetic and kingly roles. Significantly, the weapon of the utterer is "*my* mouth." Correlating with 43:8–13 and 44:6–8, the speakers have already witnessed to themselves about Yahweh's illocutionary act, which in itself adopts the servant role. At the same time, these utterances here entail functioning as Yahweh's servant/prophet by testifying to others that Yahweh alone is God. The speakers also confess Yahweh's commitment to themselves by providing protection for them. The phrase בצל ידו conveys this idea, as the term צל in Isaiah typically indicates "guarding something or someone" (e.g. 4:6; 16:3; 25:4, 5; 30:2, 3; 32:2; 34:15). Further, the Akkadian term *ṣulūlu* conveys this same idea and is used particularly in connection with the protection granted by a god.[70] This phrase only occurs in one other instance in the Old Testament, Isa 51:16a:

> And I have put my words in your mouth
> and in the shadow of my hand I have covered you.

In view of this bicolon, Yahweh's words make the weapon of the mouth like a sharp sword.

Verse 3: With this verse the speaker confesses a multidimensional illocutionary act of Yahweh. As discussed above, this bicolon resembles Ps 2:7bβ. As mentioned in Chapter 2 of the present study, Wagner correctly identifies this clause and עבדי אתה as nominal declarative illocutions.[71] Yahweh's declarative, however, is uttered by the king in the same way the speaker utters the illocution here. In this line, the name

70. *CAD* 16:242–43; *CDA*, 341; *HALOT*, 1025; see further J. Schwab, "צל," *TDOT* 12:372–82 (378–81).
71. Wagner, *Sprechaktanalyse*, 147, 148, 150, 296.

ישראל is best understood as functioning as a predicate with אתה and in parallel to עבדי, and thus should be included as part of the illocution.[72] Williamson suggests that "verse 3 is not a *description* of Israel as the servant (as though Israel were a vocative) but is rather a *designation* of the one addressed as both servant and as Israel." The prophet "is here given a new identity with a new name—or rather, an old name redefined."[73] Williamson points in the right direction as he comes close to the speech act concept that the speaker is declared as Yahweh's servant and Israel. He is also correct that the name is an old one, as Yahweh uses language here that explicitly references earlier statements about Jacob–Israel, for example, אתה ישראל עבדי (41:8aα). However, in view of the suggested prophetic strategy of Isa 40–55 and understanding the language here as a self-involving confession, the speaker is embracing the open position of Yahweh's servant. Thus, Yahweh's declarative does not consist in an old name redefined but an old name adopted by new confessors. The commission is an open call spoken earlier and embraced afresh. It is interesting that the name given is only ישראל—the parallel name יעקב is not included. Perhaps Yahweh is making a distinction between those who are servant Jacob–Israel and those who embrace his servant Israel role anew. Thus, new servant Israel is to restore servant Jacob–Israel (v. 5aβ). The phraseology of this verse further expresses covenant language between Yahweh and his people. Thus, through self-involvement, speakers claim Yahweh as their God while Yahweh claims speakers as his people.

The illocution here is a multidimensional declarative–directive–expressive–commissive expressed through a personal confession. This illocution may be the strongest type of speech act one could possibly utter, as it combines naturally strong illocutions (declarative, directive, and commissive); yet spoken through a personal confession, the utterance becomes even stronger. Although this utterance is a single confession, it contains the expressions of two different speakers. This phenomenon has not been discussed in detail, if at all, by speech act theorists. What occurs here is a type of single interdependent speech act. The utterance's primary mode as a confession makes it a single utterance, but the speaker utters

72. Similarly also Childs, *Isaiah*, 383–85; Delitzsch, *Isaiah*, 2:238; Seitz, "Isaiah 40–66," 429; Wilcox and Paton-Williams, "Servant Songs," 93; Williamson, *Variations on a Theme*, 151.

73. Williamson, *Variations on a Theme*, 151. Wilcox and Paton-Williams follow Williamson's suggestion which he apparently verbally communicated to the authors ("Servant Songs," 92–93, 102 n. 36). Seitz ("Isaiah 40–66," 429) follows Wilcox and Paton-Williams ("Prophet Isaiah," 236). Without referencing anyone Childs comes to the same basic conclusion (*Isaiah*, 384).

something Yahweh has also spoken. Further, the commissive–expressive dimensions take on different nuances as they are expressed through the two different speakers.

This confession begins with a speech formula indicating the speaker and the recipient of the message. The speaker confesses that Yahweh ויאמר לי. The speech formula authorizes the actual message as the word of Yahweh and thus the utterance is a supernatural linguistic performative.[74] At the same time, Yahweh's declarative operates through the extralinguistic institutional authority of Yahweh himself as the creator of Israel that also presupposes the brute fact that he is God. Through Yahweh's supernatural institutional utterance, the confessors create the state of affairs that they *constitute* his servant and Israel. The directive dimension is minimal at this point, but as Yahweh's servant certain entailments are involved, which will become explicit as the passage unfolds. The expressive dimension expresses Yahweh's stance that he is master and the speaker is his servant. Declaring the confessor as Israel and *my* servant means that the speaker constitutes part of Yahweh's own special people. Thus, Yahweh has obligated himself through a self-involved, commissive illocution. Yahweh has not merely attempted to persuade the reader, but, as Steven Davis emphasizes,[75] he has committed himself to his servant in the public, extralinguistic world that has imposed ethical demands upon him to perform his utterance.

For the speakers' part, they confess Yahweh's declarative–directive and thereby adopts the role of Yahweh's servant. Again, the confessors have not simply adopted an attitude, but by confessing the text the speakers *involve* them*selves* in embracing the open servant position. With the expressive dimension the speakers adopt the stance that Yahweh is master and they are his servant. By taking this stance the speaker directly contrasts Jacob–Israel, who has reversed the master–servant roles. The commissive dimension obligates the speakers to fulfill their new adopted extralinguistic responsibilities as Yahweh's servant and Israel.

To review, this verse expresses an interdependent self-involved illocutionary act uttered by Yahweh and the speaker. Both speakers mutually adopt a particular stance and commit themselves to certain entailments. In order for the utterance to operate successfully, each speaker must fulfill the obligations and responsibilities of the illocution. If one of

74. For a discussion on the nature and function of the messenger formula in prophetic writings, see Claus Westermann, *Basic Forms of Prophetic Speech* (trans. H. C. White; Louisville, Ky.: Westminster John Knox, 1991), 98–128.

75. Davis, "Anti-Individualism," 208–19.

the speakers fails in his speech act, then the utterance is infelicitous. This phenomenon is highlighted by Patrick's notion of *performative transactions*. In order for the speakers actually to experience the force of Yahweh's illocutionary act, they must first take a step of faith by embracing the call of the servant. This step puts the onus on Yahweh to fulfill his speech act. The public domain becomes the arena wherein the interdependent self-involved utterance is demonstrated and tested.

Verse 4: This is not a protest, but an expression of the struggle the confessor has and will face as Yahweh's servant. The reason for the difficulties is not explicitly stated but will become clearer in the following verse. Yet, Yahweh's illocutionary act expressed in v. 3 will counteract this opposition. Further, Yahweh's attentive commitment to his servant directly contrasts Jacob–Israel's complaint expressed in 40:27, as emphasized by the particle אכן.

Verse 5: In general, these lines summarize vv. 1–4 while explicitly identifying the task of the speaker. In the first clause following the introductory phrase, the text combines the language of vv. 1b and 3a and the speaker again confesses that Yahweh formed *me* to be his servant. The speaker essentially confesses again, "I am Israel, Yahweh's servant." The entailed extralinguistic assignment expressed by the directive of the confessor's new servant role includes first the restoration of Jacob–Israel. This assignment in part relates to the witness appointment offered to Jacob–Israel: to testify to Jacob–Israel about Yahweh's sovereignty, his sole claim to deity, and his commitment to his people. Chapters 40–48 have made it quite clear, though, that this assignment will be extremely difficult due to Jacob–Israel's self-imposed blindness and deafness.

The last lines recall vv. 3bβ and 4b, which reiterate Yahweh's commitment to those who embrace the role of his servant. Further, the speaker confesses the covenant language of "*my* God" here and in v. 4bβ, which relates to Yahweh's illocution, "you are *my* servant, you are Israel" in v. 3. The final colon also recalls 40:29–31, which expresses Yahweh's promise of sustaining strength to those who קוי יהוה (v. 31aα). Oswalt concludes that the expression "to wait for Yahweh"

> implies two things: complete dependence on God and a willingness to allow him to decide the terms. To wait on him is to admit that we have no other help, either in ourselves or in another. Therefore we are helpless until he acts. By the same token, to wait on him is to declare our confidence in his eventual action on our behalf.[76]

76. Oswalt, *Chapters 40–66*, 74.

As Israel, the speakers put their full trust in Yahweh alone, which contrasts Jacob–Israel's (40:27) and Zion–Jerusalem's stance (49:14). In addition, the utterance entails extralinguistic actions that require the speaker to demonstrate what it means to be true Israel.

Verse 6: In these final lines, Yahweh more fully discloses the responsibilities of the servant task. Verse 6aα is not expressing that the restoration of Jacob–Israel is an easy task, which has been clearly indicated as not the case. Rather, because the speaker is Yahweh's servant, to have the single goal of restoring Jacob–Israel would be trivial or too insignificant, "a rather small-scale responsibility."[77] Further, such an assignment does not resemble the nation's task of old (e.g. Gen 12:1–3; Exod 19:5–6). Thus, in addition to serving Jacob–Israel, the speaker's witness assignment includes the whole world as already laid out in 42:1–9.

In the last bicolon, the entailments of being Yahweh's servant are further expressed with a declarative–directive–commissive illocution. With the declarative dimension, Yahweh creates the institutional fact that the speaker *constitutes* light and salvation to the nations. The directive aspect exhorts the speaker to be and function as his light and salvation. Correlated with v. 3, by confessing Yahweh's declarative, the speaker *constitutes* Yahweh's servant and Israel, his light and salvation. The speaker is transformed by Yahweh's illocutionary act and, as his servant, the speaker has the assignment of operating as his illocution. The commissive dimension is expressed by both Yahweh and the speaker. For Yahweh, the speaker is "*my* servant, *my* light, *my* salvation." For the speaker, the force obligates her/him to fulfill Yahweh's directive. As Yahweh's light and salvation, the speaker transforms the world by embracing the declarative–directive dimensions of his illocution. The speaker is Yahweh's speech act! Yahweh's commissive–declarative–directive illocution is also an interdependent self-involved utterance that *transactionally* depends upon both Yahweh and the speaker to bring about its actualization.

Servant Jacob–Israel was assigned to bring משפט to the nations and teach his תורה (42:1–4). Yahweh's תורה and משפט are light and salvation (51:4–5). Each speaker who self-involvingly adopts the open call of Yahweh's servant is now under the obligation to operate as Yahweh's light and salvation. The confessor will accomplish this by functioning in the roles of both prophet and king. As a prophet, the speaker brings light to those who are blind and in darkness. As a king, the speaker brings justice to those who are oppressed. Specifically, the speaker is to point

77. Goldingay, *Isaiah*, 283.

to Yahweh, the true light (60:1–3, 19–20), the true God, and to his Torah. The speaker is to direct people to Yahweh, the only real savior (45:21–22).

Those who embrace the intended perlocutionary effect of Yahweh's Cyrus speech act do not merely fulfill Jacob–Israel's servant responsibilities on the nation's behalf; rather, they *constitute* Israel, Yahweh's servant. Accordingly, those who embrace Yahweh's call will fulfill the nation's assignment from old. For Childs, the "task that the nation Israel had been given and failed to accomplish (42:1–9) had been transferred, not away from Israel, but rather to one who would *incarnate Israel* (cf. 49:1–6)."[78] The notion of *incarnation* is exactly the goal of the prophetic strategy of Isa 40–55, but Yahweh's call to Jacob–Israel is open to any and all who will embrace being his servant. Through self-involvement with 49:1–6, speakers utter confessional speech acts and thereby incarnate the open position of Yahweh's servant which obligates them to the accompanied extralinguistic responsibilities that entail being his illocutionary act, his light and salvation to Jacob–Israel and the nations.

Isaiah 50:4–11

Translation

4The Lord Yahweh has given to me a tongue of a disciple[a]
for knowing how to help[b] the weary.
With a word[c] he awakens each morning,
each morning[d] he awakens[e] my ear
for hearing as a disciple.[f]
5The Lord Yahweh[g] has opened my ear.[h]
As for me, I have not been rebellious.
I have not turned away.
6I have given my back to those who beat
and my cheeks to those who pull out the hair.[i]
I have not hidden[j] my face from severe humiliation[k] and spitting.
7But the Lord Yahweh sustains me.
Therefore I am not humiliated.
Therefore[l] I have set my face like flint
and I know[m] that I will not be shamed.
8My vindicator is near.[n]
Who will bring an accusation against me?
Let us stand up together.
Who is my accuser?[o]
Let him come forward to me.

78. Childs, *Isaiah*, 394 (italics mine).

[9]Nevertheless, the Lord Yahweh sustains me.
Who is the one who will declare me rebellious?[p]
In fact, all of them wear out like a piece of clothing;
a moth consumes them.
[10]Who among you fears Yahweh,[q]
listens to the voice of his servant?
One who walks in pitch darkness[r] and there is no light for him,
let him trust in the name of Yahweh
and depend upon his God.
[11]However, all of you who kindle a fire,
who gird on flaming torches.[s]
Walk by the light[t] of your fire
and by the flaming torches you have lit!
From my hand this will happen to you:
You will lie down for torment.[u]

a) למודים is a pl. adj. lit. meaning "of ones who are taught." Similar to the MT, the Tg renders דמלפין ("those who teach"). Other Versions render the term as an abstract noun: LXX παιδείας; LXX[A] σοφίας; Vg *eruditam*; Syr *dywlpn*ʾ. Correspondingly, some translators understand למודים as an abstract noun (see GKC §124d, f; e.g., NIV). Others see the pl. form as an indefinite sg. (see GKC §124o) in the same way as Isa 8:16 and 54:13 (e.g. NRSV), while some understand the form as a simple plural (e.g. RSV). The translation here understands למודים as an indefinite sg., but not in the sense that the servant is a disciple of Isaiah. Overall, the point the text conveys is that the servant is in some way identified as a disciple of Yahweh, that is, one who is taught by Yahweh as in 48:17 (so Childs, *Isaiah*, 394; see further Baltzer, *Deutero-Isaiah*, 339–40; Beuken, *Isaiah II/B*, 85–86; Kaiser, *Königliche Knecht*, 69–70; Muilenburg, "Book of Isaiah," 583; Westermann, *Isaiah 40–66*, 228–29).

b) 1QIsa[a] follows the MT לדעת לעות את יעף. עות is a *hapax* which has given rise to multiple emendations (see Frederick E. Greenspahn, *Hapax Legomena in Biblical Hebrew* [SBLDS 74; Chico, Calif.: Scholars Press, 1984], 145–46). *BHS* suggests לרעת ("to teach") or alternatively a form of לעות ("to bend, make crooked") (so Rignell, *Study of Isaiah*, 69; see BDB, 736; *HALOT*, 804). The Tg confirms the former proposal with לאלפא. Korpel and de Moor emend עות to עוד ("to testify") and translate v. 4bα[1] as "to make witnesses" (*Hebrew Poetry*, 448). Rosario P. Merendino completely rejects the phrase לעות את יעף as authentic because ידע is followed by the prep. ל in only one other instance (Exod 36:1) and so דבר becomes the object of לדעת ("Allein und einzig Gottes prophetisches Wort: Israels Erbe und Auftrag für alle Zukunft [Jesaja 50:4–9a:10)," *ZAW* 97 [1985]: 344–66 [350–51]). It is possible to view the term as deriving from לעה or לעע related to the Arab *laġā*. De Boer suggests this and translates "to speak fluently" (*Second-Isaiah's Message*, 53; followed by Kaiser, *Königliche Knecht*, 67; Henk Leene, *De Stem van de Knecht als Metafoor: Beschouwingen over de Compositie van Jesaja 50* [Kampen: Kok, 1980], 5, 37 n. 43; so also apparently Beuken as he translates the term with *spreken* [*Jesaja II/B*, 79]). However, both the Heb and Arab terms convey speaking in an incomprehensible way (see Job 6:3; Prov 20:25; see further *HALOT*, 533; Hans

Wehr, *A Dictionary of Modern Written Arabic* [ed. J. M. Cowan; 4th ed.; Wiesbaden: Harrassowitz, 1979], 1021). This connotation obviously does not fit well in this context (so Koole, *Isaiah 3/2*, 107) which is also the problem of the alternative suggestion of *BHS*. The LXX renders ἐν καιρῷ ("in time"), which must have understood עות as from the noun עת. Duhm (*Jesaia*, 341–42), Westermann (*Isaiah 40–66*, 225), and Günther Schwarz ("Jesaja 50:4–5a," *ZAW* 85 [1973]: 356–57) understand the LXX translating the term ענת ("to answer"). In Aram עות means "to help" and the Arab cognate *ġwṯ* has the same meaning, but is derived from the root עוש (Joel 4:11; see BDB, 736; *HALOT*, 804). As with the majority of recent translators, the most probable understanding of לעות is "to help, sustain," which makes sense in this context and finds support with α′ ὑποστηρίσαι and Vg *sustentare*.

c) The MT ends v. 4a with דבר with the typical translation "...to help the weary with a word." Perhaps the Masoretes placed the *atnaḥ* under דבר because of their uncertainty of יעיר as evidenced by the *paseq* following it, which some translators understand as an indicator to delete יעיר (cf. *BHS*; see further Elliger, *Verhältnis*, 28–29). Following the MT, 1QIsa[a] has a ו after דבר and renders the two lines ויעיר בבוקר בבוקר ויעיר לי אוזן. Likewise, the Tg understands דבר as the object of יעף with דמשלהן לפתגמי אוריתיה חוכמא ("who faint for the words of his law"). The LXX translates דבר as the object of an infinitive which is modifying the finite verb of the clause: Κύριος δίδωσιν μοι γλῶσσαν παιδείας τοῦ γνῶναι ἐν καιρῷ ἡνίκα δεῖ εἰπεῖν λόγον ("the Lord gave to me a tongue of instruction to know in time when it is necessary to speak a word"). Building on the work of S. E. Loewenstamm ("The Expanded Colon in Ugaritic and Biblical Verse," *JSS* 14 [1969]: 176–96) and Y. Avishur ("Addenda to the Expanded Colon in Ugaritic and Biblical Verse," *UF* 4 [1972]: 1–10), P. van der Lugt argues for the validity of the MT structure ("De Strofische Structuur van het derde Knechtslied [Jes. 50:4–11]," in Grosheide et al., eds., *De Knecht: Studies rondom Deutero-Jesaja*, 102–17 [110–12]). He identifies a so-called "expanded colon" in v. 4b with three stitches as in Pss 77:17; 92:10; 93:3; Prov 31:4 Cant 4:9; Hab 3:8 (p. 111; also endorsed by Koole, *Isaiah 3/2*, 109; Leene, *Knecht als Metafoor*, 37–38 n. 43). Overall, this poetic observation belongs to the general category of climactic or staircase parallelism (see Watson, *Hebrew Poetry*, 150–56) and can be seen here; but still this suggestion does not provide sufficient reasons for following the MT accents. Furthermore, ending v. 4a with יעף produces more symmetrical cola throughout, with vv. 4–5aα producing a chiasm (see below). Thus, דבר is understood here as an adverbial accusative (see *IBHS* §10.2.2; *GBH* §126).

d) The LXX renders ἔθηκέν μοι πρωΐ ("he sets me up in the morning"), but does not include the second prep. phrase which *BHS* suggests to follow. However, α′ supports the MT with ἐγείρει ἐν πρωΐᾳ ἐν πρωΐᾳ ἐξεγείρει μοι ὠτίον (see Barthélemy, *Critique Textuelle*, 370–71) as also 1QIsa[a], Vg, and Tg. Despite this support, the repetition of בבקר בבקר is a common idiomatic construction for expressing a distributive idea (see *IBHS* §7.2.3b). Thus, בבקר בבקר conveys the notion of "morning by morning," that is, each and every morning (e.g. Isa 28:19; see *HALOT*, 151–52; see further Beuken's discussion in *Jesaja II/B*, 80, 87; see also Werner Grimm and Kurt Dittert, *Deuterojesaja: Deutung—Wirkung—Gegenwart* [CBK; Stuttgart: Calwer, 1990], 361–62). The repeating of the prep. phrase also nicely balances v. 4bα.

e) For the repeated verb יעיר the LXX renders ἔθηκέν…προσέθηκέν. According to Ottley (*Book of Isaiah*, 336), the LXX read each time עלה ("placed, offered").

f) Understanding כלמודים in the same way as v. 4a. The Vg has *magistrum* ("master, teacher") instead of repeating *eruditam*.

g) 1QIsa[a] has אלוהים instead of יהוה.

h) Either the repetitious nature or lack of parallel colon has caused some translators to consider the line secondary (*BHS*; North, *Second Isaiah*, 201; Whybray, *Isaiah 40–66*, 152) or a parallel line has been lost (Westermann, *Isaiah 40–66*, 225). However, the colon links to the preceding cola with the repetition of לי אזן and leads into what follows (see van der Lugt, "Strofische Structuur," 113; see also Koole, *Isaiah 3/2*, 110). Further, the colon completes the chiasm of vv. 4–5aα.

i) למרטים has posed semantic difficulties. The LXX translates εἰς ῥαπτυσμάτων ("for blows"), which parallels the previous phrase εἰς μάστιγας ("for lashes"). Similarly Syr has *lswqpʾ* ("to strike, beat"). 1QIsa[a] renders the MT as למטלים which Kutscher finds difficult to explain and asserts that both the LXX and Syr did not know the term in the MT (*Isaiah Scroll*, 255–56; for possible derivatives see Koole, *Isaiah 3/2*, 112). Guillaume suggests that the two liquids often interchange with subsequent metathesis. Guillaume further relates מטל to the Arab *maraṭa* and *malaṭa*, which are synonymous for "hairlessness" ("Scroll of Isaiah," 43). Joh. Hempel derives למטלים from the Ugraitic *ṭll* ("to fall" [*fallen*]) ("Zu Jes 50₆," *ZAW* 76 [1964]: 327). Following G. R. Driver's suggested Arab cognate *maṭala* ("beat metal") ("Hebrew Scrolls," *JTS* 2 [1951]: 17–30 [27]; see also BDB, 564) and in contrast to Kutscher, Robert Gundry concludes that both the LXX and Syr follow 1QIsa[a], understanding the root as מטל ("to beat, smite"), which he sees Mark 14:65 alluding to ("למטלים I Q Isaiah a 50,6 and Mark 14,65," *RevQ* 2 [1960]: 559–67). Jean Carmignac proposes that סטר, in essence meaning "to slap" (*gifler*), is the actual term behind מטל and also 1QIsa[a], Syr, and LXX ("Six passages d'Isaïe éclairs par Qumran," in *Bibel und Qumran: Beiträge zur Erforschung der Beziehungen zwischen Bible-und Qumranwissenschaft* [ed. S. Wagner; Berlin: Evangelische Aupt-Bibelgesellschaft, 1968], 37–46 [44–46]). Despite all these suggestions, the MT makes sense if למרטים is understood to derive from מרט ("to pull out *hair*") especially in syntagmatic relationship with לחי (cf. Ezra 9:3; Neh 13:25; see *HALOT*, 635). This meaning is supported by the Tg למרטין ("pluck out"), Vg *vellentibus* ("pull, pluck out"), Akk *marāṭu* ("to scratch, scrape off") (*AHw*, 610; *CAD* 10:276–77; *CDA*, 197) and the Arab *mariṭa/maraṭa* ("to tear out one's hair") (*HALOT*, 634–35; Wehr, *Written Arabic*, 1060).

j) 1QIsa[a] renders הסירותי from סור ("turn away"), which is supported by the LXX ἀπέστρεψα, Vg *averti*, and Syr *ʾpnyt*. But the Tg supports the MT with טמריה. According to Kutscher, due to the phrase הסר פנים found in 2 Chr 30:9, the LXX, and 1QIsa[a], it seems that there was a tendency during the Second Temple Period to substitute הסר פנים for הסתר פנים (*Isaiah Scroll*, 268). In the final analysis, there is not much difference between the MT and 1QIsa[a] et al.

k) מכלמות is a pl. noun, but is understood here as a plural of intensity (see GKC §124d, e; *GBH* §136f; so Beuken, *Jesaja II/B*, 80; Goldingay, *Isaiah 40–55*; Koole, *Isaiah 3/2*, 112; *pace* Oswalt, *Chapters 40–66*, 321 n. 29). The LXX translates the two nouns מכלמות ורק as a prep. phrase ἀπὸ αἰσχύνης ἐμπτυσμάτων ("from shameful spitting").

l) The LXX renders the second על־כן with ἀλλὰ thus making the last two lines dependent upon v. 7aβ. For Duhm, the LXX read a כי here, which for him is a better understanding and construction of these cola (*Jesaia*, 343). However, 1QIsa[a], Vg, Tg, and Syr all confirm the MT.

m) Waltke and O'Connor translate the verb ואדע ("for I know"), thus understanding the *wayyiqtol* following the *qatal* שמתי having a perfective value along with introducing a causal clause dependent upon v. 7aβ (*IBHS* §33.3.1b). Korpel and de Moor also see v. 7bα introducing a causal clause, but also see another causal clause in v. 7aα. This understanding is further supported by the particles forming a chiasm ו–על־כן–על־כן–ו (*Hebrew Poetry*, 448). Goldingay rejects Waltke and O'Connor's suggestion and translates the colon as "I knew I would not be shamed." Rather than seeing the colon as dependent upon the previous line, Goldingay understands the last three cola as results of the first colon. Further, due to the past tenses in lines 7aβ and 7bα, this last colon should also be understood in the past (*Isaiah 40–55*; so also P. P. Saydon, "The Use of Tenses in Deutero-Isaiah," *Bib* 40 [1959], 290–301 [298]). Goldingay's understanding that the last three cola are dependent upon v. 7aα is correct. Further, the suggestion that ואדע introduces a causal clause is difficult to affirm. However, the *yiqtol* in v. 7aα and the overall context suggest the ongoing experience of the speaker. In addition, ידע is often used like a stative verb expressing a state of mind in the present (cf. *GBH* §112a). Further, v. 7bα seems to convey the speaker's ongoing response whenever this experience would arise, since v. 7bβ conveys the present and future conviction about Yahweh's sustaining power especially indicated by the *yiqtol* in v. 7bβ[2] (see further Beuken, *Jesaja II/B*, 90; Koole, *Isaiah 3/2*, 116; Merendino, "Gottes prophetisches Wort," 356–57; Motyer, *Prophecies of Isaiah*, 400).

n) This verse with its short opening colon followed by four parallel cola portrays a ABCB'C' structure which van der Lugt has identified as a pattern in chs. 40–55 (41:17; 43:25–26; 44:8). This pattern is also utilized in other instances with the messenger formula ([כי]כה אמר [אדני/האל] יהוה) functioning as the opening line (42:5, 43:14–15, 16–18; 44:24; 45:1, 11, 14, 18; 49:8, 22, 24–25; 50:1) ("Strofische Structuur," 113–14).

o) בעל משפטי lit. means "master of my judgment," which refers to one who has raised a legal case against someone, that is, a legal adversary (*HALOT*, 651; see also Isa 41:1; also Exod 24:14; Job 31:35). The phrase *bēl dīni* also occurs in Akk texts to convey the idea of an adversary or opponent in court (*CAD* 3:155–56; *CDA*, 42; see also *AHw*, 119).

p) Labuschagne understands הן here as an interrogative extending to v. 9a ("Particles," 9); however, the parallel הן beginning v. 9b makes this suggestion difficult to adopt (so also Koole, *Isaiah 3/2*, 119).

q) There have been numerous suggestions on how v. 10 should be understood syntactically. Essentially three issues arise here: (1) the function of מי in the initial bicolon; (2) the division of the verse and the function of אשר in v. 10bα[1]; and (3) the impf. verbs in the final bicolon. Regarding מי, the question involves whether it functions as an indefinite pronoun (GKC §137c) or as an interrogative. If taken as the former, then one is compelled to follow the LXX and emend the ptc שמע in the following colon to a juss. ישמע (so Blenkinsopp, *Isaiah 40–55*, 318; Duhm, *Jesaia*, 343–44; Elliger, *Verhältnis*, 29; Morgenstern, "Suffering Servant," 310; for the suspect nature of the LXX here see R. W. Corney, "Isaiah L 10," *VT* 26 [1976]: 497–98). As with the majority of translators, the most natural way of taking the particle is as an interrogative; yet, as Goldingay notes, מי also doubtlessly functions rhetorically as an indefinite (*Isaiah 40–55*). The relative pronoun אשר has also been viewed in different ways which also impacts the syntax of the verse as a whole. Looking at the division of the verse, the MT places the *atnaḥ* at the end of the first bicolon, which may suggest that אשר begins a new clause that is joined to v. 10bβ[1] with the interrogative clause ending at v. 10a. 1QIsa[a] begins as the MT, but uses the pl. יראי in the initial colon, which is likely due to the pl. כולם in v. 9bα. The following colon has the ms ptc. שומע, but the Scroll then returns to the pl. again הלכו, which may also indicate a new clause with v. 10bα. The syntax here presents Yahweh as the one listening to the voice of his servant (see John V. Chamberlain, "The Functions of God as Messianic Titles in the Complete Qumran Isaiah Scroll," *VT* 5 [1955]: 366–72 [372]). It is possible that the MT text could be read this way, but such an understanding does not correspond with vv. 4–5aα and, as Goldingay points out, it is not suggested that listening is Yahweh's business between Isa 1:15; 30:19; 37:4, 17; 38:5 and 59:1–2; 65:24 (*Isaiah 40–55*). As noted above, the LXX begins the verse with the interrogative τίς followed by the juss. ἀκουσάτω. The second line also seems to begin a new clause as it switches from the sg. to the pl. οἱ πορευόμενοι ("the ones who walk"). This clause is then followed by two impv. verbs also in the pl. πεποίθατε ("trust")...ἀντιστηρίσασθε ("rely"). The Vg follows closely the MT, which begins with the interrogative *quis* followed by the relative pronoun *qui* in v. 10bα and in the final colon two juss. verbs *speret* ("let him trust")...*innitatur* ("let him lean"). The Tg translates v. 10 as single interrogative sentence, but in typical fashion pluralizes the servant: דשמע בקל עבדוהי נביייא ("who listen to the voice of his servants the prophets"). The division of the verse in the MT hinges on the function and the antecedent of אשר, either עבדו or מי בכם. 1QIsa[a], LXX, and the Tg clearly distinguish the addressees as the antecedent. Further, the focus of this verse in the MT is not on the speaker who has already claimed to fear, listen, trust, and lean on Yahweh, but on those who choose to fear Yahweh and listen to his servant. Thus, אשר must refer to מי בכם (cf. W. A. M. Beuken, "Jes 50 10–11: Eine kultsche Paränese zur dritten Ebedprophetie," *ZAW* 85 [1973]: 168–82 [170–74]; idem, *Jesaja II/B*, 97–98; *pace* Muilenburg, "Book of Isaiah," 587–88; Rignell, *Study of Isaiah*, 71; Seitz, "Isaiah 40–66," 438; Torrey, *Second Isaiah*, 393). Concerning the function of אשר, there are several ways it has been understood (see specifically Beuken, "Jes 50 10–11," 174–75): as a relative pronoun extending the interrogative throughout the verse or to v. 10bα[2]; as an indefinite pronoun beginning a new clause; introducing an independent relative clause (see GKC §138; *IBHS* §19.1d, 3c); or as a conditional/temporal particle. The latter three are preferred due to the division indicated in the MT, 1QIsa[a], and the LXX along with the impf. verbs in the final bicolon, which are, as with most translators, best thought as juss. (cf. LXX and Vg). It is possible to see אשר as a relative pronoun with simple *yiqtol* verbs in the last bicolon (cf. de Boer's translation [*Second-Isaiah's Message*, 29–30]); however, the RSV and NRSV felt it necessary to insert the adversative "yet" at v. 10bβ[1] in order to make sense of the verse (so also Muilenburg, "Chapters 40–66," 587; see though Baltzer's translation [*Deutero-Isaiah*, 338]).

r) Understanding חשׁבים as a plural of intensity (so also Goldingay, *Isaiah 40–55*; Koole, *Isaiah 3/2*, 127).

s) The MT has here מאזרי which is a Piel mp ptc. from אזר ("put on, gird oneself, equip"; cf. Isa 45:5; BDB, 25; *DCH* 1:172), with זיקות as its direct object (see Beuken, "Jes 50 10–11," 175), which is read by a number of translators. *BHS* suggests reading with the Syr *mgqzly* a Hiphil mp ptc. מאירי from אור ("make light"; so also, e.g., RSV; NRSV; *HALOT*, 28). The LXX similarly translates with κατισχύετε ("you overpower"). This emendation makes good sense here, but is not the more difficult reading. Further, 1QIsa[a], 1QIsa[b], Vg *accincti* ("gird, equip"), and the Tg מתקפי ("who grasp") confirm the MT (see Barthélemy, *Critique Textuelle*, 371–73). The object of the ptc. זיקות in the MT is a *hapax* which 1QIsa[a] and 1QIsa[b] again support. The LXX translates with φλόγα ("flame"), Vg *flammis* ("fire, flame"), and the Tg חרב ("sword"). Akk helps here with *zīqtu*, *zīqu* II ("torch, flame"; *AHw*, 1532; *CAD* 21:133–34; *CDA*, 448). The understanding of זיקות as "flaming torch or arrow, firebrand, lightning flash" makes sense as it parallels אשׁ in v. 11aα and is in syntagmatic relationship with בער in v. 11bα[2], which indicates that זיקות is something that is lit by fire (see BDB, 278; *DCH* 3:102; *HALOT*, 268). Thus, the MT is retained with the phrase מאזרי זיקות functioning metaphorically (so Korpel and de Moor, *Hebrew Poetry*, 449; see further Rignell, *Study of Isaiah*, 71–72).

t) The LXX τῷ φωτὶ, Vg *in lumine*, and Syr *bzhrʾ* read באור as "by/in the light of." The MT אור is lit. "flame," but in syntagmatic relationship with אשׁ, the sense is essentially the same (see *DCH* 1:161; see also Barthélemy, *Critique Textuelle*, 373).

u) למעצבה derives from the *hapax* עצב II ("hurt, pain"; *HALOT*, 865). The LXX reads ἐν λύπῃ ("in sorrow, affliction"); Vg *in doloribus dormietis* ("in sorrowful sleep"); Tg לתקלתכון תתובון ("to your stumbling you shall return"). Waltke and O'Connor note that the מ prefix (*IBHS* §5.6b) can be used in substantives of location as in "place of torment" (e.g. *DCH* 5:410; *HALOT*, 615), or instrumentally as "in/for torture, torment," or in abstraction as "in pain." Either of these translations makes sense, while the ל prefix seems also to indicate purpose or result here.

Structure and Genre

The Servant Song paradigm designates 50:4–9 as the actual Song with vv. 10–11 as a later supplementary addition.[79] Interpreters are still divided on whether or not vv. 10–11 belong to vv. 4–9.[80] The MT has a פ and a space after 50:3 and a ס and a space following v. 11. 1QIsa[a] concurs with this division by beginning a new line after v. 3 and after v. 11. The scroll

79. See Duhm, *Jesaja*, 341–44.

80. On the division among the Versions, see Korpel and de Moor, *Hebrew Poetry*, 449. Westermann (*Isaiah 40–66*, 233–34) goes so far as to relocate vv. 10–11 to follow 51:1a due to the fact that each of the first two Servant Songs have a secondary addition relating to the particular passage followed by a hymn of praise. Verses 10–11 provide a similar addition, but there is no hymn to round off the section. This suggestion again is based in Westermann's assumptions of typical patterning, but does not find any support among the Versions nor from many interpreters, if any.

also has a small space between v. 9 and v. 10, but it does not appear to be indicating a separate unit. Prior to these verses, 49:14–50:3 concerns Zion–Jerusalem while an unidentified "I/me" appears in 50:4–9 that naturally corresponds to the voice in 49:1–6. Verses 10–11 confirm that this voice refers to Yahweh's servant (v. 10aβ). Thus, vv. 4–9 depend upon vv. 10–11 and, as Melugin asserts, vv. 10–11 depend upon vv. 4–9.[81]

The obvious division of the passage falls into two sub-units: (I) a first person speech (vv. 4–9) and (II) Yahweh's speech (vv. 10–11). The first section is connected by the refrain אדני יהוה occurring in vv. 4aα^{1}, 5aα, 7aα, 9aα.[82] A division occurs between vv. 6 and 7[83] as (A) Lord Yahweh teaches the speaker in vv. 4–6 and (B) Lord Yahweh provides help for the speaker in vv. 7–9. In detail, the structure of the unit can be seen as follows:

I. Confession of Yahweh's provision and sustaining power (vv. 4–9)
   A. Confession of provision for teaching and listening and the speaker's response (vv. 4–6)
      1. Yahweh's dual provision and purpose for the speaker (vv. 4–5aα)
         a. First provision and purpose (v. 4a)
            1) Provision of a disciple's tongue (v. 4aα)
            2) Purpose of helping the weary (v. 4aβ)
         b. Second provision and purpose (vv. 4b–5aα)
            1) Provision of opening of the ear (v. 4bα)
            2) Purpose of hearing Yahweh's teaching (v. 4bβ)
            3) Restatement of provision (v. 5aα)
      2. Response to Yahweh (vv. 5aβ–6)
         a. General response of not rebelling against Yahweh's demand (v. 5aβ–b)
         b. Specific response of embracing suffering (v. 6)
            1) Physical suffering (v. 6aα)
            2) Psychological suffering (v. 6aβ–b)
   B. Confession of confidence in Yahweh (vv. 7–9)
      1. Yahweh's sustenance for enduring acts of shame and humiliation (v. 7)

81. Melugin, *Isaiah 40–55*, 73. Those who see vv. 4–11 forming a unit include, among others, Baltzer, *Deutero-Isaiah*, 338–39; Blenkinsopp, *Isaiah 40–55*, 319; Kaiser, *Königliche Knecht*, 67–68; Goldingay, *Isaiah*, 289; F. Duane Lindsey, "The Commitment of the Servant in Isaiah 50:4–11," *BSac* 139 (1982): 216–29 (216–18); McKenzie, *Second Isaiah*, 115–16; Mettinger, *Servant Songs*, 33–34; Motyer, *Prophecy of Isaiah*, 398; Willey, *Former Things*, 211–14; van der Lugt, "Strofische Structuur," 102–17.

82. See Rosenbaum, *Word-Order Variation*, 40–41, 206–7.

83. So, e.g., Beuken, *Jesaja II/B*, 82–85; Goldingay, *Isaiah*, 289–91; Koole, *Isaiah 3/2*, 104; Motyer, *Prophecy of Isaiah*, 398–401; van der Lugt, "Strofische Structuur," 106–9.

a. Confession of confidence proper (v. 7aα)
b. Dual result (v. 7aβ–b)
1) Confession of confidence (v. 7aβ)
2) Empowerment to continue enduring shameful acts (v. 7b)
a) Resolve (v. 7bα)
b) Confession of trust (v. 7bβ)
2. Dual confession about Yahweh the vindicator (vv. 8–9)
a. First confession (v. 8)
1) Yahweh the vindicator is near (v. 8aα^{1})
2) Two rhetorical calls for any accuser to step forward (v. 8aα^{2}–b)
b. Second confession (v. 9)
1) Yahweh sustains the speaker (v. 9aα)
2) Rhetorical call to present an accusation against the speaker (v. 9aβ)
3) The transitiveness of the speaker's accusers (v. 9b)
II. Yahweh's call to fear him and listen to his servant (vv. 10–11)
A. Call proper (v. 10a)
B. Two alternative responses to Yahweh's call (vv. 10b–11)
1. First response (v. 10b)
a. Identity of the addressees (v. 10bα)
b. Response proper: Trust and depend on God (v. 10bβ)
2. Second response (v. 11)
a. Response proper: Providing one's own light (v. 11a–bα)
b. Warning (v. 11bβ)

Begrich understands vv. 4–9 as an individual "lament psalm" (*Klagelied*).[84] Although these verses contain similar expressions as the laments, the typical plea for help and thanksgiving for Yahweh's expected intervention are absent here (see, e.g., Pss 13; 22; 86). Elliger, followed by others, suggests that vv. 4–9 is an individual "psalm of confidence, trust" (*Vertrauenspsalm*).[85] A substantial amount of correspondence between these verses and the psalms of trust exists (e.g. Pss 31; 35). There are also parallels between vv. 4–9 and Jeremiah's confessions.[86] As such, this section further correlates with 49:1–6.[87] In general, vv. 10–11 constitute a speech of Yahweh.[88] It is not uncommon for Yahweh to refer to himself in the third person in these chapters (e.g. 41:16, 20; 42:19); yet,

84. Begrich, *Deuterojesaja*, 54–55.

85. Elliger, *Verhältnis*, 34; so also Kaiser, *Königliche Knecht*, 67–69; Melugin, *Isaiah 40–55*, 72; Westermann, *Isaiah 40–66*, 226–27.

86. See Westermann's display of parallels between vv. 4–9 and some of Jeremiah's confessions (*Isaiah 40–66*, 227–28).

87. As with 49:1–6, Lindblom (*Servant Songs*, 32) also calls this "a prophetic confession."

88. So, e.g., Delitzsch, *Isaiah II*, 257; Goldingay, *Isaiah*, 291; Koole, *Isaiah 3/2*, 122; Melugin, *Isaiah 40–55*, 72.

the term מידי in v. 11bβ[1] explicitly indicates that he is the speaker here. The speech is a type of announcement of judgment that expresses an implicit promise to those who fear Yahweh and an explicit warning to those who do not choose to trust him.

Interpretive Analysis

This passage continues the confession of the previous servant passage. However, the election and covenant language expressed in 49:1–6 are absent from these lines. The speaker has already confessed Yahweh as his God and embraced the role of his servant. At the same time, Yahweh has declared his commitment to the speaker. Isaiah 50:4–9 focus on the relationship between Yahweh and his servant that is based on their previous interdependent self-involved speech acts. Specifically the speaker confesses the additional extralinguistic responsibilities as Yahweh's servant along with a confessional stance of trust in his faithfulness while facing opposition.

Much of the content of these verses uses similar language in Yahweh's "fear not" speech to Jacob–Israel in 41:8–16. The verb עזר occurs twice here (vv. 7aα, 9aα) and three times in ch. 41 (vv. 10bα, 13bβ, 14bα). Thus, Yahweh's promises to "help, sustain" Jacob–Israel are applied to those who self-involvingly adopt the servant role. Yahweh's intervention is needed to sustain servant Jacob–Israel (41:11–12) and this servant/speaker (vv. 6–9) in the midst of opposition. Another important link occurs with the verb בוש. Yahweh assures Jacob–Israel that their opponents will be shamed and eventually perish. The speakers here confess their confidence that their attackers as well will be shamed (v. 7), fade away, and disappear (v. 9b).

Verses 4–5aα: The refrain אדני יהוה occurs several times in chs. 40–55 (40:10aα; 48:16bα; 49:22aα[1]; 51:22aα[1]; 52:4aα). The names also appear in parallel in Zion–Jerusalem's complaint (49:14). The dominant use of the refrain in the Old Testament occurs in prophetic speeches and particularly in the messenger formulae.[89] Hence, the phrase is especially associated with the authority of the word of God.[90] Apart from ch. 50, the contexts of the refrain in Isa 40–55 concern Yahweh's promised deliverance for his people linking it to the authority of Yahweh's word and saving power. This use nicely transfers to the context of 50:4–9 with Yahweh's teaching his word to his servant and the speaker's confidence in Yahweh's sustaining power.

89. See Otto Eissfeldt, "אדון," *TDOT* 1:59–72 (62–63).
90. Terence E. Fretheim, "אדוני," *NIDOTTE* 1:275.

In 50:4–5aα, the self-involved speaker testifies to Yahweh's illocutionary acts uttered in 49:3, 6 and their responsive extralinguistic actions. The language here recalls Yahweh's critique of self-blinded and deafened Jacob–Israel, whose "ears are open but refuse to hear" (42:20b). It also references Yahweh's assertion that Jacob–Israel has not "heard" and that their "ear has not been opened" until now concerning the Cyrus event (48:8a).

Werner Grimm and Kurt Dittert identify in these lines a chiasm and a *Hysteron-proteron-Figur*.[91] The latter structure indicates a chronological inversion—"later earlier"—and thus the testimony functions in reverse order.[92] Hence, in proper chronological sequencing, Yahweh opens the ear in order for the disciple to teach his words. Yet, the chiastic or concentric structure,[93] along with the distributive expression בבקר בבקר, conveys that this is not a one-time experience but is the daily routine of both Yahweh and the speaker. The concentric structure can be seen as follows:

A אדני יהוה נתן לי לשון למודים
B לדעת לעות את־יעף
C דבר יעיר
D בבקר
D' בבקר
C' יעיר לי אזן
B' לשמע כלמודים
A' אדני יהוה פתח־לי אזן[94]

As an ongoing experience, the disciple learns and teaches, teaches and learns, learns and teaches, teaches and learns, etc. With this testimony, the speakers also confess that they are disciples of Yahweh, which involves an expressive–commissive illocution. Thus, the speakers adopt the attitude and stance of disciples (expressive) and obligate themselves to the extralinguistic behavior of listening attentively to Yahweh and teaching his words (commissive). The term למוד also occurs in 54:13a in reference to the descendents of Zion–Jerusalem, who are also identified as Yahweh's servants (54:17). The disciples of Yahweh are those who have embraced Yahweh's call to servanthhood.

Yahweh's awakening the servant with a דבר correlates with how Yahweh often reveals himself and specifically delivers his message to his prophets. This is especially true of Jeremiah since the book focuses on the

91. Grimm and Dittert, *Deuterojesaja*, 359.
92. Schökel, *Hebrew Poetics*, 186.
93. See Watson, *Hebrew Poetry*, 187–90.
94. For another possible chiastic structure, see Goldingay, *Isaiah 40–55*.

דבר יהוה (e.g. 1:4; 16:1; 18:1). Again the speaker expresses his adopted role as a prophet. Those who the disciple/servant teaches are the יעף, which points to Jacob–Israel (49:5–6), who are also explicitly identified as the "weary" (40:29). Further, it is the idol-maker who grows "weary" in his work (44:12bβ). Thus, the speaker will teach idolaters about the supremacy of Yahweh and will exhort them to entrust themselves in him alone.

Verses 5aβ–6: Following the above responsibilities of Yahweh's servant, the speakers testify to the additional extralinguistic obligations of being Yahweh's servant. Specifically, the entailment of a disciple/servant includes a complete and unalterable commitment to their master, Yahweh.

The text here does not clearly identify the servant's opponents. Jacob–Israel is expected to resist the message of Yahweh's servant/prophet. This reaction corresponds to Israel's typical opposition to Yahweh's prophets: for example, Elijah (1 Kgs 18:1–19:8), Micaiah (1 Kgs 22:1–28), Hanani (2 Chr 16:7–10), Amos (7:10–17), Zechariah son of Jehoiada (2 Chr 24:20–21). As in the case of these prophets, the resistance was often severe and violent, which characterized Jeremiah's experience (e.g. Jer 1:19; 20:2; 37:15). The attackers could also include Jacob–Israel's captors, who will be overthrown by their prisoner's deliverer. This correlates with those who oppress Jacob–Israel in 41:11–12. Nevertheless, some Babylonians may have eagerly welcomed the arrival Cyrus.[95] Ironically, Jacob–Israel is not expected to be pleased with Yahweh's appointed deliverer (45:9–13). Because of the text's silence, it seems best to understand the opponents of the speaker in a general sense as those who resist the word of Yahweh and thus his messenger.

Regarding the descriptions of violence, a person found guilty of a crime in Israel could be beaten (Deut 25:2–3). As noted above, the prophets were also often beaten and thrown in prison. Pulling out the beard and spitting in the face were used in institutionalized settings within Israel to express anger and shame (Neh 13:25; Deut 25:9; see also Num 12:14). However, such expressions could also be employed by anyone to communicate contempt of another (Job 17:6; 30:10). In addition, the

95. According to the Cyrus Cylinder, upon the arrival of the Persian king, "All the people of Babylon, all the land of Sumer and Akkad, princes and governors, bowed to him and kissed his feet. They rejoiced at his kingship and their faces shone. Ruler by whose aid the dead were revived and who had all been redeemed from hardship and difficulty, they greeted him with gladness and praised his name" (*COS* 2:314–16 [315]; for another translation see *ANET*, 315–16 [316]).

experiences portrayed here correspond to those expressed by the innocent sufferer in certain psalms of lament and confidence (e.g. Pss 22; 31; 35). The difference between these psalms or even between Jeremiah's confessions (e.g. Jer 11:18–20; 15:15–18; 18:19–23; 20:7–18) and this passage is that the speaker does not utter any protest but unreservedly embraces the suffering.

The text makes explicit that physical and psychological suffering constitutes part of the entailments of being Yahweh's servant. Through self-involvement, the reader expresses the further obligations of the commissive–expressive illocution uttered above and in 49:1–6. The commissive dimension entails the speaker's extralinguistic commitment to Yahweh, which is publicly demonstrated in uncontested suffering and dependence on Yahweh. The expressive dimension conveys the stance that Yahweh is the one and only God in whom they place their trust.

Verse 7: Here the speakers confess their confidence in Yahweh's sustaining power in the face of aggressive acts of opposition. Goldingay identifies another Hysteron-proteron in v. 7aβ–b conveying the chronological order of knowing, setting, and not being humiliated.[96] Thus, the confidence of the speaker is grounded in knowing Yahweh and trusting in his commissive illocutions. The speaker's confidence in Yahweh provides the resolve for the speaker not to hide *my* face and rather set *my* face to embrace future acts of pain and humiliation.

Verses 8–9: These lines depict a courtroom scene that recalls the earlier trial passages in chs. 40–48. The speakers confess their utmost confidence in Yahweh, "*my* vindicator." Further, the speakers confess their complete reliance upon Yahweh by essentially expressing again, "*my* judgment is with Yahweh" (49:4bα). For the speakers, Yahweh is the chief witness, the one they expect to defend their innocence regarding their level of commitment. The speakers are so confident that they utter three rhetorical questions with the self-implied answer that no one will step forward and offer evidence against them. As discussed above, rhetorical questions contain an assertive and interrogative dimension. The speakers here utter a strong self-involving assertive–expressive illocution that asserts that they have fully adopted the stance of total obedience to and dependence upon Yahweh. The utterance is an intersubjective public illocution. By voicing these rhetorical questions the speakers willingly expose themselves to public critique. The speakers call listeners either to confirm their assertion or present evidence contrary to their claim.

96. Goldingay, *Isaiah 40–55*.

The acts of violence and shame in v. 6 are directly linked to these verses. The reason for the reaction to the speaker is based on the stance taken as a disciple and servant of Yahweh. On a number of occasions the Old Testament concept of shame is associated with guilt. Consequently, interpreters tend to view בוש solely as the result of a person failing to achieve a particular goal and thus the avoidance of shame is one's own responsibility.[97] Most interpreters recognize that in this context the acts of aggression are unwarranted but they often emphasize the servant's experience in these terms.[98] Margaret S. Odell brings a balance to this tendency.[99] Without dismissing the obvious link between shame and guilt, Odell demonstrates that shame is also related to the idea of dependence or trust. In other words, shame is experienced as the result of betrayal of trust. Odell examines בוש and its Akkadian cognate *ba'āšu* in particular secular and ritual texts and concludes that the experience of shame is due to the failure of the one trusted. In theological contexts, "both the Mesopotamian and biblical literature describe the individual's relationship to the personal god as one of trust and dependence which results in the petitioner's protection of shame." It is divine abandonment, then, that brings about shame.[100]

From the Old Testament, Odell finds support for her thesis in Ps 22, which has a number of motifs that relate to this servant passage. Following the psalmist's complaint (vv. 2–3), he expresses confidence in Yahweh by referring to his ancestors' trust in him and the fact that ultimately they were not "shamed" because of this stance (vv. 4–6). The psalmist expresses that his experience of gestures of shame are based on his suffering condition, which is due to the absence of God (vv. 7–9). Following this, he confesses his confidence in Yahweh once again (vv. 10–11). Based on his assurance, the psalmist cries out:

> 12 Do not be far from me,
> for trouble is near (קרובה);
> for there is no other helper (עוזר).

The psalmist continues by describing his dire situation (vv. 13–19), cries out again for Yahweh, his helper, to not be far away (vv. 20–22), and concludes with thanks and praise (vv. 23–32). In this lament, the psalmist

97. See, e.g., Horst Seebass, "בוש," *TDOT* 2:50–60 (52–53).

98. See, e.g., Motyer, *Prophecy of Isaiah*, 400; Westermann, *Isaiah 40–66*, 230–32.

99. Margaret S. Odell, "An Exploratory Study of Shame and Dependence in the Bible and Selected Near Eastern Parallels," in Younger, Hallo, and Batto, eds., *The Biblical Canon in Comparative Perspective*, 217–33.

100. Ibid., 228.

confesses his complete dependence upon and trust in Yahweh and, for Odell, what "is mocked is precisely the psalmist's professed reliance on God" (v. 9).[101] Odell is correct in one sense, but the origin of the mocking must be based in the typical assumption that the suffering is because of sin, which is the reason for God's distance (cf. Job). Thus, it is the apparent guilt confirmed by the psalmist's sickly state that brings about the initial mocking (v. 7). The speaker's confessional trust in Yahweh adds *insult to injury*, as it prompts further mocking. Ultimate shame will occur if Yahweh remains absent from the psalmist, which will confirm the mocker's humiliating gestures. This is evidenced by the ironic, sarcastic tone of the mockers' utterance in v. 9.

Before drawing any conclusions, it will be beneficial also to examine the term בוש in Isa 40–55. The verb occurs eleven times and primarily in the first section. In brief, those who will be shamed are Jacob–Israel's opponents (41:11aα), the worshipers and manufacturers of idol-gods (42:17aα [2×]; 44:9bβ, 11aα, 11bβ; 45:16a), and those who deny that Yahweh alone is God (45:24bα). The ones who will not be shamed are those who "wait" (קוה) on Yahweh (49:23bβ). Further, Israel (45:17bα) and Zion (54:4aα) will not be shamed because Yahweh will restore his people in Jerusalem. In light of all the above, those who put their trust in idol-gods and not in Yahweh will experience the ultimate divine betrayal and thereby shame. In contrast, the speakers here are confident that they will not be shamed because Yahweh, unlike idols, is truly divine. The rhetorical questions call for anyone to find evidence against the speaker's innocence. But, in this context, any proof of wrongdoing is based on whether or not the speaker remains committed to Yahweh. Thus, the suffering and shame is derived from the speaker's association with and total trust in Yahweh. The aggressive reaction the speaker experiences confirms the opponent's assumption that Yahweh has abandoned him, which, in turn, encourages further mocking. In the face of such suffering, the speaker confesses his/her confidence in Yahweh with the hope that he/she will not be shamed because אדני יהוה יעזר־לי and he/she knows that his/her advocate is קרוב.

In sum, these verses display the entailments of the mutual self-involvement between the speaker and Yahweh. Yahweh is the master in this relationship while the speaker is his servant/disciple. The entailment of Yahweh's self-involvement includes teaching his servant and sustaining them through and ultimately delivering them from suffering. The entailments of the speaker's self-involvement include maintaining the position

101. Ibid., 227.

of a servant/disciple who listens to their master and then teaches his words. Further, Yahweh's disciple/servant is to expect and embrace opposition and suffering, but all the while remaining confident in Yahweh's commissive illocution.

Verses 10–11: With these verses Yahweh addresses again the second masculine plural audience which continues through 51:8. Those who comprise this group are identified as ones who walk in darkness and have no light. As already discussed above, this second masculine plural addressee most often refers to Jacob–Israel. Further, the nation walks in darkness, but, ironically, has access to the light of Yahweh and his law. Yahweh also promised earlier that he will lead the blind and make darkness into light before them (42:16). However, those who place their trust in idols will be shamed (v. 17). The idolatrous nations also exist in darkness and do not have any light. Thus, Yahweh issues a general call here to all those among Jacob–Israel and the nations.[102]

Yahweh exhorts individuals among the second masculine plural audience to adopt the role of his servant. To ירא יהוה means to confess sole allegiance to Yahweh, which entails obedience to his commands (e.g. Deut 6:10–25; 10:12–13).[103] Parallel to this phrase, Yahweh calls to those who שמע בקול עבדו. The phrase שמע בקול accompanied by a genitive of קול is a common construction in the Old Testament with the voice most often associated with a living person or being (e.g. Num 21:3aα; Deut 8:20b; 13:19aα; 21:18aβ). In Isa 40–55, the term קול occurs eight other times. It is used for Zion to raise her "voice" (40:9aβ[1]) and for her watchman to raise their "voice" (52:8 [2×]) to proclaim Yahweh's return to Zion. It is also used twice in reference to the "sound" of rejoicing (48:20aα[2]; 51:3bβ;). The noun occurs in ch. 40 twice and refers to the "voice" of the two unidentifiable speakers (vv. 3aα, 6aα). The other occurrence is found in the first servant passage: ולא־ישמיע בחוץ קולו (v. 2b). The servant will not make his voice heard in the streets; it must be listened to attentively.[104] In sum, when קול is used in reference to an

102. Similarly, e.g., Beuken, "Jes 50 10–11," 170–74; idem, *Jesaja II/B*, 95–101; Childs, *Isaiah*, 396; Koole, *Isaiah 3/2*, 125, 128; Motyer, *Prophecy of Isaiah*, 401. Other interpreters understand the 2mp addressee in v. 10 as Jacob–Israel and the 2mp addressee in v. 11 as those who attack the prophet (e.g. Goldingay, *Isaiah*, 291; Whybray, *Isaiah 40–66*, 153–54). With the above discussion on the servant's attackers and the fact that the 2mp addressee most often indicates Jacob–Israel, it seems impossible from a literary standpoint to distinguish two different groups here.

103. See H. F. Fuhs, "ירא," *TDOT* 6:290–315 (297–303, 306–15).

104. See Motyer, *Prophecy of Isaiah*, 320.

entity or being, it is typically anonymous as with the עבד role in the servant passages. Thus the phrase קול עבדו is functionally ambiguous.

In general, the verb שמע means "to listen" to words with one's ears. Yet, often to שמע means "to act" in response to something said (e.g. Deut 11:26–28; 28:1–2, 15; 30:17, 20; 1 Sam 15:22).[105] Further, in certain instances when the terms שמע and ירא function together, they indicate that to "hear and fear" means to comprehend the unpleasant outcome of a particular action while taking the appropriate actions to avoid the same fate (e.g. Deut 13:12; 17:13; 19:20). To listen to the voice of the servant here means to obey the words that Yahweh has taught his disciple, which is naturally his Torah (42:4b). To obey Yahweh's Torah is to acknowledge Yahweh alone. Thus, to ירא יהוה and שמע בקול עבדו is to embrace the position and entailments of Yahweh's servant. At the same time, to "listen to" this voice is to recall Yahweh's summons to the nations and Jacob–Israel to fear him alone (41:1–4; 46:3–13; 48:12–16). In addition, it involves recognizing this servant's adoption of the open call confessed in 49:1–6. The voice of the servant, then, is simultaneously identifiable and open. The voice belongs to those who have adopted the role of Yahweh's servant. Yet, at the same time, the servant position is not filled by any one person, and consequently the open voice anticipates additional self-involved incarnation.

With vv. 10–11 Yahweh utters a multidimensional declarative–assertive–directive illocution to the second masculine plural addressee. The assertive–directive dimension both exhorts and warns the addressee. As an exhortation, Yahweh calls the addressee to adopt the role of the servant (assertive), which thereby leads them to put their full trust in Yahweh alone (directive).[106] With this aspect, Yahweh also utters an implicit directive promise of his presence to accompany those who walk in the darkness (43:16). The warning aspect points to potential judgment (assertive), which prompts the addressee to take the appropriate action prescribed to those who fear Yahweh (directive). The declarative dimension aims at the future consequences of torment. This dimension depends upon the action taken by the addressee. If the warning is heeded, then the assertive–directive dimension finds success as well as the declared promise of his presence. If it is not heeded, then Yahweh will actualize the declarative dimension.

105. See H. Schult, "שמע," *TLOT* 3:1375–80.

106. On the close relationship between the assertive and directive forces, especially with warnings, see Searle and Vanderveken, *Illocutionary Logic*, 202–3.

Isaiah 52:13–53:12

Translation

13 There, my servant[a] will achieve success,[b]
he will be exalted, be lifted up and be very high.[c]
14 Just as[d] many were appalled about you,[e]
so his appearance was marred[f] beyond[g] that of any person,
and his form beyond that of humankind.[h]
15 So he will sprinkle[i] many nations,
Because of him kings will shut their mouths.
For what had not been told to them they will have seen
and what they had not heard they will have understood.
1 Who could have believed what we have heard?
And upon whom has the arm of Yahweh revealed itself?[j]
2 How he grew up[k] like a young plant[l] before him[m]
and like a root out of dry ground.
He had no form or majesty[n] so that we should look at him
and he had no appearance so that we should desire him.[o]
3 He was despised and most frail of human beings,[p]
a man of severe pains[q] and knowing[r] sickness.
And as when ones hide their faces from someone,[s]
he was despised[t] and we did not consider him.
4 Yet unexpectedly,[u] he himself bore our sicknesses
and our severe pains, he carried them.[v]
Whereas we ourselves considered him touched violently,
struck by God[w] to be humbled.[x]
5 But he was wounded[y] because of our rebellions,
crushed because of our iniquities.
The chastisement for our wholeness was upon him[z]
and by his wounds comes healing to us.
6 All of us like sheep have wandered off,
each person, we have turned, to his own way.
Yet, Yahweh laid upon him the iniquity of us all.[aa]
7 He was oppressed, but he[bb] submitted himself.[cc]
And he would not open his mouth.
Like a lamb led to slaughter
and like a ewe before its shearers is silent
and he would not open his mouth.[dd]
8 By an unjust sentence[ee] he was taken away,
but who would contemplate with his generation[ff]
that[gg] he was cut off from the land of the living,
because of the rebellion of my people,[hh] a violent touch to him;[ii]
9 how one appointed[jj] his grave with the wicked,
and in his tragic death[kk] with the rich;[ll]
although[mm] he had done no violence
and no deceit with his mouth?

10 But[nn] Yahweh set out to crush him,[oo]
whom he made sick.[pp]
When[qq] his life is placed[rr] as a reparation offering,
he will see descendents,[ss]
he will lengthen days[tt]
and the purpose of Yahweh will succeed by his hand.
11 Because of the suffering of his life
he will see[uu] and be satisfied.
By his knowledge[vv] the righteous one,[ww] my servant,[xx]
will bring righteousness for the many;
he himself bears their guilt.
12 Therefore, I will make apportion[yy] to him with the many
and the mighty he will apportion as spoil,
in return for the fact that[zz] he poured out his life to the death
and he let himself be counted with rebels.
When he himself carried the sin[aaa] of many
and will continue to intercede[bbb] for the rebels.[ccc]

a) Following עבדי, the Tg adds משיחא ("the messiah"). All the other Versions support the MT.

b) ישכיל is a Hiphil impf. 3ms. 1QIsa[a] follows the MT while the Tg renders יצלח ("he will prosper, succeed"). Mitchell Dahood identifies God as the subject of ישכיל and repoints the following colon to produce divine appellatives for God: "Behold the Exalted and Sublime and Most Lofty will prosper his servant" ("Phoenician Elements in Isaiah 52:13–53:12," in *Near Eastern Studies* [Festschrift William F. Albright; ed. H. Goedicke; Baltimore: The Johns Hopkins University Press, 1971], 63–73 [65]; see also idem, "Hebrew-Ugaritic Lexicography III," *Bib* [1965]: 311–32 [323]). The other Versions use terms conveying the idea of "understanding": LXX συνήσει; α′ ἐπιστημονισθήσεται; Vg *intelleget*; Syr *mstkl*. Torrey (*Second Isaiah*, 415) translates the term as the proper name of the servant, "The Wise One." Morgenstern ("Suffering Servant," 313) emends to ישקל "he is suspended, he is hanging." G. R. Driver also adopts this emendation, but translates "he will be bound" based on the Akk *šakkīlu* and Arab *šakala* ("Isaiah 52$_{13}$–53$_{12}$: The Servant of the Lord," in *In Memoriam Paul Kahle* [ed. M. Black and G. Fohrer; BZAW 103; Berlin: Töpelmann, 1968], 90–105 [90]). Both these interpreters understood the line to convey suffering, but this view neither corresponds to the following colon nor finds any support with the Versions. The term שכל in the Old Testament describes a person who understands (Isa 44:18; Jer 9:23) and is wise (Prov 15:24). This wisdom or insight, then, naturally leads to and in fact produces success (cf. Josh 1:8; Jer 10:21; see M. Sæbø, "שכל," *TLOT* 3:1269–72; see also *HALOT*, 1328–29).

c) The LXX translates this colon with only two verbs καὶ ὑψωθήσεται καὶ δοξασθήσεται σφοδρα ("and he will be lifted up and greatly glorified"; followed by Georg Fohrer, "Stellvertretung und Schuldopfer in Jes 52$_{13}$–53$_{12}$," in *Studien zu alttestamentlichen Texten und Themen [1966–1972]* [BZAW 155; Berlin: de Gruyter, 1981], 26; Wilson, *Nations in Deutero-Isaiah*, 290). 1QIsa[a], Vg, and Tg all support the MT along with 1QIsa[b] (but transposes the final two verbs). For discussions on the

LXX and the renderings of α′, θ′, and σ′ in relation to the MT, see Otfried Hofius, "Zur Septuaginta-Übersetzung von Jes 52,13b," *ZAW* 104 (1992): 107–10.

d) Verses 14–15a present some syntactical difficulties. The main issue here concerns the function of כאשר in the first colon and the two repeated כן particles in vv. 14aβ and 15aα. Due to meter and content, Duhm suggested that v. 14aβ originally belonged at the end of 53:2 (*Jesaia*, 355–56; so also Sigmund Mowinckel, *He That Cometh: The Messiah Concept in the Old Testament and Later Judaism* [trans. G. W. Anderson; Nashville: Abingdon, 1956], 196 n. 3; for similar suggestions see *BHS*; Blenkinsopp, *Isaiah 40–55*, 345; Driver, "Isaiah 52$_{13}$–53$_{12}$," 103; Marco Treves, "Isaiah LIII," *VT* 24 [1974], 98–108 [103, 106–7]; Westermann, *Isaiah 40–66*, 254; Whybray, *Isaiah 40–66*, 169). Wilson follows Duhm's suggestion, but also omits כאשר and כן in v. 15aα (*Nations in Deutero-Isaiah*, 290). However, any relocation, supplementation, or omission is not necessary and does not have any support from the Versions (see further Childs, *Isaiah*, 412). Dahood retains the MT verse order and understands v. 14aα to be subordinate to v. 13 and translates כאשר as "though" and understands each כן emphatically "truly" ("Phoenician Elements," 65). Dahood's understanding of כאשר is rare, if it functions at all this way. Morgenstern understands כאשר temporally, reading "even while," and as the protasis of v. 14aβ–b, but does not translate the first כן. He translates כן in v. 15aα and apparently as the result of v. 14aβ ("Suffering Servant," 313). כאשר can function temporally (see *GBH* §166n; *IBHS* §38.7a), but, as Morgenstern shows, כן then becomes difficult to incorporate (p. 298). The most common way the Old Testament indicates a comparison is through the pairing of כאשר in the protasis and כן in the apodosis (*GBH* §174a, b; cf. *IBHS* §38.5a; see Gen 41:13; Isa 31:4). Further, כאשר can be in the protasis of a comparison with two apodoses, each introduced by כן (e.g. Exod 1:12; Josh 11:15). In a similar way here, and with the majority of recent translators, כאשר in v. 14aα is the protasis with a double comparative apodosis introduced by כן, which governs v. 14aβ and v. 15aα (see M. J. Mulder, "Die Partikel כן im Alten Testament," in van der Woude, ed., *Remembering All the Way…*, 201–27 [222–23]; *pace* Delitzsch, *Isaiah* 2:282–83; F. Duane Lindsey, "The Career of the Servant in Isaiah 52:13–53:12," *BSac* 139 [1982]: 312–29 [316–17]; Oswalt, *Chapters 40–66*, 379 n. 80). Meterically, though, as Goldingay (*Isaiah 40–55*) observes, v. 14aα finds its pair in v. 15aα, while a complete bicolon comprising v. 14aβ–b intervenes, thus producing a ABB'A' pattern.

e) Two Hebrew MSS, Syr and, although quite different, the Tg read a 3ms pron. עליו ("about him"), which is adopted by a large number of translators. Dahood ("Phoenician Elements," 65) also sees a 3ms suffix here as he divides עליך to עלי ("at him"). However, 1QIsa[a], LXX, and Vg confirm the MT. Coupled with this support and the fact that the MT constitutes the more difficult reading, this alternating back and forth between personal pronouns is not uncommon in Hebrew poetry (cf. GKC §144p; see Isa 42:20; 45:8, 21; 61:7). Marjo C. A. Korpel demonstrates that this switching of person is perfectly normal in North West Semitic poetry ("Exegesis in the Work of Ilimilku of Ugarit," in *Intertextuality in Ugarit and Israel* [ed. J. C. de Moor; OTS 40; Leiden: Brill, 1998], 86–111 [cf. 99]; see also Lénart de Regt, "Person Shift in Prophetic Texts: Its Function and Its Rendering in Ancient and Modern Translations," in de Moor, ed., *The Elusive Prophet*, 214–31). Thus, the servant is the antecedent of the 2ms suffix.

f) The noun משחת only occurs in the Old Testament here, but most likely derives from שחת ("to ruin, spoil") 1QIsa[a] has משחתי derived from משח ("to anoint"; see, e.g., D. Barthélemy, "Le grand rouleau d'Isaïe trouvé près de la Mer Morte," *RB* 57 [1950]: 530–49 [546–47]; idem, *Critique Textuelle*, 387–90; Kutscher, *Isaiah Scroll*, 262). Driver, on the other hand, sees the י on משחת as simply a *ḥireq compaginis* (see GKC §90k–n), which he claims is common to 1QIsa[a] ("Isaiah 52$_{13}$–53$_{12}$," 92; so also Blenkinsopp, *Isaiah 40–55*, 347 n. 1). Guillaume connects the term to the Arab *masakha* and not *masaḥa* and translates "I mar" ("Scroll of Isaiah," 41–42). Yehuda Komlosh suggests that the origin of the term משחת in 1QIsa[a] is the Aram מִשְׁחָא and so the scroll should be emended to משחתו ("his stature") and read for the MT ("The Countenance of the Servant of the Lord, Was it Marred?," *JQR* 65 [1974–75]: 217–20; see also BDB, 602–3). The Versions in one way or another support the MT: 1QIsa[b] משחת; LXX ἀδοξήσει; Vg *inglorius*; Tg חשוך; Syr *mḥbl*. Morgenstern emends the MT to a Niphal ptc. נשחת ("to become marred, deteriorate, decay"; "Suffering Servant," 314; so also Baruch Levine, "René Girard on Job: The Question of the Scapegoat," *Semeia* 33 [1985]: 125–33 [128]; Mowinckel, *He That Cometh*, 197). Based on one MS and the Babylonian tradition, *BHS* suggests to emend the MT to a Hophal ptc. מָשְׁחָת ("spoiled, ruined"; see BDB, 1008; *HALOT*, 1472), which is followed by many translators. Goldingay reads משח here since it is unclear which meaning, "anoint" or "ruin," was original (see also Jean Koenig, *L'Herméneutique Analogique du Judaïsme Antique d'Après les Témoins Textuels d'Isaïe* [VTSup 33; Leiden: Brill, 1982], 370–71). Goldingay observes that outside this text there are no other references to either anointing or ruining someone's look or appearance. It is quite possible, as William H. Brownlee claims, that the author here could have had both meanings in mind as in Dan 8:24–25 and 9:24–27 ("The Servant of the Lord in the Qumran Scrolls. I," *BASOR* 132 [1953]: 8–15 [10–15]; see also idem, "Certainly Mašaḥti!," *BASOR* 134 [1954]: 27–28). The real problem, as Goldingay concedes, is the syntactical difficulty of the comparison made between the appalment and marring. Ruining and then appalling might work, but the reverse does not (*Isaiah 40–55*). If "anoint" is understood here, the question arises: How is an appearance anointed? (cf. Joseph Reider, "On *Mšḥty* in the Qumran Scrolls," *BASOR* 134 [1954]: 27–28). Further, the immediate context (v. 14aβb) along with the entire poem (cf. 53:3–5, 7) express severe suffering, not anointing (see James Barr, *Comparative Philology and the Text of the Old Testament* [Oxford: Clarendon, 1968], 285). Still, as Goldingay points out, the anointing of the servant parallels the account of David's anointing as a person beautiful in appearance and a man of good looks (1 Sam 16:12–13, 18; Ps 89:19–20, 50–51; see also Grimm and Dittert, *Deuterojesaja*, 408–9). Further, anointing fits the priestly dimension of this poem (Goldingay, *Isaiah 40–55*). All in all, the MT משחת understood as either a noun or verbal form from שחת (see North, *Second Isaiah*, 228) makes sense in this context (see *DCH* 5:519) and has dominant support among the Versions and is the choice among most translators. A possible way of combining the two ideas of anointing and marring is if anointing constitutes suffering that distinguishes and enables the servant to accomplish his kingly/priestly task.

g) The prefixed מן could be functioning instrumentally (Dahood, "Phoenician Elements," 65), but most translators understand the prep. as conveying some type of comparison (*pace* Koole, *Isaiah 3/2*, 270). It is taken here to express the idea of separation (see GKC §119w–z) and more specifically in a negative comparative/superlative way (see GKC §133c; *IBHS* §11.2.11e; so Blenkinsopp, *Isaiah 40–55*, 347 n. m; Goldingay, *Isaiah 40–55*).

h) Lit. מבני אדם ("beyond that of the sons of man"). 1QIsa[a] has מבני האדם while the LXX has the pl. ἀπὸ ἀνθρώπων.

i) יזה is a Hiphil impf. 3ms and most naturally from נזה I, which is used to convey the "spattering, sprinkling, splashing" of blood, water, or oil onto people or certain objects (see Exod 29:21; Lev 5:9; 8:10–11, 30; 16:14; BDB, 633; *DCH* 5:648–49; *HALOT*, 683). Because of the semantic domain of this term, a number of different emendations have been put forward. For instance, *BHS* suggests יִזּוּ ("they sprinkle"; so de Boer, *Second-Isaiah's Message*, 34, 112), יִרְגְּזוּ ("they are excited/agitated"; see BDB, 919; so G. F. Moore, "On יזה in Isaiah LII. 15," *JBL* 9 [1890]: 216–22; Elliger, *Verhältnis*, 6; Hans-Jürgen Hermisson, "Das vierte Gottesknechtslied im deuterojesajanischen Kontext," in *Der leidende Gottesknecht: Jesaja 53 und seine Wirkungsgeschichte* [ed. B. Janowski and P. Stuhlmacher; FAT 14; Tübingen: J. C. B. Mohr (Paul Siebeck), 1996], 1–25 [6]; Torrey, *Second Isaiah*, 416), or יִבְזָהוּ ("they despise"; see BDB, 102; so Jacob Leveen, "יזה in Isaiah LII. 15," *JJS* 7 [1956]: 93–94). Other suggestions include יָזוּחוּ ("they are excited/worked up"; so Fohrer, "Stellvertretung," 27; Ernst Kutsch, "Sein Leiden und Tod—unser Heil: Auslegung von Jesaja 52,13–53,12," in *Kleine Schriften zum Alten Testament* [ed. L. Schmidt and K. Eberlein; BZAW 168; Berlin: de Gruyter, 1986], 169–96 [172, 176]), ירגזו...עליו ("are perturbed at him"; Wilson, *Nations in Deutero-Isaiah*, 290–91), יֶחֱזָהוּ ("kept staring"; Morgenstern, "Suffering Servant," 314), or יזהרו/יזהר ("will be enlightened"; Treves, "Isaiah LIII," 106–7). Nevertheless, the suggestion most often adopted by recent translators is the *hapax* נזה II from the Arab *nazā* ("to spring, leap"; see BDB, 633) and typically translated as "startle" or "astonish." Despite the term being a *hapax*, it is a stretch additionally to claim that נזה II can mean "startle, astonish" (so Goldingay, *Isaiah 40–55*). Regarding the Versions, the LXX lends support to this suggestion with θαυμάσονται ("they will be amazed") The Tg has יבדר ("he will scatter") and similarly σʹ has ἀποβαλεῖ ("he will remove"). In the same way, Th. C. Vriezen sees the servant making many nations retreat in great fear ("The Term *Hizza*: Lustration and Consecration," in *Oudtestamentische Studiën 7* [ed. P. A. H. de Boer; Leiden: Brill, 1950], 201–35 [204]; so also Gerleman, "Gottesknecht," 40). Similarly, and in contrast to the LXX, Beuken (*Jesaja II/B*, 186, 203) sees a negative reaction as he translates v. 15aα: "so he will bring many nations into confusion" (*zo zal hij vele volken in verwarring brengen*). Despite these suggestions, 1QIsa[a] agrees with the MT, which also finds support from αʹ and θʹ ῥαντίσει ("he will sprinkle"); Vg *asperget* ("he will sprinkle"); Syr *mdkʾ* ("purge, purify"; see Smith, *Syriac*, 253). The main objection to translating נזה I here is that the verb does not have its usual object (type of liquid) + prep. phrase indicating what the object is splashed on. However, נזה I can be used without a prep. phrase (e.g. Lev 4:6, 17). Although no liquid is discussed, the servant is clearly depicted in terms of a sacrifice. Thus, the absence of typical syntactical elements is not enough to emend the text or choose a *hapax* and so נזה I is read, a reading which has support among the Versions and is followed by a large number of translators (see cf. Barthélemy, *Critique Textuelle*, 386–87, 394–95; E. J. Young, "The Interpretation of יזה in Isaiah 52:15," *WTJ* 3 [1941]: 125–32).

j) For v. 1b, most translators render as "and to/upon whom has the arm of Yahweh been revealed?" The verb נגלתה is a Niphal impf. 3fs with the subject זרוע יהוה. As a manifestation of Yahweh, if the verb is understood passively then someone else besides Yahweh himself is uncovering or displaying his arm. Thus, it is better to take the verb in a reflexive/causative sense (so also Goldingay, *Isaiah 40–55*).

k) ויעל is an epexegetical *wayyiqtol* that begins to answer the question issued in v. 1 (see GKC §111d; *IBHS* §33.2.2; *GBH* §118j). Thus, the following depiction of the servant constitutes the content of לשמעתנו and the disclosure of זרוע יהוה.

l) כיונק is a כ + Qal act. ptc. from ינק ("to suck"; see BDB, 413). יונק can indicate a suckling child (1 Sam 15:3; 22:19) or a young child (e.g. Deut 32:25; Isa 11:8). The Syr translates as the former with *ynwdʾ* (see Smith, *Syriac*, 192). α′ τιθῄιζόμενον and θ′ θηλάζον understand the term here indicating a suckling child along with the LXX, but renders the line quite differently from the MT: ἀνηγγείλαμεν ἐναντίον αὐτοῦ ὡς παιδίον ("we announced before him as a child"). However, other Versions understand יונק referring to a plant or branch: σ′ κλάδος ("branch"); Vg *virgultum* ("plant"); Tg כלבלבין דפרן ("as buds which sprout"). As with these translations, יונק can figuratively mean "shoot, sprout" in the Old Testament (e.g. Ezek 17:22; Hos 14:7; Ps 80:9–12). Thus, with the parallel term שרש ("root") and both terms linked to the prep. phrase מארץ ציה, it seems best, as with most translators, to understand the term in such a way (see further H. Ringgren, "ינק," *TDOT* 6:106–8 [108]).

m) *BHS* suggests reading לפנינו for לפניו and is followed by a few scholars; however, this emendation has no support from the Versions and is unwarranted. Wilson emends the prep. to the adj. לבן ("pale") to parallel the following colon (*Nations in Deutero-Isaiah*, 291). A more radical emendation has been offered by Günther Schwarz who claims that לפניו was misread for מפנה and thus the translation "…like a shoot from a battlement" ("'…wie ein Reis vor ihm'?," *ZAW* 83 [1971]: 255–56). Both these emendations have no textual support. Reading the MT, Driver suggested that לפניו is reflexive "before himself" and means here "grew straight up" ("Linguistic and Textual Problems: Isaiah I–XXXIX," *JTS* 38 [1937]: 36–50 [48]) which is followed by D. Winton Thomas ("A Consideration of Isaiah LIII in Light of Recent Textual and Philological Study," *ETL* 44 [1968]: 79–86 [81]; so also North, *Second Isaiah*, 229). R. P. Gordon further supports Driver's earlier thesis with additional Syr parallels ("Isaiah LIII 2," *VT* 20 [1970]: 491–92), which Leslie C. Allen later affirms ("Isaiah LIII 2 Again," *VT* 21 [1971]: 490). However, these suggestions are unnecessary and have not found much support among recent translators. In fact, Driver later retracted his earlier proposal and translated לפניו as "in his sight" ("Isaiah 52:13–53:12," 103). De Boer (*Second-Isaiah's Message*, 113–14) translates לפניו as "by itself," as does Beuken with *voor zich alleen* (*Jesaja II/B*, 187, 210–11) to convey the idea of the plant being alone, independent, and vulnerable, which nicely parallels the following colon and agrees with the preceding 3ms pronouns in 52:13–15. However, as with the majority of translators, the most natural way to understand the prep. לפניו is as "before" in a local sense (see *IBHS* §11.3.1a; *HALOT*, 941–42) with Yahweh in 53:1b as the explicit and immediate antecedent of the 3ms suffix. This is confirmed by α′ πρόσωπον αὐτοῦ and θ′, σ′ ἐνώπιον αὐτοῦ.

n) Following σ′, *BHS* rightly suggests moving the *atnaḥ* from הדר to ונראהו, which most translators follow (*pace* Gerleman, "Gottesknecht," 40; Korpel and de Moor, *Hebrew Poetry*, 546; Oswalt, *Chapters 40–66*, 374; Hans W. Wolff, *Jesaja 53 im Urchristentum* [Giessen: Brunnen, 1984], 19).

o) *GBH* understands the two verbs in this bicolon as indirect cohortatives (§116c).

p) The phrase וחדל אישים is difficult to translate. The MT חדל is an adj. in the construct. Most translators have understood the phrase as a subjective genitive "rejected/abandoned by men." The adj., though, in its other instances conveys an active idea rather than a passive. The verb חדל I generally means "cease" or "refrain" (BDB, 292–93; *HALOT*, 292) and so Thomas suggests that the adj. here means "leave, forsake" and translates "shunning the company of men" ("Isaiah LIII," 82; see also idem, "Some Observations on the Hebrew Root חדל," in *Congress Volume Strasbourg 1956* [ed. G. W. Anderson et al.; VTSup 4; Leiden: Brill, 1957], 8–16 [11–12]; so also Driver, "Isaiah I–XXXIX," 48–49; idem, "Isaiah 52$_{13}$–53$_{12}$," 92–93, 103; Clines, *I, He, We, and They*, 16; North, *Second Isaiah*, 64). But this idea does not correspond to the actions ascribed to the speaker in 49:1, 6, and 50:4–6. Ringell (*Study of Isaiah*, 80; see also BDB, 293), followed by Mettinger, translates the phrase "lacking men," which conveys the idea of the nation Israel as a reduced and insignificant group (*Servant Songs*, 40). This translation is possible, if one understands the servant here as collective Israel. Yet, Motyer similarly translates as " 'lacking in' adherents," with the individual servant the object of scorn (*Prophecies of Isaiah*, 428). Philip J. Calderone proposes a *hapax* adj. חדל meaning "fat" extending to "stupid, senseless" ("Supplementary Note on *ḤDL*-II," *CBQ* 24 [1962]: 412–19), which Dahood follows with the translation "He was despised as the most stupid of men" ("Phoenician Elements," 64, 66). However, as Goldingay rightly concludes, Calderone's suggestion seems to build speculation on speculation (*Isaiah 40–55*). The adj. חדל is used in a similar context to this poem in Ps 39 where the term in v. 5 conveys the idea of "transient" or "frail" (see BDB, 293; *DCH* 3:163; *HALOT*, 292–93). This meaning fits well here and corresponds to the overall context (so Goldingay, *Isaiah 40–55*; see Koole, *Isaiah 3/2*, 283–84). Regarding אישים, it is a rare form in the Old Testament which only occurs here, Ps 141:4, and Prov 8:4. *GBH* (§99b) identifies the form as the result of defective spelling as the typical pl. form is אנשים (so also Morgenstern, "Suffering Servant," 315), but is derived from a different root. Horace D. Hummel suggests that in each instance the form could simply be איש + enclitic ם ("Enclitic *Mem* in Early Northwest Semitic, Especially Hebrew," *JBL* 76 [1957]: 85–107). Hummel translates this bicolon as "despised and rejected is (the) man, a man…" (p. 101). This is possible, but Phoenician evidence shows that the form here is actually the normal pl. form (see Richard S. Tomback, *A Comparative Semitic Lexicon of the Phoenician and Punic Languages* [SBLDS 32; Missoula, Mont.: Scholars Press, 1978], 33; see also Dahood, "Phoenician Elements," 66; idem, "Proverbs 8,22–31: Translation and Commentary," *CBQ* 30 [1968]: 512–21). With this evidence, Gary A. Rendsburg concludes that the biblical form אישים is the "expected" form and "was at home in northern Israel" ("Morphological Evidence for Regional Dialects in Ancient Hebrew," in *Linguistics and Biblical Hebrew* [ed. W. R. Bodine; Winona Lake, Ind.: Eisenbrauns, 1992], 65–88 [85]). Thus, אישים is considered the pl. of איש with the phrase conveying the sense of the servant's frailty in relation to and in comparison with other human beings (so Goldingay, *Isaiah 40–55*; Koole, *Isaiah 3/2*, 284). The translation given finds support in some of the Versions: LXX ἐκλεῖπον παρὰ πάντας ἀνθρώπους ("more frail than all men"; see BDAG, 306); σʹ ἐλάχιστος ανδρῶν ("lowest/least of men"); Syr *mkykʾ dʾnšʾ* ("lowly of men"); Vg *novissimum virorum* ("the lowest of all men"). Poetically, the noun

אישים followed by איש has been understood as a classic example of assonance (see Boadt, "Intentional Alliteration," 362–63).

q) מכאבות functions here as a plural of intensity (so Goldingay, *Isaiah 40–55*; *HALOT*, 579; Koole, *Isaiah 3/2*, 284).

r) וידוע is a Qal pass. ptc. 1QIsa[a] has an act. ptc. ויודע ("and knowing"), which some Versions support: LXX εἰδὼς; Vg *scientem*; Syr *ydʿ*. 1QIsa[b] uses the verb וידע while α′, θ′, and σ′ use the adj. γνωστός. D. Winton Thomas proposed that ידע II is the term here which he relates to the Arab *waduʿa* ("still, quiet, submissive") that extends to "humiliate, punish," thus the translation "brought low by sickness" ("The Root ידע in Hebrew," *JTS* 35 [1934]: 298–306 [298–306]; idem, "More Notes on the Root ידע in Hebrew," *JTS* 38 [1937]: 404–5; cf. idem, "Isaiah LIII," 79, 82–83). This understanding has also been suggested and adopted by a number of translators. However, William Johnstone ("*Ydʿ* II, 'Be Humbled, Humiliated'?," *VT* 41 [1991]: 49–62) has definitively demonstrated that no relationship exists between the so-called ידע II and the Arab *waduʿa*, and so Thomas' theory must be abandoned (Johnstone's analysis has been confirmed in detail by J. A. Emerton, "A Further Consideration of D. W. Thomas's Theories about *Yādaʿ*," *VT* 41 [1991]: 145–63; see also Anthony Gelston, "Knowledge, Humiliation or Suffering: A Lexical, Textual and Exegetical Problem in Isaiah 53," in McKay and Clines, eds., *Of Prophets' Visions and the Wisdom of Sages*, 126–41). Thus, the verb here is ידע I ("know"; see further Clines, *I, He, We, and They*, 16–17). The majority of recent translators follow 1QIsa[a] et al. and translate "knows/acquainted with sickness" while a few read the MT as a pass, "known by sickness" (e.g. Jean Ch. Bastiaens, *Interpretaties van Jesaja 53: Een intertextueel onderzoek naar de lijdende Knecht in Jes 53 (MT/LXX) en in Lk 22:14–38, Hand 3:12–26, Hand 4:23–31 en Hand 8:26–40* [TFT-Studies 22; Tilburg University Press, 1993], 34; Koole, *Isaiah 3/2*, 285; Watts, *Isaiah 34–66*, 224; Wilson, *Nations in Deutero-Isaiah*, 292). However, the MT form ידוע can denote an inherent quality, as with בטוח ("trustful") in Isa 26:3b and זכור ("mindful") in Ps 103:14b (cf. GKC §§50f; 84[a]m), which goes well with the other expressions of the servant's suffering (so also Goldingay, *Isaiah 40–55*).

s) Lit. וכמסתר פנים ממנו ("and like hiding of face/faces from him/us").

t) For the Niphal ptc. נבזה from בזה ("despise"), 1QIsa[a] has ונבוזהו, which is either from בזז ("plunder"; *HALOT*, 118) or בוז ("show contempt/despise"; *HALOT*, 115). Similarly, Syr translates *wšṭnyhy* and so *BHS* assumes haplography in the MT and suggests reading ונבזהו (so also Morgenstern, "Suffering Servant," 315–16; Thomas, "Isaiah LIII," 83), which could in fact represent either of these roots. Dahood takes ולא as a substantive forming a hendiadys with נבזה, which he translates "a worthless nothing" ("Hebrew-Ugaritic Lexicography IV," *Bib* 47 [1966]: 403–19 [408]) and subsequently "a despicable cipher" ("Phoenician Elements," 67). The form נבזה in the MT is the identical form in v. 3aα, which provides a type of *inclusio* when retained (Koole, *Isaiah 3/2*, 287). Most translators maintain the MT which the LXX ἠτιμάσθη ("he was shamed"), Vg *despectus* ("despicable"), and Tg, although in the plural, בסירין ("they are despised"), support.

u) For the function of אכן, see 49:4bα.

v) Some 20 Hebrew MSS along with Syr and Vg repeat הוא in this bicolon, a reading which has been adopted by some translators (e.g. Fohrer, "Stellvertretung," 27; Hermisson, "Gottesknechtslied," 7; Morgenstern, "Suffering Servant," 316;

North, *Second Isaiah*, 229; Thomas, "Isaiah LIII," 80). Neither 1QIsa[a] nor 1QIsa[b] include the pronoun and is unnecessary to include.

w) The LXX omits אלהים, but α′, θ′, and σ′ all have ὑπὸ θεοῦ. Thomas ("Isaiah LIII," 83) and Whybray (*Isaiah 40–66*, 175) translate the phrase מכה אלהים as "terribly smitten" with אלהים expressing the superlative. Although divine names can express the superlative (see D. Winton Thomas, "A Consideration of Some Unusual Ways of Expressing the Superlative in Hebrew," *VT* 3 [1953]: 209–24), Clines correctly concludes that this is not such an instance here, "since it would be pointless for the 'we' to say that they 'considered' or 'esteemed' the servant to be 'terribly smitten' when there was no question but that he was (cf. 52:14)" (*I, He, We, and They*, 17).

x) ומענה is a Pual ptc. from ענה II ("bowed down, afflicted"; BDB, 776; *HALOT*, 853). The ptc. here is understood with a *factitive* nuance and thus indicating the purpose/result of God's striking the servant (cf. *IBHS* §25.2a n. 4). Rosenbaum considers v. 4b as a "[A&B] hendiadys [x]–C" (*Word-Order Variation*, 156).

y) *BHS* suggests reading a Pual ptc. מְחֻלָּל for the Poal ptc. מחלל, but this is unnecessary as both stems convey a pass. nuance (see *GBH* §59a). α′ βεβηλωμένος and the Tg דאיתחל read חלל I ("defile, profane"; see Barthélemy, *Critique Textuelle*, 396). The immediate context and the parallel term מדכא in the following colon suggests that חלל II ("pierce, wound") more appropriately belongs here, which is supported by the LXX ἐτραυματίσθη ("he was wounded") and is the choice of most translators.

z) The genitive relationship here indicates the purpose of the servant's suffering (cf. GKC §128q; *IBHS* §9.5.2c).

aa) Elliger finds multiple problems with vv. 6b–7 and so he completely reconstructs these lines ("Textkritisches zu Deuterojesaja," in Goedicke, ed., *Near Eastern Studies*, 113–19 [115–19]). Elliger's proposal, though, is hyper-critical and is not sensitive to the poetry and consequently has not found much support among recent translators.

bb) Morgenstern suggests relocating the ו to proceed the following verb נענה and read as a perf. ("Suffering Servant," 316; so also *BHS*; Wilson, *Nations in Deutero-Isaiah*, 292). This transposition produces a clause consisting of a subject and two predicates, which a few interpreters adopt. The MT, however, finds support from 1QIsa[a], 1QIsa[b] נגש והואה נענה, and σ′ προσηνέχθη καὶ αὐτὸς ὑπήκουσε. Muilenburg ("Book of Isaiah," 624) and Beuken understand the pronoun as emphatic, which is quite possible. Yet, Beuken (*Jesaja II/B*, 187, 220–21) also translates this clause to contrast the first clause as he translates "but he, himself bowed himself" (*maar hij, hij boog zich*). Similar to Beuken and a number of translators, it seems best to understand the pronoun introducing a circumstantial clause (see GKC §141e; *GBH* §171f) that contrasts the previous clause. Koole understands עון from v. 6bβ as the subject of נגש and translates "it was claimed." Consequently הוא does not introduce a circumstantial clause, but rather reintroduces the servant as subject (*Isaiah 3/2*, 300). Although Koole's suggestion is possible, it requires a grammatical leap since the servant is the obvious dominant subject within this passage and is represented by the same pronoun הוא in v. 5aα and is the object whereupon the עון is laid in v. 6b.

cc) The verb נענה is a Niphal ptc. from ענה II, which occurred earlier in v. 4bβ as a Pual ptc. Due to the change of stem and the following lines (v. 7aα[2]–b), along with the 3ms pronoun, the Niphal here is understood as reflexive, which the majority of translators recognize (see cf. Hermisson, "Gottesknechtslied," 7 n. 23).

dd) Earlier, along with a few contemporary, translators often omit or bracket off v. 7b due to its apparent unnecessary repetition (cf. *BHS*). Similarly, Wilson omits the first of the repeated lines in v. 7aα^2 due to a quite fanciful scribal error (*Nations in Deutero-Isaiah*, 293). These omissions have no support among the Versions and unfortunately disregard the poetical structure of the verse (see Muilenburg, "Chapters 40–66," 624–25; North, *Second Isaiah*, 229–30; John T. Willis, "Alternating [ABA'B'] Parallelism in the Old Testament Psalms and Prophetic Literature," in Follis, ed., *Dirctions in Biblical Hebrew Poetry*, 49–76 [67–68]).

ee) Lit. מעצר וממשפט ("by restraint and by judgment"). Others have recognized a hendiadys here which may be further indicated by the repeated מ. עצר is an abstract noun that occurs only two other times outside this text and means "oppression" as in Ps 107:39 (see Ernst Kutsch, "Die Wurzel עצר im Hebräischen," *VT* 2 [1952]: 57–69 [58]; D. P. Wright and J. Milgrom, "עצר," *TDOT* 11:310–15 [313]) or "restraint" as in Prov 30:16. The verb also typically indicates some kind negative action as "restrain, detain, holdback" (*HALOT*, 870). The noun עצר occurs once in Judg 18:7 but is obscure. Related to the verb, the noun conveys power or rule (see Shemaryahu Talmon and Weston W. Fields, "The Collocation משתין בקיר ועצור ועזוב and Its Meaning," *ZAW* 101 [1989]: 85–112). In the context of Judg 18:7 the term speaks of one who seizes power and expectedly with restraining, oppressive results (see Talmon and Fields, "Collocation," 91–92; Wright and Milgrom, *TDOT* 11:313; T. J. Meek, "Translating the Hebrew Bible," *JBL* 79 [1960]: 328–35 [328]; see also A. H. Konkel, "עצר," *NIDOTTE* 3:501–3 [501]). The Versions understand the term expressing some sense of oppression: LXX ἐν τῇ ταπεινώσει ("by humiliation"); Vg *de angustia* ("from anguish/trials"); Tg מיסורין ("from chastisements/bonds"). This said, C. F. Whitley's emendation of מעצה ("without counsel"; "Textual Notes on Deutero-Isaiah," *VT* 11 [1951]: 457–61 [459–60]) finds no support. D. F. Payne sees a fixed legal idiom here meaning "after arrest and sentence" or "from prison and lawcourt" ("The Servant of the Lord: Language and Interpretation," *EvQ* 42/43 [1970–71]: 131–43 [135]; so also, e.g., F. Duane Lindsey, "The Career of the Servant in Isaiah 52:13–53:12 [Concluded]," *BSac* 140 [1983]: 21–39 [28]; Motyer, *Prophecies of Isaiah*, 434; North, *Second Isaiah*, 65). There is, however, no evidence of such formula. With the proposed understanding of עצר, it is difficult, if not impossible, to endorse the translation "without/from protection" (e.g. Driver, "Isaiah 52$_{13}$–53$_{12}$," 94, 104; Gerleman, "Gottesknecht," 41; Koole, *Isaiah 3/2*, 303; Mowinckel, *He That Cometh*, 198) or the idea that the servant is being taken from a place of honor and power (e.g. Torrey, *Second Isaiah*, 419; Peter R. Ackroyd, "The Meaning of Hebrew דור Considered," *JSS* 13 [1968]: 3–10 [7]; G. W. Ahlström, "Notes to Isaiah 53:8f," *BZ* 13 [1969]: 95–98 [95–97]; Rignell, *Study on Isaiah*, 82). A more plausible translation is "without restraint" (Dahood, "Phoenician Elements," 64; idem, "Isaiah 53,8–12 and Massoretic Misconstructions," *Bib* 63 [1982]: 566–70 [566]; Korpel and de Moor, *Hebrew Poetry*, 547; Laato, *Servant of YHWH*, 131) or even "without delay" (de Boer, *Second-Isaiah's Message*, 35), but these do not convey the aggressive and oppressive action conveyed by the noun and especially in this context. The phrase seems best translated as "by oppressive judgment/sentence/lawsuit" (so Bastiaens, *Jesaja 53*, 31; Beuken, *Jesaja II/B*, 187, 221–22; Childs, *Isaiah*, 408; Konkel, *NIDOTTE* 3:501). This translation, however, is awkward while "legal restraint" (Goldingay, *Isaiah 40–55*) is smoother. Perhaps McKenzie captures the phrase best with "by a perverted judgment" (*Second Isaiah*, 130), which William Holladay concurs with "by a perversion of justice" (*Unbound by Time: Isaiah Still Speaks* [Cambridge: Cowley, 2002], 111); similarly Levine, "Through miscarriage of justice" ("Girard on Job," 129). Regarding the מ prefixes and with a number of translators, they are indicating the means/cause (see *IBHS* §11.2.11d) whereby the servant is taken away.

ff) The term דורו here has produced many suggestions. דור I occurs in Isa 38:12aα with the meaning of "dwelling-place" (*HALOT*, 217), which is related to the Akk *dūru* I ("city wall"; *AHw*, 178; *CAD* 3:192–97) and the Arab *dār* ("house, building, structure"; Wehr, *Written Arabic*, 344–45). Duhm sees דור I here as he translates with *Stätte* (*Jesaia*, 361), as does Wolff with *Wohnstatt* (*Jesaja 53*, 20, 24) and Levine with "abode" ("Girard on Job," 120). Driver suggests reading דור II as related to the Akk *dūru* II ("lasting state, permanent condition"; see *AHw*, 164, 178; *CAD* 3:197–98) and the Arab *dauru(n)* ("role [in life]") and *aldârâni* ("the two states") meaning here "plight, fate" ("Linguistic and Textual Problems: Isaiah XL–LXVI," *JTS* 36 [1935]: 396–406 [403]). Thus, Driver translates v. 8aβ as "and who gave a thought to his plight" ("Isaiah 52$_{13}$–53$_{12}$," 94–95, 104), which is followed by a number of translators (e.g. NRSV). This translation makes sense, but the most common use of דור II in the Old Testament refers to a "generation" (*HALOT*, 217–18). Further, the term rarely stands alone and in such instances it generally means "generation," that is, one's contemporaries, as in Isa 41:4aβ and 51:8–9 (so Korpel and de Moor, *Hebrew Poetry*, 547). This meaning also finds support with the LXX and α′ τὴν γενεὰν αὐτοῦ and Vg *generationem eius*. Dahood initially translated דורו as "his life" based on Isa 38:12 where דורי is parallel to חיי ("Phoenician Elements," 69); however, he later revised his translation with "his generation" ("Isaiah 53,8–12," 566) as with many other translators (e.g. RSV). It is possible that דור constitutes a narrower, specific group than merely general contemporaries. Following Frank J. Neuberg ("An Unrecognized Meaning of Hebrew *Dôr*[1]," *JNES* 9 [1950]: 215–17), Ackroyd identifies a close relationship between דור and the Ug *dr* ("assembly" or "community"; see also G. J. Botterweck, "דור," *TDOT* 3:170–73) in a number of Old Testament texts (cf. Isa 38:12) and so translates this colon as "that grouping to which he belongs" ("דּוֹר Considered," 6–7; similarly Gerleman, "Gottesknecht," 41; Grimm and Dittert, *Deuterojesaja*, 415). Torrey apparently understands דור II here also, but translates "his line" indicating the servant's descendents (*Second Isaiah*, 420; so also NIV; Muilenburg, "Chapters 40–66," 626; Westermann, *Isaiah 40–66*, 265). However, this meaning is suspect and is not conclusive when translated as such (for possible instances see Deut 32:20; Isa 38:12; Pss 73:15; 112:2; see D. N. Freedman and J. Lundbom, "דור," *TDOT* 3:169–70, 173–80 [cf. 173–75]). Further, the more common term for "offspring, descendents" is זרע, which occurs in v. 10aβ and raises the question of why this term was not be used here also if that is what the author wanted clearly to indicate.

gg) כי here is understood to introduce the content of the interrogative concerning what is thought of, contemplated (see BDB, 471; *HALOT*, 47). Most translators see the interrogative ending at v. 8a while others extend it to the end of v. 8 (e.g. Delitzsch, *Isaiah* 2:297; Kaiser, *Königliche Knecht*, 85; Morgenstern, "Suffering Servant," 299; Treves, "Isaiah LIII," 80). It seems best, though, to extend the interrogative to the end of v. 9 since there is no clear break in theme until v. 10 (so Driver, "Isaiah 52₁₃–53₁₂," 104; see also Clines, *I, He, We, and They*, 13).

hh) Multiple emendations have been offered for מפשע עמי. For instance, *BHS* suggests מפשעם ("because of their rebellion"). Elliger emends מפשעימו ("*für ihre Sünden*"; "Nochmals Textkritisches zu Jes 53," in Schreiner, ed., *Wort, Lied und Gottesspruch*, 137–44 [140]). Fohrer emends to מפשענו ("*'unserer' Auflehnung 'en'*"; "Stellvertretung," 28). North suggests מִפֶּשַׁע עַמִּי and translates the line "for the sin/transgression of peoples who deserved to be stricken themselves" (*Second Isaiah*, 65, 230). Whitley emends to מפשעים ("by transgressors"; "Textual Notes," 460). *BHS* also cites 1QIsa[a] reading עמו and confirmed by a good number of translators, but again distinguishing between the י and ו is difficult to determine in 1QIsa[a], which is also true in this instance in 1QIsa[b] and 4QIsa[d]. Further, the entire line in 1QIsa[a] appears to be a subsequent addition. Dahood claims that עמי is another instance of the Phoenician *î* indicating the 3ms suffix ("Phoenician Elements," 69; idem, "Isaiah 53,8–12," 566). However, this type of suffix is extremely rare in the MT, if it occurs at all (Mic 3:5?), while the MT "my people" finds dominant support among the Versions: LXX, α′, θ′, and σ′ τοῦ λαοῦ μου; Vg *populi mei*; Tg עמי; Syr *dʿmy*.

ii) The phrase נגע למו is a noun + prep. phrase. The noun is understood as a verb in the Versions—which *BHS* suggests to follow—but they all seem to be paraphrasing. For למו the LXX has εἰς θάνατον, which suggests למות, which many translators adopt (see cf. *BHS*; Barthélemy, *Critique Textuelle*, 398). Yet, the Hebrew prep. phrase frequently stands for להם in poetry, which is how α′, θ′, σ′, and Tg understand it; still, the rendering "because of the rebellion of my people a violent touch to them" (similarly Korpel and de Moor, *Hebrew Poetry*, 547; North, *Second Isaiah*, 65, 230) does not work with what has preceded and what follows. The form למו, though, can function as a pausal for לו (cf. Isa 44:15bβ; see GKC §103f n. 3; *GBH* §103f; *IBHS* §11.2.10a) which is how the Vg and Syr understand it as well as a number of translators. Nevertheless, the use of the form here could indicate purposeful ambiguity (see Motyer, *Prophecies of Isaiah*, 435).

jj) *BHS* suggests וַיֻּתַּן for ויתן (so also, e.g., Blenkinsopp, *Isaiah 40–55*, 345; Clines, *I, He, We, and They*, 13; Elliger, *Verhältnis*, 7; Laato, *Servant of YHWH*, 131). This is, however, unnecessary since the verb can simply function impersonally (see *IBHS* §4.4.2), which is how the majority of recent translators understand the verb and also 1QIsa[a] may confirm with the 3mp ויתנו. Dahood understands עמי ("his people") as the subject of the verb יתן and translates "It appointed his grave with the wicked" ("Isaiah 53,8–12," 567–68). This is quite possible, but the impersonal remains the preferred reading.

kk) Interpreters are divided on whether במתיו is either מות + ב ("in his deaths"—typically translated in the sg.) or related to במה ("his burial mound/grave"). 1QIsa[a] follows the latter, but in the sg. (Kutscher, *Isaiah Scroll*, 225), while the LXX, Vg, Tg, and Syr all read the former. The parallel term קבר suggests במה should be read. Yet, the MT has textual support and so is read here as an intensive plural (similarly Motyer, *Prophecies of Isaiah*, 435–36).

ll) For עשיר the LXX has the pl. τοὺς πλουσίους. 1QIsa[a] may also have the pl. [עשיר[ים. The MT should be retained (*pace* Wilson, *Nations in Deutero-Isaiah*, 294), as Ahlström observes that the consonants of the parallel terms have the same letters

רשעים עשיר, but transpose the order of the consonants. This clearly displays a word play and specifically assonance which the pl. ending would disrupt ("Isaiah 53:8f," 98; so also Goldingay, *Isaiah 40–55*). Holladay also sees the assonance with these two terms here and in Jer 5 with רשעים ("criminals," v. 26a) and ויעשירו ("and they grow rich," v. 27b) (*Jeremiah 1*, 198).

mm) The majority of translators understand על here functioning in a concessive sense (see GKC §160c; *GBH* §172e). This is a rare function of the prep. (Job 16:17) and so Clines translates it causally (so also Delitzsch, *Isaiah* 2:301), but understands it functioning in an ironic sense (*I, He, We, and They*, 20; so also Koole, *Isaiah 3/2*, 317). Although this suggestion is plausible and appealing, the concessive idea is the more natural reading.

nn) The following verses and in particular v. 10 has produced a number of various emendations and reconstructions, with the most radical proposed by H. L. Ginsberg ("The Arm of YHWH in Isaiah 51–63 and the Text of Isa 53 10–11," *JBL* [1958]: 152–56 [155–56]), Hans-P. Müller ("Ein Vorschlag zu Jes 53 10f," *ZAW* 81 [1969]: 377–80), and Isaiah Sonne ("Isaiah 53 10–12," *JBL* 78 [1959]: 335–42).

oo) דכאו is a Piel inf. const. + 3ms suffix. Based on the LXX καθαρίσαι ("to purify"), Duhm (*Jesaia*, 363–64) and later Driver suggest that the term דכא is an Aramaizing term דכה/דכא equal to זכה ("was pure, innocent, justified"; "Isaiah 52:13–53:12," 96). Similarly Kutscher claims that 1QIsa[a] דכאו read the Aram טהר, which corresponds to the LXX (*Isaiah Scroll*, 236). These Versions, though, could be attempting to soften the MT that presents Yahweh as the direct cause of the servant's suffering (see J. Lust, "The Demonic Character of Jahweh and the Septuagint of Isaiah," *Bijdragen* 40 [1979]: 2–14), which is exactly North's reasoning for his translation "...he should be broken by suffering" (*Second Isaiah*, 65, 242; see also Wilson, *Nations in Deutero-Isaiah*, 295). The root דכא also occurs in v. 5aβ with the same appropriate meaning of "crush" and is supported by σ′ ἐλεῆσαι αὐτὸν and Vg *conterere eum*. It is also unnecessary to adopt Elliger's repointing to דַּכָּאוֹ ("who was crushed"; *Verhältnis*, 7; so also Westermann, *Isaiah 40–66*, 254).

pp) החלי is a Hiphil pf. 3ms from חלה/חלא (cf. GKC §§74k; 75ii, rr) meaning "sick" (*HALOT*, 315, 317). Thomas ("Isaiah LIII," 85) followed by Clines (*I, He, We, and They*, 13, 20) consider the form an inf. abs. הַחֲלִי and translate "through sickness," "God puts him to grief" respectively. 1QIsa[a] has ויחללהו from either חלל I ("and he profaned him") or חלל II ("he pierced him"; see Kutscher, *Isaiah Scroll*, 236–37). Morgenstern reads 1QIsa[a] and adopts the latter root ("Suffering Servant," 318), as does Dahood, but reads the MT which he repoints to a Hiphil inf. const. + 3ms suffix הָחֲלִי ("to pierce him"; "Phoenician Elements," 71; idem, "Isaiah 53,8–12," 568–69). Some translators simply omit the term (e.g. Fohrer, "Stellvertretung," 28; Kaiser, *Königliche Knecht*, 86; Kutsch, "Leiden und Tod," 173). However, 4QIsa[d] confirms the MT and finds further support among the Versions: LXX τῆς πληγῆς ("from a blow/wound"); α′ ἀρρωστία/ἀρρώστημα ("sick/illness"); σ′ ἐν τῷ τραυματισμῷ ("by a wound"); Vg *in infirmitate* ("in/by illness"; see further Barthélemy, *Critique Textuelle*, 400–402). These renderings may support Müller's suggestion of מחלי ("Jes 53 10f," 380). Following Begrich's emendation of v. 10aα[1]–aα[2], החלים את־שם אשם נפשו (*Deuterojesaja*, 64), Driver sees החלי אם deriving from חלם ("to grow strong"), which occurs in the Qal in Job 39:4a "was healthy" and the Hiphil in Isa 38:16bβ "restored to health." Thus, Driver translates, "and restored him who had made himself an offering for sin" ("Isaiah 52$_{13}$–53$_{12}$," 96–97, 104; so also *BHS*; Westermann, *Isaiah 40–66*, 254; for Driver's earlier suggestion, see "Isaiah XL–LXVI," 403–4). Despite the apparent problems of reworking the MT in such a manner along with the consequential emendations required, this suggestion has no support among the Versions (see further Baltzer, *Deutero-Isaiah*, 419).

qq) אם is supported by all the Versions except Syr.

rr) תשים is either a Qal impf. 3fs or 2ms. The issue here is what or who is the subject of the verb. In his earlier work, Dahood redivided אם־תשים to produce אמת שם and translated the colon "Truly, he made himself an offering for sin" ("Textual Problems in Isaia," *CBQ* 22 [1960]: 400–409 [406]; "Phoenician Elements," 71). James Battenfield later confirmed Dahood's redivision by noting that 1QIsa[a] has אמ instead of the MT אם ("Isaiah LIII 10: Taking an 'If' Out of the Sacrifice of the Servant," *VT* 32 [1982]: 485; so also Bastiaens, *Jesaja 53*, 36; Beuken, *Jesaja II/B*, 190–91). This suggestion produces an awkward and sudden interjection that does not fit well with what has proceeded along with what follows. Further, the lack of a final ם does not constitute enough evidence for such emendation since the medial מ is used instead of a final ם in other instances throughout the scroll (e.g. 40:28). H. J. van Dijk suggests that the ת performative is a 3ms based on instances in Ugaritic ("Does Third Masculine Singular **TAQTUL* Exist in Hebrew?," *VT* 19 [1969]: 440–47 [cf. 442–43]). Dahood abandoned his earlier suggestion and follows van Dijk and emends אם to the ptc. אים, which becomes the subject of the verb, God, and translates as "the Awesome" ("Third Masculine Singular with Preformative *t-* in Northwest Semitic," *Or* 48 [1979]: 97–106 [100]; "Isaiah 53,8–12," 568–69). However, this form is extremely rare and highly unlikely here (so Korpel and de Moor, *Hebrew Poetry*, 548 n. 16). 1QIsa[a] and 4QIsa[d] confirm the MT while the LXX differs from the MT, but reads the verb as a 2p δῶτε. The Vg translates the colon as the action of the servant *si posuerit pro peccato animam suam* ("if he will lay down his life for sin"). The MT colon could be translated as "if you make his life/soul a guilt offering" with Yahweh as the antecedent of the 2ms (e.g. NIV; Korpel and de Moor, *Hebrew Poetry*, 548; Lindsey, "52:13–53:12 [Concluded]," 30–31; Motyer, *Prophecies of Isaiah*, 439) or the reader/hearer (cf. LXX; Oswalt, *Chapters 40–66*, 401–2). Yet, the most plausible and natural syntax is to understand נפשו as the subject of the verb (*pace* R. N. Whybray, *Thanksgiving for a Liberated Prophet: An Interpretation of Isaiah Chapter 53* [JSOTSup 4; Sheffield: JSOT Press, 1978], 63–65). Similarly and closely to the Vg, a number of translators translate נפשו as the direct object of the servant's "placing/setting" (e.g. Baltzer, *Deutero-Isaiah*, 393, 420; Fohrer, "Stellvertretung," 28; Morgenstern, "Suffering Servant," 299; Wolff, *Jesaja 53*, 20). Understanding נפשו as the subject of the verb תשים does not require repointing it to a Qal pass. as suggested by Thomas ("Isaiah LIII," 85) and Blenkinsopp (*Isaiah 40–55*, 348 n. bb). De Boer's emendation of אם ת(א)שם אשם נפשו ("when he has made atonement"; *Second-Isaiah's Message*, 55) is also unnecessary.

ss) Based on certain Psalms (cf. Ps 91:15–16) and the prominence of Yahweh's arm in Isa 51–63 along with its reference in v. 1b, Ginsberg suggests that זרע should be revocalized as זְרוֹעַ ("arm"; "Arm of YHWH," 155–56). However, this suggestion finds no support among the Versions.

tt) Based on 1QIsa[a], 4QIsa[d], and the Tg, most translators understand the servant as the subject of the verb and so the servant's days are lengthened.

uu) 1QIsa[a], 1QIsa[b], 4QIsa[d] (see Barthélemy, *Critique Textuelle*, 403), and the LXX all include אור as the direct object of the verb. For some translators, the MT is the result of haplography and so אור should be read (e.g. NRSV; NJB; NIV; Blenkinsopp, *Isaiah 40–55*, 346; I. Blythin, "A Consideration of Difficulties in the Hebrew Text of Isaiah 53:11," *BT* 17 [1966]: 27–31; Driver, "Isaiah 52₁₃–53₁₂," 97; Grimm and Dittert, *Deuterojesaja*, 416–17; Hermisson, "Gottesknechtslied," 8 n. 37; Kutsch, "Leiden und Tod," 188; Lindsey, "52:13–53:12 (Concluded)," 33; North, *Second Isaiah*, 233–34; Oswalt, *Chapters 40–66*, 399 n. 43; Whybray, *Isaiah 40–66*, 180; Wolff, *Jesaja 53*, 25). However, אור is not found in α′, θ′, σ′, Vg, Tg, and Syr. Consequently, no one reading has dominant textual support and so the MT is maintained here. For an explanation for reading the MT and why some of the Versions included אור, see Korpel and de Moor, *Hebrew Poetry*, 549 n. 17. For a more radical reworking of v. 11a, see Wilson, *Nations in Deutero-Isaiah*, 295–96.

vv) A large number of translators follow the MT pausal accent and connect בדעתו with the subsequent colon which is supported by 1QIsa[a] with ובדעתו the LXX with καὶ..., and implicitly the Vg and Tg. Concerning the term ידע, both de Boer (*Second-Isaiah's Message*, 55) and H. G. M. Williamson ("*Daʿaṯ* in Isaiah LIII 11," *VT* 28 [1978]: 118–21) follow Thomas' earlier studies on this root and translate the prep. phrase as "with his rest." Although this avoids translating ידע as "humiliation," which Thomas and others suggest, the translation still adopts the erroneous connection between ידע and the Arab *waduʿa*. Gelston also recognizes the failure of Thomas' proposal, but still finds the MT unsatisfactory. Thus, he emends to ברעתו ("by his suffering"; see Gelston, "Knowledge, Humiliation or Suffering," 140–41). Although this suggestion makes some sense here, the Versions support the MT.

ww) A number of translators omit צדיק due to dittography (see A. Gelston, "Some Notes on Second Isaiah," *VT* 21 [1971]: 517–27 [524–27]). However, the term is included in 1QIsa[a], 1QIsa[b], LXX, and Vg and does not pose any substantial syntactical difficulties as most translators recognize (see GKC §132b; *IBHS* §14.3.3c).

xx) The phrase צדיק עבדי can be translated in a number of different ways which Waltke and O'Connor attribute to purposeful grammatical ambiguity (*IBHS* §11.4.3b).

yy) The verb אחלק and the verb יחלק in the following bicolon are in the Piel, which is conveying a resultative nuance here as is typical with the verb חלק (cf. *IBHS* §24.3.1a).

zz) This translation of תחת אשר comes from Goldingay (*Isaiah 40–55*; see also Motyer, *Prophecies of Isaiah*, 443). For the use of תחת, see BDB, 1065–66; *IBHS* §11.2.15; cf. *GBH* §170g).

aaa) 1QIsa[a], 1QIsa[b], 1QIsa[d], LXX, σ′, Tg, and Syr all read a pl. חטאי here.

bbb) יפגיע is a Hiphil impf. 3ms from פגע ("to come, meet"; *HALOT*, 910). Based on the LXX παρεδόθη and 1QIsa[a] יפגע, Elliger claims that the MT form is a Niphal conveying a pass. nuance ("Textkritisches zu Jes 53," 143–44). However, the form יפגע could simply be a defective Hiphil (see Dahood, "Phoenician Elements," 72–73; Kutscher, *Isaiah Scroll*, 362–63). 1QIsa[b] יפגיע confirms the MT. The Hiphil makes sense here and corresponds with the rest of the poem which the majority of translators recognize.

ccc) For ולפשעים, 1QIsa[a], 1QIsa[b], and 4QIsa[d] read ולפשעיהם/לפשעיהמה ("for their rebellions"), which Kutscher claims is a result of attempting to emend the second part of the verse to accord with the first half (*Isaiah Scroll*, 383). The LXX translates καὶ διὰ τὰς ἁμαρτίας αὐτῶν παρεδόθη ("and because of their sins he was delivered"). Driver originally understood 1QIsa[a] and the LXX ("Once Again Abbreviations," *Textus* 4 [1964]: 76–94 [80]) as the authentic reading which a few translators adopt (e.g. *BHS*; Baltzer, *Deutero-Isaiah*, 393; Barthélemy, *Critique Textuelle*, 405–6; Blenkinsopp, *Isaiah 40–55*, 349 n. ff; Oswalt, *Chapters 40–66*, 399 n. 49; Wilson, *Nations in Deutero-Isaiah*, 296). Similarly, Elliger emends to ולפשעם ("*und für ihre Frevel*"; "Textkritisches zu Jes 53," 143–44). As with most recent translators, Driver later reads the MT as "for transgressors" ("Isaiah 52$_{13}$–53$_{12}$," 104), which is confirmed by α′, θ′, σ′, Vg, and Syr.

Structure and Genre

The parameters of this passage have generally been accepted by modern interpreters since Duhm. The MT concurs by placing a space and a ס after 52:12 and 53:12.[107] 1QIsa[a] also recognizes this break by beginning a new line after 52:12 and 53:12 but also begins a new line at 53:1. 52:13–53:12 is found in the middle of sections 51:9–52:12 and 54:1–17 that concern Zion–Jerusalem. 52:13 begins with הנה, which introduces a section concerning Yahweh's servant, which is made explicit in the opening verse and 53:11aβ. Regarding the internal structure, 1QIsa[a] begins and indents a new line at 53:9 and indents v. 10aβ. The scroll also has a small space after vv. 6a and 11. A definite break occurs at the end of ch. 52, but vv. 13–15 do not constitute a separate unit.[108] The simplest and most obvious division of the passage is based on the two different voices within the unit: Yahweh and a first person plural. Thus, there are three main units: (I) Yahweh's first speech about his servant (52:13–15); (II) a "we/us/our" speech about the servant (53:1–11aα); and (III) Yahweh's second speech about his servant (53:11aβ–12).[109] The middle section divides into two main sub-units with v. 1 functioning as an introduction for the rest of the speech. Verses 2–11aα naturally fall into four sub-units (vv. 2–3, 4–6, 7–9, 10–11aα).[110] A detailed structure can be seen as follows:

107. In general, the MT tradition recognizes 52:13–53:12 as a unit (see Gelston, "Isaiah 52:13–53:12," 187–204).

108. See further Korpel and de Moor, *Hebrew Poetry*, 550–59.

109. So, e.g., Beuken, *Jesaja II/B*, 193–200; Childs, *Isaiah*, 411; Goldingay, *Isaiah 40–55*; Hermisson, "Gottesknechtslied," 10; Bernd Janowski, "Er trug unsere Sünden—Stellvertretung nach Jes 52,13–53,12," in idem, *Stellvertretung: Alttestamentliche Studien zu einem theologischen Grundbegriff* (SBS 165; Stuttgart: Katholisches Bibelwerk, 1997), 67–95 (78–81); Westermann, *Isaiah 40–66*, 255–56; similarly Koole, *Isaiah 3/2*, 262.

110. Similarly, e.g., Goldingay, *Isaiah 40–55*; Muilenburg, "Chapters 40–66," 614; Oswalt, *Chapters 40–66*, 376; Westermann, *Isaiah 40–66*, 255–56.

I. Yahweh's speech concerning his servant's exaltation (52:13–15)
A. Exaltation proper (v. 13)
B. Comparative reason for the servant's exaltation (vv. 14–15aα)
1. Comparison to the extent of the servant's suffering (v. 14)
2. Comparison to the extent of the servant's priestly work (v. 15aα)
C. Royal reaction to the servant's work and exaltation (v. 15aβ–b)
II. Corporate confession and testimony of the servant's priestly work (53:1–11aα)
A. Rhetorical introduction (v. 1)
B. Confession/testimony proper (vv. 2–11aα)
1. Description and misconception of the servant (vv. 2–3)
a. Description (v. 2)
1) Barren origin (v. 2aα)
2) Purposeful humiliation (v. 2aβ–b)
b. Misconception (v. 3)
1) General rejection (v. 3a)
a) Rejection proper (v. 3aα)
b) Reason (v. 3aβ)
2) Confession of personal rejection (v. 3b)
a) Comparison (v. 3bα)
b) Confession proper (v. 3bβ)
2. The explanatory reason for the servant's suffering (vv. 4–6)
a. Explanation and misconception of suffering (v. 4)
1) Explanation (v. 4a)
2) Misconception (v. 4b)
b. Expansion of explanation (vv. 5–6)
1) Negative/positive reasons for suffering (v. 5)
a) Negative (v. 5a)
b) Positive (v. 5b)
2) Illustrative confessional reason for suffering (v. 6)
a) Illustrative confession (v. 6a)
b) The source of suffering (v. 6b)
3. The voluntary suffering of the servant (vv. 7–9)
a. Physical suffering (v. 7)
1) Suffering proper (v. 7aα^{1a})
2) Voluntary response (v. 7aα^{1b}–b)
a) Response proper (v. 7aα^{1b})
b) Concentric illustration (v. 7aα^{2}–b)
b. Unjust sentence, death, and burial of the servant (vv. 8–9a)
1) Unjust sentence of the servant (v. 8aα)
2) Death of the servant (v. 8aβ–b)
a) Introductory phrase (v. 8aβ)
b) Death proper (v. 8b)
(1) The servant was cut off (v. 8bα)
(2) Reason (v. 8bβ)
3) Death and burial (v. 9a)
c. The servant's innocence (v. 9b)

4. The promise of the servant's sacrificial work (vv. 10–11aα)
a. Work proper (v. 10aα)
1) Yahweh's role in the servant's suffering (v. 10aα^{1})
2) The servant's voluntary sacrifice (v. 10aα^{2})
b. Promised results (vv. 10aβ–11aα)
1) Descendents (v. 10aβ^{1})
2) Lengthened days (v. 10aβ^{2})
3) Yahweh's purpose will succeed (v. 10b)
4) The servant will see and be satisfied (v. 11aα)
a) Reason (v. 11aα^{1})
b) Seeing and satisfaction proper (v. 11aα^{2})
III. Yahweh's speech concerning his servant's priestly work, rewards, and royal actions (vv. 11aβ–12)
A. Righteousness for many (v. 11aβ–b)
1. Righteousness proper (v. 11aβ)
2. Means of righteousness (v. 11b)
B. Distribution of the spoils of victory (v. 12)
1. Distribution proper (v. 12aα)
a) Yahweh to the servant and the many (v. 12aα^{1})
b) The servant to Yahweh (v. 12aα^{2})
2. The reason for the distribution (v. 12aβ–b)
a) The servant's voluntary death (v. 12aβ^{1})
b) Purpose of sacrificial death (v. 12aβ^{2}–b)
(1) Identified himself with rebels (v. 12aβ^{2})
(2) Carried the sin of the many (v. 12bα)
(3) Continuance of intercession for the rebels (v. 12bβ)

Elliger recognizes the above division and identifies the whole as a "prophetic liturgy." The middle section is a mixture of a "mourning song" (*Leichenlied*) and "lament of the people" (*Volksklagelied*) expressed in the general form of a "penitence song" (*Bußliedes*).[111] Begrich divides this unit similarly (52:13–15; 53:1–10, 11–12) and sees the two speeches of Yahweh surrounding a "song of a group" (*Lied einer Mehrheit*).[112] This song resembles a psalm of thanksgiving with vv. 2–3 containing expressions of a lament.[113] Whybray claims that the entire unit is an individual psalm of thanksgiving which was composed in response to Deutero-Isaiah's deliverance from a Babylonian prison and his own thanksgiving psalm.[114] Whybray also follows Begrich's lead and appeals to Ps 118 as a parallel psalm of thanksgiving to account for the poem's third person

111. Elliger, *Verhältnis*, 19.
112. Begrich, *Deuterojesaja*, 62.
113. Ibid., 63–66.
114. Whybray, *Liberated Prophet*, 110–28, cf. 134–35.

language.[115] Kaiser identifies the poem as an "oracle of salvation" (*Heilsorakel*) with 53:1–6 composing a thanksgiving psalm.[116] Melugin sees the poem as a unique creation of the prophet which employs the language and imagery of the psalms of thanksgiving and lament. Essentially the poem "functions as a speech of salvation."[117] Overall, this poem has a number of parallels with the lament and thanksgiving psalms that typically revolve around the central concern of deliverance. As with the other servant passages, however, this unit is not a song and does not correspond to any one formal genre.

Working outside of form-critical concerns, Clines observes that the poem is expressed in highly visual language. The poem "is concerned with how to see, i.e., how the servant should be seen."[118] Lindblom somewhat anticipated Clines's assessment by identifying the song as "a symbolic narrative, an allegorical picture."[119] More in line with Clines, Goldingay identifies this poem as a "vision" and essentially it is a "job-description" for Yahweh's servant.[120] Behind this vision is a fourfold background expressed in the language of the lament as in Jer 15 and Hos 6, thanksgiving as in Ps 118, Yahweh's divine promise to his king, and the language of Lev 1–16.[121]

The conclusions of Clines and Goldingay are correct. The first person singular voice of the second and third servant passages has disappeared. Others tell the servant's story in a similar way as Yahweh speaks about his servant in 42:1–4. They speak about their relationship with him, his suffering, his assignment, and his success while the servant himself remains silent (cf. 53:7).[122] Characteristic of visions, what is portrayed is obscure, ambiguous, and not confined to space or time.[123] The voices concentrate on describing the servant's actions in vivid language and imagery, which display what it means to be Yahweh's servant. The voices utter promises, confessions, and testimonies about the servant utilizing various

115. Ibid., 128–34; see Begrich, *Deuterojesaja*, 65.

116. Kaiser, *Königliche Knecht*, 88.

117. Melugin, *Isaiah 40–55*, 74.

118. Clines, *I, He, We, and They*, 40–41.

119. Lindblom, *Servant Songs*, 47.

120. Goldingay, *Isaiah*, 301.

121. Ibid.

122. For a graph displaying the various personae in this passage, see Christina Spaller, "Syntaktische und stilistische Relationen im Vierten Gottesknechtslied und deren exegetische Relevanz," in F. V. Reiterer and P. Eder, eds., *Liebe zum Wort: Beiträge zur klassischen und biblischen Philologie* (Festschrift P. Ludger Bernhard; Salzburg: Müller, 1993), 275–92 (282–83).

123. See Clines, *I, He, We, and They*, 37–49.

types of formal language, and specifically, the four types identified by Goldingay. These voices are not outside, unaffected observers of Yahweh's servant; they are self-involved speakers who utter speech acts about and in reference to him.

Interpretive Analysis

When attempting to make sense of this passage, almost every interpreter wisely prefaces their analysis with words of caution and personal confession of bewilderment. There is no difference here, except for maybe more fear and trepidation. Walter Brueggemann most appropriately states that "we are very close here to what seems to be quintessential holy ground."[124] This text is unquestionably enigmatic and mysterious. The poem's dense perplexity is produced by its visionary nature and opaque poetical language and imagery. Its obscurity is further enhanced by its textual, grammatical, and semantic complexities that seemingly appear with each and every colon. To make matters worse, 52:13–53:12 is one of, if not, the most disputed block of text in the entire Bible. Speech act theory and the notion of self-involvement will help towards understanding how this text functions and its role within the overarching prophetic strategy of chs. 40–55. As already clearly displayed, however, these concepts cannot and will not solve all of the interpretive issues at stake.

In line with Clines's observations, Goldingay, Brueggemann, and others have also recognized the clear self-involving nature of this passage.[125] I am suggesting that the way readers find their place within this poem is by first following the prophetic strategy of Isa 40–55. The self-involvement of the addressees/readers occurs on two different plains or with two different, but related personae. The poem opens with הנה ישכיל עבדי, which closely resembles the beginning of the first servant passage, הן עבדי. Yahweh identifies his servant in this poem with the identical phrase he uses for his servant Jacob–Israel and the speaker in the other servant passages—עבדי. Those who heed Yahweh's open call to return to him embrace the position of עבדי through confessionary utterances. Unlike the second and third servant passages, the servant here is silent. Thus, the addressees' self-involvement with this vision occurs through *identification* with the servant since they are Yahweh's עבד.

The addressees/readers also identify with the "we/us/our" group. There are a number of different suggestions concerning this voice: the kings of the nations in 52:15; the prophet or prophets on behalf of Jacob–Israel;

124. Walter Brueggemann, *Isaiah 40–66* (Westminster Bible Companion; Louisville, Ky.: Westminster John Knox, 1998), 149.

125. See Goldingay, *Isaiah*, 301–9; Brueggemann, *Isaiah 40–66*, 141–50.

Jacob–Israel; or the nations.[126] From a literary standpoint, this plural entity predominantly refers to Jacob–Israel throughout these chapters (e.g. 40:3, 8; 42:24; 47:4). The difficulty with this conclusion is the term עמי in 53:8bβ. Outside the mouth of Yahweh or one of his prophets, this expression is used when describing a particular people group one is associated with (e.g. Gen 23:11; 49:29; Judg 14:16; 1 Sam 15:30). The plural form עמנו rarely occurs (2 Sam 10:12aα//1 Chr 19:13aα; Jer 46:16bβ) and thus the singular form is found even when the plural form could be used (e.g. Judg 14:3). Therefore, a switch from first person plural language to the singular עמי would be expected.

This "we/us/our" entity appeared for the first time as the anonymous witnesses in 41:21–29. To recall, Yahweh assigned Jacob–Israel as his witnesses to his Cyrus speech act. But included in this group are the nations who will also witness Yahweh's demonstration of power. The intended perlocutionary effect of Yahweh's speech act was for Jacob–Israel and the nations to confess Yahweh as their sole savior and God. Although this first person plural voice naturally points to Jacob–Israel, the nations cannot be excluded. As with the unidentified "I/me" in the second and third servant passages, this voice is functionally anonymous.

Addressees/readers readily *involve* them*selves* with this plural group because of its anonymous nature and due to the voice's central concern: *sin*. Throughout chs. 40–55, Yahweh has issued a call to return to him. The second and third servant passages have provided practical ways for addressees/readers publicly to adopt the servant role through self-involvement. The open "we/us/our" group allows the addressees/readers to confess their sin, find forgiveness, and express their thankfulness and surprised astonishment.[127] This group previously confessed their sin in 42:24. This utterance is surrounded by concerns of idolatry, Jacob–Israel's refusal to recognize Yahweh as God alone (42:14–22), and Yahweh's Cyrus speech act (43:1–13). In the final servant passage, the confession is directly related to the task of Yahweh's servant. Confession here is birthed by the sacrificial and saving work of this servant. Throughout Isa 40–55, Yahweh calls for all to forsake their sin and turn to him, as their sin has been removed (40:2aβ–b). In addition, Yahweh promises that he will continue to wipe away all their sins, which will not be remembered (43:25). This vision points to a time when forgiveness will be realized through Yahweh's servant and the confession of sin is based

126. See Clines, *I, He, We, and They*, 29–33.

127. Similarly, Brueggemann, *Isaiah 40–66*, 146; see also Beverly J. Stratton, "Engaging Metaphors: Suffering with Zion and the Servant in Isaiah 52–53," in Fowl, ed., *The Theological Interpretation of Scripture*, 219–37.

on his provision of deliverance. There is no explanation given for why Yahweh needs to take this course of action. However, what becomes clear in Isa 56–66 is that Jacob–Israel remains rebellious. This indicates that Yahweh's people have, for the most part, decided not to return to Yahweh with their whole heart. Moreover, the problem of sin has plagued Israel's entire existence, as well as the whole of humanity, and so perhaps Yahweh anticipates a mediocre response at best and initiates their return, along with the nations, by providing forgiveness despite their ongoing rebellion.

The prophetic strategy of Isa 40–55 leads the addressees/readers to *identify* with the servant described in the vision as they are Yahweh's servant. At the same time, they actively participate in the confession which tells the servant's story. Consequently, self-involved addressees of 52:13–53:12 are simultaneously identified as and distinct from Yahweh's servant. This paradox recalls the individual/collective dilemma highlighted in 49:1–6. Again, the Servant Song answer that the figure is an individual in each of the passages is inadequate. Nevertheless, in this poem Yahweh's servant is clearly an individual. The individuality of this figure is seen in the contrastive phrases between the singular servant and the plural confessors: for example, "*we* did not consider *him*," "*he* bore *our* sicknesses," "*he* was wounded because of *our* rebellions," "by *his* wounds comes healing to *us*," "Yahweh laid upon *him* the iniquity of *us* all." These contrasts, though, do not definitively identify this figure as an individual, for Yahweh uses singular pronouns for collective Jacob–Israel and calls the nation עבדי. Further, the servant is distinguished from the nations and kings in 52:15a. This distinction could be seen as reflecting the Old Testament tradition of drawing clear lines between Israel and the גוים. Thus, the servant would naturally be understood here as the nation of Israel in contrast to the foreign nations. Still, the distinction between the servant and the first person plural group is made clear by the fact that the latter is characterized as sinful. From the perspective of Isa 40–55, and the entire Old Testament for that matter, those who find themselves in this category must include every person among Jacob–Israel, Zion–Jerusalem, and the nations, that is, humanity. This servant is distinguished from this group because he is sinless in word and deed (53:9b).

What the final servant passage describes is an individual who has embraced the open servant role at another dimension. As with other addressees/readers, this person adopts the same servant position and designates Yahweh as his master. But this master–servant relationship is stretched to its limits. Yahweh's servant also has opponents and experiences the absence of God similar to 50:6–9, but here Yahweh also becomes his greatest oppressor and attacker. This servant embraces everything Yahweh lays upon him, without a single word of protest, or even hope. This servant operates in the kingly role as expressed in the other servant passages, but he does not overtly function as a prophet. Here he acts as a priest by presenting himself as a sacrifice for sin on behalf of the rebellious. As a priest, though, he points to the original priestly call of Yahweh's servant (Exod 19:6). Each speaker of the second servant passage is Yahweh's light and salvation to Jacob–Israel and the nations. This servant also functions in these capacities, but it is his suffering and death that *constitutes* Yahweh's salvation and light. Because of the extraordinary character of this servant and his special priestly assignment, he alone ends up designated as עבד יהוה while all the others who have embraced Yahweh's call form a group identified as עבדי יהוה.

In sum, this poem presents an unidentified individual as Yahweh's servant and, as a vision, it openly awaits for one to fulfill these unique responsibilities. One among the many of Yahweh's servant(s) will distinguish himself in his conduct and will embrace the specific task of providing forgiveness to the rebellious. Yet, the self-involved fulfillment of the servant's task does not exhaust the descriptive portrayal of the servant role. Although the sacrificial task will be accomplished by one, the vision presents the general stance and entailments of what it means to be Yahweh's servant. Upon fulfillment of these unique entailments, this individual will put flesh on the faceless servant of Yahweh and will become a model to exemplify. At the same time, his work of deliverance will continue to prompt the rebellious to confess their sins with gratefulness and wonderment as they receive miraculous healing and restoration. Thus, self-involved addressees identify themselves as Yahweh's servant and simultaneously remain distinct from Yahweh's servant as they *involve* them*selves* with and become recipients of his sacrificial work.

52:13: Yahweh tells his servant's story by beginning at the end. The servant is elevated to the highest position possible—Yahweh's. The level of exaltation is expressed by the phrase ירום ונשא וגבה מאד. The initial two verbs occur together three other times, only in Isaiah, and always in reference to Yahweh (6:1aβ; 33:10; 57:15aα[1]). This exaltation answers the servant's confidence in Yahweh, and specifically, will demonstrate that Yahweh has drawn near and vindicated the servant's trust in him, thus removing forever any temporary shame.

The servant's insight is demonstrated by his actions which display a total submission to Yahweh's assignment. The reason for the servant's elevated status is the implementation of his insight. Because of his wise actions, the Niphal verb נשא could indicate that the servant exalted himself.[128] However, as Clines has observed, "there is *no concrete action* that the servant does—apart from letting everything happen to him."[129] Coupled with this and because of the servant's posture as *servant* and the level of exaltation, it seems that only Yahweh would elevate him to such a place. Yet, the servant's exaltation is based on his own submissive actions. Thus, this exaltation reflects the mutual self-involvement of Yahweh and his servant.

Verses 14–15: With these lines Yahweh alludes to the work of his servant in the subsequent verses. The reaction is based on the servant's suffering condition described in the second section of the vision (see Job 17:6–8).[130] The comparison between the first colon and the following bicolon (v. 14aβ–b) conveys that the extent of the people's disgust in the servant's condition is the degree to which he experiences suffering. Goldingay rightly concludes that these lines are not necessarily asserting that the servant suffered more than any other human being nor ceased to look like a human being, but that he suffered in a way that marked him more than any other human being. Thus, because he suffered as if he were the worst of human beings, people can treat him as such (53:2–3, 8).[131]

Verse 15aα parallels with v. 14aα while extending the comparison of v. 14aβ–b. This colon briefly introduces the priestly aspect of the servant's task. The appalling reaction to the servant's suffering is directly proportionate to the extent of his priestly work. In regards to sacrifice, blood is typically נזה, but the poem does not disclose any spattered substance. Yahweh's speech ends by specifically describing the royal reaction to the servant's exaltation. Isolating this response emphasizes the servant's unexpected elevation to the position of a king, the true King. The phrase קפץ פי is a typical way of indicating "to stop speaking"[132] and in certain instances it means "to stop mocking, slandering" (Ps 107:42; Job 5:16). Interestingly, similar expressions are accompanied with the verb בוש (Ezek 16:63; Mic 7:16).[133] In one of Jeremiah's confessions, he asserts his confidence in Yahweh and speaks of the outcome of those

128. Goldingay, *Isaiah 40–55*.

129. Clines, *I, He, We, and They*, 42.

130. Jean C. Bastiaens ("The Language of Suffering in Job 16–19 and in the Suffering Servant Passages of Deutero-Isaiah," in van Ruiten and Vervenne, eds., *Studies in the Book of Isaiah*, 421–32 [426]) suggests that Job 17:6–8 is "reminiscent" of v. 14.

131. Goldingay, *Isaiah 40–55*.

132. See C. J. Labuschagne, "פה," *TLOT* 2:976–79 (979).

133. Koole, *Isaiah 3/2*, 274.

who persecute him: בשו מאד כי־לא השכילו (20:11bα). Thus, although the reaction to the servant would naturally be one of astonishment, more specifically the response will be the ceasing of mocking and humiliating gestures. The servant's knowledge will prove to be wise whereas those who oppose him will be shamed. Interestingly, it is the kings who *shut their mouths* because they had not heard the message. In one sense, this argues against the kings being the "we/us/our" group who *confess* the message in vv. 1–11aα.[134] Also, why isolate kings as the ones responding to the servant in silence? Perhaps there is an emphasis being placed on the distinction between those who confess—servants—and those who shut their mouths—kings.

53:1: This weak, double rhetorical question introduces the confession and testimony of the first person plural voice. The majority of interpreters all concur that the self-implied answer is, "No one." No person could have anticipated or believed that Yahweh's power of deliverance would be manifested in such a way.

The phrase זרוע יהוה is typically a metonymy for God's power, which is specifically displayed in his mighty acts of deliverance (e.g. Exod 6:6bα; 15:16aβ; Deut 4:34aβ; 33:27aβ; Isa 30:30aα^2; 51:5aβ; 52:10a).[135] In certain instances Yahweh's arm comes close to a hypostatization (e.g. Pss 44:4b; 98:1bβ), as it is here and in Isa 40:10aβ, 11aα^2; 48:14bβ; 51:9aα; and 59:16bα.[136] In this poem, the arm of Yahweh constitutes the work of his servant and so he is a display of Yahweh's power. In the first section of Isa 40–55, the arm of Yahweh is related to the deliverance of Jacob–Israel from Babylon. In chs. 49–55, the second Zion section (51:9–52:12) begins with a call to the arm of Yahweh to rouse itself and put on strength. This exhortation is a direct response to Zion–Jerusalem's rephrasing of Jacob–Israel's complaint, which begins the first Zion section (49:14). In the second Zion section, the city is also exhorted to rouse herself and put on strength in preparation for her redemption and Yahweh's return (51:17; 52:1–2). At the close of this section, and similar to 40:1–11, Yahweh again announces his return to and redemption of Zion–Jerusalem (52:7–9) and then proclaims:

134. So also, e.g., Goldingay, *Isaiah*, 304.

135. See F. J. Helfmeyer, "זרוע," *TDOT* 4:131–40 (133–40).

136. So also Goldingay, *Isaiah 40–55*; Motyer, *Prophecy of Isaiah*, 427. See further Michael Fishbane, "Arm of the Lord: Biblical Myth, Rabbinic Midrash, and the Mystery of History," in Balentine and Barton, eds., *Language, Theology, and the Bible*, 271–92.

[10]Yahweh bares his holy arm before all the nations
and all the ends of the earth see the salvation of our God.

These lines also resemble Yahweh's salvific call to the all the peoples of the earth (45:20–25). As in the first exodus, Yahweh bared his arm in the Cyrus event, but the work of his arm here will execute another deliverance and not through offensive, aggressive action, but in passive submissiveness.

The declarative–directive dimension of Yahweh's illocutionary act in 49:3, 5–6 finds further expression in this poem. As a vision, this poem expresses the directive dimension as it lays out the unique task of Yahweh's servant. The declarative dimension builds upon his previous illocutions that the speaker *constitutes* his servant and Israel, his light and salvation. In this poem the suffering and death of Yahweh's arm/servant *constitutes* his salvation and light. The servant who embraces this assignment will simultaneously fulfill the directive and declarative dimensions. The extralinguistic actualization of Yahweh's illocutionary act will bring about a transformation in the world. The servant is Yahweh's illocutionary act. The servant *constitutes* Yahweh's promise of salvation! This promise is realized through the interdependent self-involved utterances spoken by Yahweh and his servant. Upon the fulfillment of this vision the servant will realize to the fullest extent Yahweh's promise that he will wipe away transgressions and remember them no more (43:25).

Verse 2: With these lines the first person plural group begins to explain the servant's task. In the first bicolon, the servant grows up before Yahweh. The prepositional phrase לפניו conveys the idea that the servant is under the watchful eye of Yahweh (e.g. Ps 61:8a).[137] Interestingly, the phrase occurs multiple times throughout Lev 1–16 and specifically indicates the location where sacrifices are offered—לפני יהוה. The servant is described here as a יונק and a שרש. The latter term could be pointing back to the messianic root of Jesse in Isa 11:1b, 10aα, but the noun can also refer to a person (Job 29:19a) or people (Ps 80:10b). The plural group further describes the origin of the servant as barren and unhealthy; ארץ ציה is a waterless place where life cannot be sustained (Jer 51:43; Hos 2:5b).[138]

In the second bicolon, the "we/us/our" entity speaks of the servant's purposeful modest appearance. The noun הדר refers to Yahweh's own splendor and majesty (e.g. Isa 2:10bβ, 19bβ; Pss 96:6a; 104:1b) which he

137. Goldingay, *Isaiah 40–55*.

138. See G. Fleischer, "ציה," *TDOT* 12:330–33.

has placed on human beings in general (e.g. Ps 8:6b) and upon the king (e.g. Pss 21:6b; 45:4b). Unlike Joseph who was יפה־תאר ויפה מראה (Gen 39:6b) and David who was עם־יפה עינים וטוב ראי (1 Sam 16:12), this servant does not possess the outward qualifications that typify a key leader or king (cf. 1 Sam 9:2). The kingly qualities of this servant are hidden from the naked eye. This servant, though, walks before Yahweh who does not look on the outward form as human beings do, but looks at the heart (1 Sam 16:7b).

Verse 3: The plural voice testifies here about the sickly state of Yahweh's servant and confesses its own despising of him. Moreover, these speakers confess that they rejected him, which is highlighted by the phrase וכמסתר פנים ממנו (see, e.g., Isa 8:17; 54:8a).

Verses 4–5: With these lines, confessors exclaim their unexpected astonishment, which completely contradicts their first impression of the servant. In his analysis of the functional grammar of Isa 40–55, Michael Rosenbaum remarks that vv. 4a, 5, 6b contain "*Replacing Foci*" which indicates a change in the pragmatic information of the speaker.[139] In v. 4a, the replacing focus is triply marked by the particle אכן, the word order of object verb, and the pronoun הוא functioning as an enclitic highlighting the previous word.[140] For Rosenbaum, this grammatical construction is "designed to replace one set of assumptions about the Servant with another." It "focuses attention on the *our-ness* and points to the true cause of the Servant's suffering."[141] Rosenbaum's analysis highlights the speakers' sudden and unexpected reversal of their opinion concerning the servant's condition. Like Job's friends, the plural voice thought that the servant was sick because of his own sin. In fact, the servant is violently struck (נגע) like Job who cried out: כי יד־אלוה נגעה בי (19:21b).[142]

139. See Rosenbaum, *Word-Order Variation*, 66–78.

140. Rosenbaum notes that Stephen A. Geller identifies the use of the pleonastic pronoun הוא in 53:4a as "quasi-clefting"; see Geller's "Cleft Sentences with Pleonastic Pronoun: A Syntactic Construction of Biblical Hebrew and Some of its Literary Uses," *JANESCU* 20 (1991): 15–33 (30). Geller (ibid., 31 n. 56) and Takamitsu Muraoka (*Classical Syriac for Hebraists* [Wiesbaden: Harrassowitz, 1987], §103) also remark that the Syriac enclitic pronoun *hûʾ* functions in a similar manner.

141. Rosenbaum, *Word-Order Variation*, 82–83.

142. Bastiaens ("Language of Suffering," 429) sees the verb נגע in Job 19:21 as reminiscent of its use here. For some interpreters the term נגוע indicates that the servant suffered a skin disease which the Vg understands as *leprosum* (so, e.g., Duhm, *Jesaja*, 359; Lindblom, *Servant Songs*, 44; see also Baltzer, *Deutero-Isaiah*, 408). In Lev 13–14, the term נגע refers to some type of skin disease (cf. 13:2). In

Like the mockers of the innocent sufferer in the lament psalms, the plural voice despised and rejected the servant because of his sickly, sinful state (e.g. Ps 22:7, 24). They despised him and did not "consider him" (חשבנהו) because they "considered him" (חשבנהו) stricken by Yahweh for disciplinary reasons. The plural voice, though, acknowledges that their assumptions could not be farther from the truth. Rather, the servant's intimate experience of "sickness" (חלי) was "our sicknesses" (חלינו). The servant was a "man of severe pains" (איש מכאבות) because he carried "our severe pains" (מכאבינו).[143]

In the first bicolon of v. 5 the plural voice discloses the reason for the servant's condition. He was struck by God with disease and sickness like those who have sinned against Yahweh (see Deut 28:22, 27, 35, 59, 61; Mic 6:13). Here the servant shares in the suffering of Yahweh's people. Yet, the sickness of this servant is not caused by his own rebellion or iniquity, but because of "our rebellions" (מפשענו) and "our iniquities" (מעונתינו). Thus, others deserved the sickness and suffering he experiences.

The task of the servant consists of absorbing the rebellions of others into himself. He vicariously suffers the consequences of others' sin. This substitutionary task is made clear in the final bicolon of v. 5, as the speakers assert that their sins have been transferred to the innocent servant, and somehow in exchange wholeness and health have been transmitted to them. The term מוסר is often used to indicate the instruction, rebuke, or physical discipline of a child by a parent in order to correct and deter a certain type of behavior (see Prov 13:24; 22:15; 23:13).[144] Yahweh also disciplines (יסר) sinners in order to turn them from their wickedness (cf. Ps 39:11–12; see also Job 5:17). Yahweh has on a number of occasions struck Israel because of their sin, but the nation has refused to turn back to him (e.g. Jer 2:30; 5:30; 30:14). Here, Yahweh disciplines his undeserving servant. At the close of ch. 48 Yahweh makes it clear that those who oppose him will not find שלום. The wicked will only experience chaos and sickness; however, the servant's undeserved suffering will replace these with peace and health.

2 Kgs 15:5 and 2 Chr 26:20 the Piel form of נגע is used to indicate a skin disease. However, the term can also be used simply to indicate that harm has been done to someone (e.g. Gen 12:17; 26:29; 1 Sam 6:9). Further, as the majority of interpreters concur, there is not enough information given in this text even to suggest that the servant is described as having a skin disease or leprosy.

143. On the various repeated ideas that produce interpretive contrasts in this poem, see Paul R. Raabe, "The Effect of Repetition in the Suffering Servant Song," *JBL* 103 (1984): 77–84.

144. See further R. D. Branson, "יסר," *TDOT* 6:129–34 (131–34).

Verse 6: The prepositional phrase כלנו forms an *inclusio* around this verse that completes the replacement focus of the speaker's mistaken assumptions.[145] The phrase emphasizes the fact that no one is excluded from the category of sin; "all of *us*" have turned from Yahweh. With the first bicolon, speakers explicitly confess their sin against Yahweh. The phrase איש לדרכו פנינו clearly indicates that while the confession is corporate, each individual person is culpable and responsible to confess his own sin. This confession is a strong self-involving speech act that expresses an assertive–expressive–commissive illocution. With the assertive dimension, speakers assert that they have in fact committed certain rebellious acts against Yahweh. One aspect of the expressive conveys the attitude of remorse and stance of humbleness. The speakers also publicly confess their culpability and thereby adopt a stance concerning sin. They perform the act of separating themselves from rebellious actions by expressing their stance concerning those actions. As Briggs remarks, to label something as sin "is a self-involving act indicative of one's stance towards that sin."[146] The commissive dimension involves the entailments of retaining that stance. Thus, self-involved speakers utter a multidimensional illocutionary act whereby they confess their sin and obligate themselves to a lifelong stance of walking in the ways of Yahweh and not their own.

With the final colon, the speakers make it unmistakably clear that they deserved the suffering that the servant is experiencing. Their iniquity is upon the servant. The speakers also testify that Yahweh himself is orchestrating their forgiveness through the servant. Yahweh is the one who has provided deliverance despite the speakers' rebellion against him.

Verse 7: This verse begins the next sub-unit that testifies to the servant's complete innocence in his behavior and his speech. The plural voice also speaks about the unreserved submissiveness of the servant to Yahweh. In the initial colon they testify that the servant willingly embraced the suffering task. Yahweh's servant is not a victim of circumstance, but he knowingly and willingly volunteers for the assigned suffering. In a concentric structure, the remainder of the verse illustrates the silent stance of the servant:

A ולא יפתח־פיו
B כשה לטבח יובל
B' וכרחל לפני גזזיה נאלמה
A' ולא יפתח פיו

145. Rosenbaum, *Word-Order Variation*, 201–2.
146. Briggs, *Words in Action*, 247; see also p. 215.

"The thrust of this verse is the patient resilience with which Yahweh's servant absorbs the suffering which is heaped upon him, which is emphasized in B and B'."[147] With this imagery, the servant's stance directly contrasts the confessors' previous actions, who like sheep went in their own rebellious direction. This servant goes in the way Yahweh directs. Jeremiah uses the same metaphor in the central lines BB' to describe his own experience (11:19a), but he confesses that he was not aware of such plots against him (v. 19b). Moreover, he asks Yahweh to carry off his wicked opponents like sheep for the slaughter (12:3bα).

Verses 8–9: The language here corresponds with a number of expressions found in the lament psalms, and thus some interpreters argue that these verses, along with the entire poem, do not describe a death of the servant nor any vicarious suffering.[148] Whybray has presented the most extensive and rigorous arguments in support of this position.[149] Space does not allow for a detailed analysis of Whybray's conclusions.[150] In brief, looking at each expression that describes death in isolation could lead to the conclusion that they are hyperbolic metaphors. For instance, the term נגזר can indicate death (e.g. Ps 88:5b) or simply a dire situation (Ezek 37:11bβ; Lam 3:54b). King Uzziah is נגזר from the temple because of his skin disease (2 Chr 26:20–21). The phrase נגזר מארץ היים can indicate death, which even Whybray concedes,[151] but some of its occurrences are less conclusive (see Isa 38:11aβ; Jer 11:19bβ; Ezek 26:20b; 32:23bβ, 24bβ; Pss 27:13; 52:7b; 116:9b; 142:6b). Nevertheless, the combination of all the expressions referencing death in this passage coupled with the notion that the servant becomes a sacrifice, makes its seem quite clear that the servant in fact dies.[152] The vicarious language in

147. Willis, "Alternating Parallelism," 68.

148. E.g. Driver, "Isaiah 52$_{13}$–53$_{12}$," 104–5; Gerleman, "Gottesknecht," 41–42; Jeppesen, "Mother Zion," 109–10, 120–21; Orlinsky, "So-Called 'Servant,'" 51–66; J. Alberto Soggin, "Tod und Auferstehung des Leidenden Gottesknechtes: Jesaja 53:8–10," *ZAW* 87 (1975): 346–55; Torrey, *Second Isaiah*, 420–21.

149. Whybray, *Liberated Prophet*, 29–106.

150. For critiques of Whybray's position, see, in particular, Laato, *Servant of YHWH*, 138–50; see also Oswalt, *Chapters 40–66*, 392–98.

151. Whybray, *Liberated Prophet*, 106; *pace* Soggin, "Tod und Auferstehung," 351–54.

152. Along with the above, those who understand the servant dying include Beuken, *Jesaja II/B*, 222–27; Blenkinsopp, *Isaiah 40–55*, 353–54; Brueggemann, *Isaiah 40–66*, 147; Childs, *Isaiah*, 416–17; Dahood, "Phoenician Elements," 69–71; idem, "Isaiah 53,8–12," 568; Delitzsch, *Isaiah*, 2:297–303; Elliger, *Verhältnis*, 22; Ivan Engnell, "The 'Ebed Yahweh Songs and the Suffering Messiah in 'Deutero-Isaiah,'" *BJRL* 31 (1948): 54–93 (76–89); Fohrer, "Stellvertretung," 33–35;

the preceding verses along with the servant's death signifies that his sacrifice is also substitutionary.[153]

The speakers ask another weak rhetorical question with the implied answer that no one would have given the servant's death a second thought because he was obviously guilty. The speakers testify that human opponents aggressively and unjustly sought out his execution. Like 50:6–9, the servant suffers at the hands of those who oppose Yahweh. In this poem, the servant has two opponents: human beings and Yahweh. The text does not clearly distinguish between these two; who did what and when to the servant. In these verses, human beings are responsible for the death of the servant, yet, as the following verses show, the servant is the one who offers himself unto Yahweh who caused his sickness and purposed his death.

The servant is appointed a grave with the רשעים and the עשיר. As seen above, at the close of the first section of Isa 40–55 Jacob–Israel is identified as the רשעים (48:22). Near the close of the second section Yahweh issues a call to the רשע to forsake their sin and return to him (55:7aα). As most agree, the parallel term עשיר does not indicate a righteous person or group.[154] This does not make sense in this context and it is not unusual for the rich to be equated with the wicked, especially in the prophets (e.g. Jer 5:26–28; Mic 6:11–12; Job 27:13–19). Although the servant is innocent, he suffers as one who is guilty and naturally his grave is placed with the rebellious.

Verses 10–11aα: The speakers reiterate that the suffering of the servant was purposed and accomplished by Yahweh with the cooperation of his servant. Yet, the speakers introduce a new aspect of this suffering—the servant himself is a sacrificial offering. Interpreters have been generally puzzled by the use of אשם to define the servant's sacrificial death. Such a designation, however, is quite appropriate and significant for a number of reasons. The verb אשם indicates that one who has acted wrongly, has

Goldingay, *Isaiah*, 306; Hermisson, "Gottesknechtslied," 15–16; Janowski, "Er trug unsere Sünden," 85–90; Koole, *Isaiah 3/2*, 303–17; Kutsch, "Leiden und Tod," 182–85; Lindblom, *Servant Songs*, 44; Lindsey, "Isaiah 52:13–53:12 (Concluded)," 26–30; McKenzie, *Second Isaiah*, 135; Motyer, *Prophecy of Isaiah*, 433–36; Mowinckel, *He That Cometh*, 200–5; Muilenburg, "Chapters 40–66," 625–27; Payne, "Servant of the Lord," 136–39; Seitz, "Isaiah 40–66," 466–67; Westermann, *Isaiah 40–66*, 266; Wilcox and Paton-Williams, "Servant Songs," 96.

153. In general, interpreters who acknowledge that the servant dies also recognize that the nature of his suffering and death is vicarious.

154. *Pace*, e.g., Delitzsch, *Isaiah*, 2:301–2; Lindsey, "52:13–53:12 (Concluded)," 29–30; Motyer, *Prophecy of Isaiah*, 435–36.

become guilty, and thus culpable.[155] For instance, in Hosea, those who rebel against Yahweh and engage in the worship of Baal are אשם before him (Hos 4:15aβ; 5:15aβ; 10:2a; 13:1b; 14:1bα).[156] The noun expresses the "guilt-obligation" of the offender, "it is *the obligation, the duty, the liability, that results from incurring guilt.*"[157] In the sacrificial system, אשם is a technical term that specifically dealt with sinful acts identified by the verb מעל (cf. Lev 5:15–16, 21; Num 5:6–7; Ezra 10:10, 19).[158] In general, מעל conveys unfaithfulness to Yahweh (e.g. Josh 7:1) or to another human being (e.g. Num 5:12).[159] The phrase מעל ביהוה essentially means "to commit unfaithfulness against Yahweh" (e.g. Lev 5:15, 21; 26:40; Num 5:6; Josh 22:16).[160] מעל is a "breach of faith" against Yahweh.[161] In relation to the nation Israel, Yahweh considers the violation of their covenant oath as an act of מעל, and consequently he sent them into captivity (Lev 26:40; Ezek 15:8; 2 Chr 36:14; Neh 1:8; Dan 9:7; see also Ezek 17:19–20).[162]

Important for Whybray's overall argument against the notion of vicarious suffering and sacrifice is his claim that the אשם was extremely limited and was ineffective to atone for those who had sinned ביד רמה or intentionally (Num 15:30). Such defiant acts denoted contempt for the word of Yahweh and the breaking of his commandments (v. 31). "The sins of Israel which had led to the punishment of the Exile were certainly of this kind" and there was no sacrifice whatsoever that could "atone for Israel's wanton rejection of God."[163] Whybray is correct in one sense that intentional sins fell outside the regular provision of the sacrificial system. Yet, as noted above, some texts identify Israel's sin against Yahweh as מעל, which the אשם could expiate.

Jacob Milgrom has produced the most thorough examination of the אשם sacrifice and demonstrates that it reduces intentional sins to an inadvertence, thereby rendering it eligible for sacrificial expiation.[164] The

155. See R. Knierim, "אשם," *TLOT* 1:191–95 (192–93).

156. D. Kellermann, "אשם," *TDOT* 1:429–37 (435–36).

157. Knierim, *TLOT* 1:193.

158. John E. Hartley, *Leviticus* (WBC 4; Dallas: Word, 1992), 77. For a in depth study on מעל in relation to אשם, see Jacob Milgrom, *Cult and Conscience: The Asham and the Priestly Doctrine of Repentance* (SJLA 18; Leiden: Brill, 1976), 16–35; idem, *Leviticus 1–16* (AB 3; New York: Doubleday, 1991), 345–56.

159. See R. Knierim, "מעל," *TLOT* 2:680–82; H. Ringgren, "מעל," *TDOT* 8:460–63.

160. Knierim, *TLOT* 2:681–82.

161. Hartley, *Leviticus*, 77.

162. See Hartley, *Leviticus*, 81; Knierim, *TLOT* 2:681–82.

163. Whybray, *Liberated Prophet*, 65–66.

164. Milgrom, *Cult and Conscience*, 104–27; idem, *Leviticus 1–16*, 339–78.

key component or principle of an אשם for expiating an intentional sin is the requisite confession of sin. According to Milgrom, for "involuntary sin, *ʾšm* or remorse alone suffices; it renders confession superfluous. But for deliberate sin there is the *added requirement that remorse be verbalized*; the sin must be articulated and responsibility assumed."[165] He goes on to say that "*confession is the legal device* fashioned by the Priestly legislators to convert deliberate sins into inadvertencies, thereby qualifying them for sacrificial expiation."[166]

The servant offers himself as an אשם, which means that he bears the guilt-obligation of those who have wronged Yahweh in some way. As a sacrifice, he absorbs the guilt of others and thus dies on behalf of or in place of the rebellious. In addition, the servant's sacrificial death provides for both unintentional and intentional sins. Thus, any and all sins are atoned for by this אשם.[167] Yet, in this text the sin confessed is labeled as intentional, defiant rebellion (53:6). Operating through the conventional institution of Yahweh's sacrificial system, the אשם provides forgiveness for intentional sins when accompanied by confession, which these verses implore the addressee/reader to do. In speech act terms, the servant's death is an אשם which operates through the extralinguistic convention of the sacrificial legislation. But the sacrifice performs its intended expiatory purpose only when accompanied with the linguistic confession of sin. Thus, the institutionally required confession in conjunction with a אשם creates the states of affairs that the speaker is *counted as* forgiven.

The servant's death as אשם is the provision of forgiveness, but the accompanied speech act of confession transforms the speaker as forgiven. Through the self-involved confession of sin speakers separate themselves from sinful acts and receive forgiveness of that sin. Following Briggs' discussion on forgiveness, through this speech act Yahweh removes the institutional fact of sin, which also changes the brute facts. Thus, the identity of the sinful person is *refigured*. In other words, the confessor's identity as *rebellious* is changed to *forgiven*. As a result, the sickly condition of the confessor has been transformed into health and vitality. Yahweh has not been persuaded to forgive nor are confessors merely convinced of their forgiveness. Rather, Yahweh's servant has actualized their illocutionary act that brings about a transformation in the world whereby one can become transformed as forgiven and restored through personal confession of sin and the servant's אשם sacrifice.

165. Ibid., 109 (italics mine).
166. Ibid., 119 (italics mine).
167. Hartley, *Leviticus*, 80.

The result of the servant's sacrifice includes descendents, lengthened days, and the continued success of Yahweh's purpose. Oswalt points out that the phrases in v. 10aβ–b are typically used of a person favored by God: they will see descendents (Pss 127:3–5; 128:6; Prov 17:6), they will live a long life (Pss 21:5; 34:13; Prov 3:2), and they will accomplish God's purposes for they life (Josh 1:7; 2 Chr 20:20; Pss 1:3; 91:16).[168] Regarding the phrase יראה זרע, most interpreters conclude that the servant will have descendents, but the text does not explicitly identify them as "his" descendents. In light of the previous chapter, the future people of God will be those descendents of Jacob–Israel who witness to Yahweh's power and confess him alone. These descendents are also identified as the children of Zion, Yahweh's disciples, Yahweh's servants. Yet, correlated with the confessional nature of Yahweh's community, those who confess their sins in relation to the servant will be in a sense "birthed" into the people of God. In this way, the servant will have descendents who will form the confessional community of Yahweh. Thus, this servant plays a significant role in the formation of Yahweh's people.

The phrase יאריך ימים is obscure. What seems to be suggested is that Yahweh will lengthen days because of the servant's work which directly impacts the lifespan of the servant and the confessors. In the last colon of the verse, the speakers testify that as Yahweh "purposed" (חפץ) to crush the servant and make him sick (v. 10aα[1]), so Yahweh's "purpose" (חפץ) will continue to succeed through the servant. With the final line of the plural voice, the speakers testify that the servant will see again and will be satisfied with the outcome of his suffering. Thus, the servant dies and will live again.

Verse 11aβ–b: The first plural voice has completed its confession/testimony and Yahweh finishes the servant's story. The term צדק is significant in the book of Isaiah and especially in chs. 40–55. In these chapters the noun צדקה/צדק often occurs in parallel with ישועה (e.g. 45:8; 46:12–13; 51:5aα, 6b, 8b). Yet, even without this parallel, the noun can convey the idea of deliverance (e.g. 54:14a, 17bβ). In these instances, the צדקה/צדק of Yahweh concerns his faithfulness to his covenant promises which he demonstrates in his saving action that aims at restoring relationship.[169]

168. Oswalt, *Chapters 40–66*, 402.

169. See John J. Scullion, "*Ṣeded-Ṣedeqah* in Isaiah cc. 40–66 with Special Reference to the Continuity in Meaning Between Second and Third Isaiah," *UF* 3 (1971): 335–48 (340–41); idem, "Righteousness (Old Testament)," *ABD* 5:724–36 (733).

The Hiphil form of the verb occurs here and eleven other times throughout the Old Testament (Exod 23:7bα; Deut 25:1bα; 2 Sam 15:4bβ; 1 Kgs 8:32b; Isa 5:23a; 50:8aα; Ps 82:3b; Job 27:5a; Prov 17:15a; Dan 12:3b; 2 Chr 6:23b). According to a number of semantic analysts, the predominant meaning of the verb in this stem is that of "acquit, declare righteous, justify, make right, vindicate."[170] However, the construction יצדיק...לרבים in this colon is unique and thus suggests a different idea.[171] In all other instances, the ל does not appear and without the preposition the term clearly functions as a direct object and possibly a forensic idea, for example, justifying the unjust (cf. Dan 12:3). Because of its typical usage, a number of translators understand the verb יצדיק here in a forensic sense, that is, the servant justifies, accounts as righteous the many.[172] The grammatical construction argues against this as well as probably imposing too much of a forensic understanding on the verbal form.[173] Some interpreters understand the verb as intransitive or reflexive/causative, indicating that the servant showed or proved himself to be righteous to the many.[174] The appealing aspect of this suggestion is its correspondence with the opening line of Yahweh's first speech. Still, the main concern of this passage is salvation from sin and the restoration

170. E.g. *HALOT*, 1003–4; B. Johnson, "צדק," *TDOT* 12:239–64 (250); K. Koch, "צדק," *TLOT* 2:1046–62 (1051); Scullion, *ABD* 5:726.

171. 1QIsa[a] reads ובדעתו יצדיק צדיק עבדו לרבים, which is identical to the MT except for the initial copula and the 3ms suffix on עבד. As discussed above, the suffix could be a י in 1QIsa[a], which is a preferred reading here (see Barthélemy, *Critique Textuelle*, 405). The LXX is ambiguous δικαιῶσαι δίκαιον εὖ δουλεύοντα πολλοῖς. John W. Olley understands God as the subject of the inf. and the servant as the object and interprets the line, "'to vindicate or acquit one who has served well,' so correcting the injustice of v. 8a" (*"Righteousness" in the Septuagint of Isaiah: A Contextual Study* [SBLSCS; Missoula, Mont.: Scholars Press, 1979], 51). Yet, δίκαιον could be taken as the subject of the inf. and translated as "a righteous person justifies well by serving many." The Tg reads בחכמתיה יזכי זכאין ("by his wisdom he will vindicate/justify the just").

172. E.g. Baltzer, *Deutero-Isaiah*, 393; Blenkinsopp, *Isaiah 40–55*, 346; Childs, *Isaiah*, 419; Delitzsch, *Isaiah*, 2:309–10; Hermisson, "Gottesknechtslied," 8, 19; Koole, *Isaiah 3/2*, 332–33; Muilenburg, "Chapters 40–66," 630; Oswalt, *Chapters 40–66*, 405; Watts, *Isaiah 34–66*, 232.

173. See Olley, *Septuagint of Isaiah*, 61–62.

174. Mowinckel is typically attributed as the first to interpret the phrase this way (*He That Cometh*, 199). Those who adopt this idea include, among others, Beuken, *Jesaja II/B*, 188, 232–33; Clines, *I, He, We, and They*, 21–22; Goldingay, *Isaiah*, 308; Bo Reicke, "The Knowledge of the Suffering Servant," in *Das Ferne und Nahe Wort* (Festschrift Leonhard Rost; ed. F. Maass; BZAW 105; Berlin: Töpelmann, 1967), 186–99 (cf. 189–91); Stratton, "Engaging Metaphors," 225; Westermann, *Isaiah 40–66*, 267–68; Whybray, *Isaiah 40–66*, 181.

of relationship. This theme correlates with the primary use of the noun צדקה/צדק in Isa 40–55. Thus, more likely the servant is bringing or providing righteousness/salvation for many.[175] In ch. 51, Yahweh has promised to the second masculine plural addressee that יצא ישעי and קרוב צדקי (v. 5aα). His servant will realize this promise by offering himself as an אשם and thereby bringing righteousness to many, which results in the forgiveness of sin, wholeness, health, and restored relationship with Yahweh. Briggs' conclusions concerning the dual aspect of self-involved forgiveness correspond to this passage: Yahweh has taken the *stance* of providing forgiveness which results in the *entailment* of restored relationship.

The final colon reiterates the means of this provided righteousness. The phrase ועונתם הוא יסבל is very similar to the phrase in Lam 5:7, אנחנו עונתיהם סבלנו. As the speakers bore the iniquities of their fathers, so the servant bears the iniquities of others. The noun רבים here and in 52:14aα along with the antecedent of the third masculine plural has given rise to a number of suggestions as to their identities. The most logical conclusion is that they both correspond to the "we/us/our" group. As already seen, this is not the first time that a switch in personal pronouns has occurred. An identical switch from "we" to "their" occurs in 42:24aβ–b, which refers to the same entity.[176] In addition, Yahweh as the speaker would naturally speak about the plural group in the third person. Clines further observes that within the poem "the identity of the 'we' and the 'they' virtually merges as 'he' is shown to have the same relationship to both groups: that is, 'he' bears (*nāśā'*, *sābal*) the sufferings and pains of the 'we' (53:4), and also bears (*sābal*, *nāśā'*) the guilt (*'āwôn*) and sin (*ḥēṭ'*) of the 'they', the *rabbîm* (53:11b, 12b)."[177] Thus, the רבים are those for whom the servant bears sin, who are the first person plural confessors and in the context of Isa 40–55 are those among Jacob–Israel and the nations.[178]

Verse 12: In the first bicolon Yahweh again discusses the servant in royal language while summarizing his priestly work. The arm/servant of Yahweh has triumphed over sin. After the conquest Yahweh the victor

175. A few interpreters understand the verb in a similar way, for example, Fohrer, "Stellvertretung," 28; Gerleman, "Gottesknecht," 43; Kutsch, "Leiden und Tod," 173, 189; McKenzie, *Second Isaiah*, 131; Motyer, *Prophecy of Isaiah*, 441–42; North, *Second Isaiah*, 65.

176. See further de Regt, "Person Shift," 227.

177. Clines, *I, He, We, and They*, 40.

178. John W. Olley, "'The Many': How is Isa 53,12a to be Understood?," *Bib* 68 (1987): 330–56.

and his servant distribute the spoils. What the actual שלל consists of is not exactly clear. In general, interpreters either understand the "spoil" as the רבים and עצומים for Yahweh and his servant or something distributed to these people.[179] It seems best, though, that the text is conveying both ideas. In the first colon, Yahweh distributes the spoils to the servant with the many. For the servant, perhaps the spoils include his exaltation, long life, and the unique role he has in continuing to execute the purpose of Yahweh. For the confessors, Yahweh has promised to Jacob–Israel that he will restore the land and they will inherit the desolate heritages (49:8bβ). In addition, the spoils would be the effects of the servant bringing them righteousness. Conceivably the spoils also include free access to Yahweh's banquet (55:1–2). In the second colon, the servant apportions the mighty as spoil. In 40:10bα, Yahweh's "reward, booty" (שכר) constitutes those who return with him to Zion. Further, the goal of Isa 40–55 is for Yahweh to have a people for himself. Thus, the spoils of victory for Yahweh are the confessors who in turn receive the spoils of relationship with him.

With the remainder of the verse, Yahweh rehearses the vicarious work of the servant. He identified with rebels, he took their place in death, and carried their sin. By taking on the burden of sin the servant will forever relieve Yahweh of his servant role (43:24b). The verb יפגיע also conveys that the servant's intercessory work will continue on into the future.[180]

Conclusion

These four texts integrally function within the overarching prophetic strategy of Isaiah 40–55: *the call to return to Yahweh* which occurs by *forsaking sin, acknowledging and confessing Yahweh as God alone*, and *embracing the role of his servant*. Jacob–Israel is blind, deaf, and Israel in name only because of their chosen objects of worship. Consequently Yahweh's people are unable to fulfill their servant responsibilities. Yet, Yahweh remains faithful to his chosen nation and provides a way to

179. The most natural way to understand עצומים is in the sense of "people" as it is parallel to רבים (see N. Lohfink, "עצם," *TDOT* 11:289–303 [290–93], 301–2; Olley, "Isa 53,12a," 333–48). The two parallel terms also seem to indicate the large size of the confessors (see further Adele Berlin, "On the Meaning of *rb*," *JBL* 100 [1981]: 90–93 [91]).

180. Robert L. Hubbard's study on the root פגע is intriguing. He examines the verb in the Qal within judicial contexts and concludes that the verb is a legal technical term indicating "put to death, execute" ("The Hebrew Root *Pgʿ* as a Legal Term," *JETS* 27 [1984]: 129–33).

return to him physically and spiritually. His provided deliverance also functions as a way to demonstrate his sole claim to deity. Yet, this act is not reserved solely for Jacob–Israel; the nations are also included as witnesses to his power. Yahweh's illocutionary act of the Cyrus event will provide a way to return to him as the intended perlocutionary effect aims at convincing witnesses to acknowledge and confess him alone.

In the first section of Isa 40–55, Yahweh looks to the descendents of Jacob–Israel to form the future people of God. This occurs through a personal confession of him alone and by each individual entitling themselves with the name "Israel." Yahweh's future people constitute a confessional community. Through self-involvement with the second and third servant passages, speakers confess and embrace the open role of Yahweh's servant. Through their confession, they move from Babylon to the community of Yahweh's servants. Confessors incarnate the servant of Yahweh by uttering various illocutionary acts and thereby adopting particular stances and obligating themselves to the accompanied entailments. The final servant passage presents one last aspect of the confessors' return—sin. This visionary description of Yahweh's servant points to a time when forgiveness will be realized through one person's vicarious sacrifice. This individual will embrace Yahweh's unique assignment of priest and sacrifice. The text implores readers to confess their sin in accordance with his sacrifice in order to receive wholeness and restoration. Through self-involvement speakers will create the state of affairs that they are forgiven and are part of the people of God. At the same time, this vision offers other descriptions of what it means to be Yahweh's servant. The previous two servant passages have displayed that complete trust in Yahweh is one of the key hallmarks of being his servant. This is expressed here in the servant's silent trust in the face of unjust suffering. This servant stands alone in his commitment to Yahweh as everyone else opposes him. But even more incredibly, the servant's life completely revolves around others. His entire existence is for the benefit of others.[181] The servant entailments include silent trust in isolation that remains committed to Yahweh's way for the sake of others, even for those who oppose such unselfish action.

In sum, by participating in the prophetic function of Isa 40–55 and in particular with 41:21–29; 49:1–6; 50:4–11; and 52:13–53:12, confessors return to Yahweh, forsake sin, profess him alone, and embrace the role of his servant. Through self-involvement speakers utter illocutionary acts and thereby create the states of affairs that they are Yahweh's people.

181. See Brueggemann, *Isaiah 40–66*, 150.

Through their confession they will become Yahweh's disciples, the children of Zion, Yahweh's servants. Through interdependent self-involved illocutionary acts Yahweh will realize his goal: "You will be my people and I will be your God." Yahweh will have a people, a kingdom of priests, a holy nation, a community of servants.

CONCLUSION

This study began with a short essay comparing the interpretive outcomes of speech act theory and form criticism. I examined Isa 41:21–29 because of its obvious performative nature, but I soon began to notice other communicative acts in Isa 40–55 along with the overall self-involving nature of these chapters. In my research I also discovered that speech act theory had been used in a number of New Testament studies but was only utilized in a few Old Testament studies. In addition, I began to notice the minimal amount of research done on speech act theory by Old Testament interpreters. I also quickly deduced that the reason for this partial investigation was most likely due to the dense complexities of speech act theory and the daunting task of trying to comprehend the theory from the philosophical literature.

All of these initial discoveries helped formulate the goals of this study. In the first chapter I attempted to present the basic notions of speech act theory in an overarching manner. This study concentrated on the important distinction between illocutionary acts and perlocutionary effects. In short, an illocution is a type of utterance that *counts as* doing that may or may not involve formal non-linguistic conventions. I also endorsed, with certain clarifications and qualifications, the conceptual framework of illocutions operating along a spectrum of strengths with the constative and performative lying at each end. From the studies of Evans, Thiselton, and Briggs, the notion of self-involvement also comprises a strong speech act category that often includes several illocutionary forces, as the speaker adopts a stance towards a particular state of affairs that includes obligatory entailments.

I also explored how speech act theory has been appropriately and successfully utilized in biblical interpretation. Despite some of Evans's flawed notions of speech act theory proper, both Thiselton and especially Briggs have demonstrated the significance of his work in the development of a hermeneutic of self-involvement. These three studies provide a way to envision how to incorporate the central ideas of speech act theory into biblical interpretation. This working framework also displays the limitations of speech act theory as discussed in the Introduction. The notions espoused by speech act theorists translate into unique tools for the exegete, but they must be used with a certain amount of discrimination. Most Old Testament interpreters utilize speech act theory as a means of determining the persuasive aspects of biblical texts. This use not only distorts the nature of illocutionary acts, but it also discounts the unique contribution speech act theory can provide for the interpreter.

The ultimate goal of this study has been to press beyond the theoretical postulation of speech act theory and biblical interpretation to explore its usefulness in biblical exegesis. The contents of Isa 40–55 provide some of the most salient texts for conducting such a study. This is evidenced by this section's visionary character, which contains varied images, identities, and voices which are all laden with ambiguity and paradox. Rather than attempting to separate these so-called problems, reading the final form of the text allows one to embrace these tensions and consider them intentional.

I have suggested that the prophetic strategy of these chapters is a *call to return to Yahweh*. This occurs by *forsaking sin*, *acknowledging and confessing Yahweh as God alone*, and *embracing the role of his servant*. The way that the addressee/reader engages with this prophetic strategy is by closely following the text's literary structure and performative nature. Self-involved addressees/readers of Isa 40–55 utter speech acts whereby they adopt particular stances and obligate themselves to specific entailments. This is especially seen in the servant passages. One of the unique outcomes of this study is the notion of a single interdependent illocutionary act spoken by two different speakers. In certain instances, Yahweh and a speaker utter the same illocutions and thereby place themselves under particular obligations to fulfill that utterance. By uttering the illocution the addressee/reader *constitutes* Yahweh's illocutionary act. If either Yahweh or the speaker fails in the actualization of the illocution, it becomes infelicitous. Speech act theory has also shed further light on why the servant's sacrifice in ch. 53 is identified as an אשם. This special type of sacrifice requires a confessional component which is exactly what the addressee/reader is implored to do in vv. 1–11aα. Another important discovery is the self-involving nature of rhetorical questions. Speech act theorists have discussed the illocutionary dimension of both real and rhetorical questions but not from the perspective of self-involvement or evaluating their force along a spectrum of strengths. With a strong self-involving rhetorical question the speaker typically expresses an assertive–expressive–directive illocution that naturally also includes a commissive dimension. The hearer either co-expresses that illocution through self-involvement or offers a contrasting assertion with both including non-linguistic stances and entailments.

The self-involving nature of the biblical text, however, is not a new phenomenon as countless generations of readers have recognized this dynamic dimension in one way or another. This is especially true with the servant passages. For instance, language from these texts, particularly the fourth, is found in Dan 11 and 12[1] along with Zech 9–13.[2] There are also parallels between the righteous sufferers in Wisdom of Solomon 2:10–5:23 and the servant in Isa 52:13–53:12.[3] These texts display that people readily identified themselves with and/or as the Suffering Servant. The final servant passage has also played an important role within the Jewish community beyond that which is located in the Hebrew Bible.[4] Throughout the centuries the Jewish people identified with the servant in this text. Specifically, in the context of the atrocities of the Christian crusades and the unspeakable sufferings of the holocaust, the Jewish people naturally identified themselves with the Suffering Servant and thus have found solace and meaning in and for their sufferings.

1. See, e.g., Leslie C. Allen, "Isaiah LIII. 11 and its Echoes," *Vox Evangelica* 1 (1962): 24–28 (25–26); W. H. Brownlee, "Servant of the Lord," 12–15; John Day, "*Daʿat̲* 'Humiliation' in Isaiah LIII 11 in the Light of Isaiah LIII 3 and Daniel XII 4, and the Oldest Known Interpretation of the Suffering Servant," *VT* 30 (1980): 97–103; H. L. Ginsberg, "The Oldest Interpretation of the Suffering Servant," *VT* 3 (1953): 400–404; Martin Hengel, "Zur Wirkungsgeschichte von Jes 53 in vorchristlicher Zeit," in Janowski and Stuhlmacher, eds., *Der leidende Gottesknecht*, 49–91 (60–64); Wolff, *Jesaja 53*, 38–39.

2. See Adrian M. Leske, "Isaiah and Matthew: *The Prophetic Influence in the First Gospel.* A Report on Current Research," in Bellinger and Farmer, eds., *Jesus and the Suffering Servant*, 152–69 (158–60); Hengel, "Wirkungsgeschichte," 56–60; Wolff, *Jesaja 53*, 40.

3. See Pancratius C. Beentjes, "Wisdom of Solomon 3,1–4,19 and the Book of Isaiah," in van Ruiten and Vervenne, eds., *Studies in the Book of Isaiah*, 413–20; Leske, "Isaiah and Matthew," 161; M. Jack Suggs, "Wisdom of Solomon 2 10–5: A Homily Based on the Fourth Servant Song," *JBL* 76 (1957): 26–33; Wolff, *Jesaja 53*, 45–47.

4. See Joseph Alobaidi, *The Messiah in Isaiah 53: The Commentaries of Saadia Gaon, Salmon be Yeruham and Yefet ben Eli on Is 52:13–53:12* (Bern: Peter Lang, 1998); S. R. Driver and Adolf Neubauer, *The Fifty-Third Chapter of Isaiah According to the Jewish Interpreters* (2 vols.; The Library of Biblical Studies; New York: Ktav, 1969); Hengel, "Wirkungsgeschichte von Jes 53," 64–91; Kurt Hruby, "Die Rabbinische Exegese Messianischer Schriftstellen," *Judaica* 21 (1965): 100–122; Joel E. Rembaum, "The Development of a Jewish Exegetical Tradition Regarding Isaiah 53," *HTR* 75 (1982): 289–311. For a broader analysis of the Jewish community reading Isaiah, see Holladay, *Unbound by Time*, 131–57.

I am convinced that Jesus Christ is the supreme incarnation of the open servant role (cf. Acts 8:26–35).[5] But following the prophetic strategy of Isa 40–55, the role of Yahweh's servant is not restricted to one person; rather it is an open call for all those who desire to become the people of God. Such an understanding corresponds to how the servant passages have often been interpreted and used throughout history. This is also the view of the New Testament writers who do not consider the servant passages as sole descriptions of the person and mission of Jesus Christ. For instance, Paul in the book of Acts defends his preaching of the gospel to the Gentiles (13:44–48), and in response to criticism by some Antioch Jews he claims that the Lord commanded *us* and then quotes Isa 49:6b (leaving out from the LXX εἰς διαθήκην γένους). Paul understands this servant passage as a direct command to him and his co-workers. Through self-involvement Paul and others have embraced the servant role and the declarative–directive of being lights and bringing the salvation of Jesus Christ to the Gentiles.

Ongoing self-involvement with the final servant passage can be seen explicitly in Peter's use of the text. Peter calls the churches in Asia Minor to follow the example of Christ as depicted in this passage (1 Pet 2:21–25). Peter exhorts the churches to embrace the role of the servant in the face of severe suffering. The readers should follow the example of Christ who suffered on behalf of them (v. 21), was sinless (v. 22), and entrusted himself completely to God (v. 23). In contrast to this, he identifies his readers with those who strayed like sheep (v. 25), which gave reason for his atoning sacrifice (v. 24). Thus, while Peter implores his readers to exemplify Jesus Christ and thereby embrace the role of the servant, he also clearly distinguishes his readers from the servant.

For some scholars, the servant passages, in connection with prophecies about a future Davidic ruler (e.g. Isa 11:1–10), describe a future Messiah or specifically Jesus Christ.[6] Such an approach misses the text's self-involving nature and the openness of the servant role while at the same time it disregards how even the New Testament writers interpreted them. From the perspective of the New Testament, the coming of Jesus Christ has forever changed the servant passages and the servant figure.

5. For recent essays on the debate whether or not Jesus Christ knowingly understood his mission as the suffering servant of Isa 52:13–53:12, see Bellinger and Farmer, eds., *Jesus and the Suffering Servant*, 70–169.

6. E.g. Koole, *Isaiah 3/1*, 210; Lindsey, "Isaiah 42.1–9," 12–13; Motyer, *Prophecies of Isaiah*, 13–16; Oswalt, *Isaiah Chapters 40–66*, 108; Barry G. Webb, *The Message of Isaiah: On Eagle's Wings* (BST; Downers Grove, Ill.: InterVarsity, 1996), 29, 169–71.

Jesus Christ fulfilled the servant passages on a dimension that is humanly impossible. Yet, neither Jesus Christ nor the New Testament ever even faintly suggest that the servant passages no longer have any further significance. Rather, as with Jacob–Israel, readers are to still embrace the servant role but now in relation to and with an eye on Jesus Christ, the servant *par excellence*. The Christian Church is a confessional community of servants who have been delivered by and who are to exemplify their deliverer.[7]

In this study I have attempted to present a more defined understanding of speech act theory and to demonstrate its usefulness along with its limitations for biblical interpretation. Such analysis should not be confined to Isa 40–55, but the notions of speech act theory and its overarching concept of self-involvement should be explored wherever the biblical text expresses communicative action. By understanding the language of the Bible as performative and not solely as descriptive, readers of every generation have the opportunity to be exhorted, promised, confronted, and commissioned by God as well as to confess, promise, pray, lament, and offer praise to him.

7. John Goldingay anticipates the above conclusions in his book *God's Prophet, God's Servant: A Study in Jeremiah and Isaiah 40–55* (rev ed.; Toronto: Clements, 2002), cf. 113–14.

BIBLIOGRAPHY

Abma, Richtsje. "Traveling from Babylon to Zion: Location and Its Function in Isaiah 49–55." *JSOT* 74 (1997): 3–28.

Ackroyd, Peter R. "Isaiah 36–39: Structure and Function." Pages 3–21 in *Von Kanaan bis Kerala*. Festschrift J. P. M. van der Ploeg. Edited by W. C. Delsman. AOAT 211. Neukirchen–Vluyn: Neukirchener, 1982.

—"The Meaning of Hebrew דור Considered." *JSS* 13 (1968): 3–10.

Adams, Jim W. "Speech Act Theory, Biblical Interpretation, and Isaiah 40–55." Ph.D. diss., Fuller Theological Seminary, 2004.

Ahlström, G. W. "Notes to Isaiah 53:8f." *BZ* 13 (1969): 95–98.

Allen, Leslie C. "Isaiah LIII 2." *VT* 20 (1970): 491–92.

—"Isaiah LIII 2 Again." *VT* 21 (1971): 490.

—"Isaiah LIII 11 and its Echoes." *Vox Evangelica* 1 (1962): 24–28.

Alobaidi, Joseph. *The Messiah in Isaiah 53. The Commentaries of Saadia Gaon, Salmon ben Yeruham and Yefet ben Eli on Is 52:13–53:12*. La Bible dans l'histoire. Textes et etudes. Bern: Peter Lang, 1998.

Alston, William P. "Illocutionary Acts and Linguistic Meaning." Pages 29–49 in Tsohatzidis, ed., *Foundations of Speech Act Theory*.

—*Illocutionary Acts and Sentence Meaning*. Ithaca, N.Y.: Cornell University Press, 2000.

—"Linguistic Acts." *American Philosophical Quarterly* 1 (1964): 1–9.

—"Meaning and Use." *PhQ* 13 (1963): 107–24.

—*Philosophy of Language*. Englewood Cliffs, N.J.: Prentice–Hall, 1964.

—"Searle on Illocutionary Acts." Pages 57–80 in Lepore and van Gulick, eds., *John Searle and His Critics*.

—"Sentence Meaning and Illocutionary Act Potential." *PhEx* 2 (1977): 17–35.

Anscombe, G. E. M. *Intention*. 2d ed. Oxford: Blackwell. Ithaca, N.Y.: Cornell University Press, 1963.

—"On Brute Facts." *Analysis* 18 (1958): 69–72.

Anzilotti, Gloria I. "The Rhetorical Question as an Indirect Speech Device in English and Italian." *Canadian Modern Language Review* 38 (1982): 290–302.

Austin, J. L. *How To Do Things With Words*. Edited by J. O. Urmson and Marina Sbisà. 2d ed. Cambridge, Mass.: Harvard University Press, 1975.

—"How to Talk—Some Simple Ways." Pages 134–53 in *Philosophical Papers*. Edited by J. O. Urmson and G. J. Warnock. 3d ed. Oxford: Clarendon, 1979.

—"Performative-Constative." Pages 13–22 in Searle, ed., *Philosophy of Language*. Reprint from pages 22–33, 33–54 in *Philosophy and Ordinary Language*. Edited by C. E. Caton. Urbana, Ill.: University of Illinois Press, 1963.

—*Sense and Sensibilia. Reconstructed from the Manuscript Notes by G. J. Warnock*. Oxford: Clarendon, 1962.

Avishur, Y. "Addenda to the Expanded Colon in Ugaritic and Biblical Verse." *UF* 4 (1972): 1–10.

Bach, Kent, and Robert M. Harnish. *Linguistic Communication and Speech Acts*. Cambridge: MIT, 1979.

Bachmann, J. *Praeparation und Commentar zum Deutero-Jesaja, Heft 2: Jesaja Kap. 49–58*. Berlin, 1891.

Balentine, Samuel E., and John Barton, eds. *Language, Theology, and the Bible*. Festschrift James Barr. Oxford: Clarendon, 1994.

Baltzer, Klaus. *Deutero-Isaiah: A Commentary on Isaiah 40–55*. Translated by Margaret Kohl. Hermeneia. Minneapolis: Fortress, 2001.

—"Stadt-Tyche oder Zion–Jerusalem? Die Auseinandersetzung mit den Göttern der Zeit bei Deuterojesaja." Pages 114–20 in *Alttestamentlicher Glaube und Biblische Theologie*. Festschrift Horst D. Preuss. Edited by J. Hausmann and H.-J. Zöbel. Stuttgart: Kohlhammer, 1992.

—"Zur formgeschichtlichen Bestimmung der Texte vom Gottesknecht im Deuterojesaja-Buch." Pages 27–43 in *Probleme biblischer Theologie*. Festschrift Gerhard von Rad. Edited by Hans W. Wolff. Munich: Kaiser, 1971.

Barbour, Ian G., ed. *Science and Religion: New Perspectives on the Dialogue*. New York: Harper & Row, 1968.

Barr, James. *Comparative Philology and the Text of the Old Testament*. Oxford: Clarendon, 1968.

Barstad, Hans M. "The Future of the "Servant Songs": Some Reflections on the Relationship of Biblical Scholarship to its Own Tradition." Pages 261–70 in Balentine and Barton, eds., *Language, Theology, and the Bible*.

—"Isa. 40,1–11. Another Reading." Pages 225–40 in Lemaire, ed., *Congress Volume: Basel, 2001*.

—"On the So-Called Babylonian Literary Influence in Second Isaiah." *SJOT* 2 (1987): 90–110.

—"No Prophets? Recent Developments in Biblical Prophetic Research and Ancient Near Eastern Prophecy." *JSOT* 57 (1993): 39–60.

—*A Way in the Wilderness. The "Second Exodus" in the Message of Second Isaiah*. JSSM 12. Manchester: University of Manchester Press, 1989.

Bartholomew, Craig G., Colin Greene, and Karl Möller, eds. *After Pentecost: Language and Biblical Interpretation*. Scripture and Hermeneutics 2. Carlisle: Paternoster. Grand Rapids: Zondervan, 2001.

Barthélemy, Dominique. *Critique Textuelle de L'Ancien Testament*. Vol. 2, *Isaïe, Jérémie, Lamentations*. OBO 50/2. Göttingen: Vandenhoeck & Ruprecht, 1986.

—"Le grand rouleau d'Isaïe trouvé près de la Mer Morte." *RB* 57 (1950): 530–49.

Bastiaens, Jean Ch. *Interpretaties van Jesaja 53: Een intertextueel onderzoek naar de lijdende Knecht in Jes 53. MT/LXX) en in Lk 22:14–38, Hand 3:12–26, Hand 4:23–31 en Hand 8:26–40*. TFT-Studies 22. Tilburg University Press, 1993.

—"The Language of Suffering in Job 16–19 and in the Suffering Servant Passages of Deutero-Isaiah." Pages 421–32 in van Ruiten and Vervenne, eds., *Studies in the Book of Isaiah*.

Battenfield, James R. "Isaiah LIII 10: Taking an 'If' Out of the Sacrifice of the Servant." *VT* 32 (1982): 485.

Baumgartner, Wilhelm, and Jörg Klawitter. "Intentionality of Perception: An Inquiry Concerning J. R. Searle's Conception of Intentionality with Special Reference to Husserl." Pages 210–25 in Burkhardt, ed., *Speech Acts, Meaning and Intentions*.

Beentjes, Pancratius C. "Wisdom of Solomon 3,1–4,19 and the Book of Isaiah." Pages 413–20 in van Ruiten and Vervenne, eds., *Studies in the Book of Isaiah*.

Begrich, Joachim. *Studien zu Deuterojesaja*. TBü 20. Munich: Kaiser, 1963.

Bellinger, William H., Jr., and William R. Farmer, eds. *Jesus and the Suffering Servant: Isaiah 53 and Christian Origins*. Harrisburg, Pa.: Trinity, 1998.

Bentzen, Aage. "On the Ideas of 'the old' and 'the new' in Deutero-Isaiah." *ST* 1 (1947–48): 183–87.

Berlin, Adele. "On the Meaning of *rb*." *JBL* 100 (1981): 90–93.

Berlin, Isaiah, et al. *Essays on J. L. Austin*. Oxford: Clarendon, 1973.

Berry, Donald K. *The Psalms and Their Readers: Interpretive Strategies for Psalm 18*. JSOTSup 153. Sheffield: Sheffield Academic Press, 1993.

Berges, Ulrich. "Personifications and Prophetic Voices of Zion in Isaiah and Beyond." Pages 54–82 in de Moor, ed., *The Elusive Prophet*.

Bertolet, Rod. "Are There Indirect Speech Acts?" Pages 335–49 in Tsohatzidis, ed., *Foundations of Speech Act Theory*.

Beuken, Willem A. M., ed., *The Book of Job*. BETL 114; Leuven: Leuven University Press, 1994.

—"The Confession of God's Exclusivity by All Mankind: A Reappraisal of Is. 45,18–25." *Bijdragen* 35 (1974): 335–56.

—"Jes 50 10–11: Eine kultsche Paränese zur dritten Ebedprophetie." *ZAW* 85 (1973): 168–82.

—*Jesaja deel II A*. POT. Nijkerk: Callenbach, 1979.

—*Jesaja deel II B*. POT. Nijkerk: Callenbach, 1983.

—"The Main Theme of Tritio-Isaiah: 'The Servants of YHWH.'" *JSOT* 47 (1990): 67–87.

—"Mišpāt: The First Servant Song and Its Context." *VT* 22 (1972): 1–30.

—"De Vergeefse Moeite van de Knecht. Gadachten over de Plaats van Jesaja 49:1–6 in de Context." Pages 23–40 in Grosheide et al., eds., *De Knecht: Studies rondom Deutero-Jesaja*.

Bewer, Julius A. "Two Notes on Isaiah 49.1–6." Pages 86–90 in *Jewish Studies*. Festschrift George A. Kohut. Edited by Salo W. Baron and Alexander Marx. New York: Alexander Kohut Memorial Foundation, 1935.

Beyerlin, Walter, ed. *Near Eastern Religious Texts Relating to the Old Testament*. Translated by John Bowden. OTL. Philadelphia: Westminster, 1978.

Biddle, Mark E. "The Figure of Lady Jerusalem: Identification, Deification and Personification of Cities in the Ancient Near East." Pages 172–94 in Younger, Hallo, and Batto, eds., *The Biblical Canon in Comparative Perspective*.

—"Lady Zion's Alter Egos: Isaiah 47.1–15 and 57.6–13 as Structural Counterparts." Pages 124–36 in Melugin and Sweeney, eds., *New Visions of Isaiah*.

Black, Max. "Austin on Performatives." Pages 401–11 in Fann, ed., *Symposium on J. L. Austin*. Reprint from *Philosophy* 38 (1963): 217–26.

Blank, Sheldon H. "Studies in Deutero-Isaiah." *HUCA* 15 (1940): 1–46.

Blenkinsopp, Joseph. *Isaiah 40–55*. AB 19A. New York: Doubleday, 2002.

—"Second Isaiah—Prophet of Universalism." *JSOT* 41 (1988): 83–103.

—"The Servant and the Servants in Isaiah and the Formation of the Book." Pages 155–75 in vol. 1 of Broyles and Evans, eds., *Writing and Reading the Scroll of Isaiah*.

Blythin, Islwyn. "A Consideration of Difficulties in the Hebrew Text of Isaiah 53:11." *BT* 17 (1966): 27–31.

Boadt, Lawrence. "Intentional Alliteration in Second Isaiah." *CBQ* 45 (1983): 353–63.

Briggs, Richard S. "The Uses of Speech-Act Theory in Biblical Interpretation." *CRBS* 9 (2001): 229–76.

—*Words in Action: Speech Act Theory and Biblical Interpretation. Toward a Hermeneutic of Self-Involvement.* Edinburgh: T. & T. Clark, 2001.

Brock, S. P. *The Old Testament in Syriac according to the Peshiṭta Version III/1: Isaiah.* Leiden: Brill, 1993.

Brown, Colin. "The Hermeneutics of Confession and Accusation." *CTJ* 30 (1995): 460–71.

Brownlee, William H. "Certainly *Mašaḥti*!" *BASOR* 134 (1954): 27–28.

—"The Manuscripts of Isaiah from which DSIa was Copied." *BASOR* 127 (1952): 16–21.

—"The Servant of the Lord in the Qumran Scrolls. I." *BASOR* 132 (1953): 8–15.

—"The Servant of the Lord in the Qumran Scrolls. II." *BASOR* 135 (1954): 33–38.

Broyles, Craig C., and Craig A. Evans, eds. *Writing and Reading the Scroll of Isaiah: Studies of an Interpretive Tradition.* 2 vols. VTSup 70. Leiden: Brill, 1997.

Brueggemann, Walter. *Isaiah 40–66.* Westminster Bible Companion. Louisville, Ky.: Westminster John Knox, 1998.

—"Jeremiah's Use of Rhetorical Questions." *JBL* 92 (1973): 358–74.

Burkhardt, Armin. "Speech Act Theory—The Decline of a Paradigm." Pages 91–128 in idem, ed., *Speech Acts, Meaning and Intentions.*

—ed., *Speech Acts, Meaning and Intentions: Critical Approaches to the Philosophy of John R. Searle.* Berlin: de Gruyter, 1990.

Buss, Martin J. "Potential and Actual Interactions between Speech Act Theory and Biblical Studies." *Semeia* 41 (1988): 125–34.

Caird, G. B. *The Language and Imagery of the Bible with a New Introduction by N. T. Wright.* Grand Rapids: Eerdmans, 1980.

Calderone, Philip J. "Supplementary Note on *ḤDL*-II." *CBQ* 24 (1962): 412–19.

Campbell, J. Gordon, "Are all Speech-Acts Self-Involving?" *RelS* 8 (1972): 161–64.

Campbell, P. N. "A Rhetorical View of Locutionary, Illocutionary, and Perlocutionary Acts." *QJS* 59 (1973): 284–96.

Carmignac, Jean. "Six passages d'Isaïe éclairés par Qumran (Isaïe 14,11. 21,10. 22,5. 25,4. 26,3. 50,6." Pages 37–46 in *Bibel und Qumran: Beiträge zur Erforschung der Beziehungen zwischen Bibel-und Qumranwissenschaft.* Edited by Siegfried Wagner. Berlin: Evangelische Aupt-Bibelgesellschaft, 1968.

Carroll, Robert P. "Second Isaiah and the Failure of Prophecy." *ST* 32 (1978): 119–31.

—*When Prophecy Failed: Reactions and Responses to Failure in the Old Testament Prophetic Traditions.* London: SCM Press, 1979.

Ceresko, Anthony R. "The Rhetorical Strategy of the Fourth Servant Song (Isaiah 52:13–53:12): Poetry and the Exodus–New Exodus." *CBQ* 56 (1994): 42–55.

Chafe, Wallace L. *Meaning and the Structure of Language.* Chicago: University of Chicago Press, 1970.

Chamberlain, John V. "The Functions of God as Messianic Titles in the Complete Qumran Isaiah Scroll." *VT* 5 (1955): 366–72.

Childs, Brevard S. *Introduction to the Old Testament as Scripture.* Philadelphia: Fortress, 1979.

—*Isaiah.* OTL. Louisville, Ky.: Westminster John Knox, 2001.

—"Retrospective Reading of the Old Testament Prophets." *ZAW* 108 (1996): 362–77.

Chilton, Bruce D. *The Isaiah Targum: Introduction, Translation, Apparatus and Notes*. The Aramaic Bible 11. Wilmington: Glazier, 1987.

Claassen, W. T. "Speaker-Oriented Functions of Kî in Biblical Hebrew." *JNSL* 11 (1983): 29–46.

Clements, Ronald E. "Beyond Tradition-History: Deutero-Isaianic Development of First Isaiah's Themes." *JSOT* 31 (1985): 91–113.

—"Isaiah 45:20–25: The Goal of Faith." *Int* 40 (1986): 392–97.

—"Isaiah 53 and the Restoration of Israel." Pages 39–54 in Bellinger and Farmer, eds., *Jesus and the Suffering Servant*.

—Review of Tryggve N. D. Mettinger, *A Farewell to the Servant Songs: A Critical Examination of an Exegetical Axiom*. *JSS* 29 (1984): 293–95.

—"The Unity of the Book of Isaiah." *Int* 36 (1982): 117–29.

—"Zion as Symbol and Political Reality: A Central Isaianic Quest." Pages 3–17 in van Ruiten and Vervenne, eds., *Studies in the Book of Isaiah*.

Clifford, Richard J. *Fair Spoken and Persuading: An Interpretation of Second Isaiah*. New York: Paulist, 1984.

—"The Function of Idol Passages in Second Isaiah." *CBQ* 42 (1980): 450–64.

—"Isaiah, Book of (Second Isaiah)." *ABD* 3:490–501.

—"Rhetorical Criticism in the Exegesis of Hebrew Poetry." Pages 17–28 in *SBL Seminar Papers, 1980*. Edited by Kent H. Richards. SBLSP 19. Chico, Calif.: Scholars Press, 1980.

Clines, David J. A. *I, He, We, and They: A Literary Approach to Isaiah 53*. JSOTSup 1. Sheffield: JSOT Press, 1976.

—"The Parallelism of Greater Precision. Notes from Isaiah 40 for a Theory of Hebrew Poetry." Pages 77–100 in Follis, ed., *Directions in Biblical Hebrew Poetry*.

Cohen, L. Jonathan. "Do Illocutionary Forces Exist?" Pages 420–44 in Fann, ed., *Symposium on J. L. Austin*. Reprint from *PhQ* 14 (1964): 118–37.

Cohen, Ted. "Illocutions and Perlocutions." *FL* 9 (1973): 492–503.

Conrad, Edgar W. "The Community as King in Second Isaiah." Pages 99–111 in *Understanding the Word*. Festschrift Bernhard W. Anderson. Edited by James T. Butler, Edgar W. Conrad, and Ben. C. Ollenburger. JSOTSup 37. Sheffield: Sheffield Academic Press, 1985.

—"The 'Fear Not' Oracles in Second Isaiah." *VT* 34 (1984): 129–52.

—*Fear Not Warrior: A Study of 'al tîrā' Pericopes in the Hebrew Scriptures*. BJS 75. Chico, Calif.: Scholars Press, 1985.

—"Prophet, Redactor and Audience: Reforming the Notion of Isaiah's Formation." Pages 306–26 in Melugin and Sweeney, eds., *New Visions of Isaiah*.

—*Reading Isaiah*. OBT. Minneapolis: Fortress, 1991.

—"The Royal Narratives and the Structure of the Book of Isaiah." *JSOT* 41 (1988): 67–81.

—"Second Isaiah and the Priestly Oracle of Salvation." *ZAW* 93 (1981): 234–46.

Cooke, Gerald. "The Sons of (the) God(s)." *ZAW* 76 (1974): 22–47.

Corney, R. W. "Isaiah L 10." *VT* 26 (1976): 497–98.

Cross, Frank M. *Canaanite Myth and Hebrew Epic: Essays in the History of the Religion of Israel*. Cambridge, Mass.: Harvard University Press, 1973.

—"The Council of Yahweh in Second Isaiah." *JNES* 12 (1953): 247–77.

Crystal, David. "Liturgical Language in a Sociolinguistic Perspective." Pages 120–46 in *Language and the Worship of the Church*. Edited by David Jasper and R. C. D. Jasper. London: Macmillan, 1990.

Dahood, Mitchell. "Hebrew–Ugaritic Lexicography III." *Bib* 46 (1965): 311–32.

—"Hebrew–Ugaritic Lexicography IV." *Bib* 47 (1966): 403–19.

—"Isaiah 53,8–12 and Massoretic Misconstructions." *Bib* 63 (1982): 566–70.

—"Phoenician Elements in Isaiah 52:13–53:12." Pages 63–73 in Goedicke, ed., *Near Eastern Studies*.

—"Proverbs 8, 22–31: Translation and Commentary." *CBQ* 30 (1968): 512–21.

—"Textual Problems in Isaiah." *CBQ* 22 (1960): 400–409.

—"Third Masculine Singular with Preformative *t*- in Northwest Semitic." *Or* 48 (1979): 97–106.

Dascal, Marcelo. "Speech Act Theory and Gricean Pragmatics: Some Differences of Detail that Make a Difference." Pages 323–34 in Tsohatzidis, ed., *Foundations of Speech Act Theory*.

Davidson, Robert. "Universalism in Second Isaiah." *SJT* 16 (1963): 166–85.

Davies, Philip R. "God of Cyrus, God of Israel: Some Religio-Historical Reflections on Isaiah 40–55." Pages 207–25 in *Words Remembered, Texts Renewed*. Festschrift John F. A. Sawyer. Edited by Jon Davies, Graham Harvey, and Wilfred G. E. Watson. JSOTSup 195. Sheffield: Sheffield Academic Press, 1995.

Davies, Philip R., and David J. A. Clines, eds. *Among the Prophets: Language, Image and Structure in the Prophetic Writings*. JSOTSup 144. Sheffield: Sheffield Academic Press, 1993.

Davis, Steven. "Anti-Individualism and Speech Act Theory." Pages 208–19 in Tsohatzidis, ed., *Foundations of Speech Act Theory*.

—"Perlocutions." Pages 37–55 in Searle, Kiefer, and Bierwisch, eds., *Speech Act Theory and Pragmatics*.

Day, John. "*Daʿaṯ* 'Humiliation' in Isaiah LIII 11 in the Light of Isaiah LIII 3 and Daniel XII 4, and the Oldest Known Interpretation of the Suffering Servant." *VT* 30 (1980): 97–103.

De Boer, P. A. H. *The Elusive Prophet: The Prophet as Historical Person, Literary Character and Anonymous Artist*. OTS 45. Leiden: Brill, 2001.

—*Second-Isaiah's Message*. OTS 11. Leiden: Brill, 1956.

De Regt, L. J. "Discourse Implications of Rhetorical Questions in Job, Deuteronomy and the Minor Prophets." Pages 51–78 in de Regt, de Waard, and Fokkelman, eds., *Literary Structure and Rhetorical Strategies in the Hebrew Bible*.

—"Implications of Rhetorical Questions in Strophes in Job 11 and 15." Pages 321–28 in Beuken, ed., *The Book of Job*.

—"Person Shift in Prophetic Texts: Its Function and Its Rendering in Ancient and Modern Translations." Pages 214–31 in de Moor, ed., *The Elusive Prophet*.

De Regt, L. J., J. de Waard, and J. P. Fokkelman, eds. *Literary Structure and Rhetorical Strategies in the Hebrew Bible*. Assen: Van Gorcum, 1996.

De Waard, Jan. *A Handbook on Isaiah*. Textual Criticism and the Translator 1. Winona Lake, Ind.: Eisenbrauns, 1997.

Delekat, Lienhard. "Die Syropalästinische Jesaja-Übersetuzung." *ZAW* 71 (1959): 165–201.

Delitzsch, Franz. *Biblical Commentary on The Prophecies of Isaiah. With an Introduction by S. R. Driver*. 2 vols. 4th ed. Edinburgh: T. & T. Clark, 1892.

Derrida, Jacques. *Limited Inc.* Edited by Gerald Graff. Evanston, Ill.: Northwestern University Press, 1988.

—"Limited Inc abc..." *Glyph* 2 (1977): 162–254.

—"Signature Event Context." *Glyph* 1 (1977): 172–97.

Dijk, H. J. van. "Does Third Masculine Singular **Taqtul* Exist in Hebrew?" *VT* 19 (1969): 440–47.

Dion, Paul-Eugène. "L'universalisme religieux dans les différentes couches rédactionnelles d'Isaïe 40–55." *Bib* 51 (1970): 161–82.

Driver, Godfrey R. "Abbreviations in the Massoretic Text." *Textus* 1 (1960): 112–31.

—"Hebrew Scrolls." *JTS* 2 (1951): 17–30.

—"Isaiah 52_{13}–53_{12}: The Servant of the Lord." Pages 90–105 in *In Memoriam Paul Kahle*. Edited by Matthew Black and Georg Fohrer. BZAW 103. Berlin: Töpelmann, 1968.

—"Linguistic and Textual Problems: Isaiah I–XXXIX." *JTS* 38 (1937): 36–50.

—"Linguistic and Textual Problems: Isaiah XL–LXVI." *JTS* 36 (1935): 396–406.

—"Once Again Abbreviations." *Textus* 4 (1964): 76–94.

—"Problems of the Hebrew Text and Language." Pages 46–61 in *Alttestamentliche Studien*. Edited by Hubert Junker and Johannes Botterweck. Bonn: Hanstein, 1950.

Driver, S. R., and Adolf Neubauer. *The Fifty-Third Chapter of Isaiah According to the Jewish Interpreters*. 2 vols. The Library of Biblical Studies. New York: Ktav, 1969.

Duhm, D. Bernhard. *Das Buch Jesaia*. 2d ed. HKAT 3/1. Göttingen: Vandenhoeck & Ruprecht, 1902.

Dürr, Lorenz. *Die Wertung des göttlichen Wortes im Alten Testament und im antiken Orient*. Leipzig: Hinrichs, 1938.

Eagleton, Terry. "J. L. Austin and the Book of Jonah." Pages 231–36 in *The Book and the Text: The Bible and Literary Theory*. Edited by Regina M. Schwartz. Oxford: Blackwell, 1990.

Eaton, Marcia. "Speech Acts: A Bibliography." *Centrum* 2 (1974): 57–72.

Ehrlich, A. B. *Randglossen zur hebräischen Bibel*, vol. 5. Leipzig, 1912.

Eissfeldt, Otto. "The Ebed-Jahwe in Isaiah xl.–lv. in the Light of the Israelite Conceptions of the Community and the Individual, the Ideal and the Real." *ExpTim* 44 (1932–33): 261–68.

—*The Old Testament: An Introduction*. Translated by P. R. Ackroyd. New York: Harper & Row, 1965.

Eitan, Israel. "Hebrew and Semitic Particles: Comparative Studies in Semitic Philology." *AJSL* 44 (1928): 177–205, 254–60; 45 (1929): 48–63, 130–45, 197–211.

Elliger, Karl. *Deuterojesaja*. BKAT 11/1. Neukirchen–Vluyn: Neukirchener, 1978.

—*Deuterojesaja in seinem Verhältnis zu Tritojesaja*. BWANT 63. Stuttgart: Kohlhammer, 1933.

—"Nochmals Textkritisches zu Jes 53." Pages 137–44 in Schreiner, ed., *Wort, Lied und Gottesspruch*.

—"Textkritisches zu Deuterojesaja." Pages 113–19 in Goedicke, ed., *Near Eastern Studies*.

Emerton, John A. "Are There Examples of Enclitic *mem* in the Hebrew Bible?" Pages 321–38 in Fox et al., eds., *Texts, Temples, and Traditions*.

—"A Consideration of Some Alleged Meanings of ידע in Hebrew." *JSS* 15 (1970): 145–81.

—"A Further Considertion of D. W. Thomas's Theories about *Yādaʿ*." *VT* 41 (1991): 145–63.

Engnell, Ivan. "The 'Ebed Yahweh Songs and the Suffering Messiah in 'Deutero-Isaiah.'" *BJRL* 31 (1948): 54–93.

Evans, Donald D. "Barth on Talk about God." *CJT* 16 (1970): 175–90.

—*Communist Faith and Christian Faith*. London: SCM Press, 1965.

—"Differences between Scientific and Religious Assertions." Pages 101–33 in Barbour, ed., *Science and Religion*.

—*Faith, Authenticity and Morality*. Toronto: University of Toronto Press, 1980.

—*The Logic of Self-Involvement: A Philosophical Study of Everyday Language with Special Reference to the Christian Use of Language about God as Creator*. London: SCM Press, 1963.

—"Reply to J. Gordon Campbell." *RelS* 9 (1973): 469–72.

—*Spirituality and Human Nature*. Suny Series in Religious Studies. Albany: SUNY Press, 1993.

—*Struggle and Fulfillment: The Inner Dynamics of Religion and Morality*. Cleveland: Collins, 1979.

Evans, Geoffrey. "Ancient Mesopotamian Assemblies." *JAOS* 78 (1958): 1–11.

—"Ancient Mesopotamian Assemblies: An Addendum." *JAOS* 78 (1958): 114–15.

Fann, K. T., ed. *Symposium on J. L. Austin*. London: Routledge & Kegan Paul, 1969.

Fenton, Terry L. "Israelite Prophecy: Characteristics of the First Protest Movement." Pages 129–41 in de Moor, ed., *The Elusive Prophet*.

Field, Fridericus. *Origenis Hexaplorum*. 2 vols. Hildesheim: Georg Olms, 1964.

Fischer, Johann. "Das Problem des neuen Exodus in Isaias c. 40–55." *TQ* 110 (1929): 111–30.

Fish, Stanley. "How To Do Things with Austin and Searle: Speech-Act Theory and Literary Criticism." Pages 197–245 in idem, *Is There a Text in This Class? The Authority of Interpretive Communities*. Cambridge, Mass.: Harvard University Press, 1980.

Fishbane, Michael. "Arm of the Lord: Biblical Myth, Rabbinic Midrash, and the Mystery of History." Pages 271–92 in Balentine and Barton, eds., *Language, Theology, and the Bible*.

Fitzgerald, Aloysius. "*Btwlt* and *Bt* as Titles for Capital Cities." *CBQ* 37 (1975): 167–83.

—"The Mythological Background for the Presentation of Jerusalem as a Queen and False Worship as Adultery in the OT." *CBQ* 34 (1972): 403–16.

Fohrer, Georg. "Stellvertretung und Schuldopfer in Jes 52$_{13}$–53$_{12}$." Pages 24–43 in *Studien zu alttestamentlichen Texten und Themen (1966–1972)*. BZAW 155. Berlin: de Gruyter, 1981.

Fokkelman, Jan P. "Stylistic Analysis of Isaiah 40:1–11." Pages 68–90 in van der Woude, ed., *Remembering All the Way…*

Follis, Elaine R. ed. *Directions in Biblical Hebrew Poetry*. JSOTSup 40. Sheffield: JSOT Press, 1987.

—"The Holy City as Daughter." Pages 173–84 in idem, ed., *Directions in Biblical Hebrew Poetry*.

Forguson, L. W. "Locutionary and Illocutionary Acts." Pages 160–85 in Berlin et al., eds., *Essays on J. L. Austin*.

—"In Pursuit of Performatives." Pages 412–19 in Fann, ed., *Symposium on J. L. Austin*. Reprint from *Philosophy* 41 (1966): 341–47.

Fowl, Stephen E., ed. *The Theological Interpretation of Scripture: Classic and Contemporary Readings*. Blackwell Readings in Modern Theology. Cambridge: Blackwell, 1997.

Franke, Chris. *Isaiah 46, 47, and 48: A New Literary-Critical Reading*. Biblical and Judaic Studies 3. Winona Lake, Ind.: Eisenbrauns, 1994.

—"Reversals of Fortune in the Ancient Near East: A Study of the Babylon Oracles in the Book of Isaiah." Pages 104–23 in Melugin and Sweeney, eds., *New Visions of Isaiah*.

Furberg, Mats. "Meaning and Illocutionary Force." Pages 445–67 in Fann, ed., *Symposium on J. L. Austin*.

Gadamer, Hans-Georg. *Truth and Method*. Translated and revised by J. Weinsheimer and D. G. Marshall. 2d ed. New York: Continuum, 2000.

Gaines, R. N. "Doing by Saying: Toward a Theory of Perlocution." *QJS* 65 (1979): 207–17.

Geller, Stephen A. "Cleft Sentences with Pleonastic Pronoun: A Syntactic Construction of Biblical Hebrew and Some of its Literary Uses." *JANESCU* 20 (1991): 15–33.

—"A Poetic Analysis of Isaiah 40:1–2." *HTR* 77 (1984): 413–20.

Gelston, Anthony. "'Behold the Speaker': A Note on Isaiah XLI 27." *VT* 43 (1993): 405–8.

—"Isaiah 52:13–53:12: An Eclectic Text and a Supplementary Note on the Hebrew Manuscript Kennicott 96." *JSS* 35 (1990): 187–211.

—"Knowledge, Humiliation or Suffering: A Lexical, Textual and Exegetical Problem in Isaiah 53." Pages 126–41 in McKay and Clines, eds., *Of Prophets' Visions and the Wisdom of Sages*.

—"The Missionary Message of Second Isaiah." *SJT* 18 (1965): 308–18.

—"Some Notes on Second Isaiah." *VT* 21 (1971): 517–27.

Gerleman, Gillis. "Der Gottesknecht bei Deuterojesaja." Pages 38–60 in *Studien zur alttestamentlichen Theologie*. FDVNF. Heidelberg: Schneider, 1980.

Giblin, Charles H. "A Note on the Composition of Isaias 49,1–6(9a)." *CBQ* 21 (1959): 207–12.

Gill, J. H. "J. L. Austin and the Religious Use of Language." *Sophia* 8 (1969): 29–37.

Ginsberg, H. L. "The Arm of YHWH in Isaiah 51–63 and the Text of Isa 53 10–11." *JBL* 77 (1958): 152–56.

—"The Oldest Interpretation of the Suffering Servant." *VT* 3 (1953): 400–404.

—"Some Emendations in Isaiah." *JBL* 69 (1950): 51–60.

Gitay, Yehoshua. *Prophecy and Persuasion: A Study of Isaiah 40–48*. FTL 14. Bonn: Linguistica Biblica, 1981.

—ed., *Prophecy and Prophets: The Diversity of Contemporary Issues in Scholarship*. SBLSS. Atlanta: Scholars Press, 1997.

—"A Study of Amos's Art of Speech: A Rhetorical Analysis of Amos 3:1–15." *CBQ* 42 (1980): 293–309.

Goedicke, Hans, ed. *Near Eastern Studies*. Festschrift William F. Albright. Baltimore: The Johns Hopkins University Press, 1971.

Goldbaum, Fredric J. "Two Hebrew Quasi-Adverbs: לכן and אכן." *JNES* 23 (1964): 132–35.

Goldingay, John. "The Arrangement of Isaiah XLI–XLV." *VT* 29 (1979): 289–99.

—*God's Prophet, God's Servant: A Study in Jeremiah and Isaiah 40–55*. Rev. ed. Toronto: Clements, 2002.

—*Isaiah*. NIBC 13. Peabody, Mass.: Hendrickson, 2001.
—*Isaiah 40–55*. ICC. London: T. & T. Clark, 2006.
—"Isaiah 40–55 in the 1990s: Among Other Things, Deconstructing, Mystifying, Intertextual, Socio-Critical, and Hearer-Involving." *BibInt* 5 (1997): 225–46.
—"Isaiah 43,22–28." *ZAW* 110 (1998): 173–91.
—"Isaiah I 1 and II 1." *VT* 48 (1998): 326–32.
Gordis, Robert. "Job XL 29—An Additional Note." *VT* 14 (1964): 491–94.
—"A Rhetorical Use of Interrogative Sentences in Biblical Hebrew." *AJSL* 49 (1932–33): 212–17.
Gordon, R. P. "Isaiah LIII 2." *VT* 20 (1970): 491–92.
—"Where Have All the Prophets Gone? The 'Disappearing' Israelite Prophet Against the Background of Ancient Near East Prophecy." *BBR* 5 (1995): 67–86.
Gosse, Bernard, "Isaïe 52,13–53,12 et Isaïe 6." *RB* 98 (1991): 537–43.
—"Isaïe VI et la Tradition Isaïenne." *VT* 42 (1992): 340–49.
Greenspahn, Frederick E. *Hapax Legomena in Biblical Hebrew: A Study of the Phenomenon and Its Treatment Since Antiquity with Special Reference to Verbal Forms*. SBLDS 74. Chico, Calif.: Scholars Press, 1984.
Grésillon, Almuth. "Zum Linguistischen Status Rhetorischer Fragen." *Zeitschrift für Germanistische Linguistik* 8 (1980): 273–89.
Grice, H. P. *Studies in the Way of Words*. Cambridge, Mass.: Harvard University Press, 1989.
Grimes, Ronald L. "Infelicitous Performances and Ritual Criticism." *Semeia* 41 (1988): 103–22.
Grimm, Werner, and Kurt Dittert. *Deuterojesaja. Deutung–Wirkung–Gegenwart*. CBK. Stuttgart: Calwer, 1990.
Grosheide, H. H. et al., eds. *De Knecht: Studies rondom Deutero-Jesaja*. Festschrift J. L. Koole. Kampen: Kok, 1978.
Gu, Yueguo. "The Impasse of Perlocution." *JP* 20 (1993): 405–32.
Guillaume, Alfred. "Some Readings in the Dead Sea Scroll of Isaiah." *JBL* 76 (1957): 40–43.
Guillet, Jacques. "La Polemique contre les Idoles et le Serviteur de Yahve." *Bib* 40 (1959): 428–34.
Gundry, Robert H. "למטלים I Q Isaiah a 50,6 and Mark 14,65." *RevQ* 2 (1960): 559–67.
Haag, Ernst. "Die Botschaft vom Gottesknecht—ein Weg zur Überwindung der Gewalt." Pages 159–213 in *Gewalt und Gewaltlosigkeit im Alten Testament*. Edited by Norbert Lohfink. Quaestiones Disputatae 96. Freiburg: Herder, 1983.
—*Der Gottesknecht bei Deuterojesaja*. EdF 233. Darmstadt: Wissenschaftliche Buchgesellschaft, 1985.
Habel, Norman C. "The Form and Significance of the Call Narratives." *ZAW* 77 (1965): 297–323.
Halas, Roman. "The Universalim of Isaias." *CBQ* 12 (1950): 162–70.
Hallo, William W., ed. *The Context of Scripture*. 3 vols. Leiden: Brill, 1997–2002.
Hartley, John E. *Leviticus*. WBC 4. Dallas: Word, 1992.
Hauerwas, Stanley, and Richard Bondi. "Language, Experience and the Life Well-Lived: A Review of the Work of Donald Evans." *RelSRev* 9 (1983): 33–37.
Held, Moshe. "Rhetorical Questions in Ugaritic and Biblical Hebrew." *Eretz-Israel* 9 (1969): 71–79.
Hempel, Joh. "Zu Jes 50$_6$." *ZAW* 76 (1964): 327.

Hengel, Martin. "Zur Wirkungsgeschichte von Jes 53 in vorchristlicher Zeit." Pages 49–91 in Janowski and Stuhlmacher, eds., *Der leidende Gottesknecht.*

Henning-Hess, Heike. "Bemerkungen zum *Ascham*-Begriff in Jes 53,10." *ZAW* 109 (1997): 618–26.

Hermisson, Hans-Jürgen. "Die Frau Zion." Pages 19–39 in van Ruiten and Vervenne, eds., *Studies in the Book of Isaiah.*

—"Israel und der Gottesknecht bei Deuterojesaja." *ZTK* 79 (1982): 1–24.

—"Der Lohn des Knechts." Pages 269–87 in *Die Botschaft und die Boten.* Festschrift Hans Walter Wolff. Edited by Jörg Jeremias and Lothar Perlitt. Neukirchen–Vluyn: Neukirchener, 1981.

—"Neue Literatur zu Deuterojesaja (I)/(II)." *Tru* 65 (2000): 237–84, 379–430.

—"Das vierte Gottesknechtslied im deuterojesajanischen Kontext." Pages 1–25 in Janowski and Stuhlmacher, eds., *Der leidende Gottesknecht.*

—"Voreiliger Abschied von den Gottesknechtsliedern." *Tru* 49 (1984): 209–22.

Hilborn, David. "From Performativity to Pedagogy: Jean Ladriere and the Pragmatics of Reformed Worship Discourse." Pages 170–200 in Porter, ed., *The Nature of Religious Language: A Colloquium.*

Hillers, Dilbert R. "Some Performative Utterances in the Bible." Pages 757–66 in *Pomegranates and Golden Bells.* Festschrift Jacob Milgrom. Edited by David P. Wright, David N. Freedman, and Avi Hurvitz. Winona Lake, Ind.: Eisenbrauns, 1995.

Hofius, Otfried. "Zur Septuaginta-Übersetzung von Jes 52,13b." *ZAW* 104 (1992): 107–10.

Holdcroft, David. "Indirect Speech Acts and Propositional Content." Pages 350–64 in Tsohatzidis, ed., *Foundations of Speech Act Theory.*

Holladay, William L. *Jeremiah 1.* Hermeneia. Philadelphia: Fortress, 1986.

—*Unbound by Time: Isaiah Still Speaks.* Cambridge: Cowley, 2002.

Hollenberg, D. E. "Nationalism and 'The Nations' in Isaiah XL–LV." *VT* 19 (1969): 23–36.

Holter, Knut. *Second Isaiah's Idol-Fabrication Passages.* BBET 28. Frankfurt: Peter Lang, 1995.

—"The Wordplay on אֵל ('God') in Isaiah 45,20–21." *SJOT* 7 (1993): 88–98.

—"Zur Funktion der Städte Judas in Jesaja XL 9." *VT* 46 (1996): 119–21.

Hornsby, Jennifer. "Illocution and its Significance." Pages 187–207 in Tsohatzidis, ed., *Foundations of Speech Act Theory.*

—"Things Done With Words." Pages 27–46, 283–88 in *Human Agency: Language, Duty, and Value.* Festschrift J. O. Urmson. Edited by Jonathan Dancy, J. M. E. Moravcsik, and C. C. W. Taylor. Stanford: Stanford University Press, 1988.

Houston, Walter. "'Today, in Your Very Hearing': Some Comments on the Christological Use of the Old Testament." Pages 37–47 in *The Glory of Christ in the New Testament: Studies in Christology.* Festschrift George B. Caird. Edited by L. D. Hurst and N. T. Wright. Oxford: Clarendon, 1987.

—"What Did the Prophets Think They Were Doing? Speech Acts and Prophetic Discourse in the Old Testament." *BibInt* 1 (1993): 167–88.

Hruby, Kurt. "Die Rabbinische Exegese Messianischer Schriftstellen." *Judaica* 21 (1965): 100–122.

Hubbard, Robert L. "The Hebrew Root *Pgʿ* as a Legal Term." *JETS* 27 (1984): 129–33.

Hummel, Horace D. "Enclitic *Mem* in Early Northwest Semitic, Especially Hebrew." *JBL* 76 (1957): 85–107.

Iwry, Samuel. "New Evidence for Belomancy in Ancient Palestine and Phoenicia." *JAOS* 81 (1961): 27–34.

Jacobsen, Thorkild. "Primitive Democracy in Ancient Mesopotamia." Pages 157–70 in *Toward the Image of Tammuz and Other Essays on Mesopotamian History and Culture*. Cambridge, Mass.: Harvard University Press, 1970. Reprint from *JNES* 2 (1943): 159–72.

—*The Treasures of Darkness: A History of Mesopotamian Religion*. New Haven: Yale University Press, 1976.

Janowski, Bernd. "Er trug unsere Sünden—Stellvertretung nach Jes 52,13–53,12." Pages 67–95 in idem, *Stellvertretung: Alttestamentliche Studien zu einem theologischen Grundbegriff*. SBS 165. Stuttgart: Katholisches Bibelwerk, 1997. Revised ed. of "Er trug unsere Sünden: Jesaja 53 und die Dramatik der Stellvertretung." *ZTK* 90 (1993): 1–24.

—*Sühne als Heilsgeschehen: Traditions- und religionsgeschichtliche Studien zur priesterschriftlichen Sühnetheologie*. WMANT 55. Neukirchen–Vluyn: Neukirchener, 1982.

Janowski, Bernd, and Peter Stuhlmacher, eds. *Der leidende Gottesknecht: Jesaja 53 und seine Wirkungsgeschichte*. FAT 14. Tübingen: J. C. B. Mohr (Paul Siebeck), 1996.

Janzen, J. Gerald. "Isaiah 41:27: Reading הנה הנומה in 1QIsa[a] and הנה הנם in the Masoretic Text." *JBL* 113 (1994): 597–607.

Jeppesen, Knud. "From 'You, My Servant' to 'The Hand of the Lord is with My Servants': A Discussion of Is 40–66." *SJOT* 1 (1990): 113–29.

—"Mother Zion, Father Servant: A Reading of Isaiah 49–55." Pages 109–25 in McKay and Clines, eds., *Of Prophets' Visions and the Wisdom of Sages*.

Johnstone, William. "*Yd‘* II, 'Be Humbled, Humiliated'?" *VT* 41 (1991): 49–62.

Jones, Gwilym H. "Abraham and Cyrus: Type and Anti-Type?" *VT* 22 (1972): 304–19.

Kaiser, Otto. *Der Königliche Knecht: Eine Traditionsgeschichtlich-exegetische Studie über die Ebed–Jahwe–Lieder bei Deuterojesaja*. FRLANT 70. Göttingen: Vandenhoeck & Ruprecht, 1962.

Kiefer, Ferenc. "Yes–No Questions as Wh–Questions." Pages 97–119 in Searle, Kiefer, and Bierwisch, eds., *Speech Act Theory and Pragmatics*.

Kingsbury, Edwin C. "The Prophets and the Council of Yahweh." *JBL* 83 (1964): 279–86.

Knierim, Rolf P. "Cosmos and History in Israel's Theology." *HBT* 3 (1981): 59–123.

Koenig, Jean. *L'Herméneutique Analogique du Judaïsme Antique D'Après les Témoins Textuels D'Isaïe*. VTSup 33. Leiden: Brill, 1982.

Komlosh, Yehuda. "The Countenance of the Servant of the Lord, Was it Marred?" *JQR* 65 (1974–75): 217–20.

Koole, Jan L. *Isaiah*. Part 3, Vol. 1, *Isaiah 40–48*. Translated by A. P. Runia. HCOT. Kampen: Kok, 1997.

—*Isaiah*. Part 3 Vol. 2, *Isaiah 49–55*. Translated by A. P. Runia. HCOT. Leuven: Peeters, 1998.

—*Jesaja II. Deel I: Jesaja 40 tot en met 48*. Commentaar op het Oude Testament. Kampen: Kok, 1985.

Korpel, Marjo C. A. "Exegesis in the Work of Ilimilku of Ugarit." Pages 86–111 in *Intertextuality in Ugarit and Israel*. Edited by Johannes C. de Moor. OTS 40. Leiden: Brill, 1998.

—"Metaphors in Isaiah LV." *VT* 46 (1996): 43–55.

—"Second Isaiah's Coping with the Religious Crisis: Reading Isaiah 40 and 55." Pages 90–113 in *The Crisis of Israelite Religion: Transformation of Religious Tradition in Exilic and Post-Exilic Times*. Edited by Johannes C. de Moor. OTS 42. Leiden: Brill, 1999.

Korpel, Marjo C. A., and Johannes C. de Moor. *The Structure of Classical Hebrew Poetry: Isaiah 40–55*. Edited by J. C. de Moor. OTS 41. Leiden: Brill, 1998.

Krašovec, Jože, ed. *The Interpretation of the Bible: The International Symposium in Slovenia*. JSOTSup 289. Sheffield: Sheffield Academic Press, 1998.

Kratz, Reinhard G. "Der Anfang des Zweiten Jesaja in Jes 40,1f. und seine literarischen Horizonte." *ZAW* 105 (1993): 400–419.

—*Kyros im Deuterojesaja-Buch: Redaktionsgeschichtliche Untersuchungen zu Entstehung und Theologie von 40–55*. FAT 1. Tübingen: J. C. B. Mohr (Paul Siebeck), 1991.

Kruse, C. G. "The Servant Songs: Interpretive Trends Since C. R. North." *SBibT* 8 (1978): 3–27.

Kuntz, J. Kenneth. "The Form, Location, and Function of Rhetorical Questions in Deutero-Isaiah." Pages 121–41 in vol. 1 of Broyles and Evans, eds., *Writing and Reading the Scroll of Isaiah*.

Kutsch, Ernst. "Sein Leiden und Tod—unser Heil: Auslegung von Jesaja 52,13–53,12." Pages 169–96 in *Kleine Schriften zum Alten Testament*. Edited by Ludwig Schmidt and Karl Eberlein. BZAW 168. Berlin: de Gruyter, 1986.

—"Die Wurzel עצר im Hebräischen." *VT* 2 (1952): 57–69.

Kutscher, E. Y. *The Language and Linguistic Background of the Isaiah Scroll (I Q Isa[a])*. STDJ 6. Leiden: Brill, 1974.

Laato, Antti. "The Composition of Isaiah 40–55." *JBL* 109 (1990): 207–28.

—*The Servant of* YHWH *and Cyrus: A Reinterpretation of the Exilic Messianic Programme in Isaiah 40–55*. ConBOT 35. Stockholm: Almqvist & Wiksell, 1992.

Labuschagne, C. J. *The Incomparability of Yahweh in the Old Testament*. Pretoria Oriental Series 5. Leiden: Brill, 1966.

—"The Particles הֵן and הִנֵּה." Pages 1–14 in *Syntax and Meaning: Studies in Hebrew Syntax and Biblical Exegesis*. Edited by A. S. van der Woude. OTS 18. Leiden: Brill, 1973.

Ladrière, Jean. "The Performativity of Liturgical Language." *Concilium* 9 (1973): 50–62.

Landy, Francis. "The Construction of the Subject and the Symbolic Order: A Reading of the Last Three Suffering Servant Songs." Pages 60–71 in Davies and Clines, eds., *Among the Prophets: Language, Image and Structure in the Prophetic Writings*.

Leene, Henk. "History and Eschatology in Deutero-Isaiah." Pages 223–49 in van Ruiten and Vervenne, eds., *Studies in the Book of Isaiah*.

—*De Stem van de Knecht als Metafoor: Beschouwingen over de Compositie van Jesaja 50*. Kampen: Kok, 1980.

Lemaire, A., ed. *Congress Volume: Basel, 2001*. VTSup 92. Leiden: Brill, 2002.

Lepore, Ernest, and Robert van Gulick, eds. *John Searle and His Critics*. Oxford: Blackwell, 1991.

Leske, Adrian M. "Isaiah and Matthew: *The Prophetic Influence in the First Gospel*. A Report on the Current Research." Pages 152–69 in Bellinger and Farmer, eds., *Jesus and the Suffering Servant*.

Leveen, Jacob. "יזה in Isaiah LII. 15." *JBL* 7 (1956): 93–94.

Levine, Baruch. "René Girard on Job: The Question of the Scapegoat." *Semeia* 33 (1985): 125–33.

Linafelt, Tod. "Speech and Silence in the Servant Passages: Towards a Final-Form Reading of the Book of Isaiah." Pages 199–209 in Fowl, ed., *The Theological Interpretation of Scripture: Classic and Contemporary Readings*. Reprint from *Koinonia* 2 (1993): 174–90.

Linafelt, Tod, and Timothy K. Beal, eds. *God in the Fray*. Festschrift Walter Brueggemann. Minneapolis: Fortress, 1998.

Lindblad, U. "A Note on the Nameless Servant in Isaiah XLII 1–4." *VT* 43 (1993): 115–19.

Lindblom, Joh. *The Servant Songs in Deutero-Isaiah: A New Attempt to Solve an Old Problem*. LUÅ 47. Lund: Gleerup, 1951.

Lindsey, F. Duane. "The Call of the Servant in Isaiah 42:1–9." *BSac* 139 (1982): 12–31.

—"The Career of the Servant in Isaiah 52:13–53:12." *BSac* 139 (1982): 312–29.

—"The Career of the Servant in Isaiah 52:13–53:12 (Concluded)." *BSac* 140 (1983): 21–39.

—"The Commission of the Servant in Isaiah 49:1–13." *BSac* 139 (1982): 129–45.

—"The Commitment of the Servant in Isaiah 50:4–11." *BSac* 139 (1982): 216–29.

Loewenstamm, Samuel E. "The Expanded Colon in Ugaritic and Biblical Verse." *JSS* 14 (1969): 176–96.

Lohfink, Norbert. "Bund als Vertrag im Deuteronomium." *ZAW* 107 (1995): 215–39.

—"'Israel' in Jes 49,3." Pages 217–29 in Schreiner, ed., *Wort, Lied und Gottesspruch*.

Lovering, Eugene H., Jr., ed. *SBL Seminar Papers, 1991*. SBLSP 30. Atlanta: Scholars Press, 1991.

—ed., *SBL Seminar Papers, 1993*. SBLSP 32. Atlanta: Scholars Press, 1993.

Lugt, P. van der. *Remembering All the Way…* OTS 21. Leiden: Brill, 1981.

—"De Strofische Structuur van het derde Knechtslied (Jes. 50:4–11." Pages 102–17 in Grosheide et al., eds., *De Knecht: Studies rondom Deutero-Jesaja*.

Lundin, Roger, Clarence Walhout, and Anthony C. Thiselton. *The Promise of Hermeneutics*. Carlisle: Paternoster. Grand Rapids: Eerdmans, 1999.

Lust, J. "The Demonic Character of Jahweh and the Septuagint of Isaiah." *Bijdragen* 40 (1979): 2–14.

Macdonald, John. "An Assembly at Ugarit?" *UF* 11 (1979): 515–26.

Martinich, A. P. "Sacraments and Speech Act." *HeyJ* 16 (1975): 289–303, 405–17.

May, Herbert G. "Theological Universalism in the Old Testament." *JBR* 16 (1948): 3–15.

Mayer, Werner. *Untersuchungen zur Formensprache der babylonischen "Gebetsbeschwörungen"*. Studia Pohl: Series Major 5. Rome: Pontifical Biblical Institute, 1976.

McCarthy, Dennis J. "The Uses of *wᵉhinnēh* in Biblical Hebrew." *Bib* 61 (1980): 330–42.

McEleney, Neil J. "The Translation of Isaias 41,27." *CBQ* 19 (1957): 441–43.

McEvenue, Sean. "Who Was Second Isaiah?" Pages 213–22 in van Ruiten and Vervenne, eds., *Studies in the Book of Isaiah*.

McKay, Heather A., and David J. A. Clines, eds. *Of Prophets' Visions and the Wisdom of Sages*. Festschrift R. Norman Whybray. JSOTSup 162. Sheffield: JSOT Press, 1993.

McKenzie, John L. *Second Isaiah*. AB 20. Garden City, N.Y.: Doubleday, 1968.
Meek, Theophile J. "Translating the Hebrew Bible." *JBL* 79 (1960): 328–35.
Melugin, Roy F. "The Book of Isaiah and the Construction of Meaning." Pages 39–55 in vol. 1 of Broyles and Evans, eds., *Writing and Reading the Scroll of Isaiah*.
—"The Conventional and the Creative in Isaiah's Judgment Oracles." *CBQ* 36 (1974): 301–11.
—"Deutero-Isaiah and Form Criticism." *VT* 21 (1971): 326–37.
—"Figurative Speech and the Reading of Isaiah 1 as Scripture." Pages 282–305 in Melugin and Sweeney, eds., *New Visions of Isaiah*.
—*The Formation of Isaiah 40–55*. BZAW 141. Berlin: de Gruyter, 1976.
—"Muilenburg, Form Criticism, and Theological Exegesis." Pages 91–99 in *Encounter with the Text: Form and History in the Hebrew Bible*. Edited by Martin J. Buss. SBLSS 8. Missoula, Mont.: Scholars Press, 1979.
—"On Reading Isaiah 53 as Christian Scripture." Pages 55–69 in Bellinger and Farmer, eds., *Jesus and the Suffering Servant*.
—"Prophetic Books and the Problem of Historical Reconstruction." Pages 63–78 in Reid, ed., *Prophets and Paradigms*.
—"The Servant, God's Call, and the Structure of Isaiah 40–48." Pages 21–30 in Lovering, ed., *SBL Seminar Papers, 1991*.
Melugin, Roy F., and Marvin A. Sweeney, eds. *New Visions of Isaiah*. JSOTSup 214. Sheffield: Sheffield Academic Press, 1996.
Merendino, Rosario P. "Allein und einzig Gottes prophetisches Wort: Israels Erbe und Auftrag für alle Zukunft (Jesaja 50:4–9a.10)." *ZAW* 97 (1985): 344–66.
—*Der Erste und der Letzte: Eine Untersuchung von Jes 40–48*. VTSup 31. Leiden: Brill, 1981.
—"Jes 49:1–6: ein Gottesknechtslied?" *ZAW* 92 (1980): 236–43.
Merrill, Eugene H. "The Literary Character of Isaiah 40–55, Part 1: Survey of a Century of Studies on Isaiah 40–55." *BSac* 144 (1987): 24–43.
—The Literary Character of Isaiah 40–55, Part 2: Literary Genres in Isaiah 40–55." *BSac* 144 (1987): 144–56.
Mettinger, Tryggve N. D. *A Farewell to the Servant Songs: A Critical Examination of an Exegetical Axiom*. SM 1982–1983: 3. Lund: Gleerup, 1983.
—*King and Messiah: The Civil and Sacral Legitimation of the Israelite Kings*. ConBOT 8. Lund: Gleerup, 1976.
—"In Search of the Hidden Structure: YHWH as King in Isaiah 40–55." Pages 143–54 in vol. 1 of Broyles and Evans, eds., *Writing and Reading the Scroll of Isaiah*.
Meyers, Robert. B., and Karen Hopkins. "A Speech-Act Theory Bibliography." *Centrum* 5 (1977): 73–108.
Mijoga, Hilary B. P. "Some Notes on the Septuagint Translation of Isaiah 53." *Africa Theological Journal* 19 (1990): 85–90.
Milgrom, Jacob. *Cult and Conscience: The Asham and the Priestly Doctrine of Repentance*. SJLA 18. Leiden: Brill, 1976.
—*Leviticus 1–16*. AB 3. New York: Doubleday, 1991.
Millard, A. R. "Isaiah 53:2." *TynBul* 20 (1969): 127.
Miller, John W. "Prophetic Conflict in Second Isaiah: The Servant Songs in the Light of their Context." Pages 77–85 in Strobe, ed., *Wort—Gebot—Glaube*.
Miller, Patrick D. "Cosmology and World Order in the Old Testament: The Divine Council as Cosmic-Political Symbol." *HBT* 9 (1987): 53–87.

—"The Divine Council and the Prophetic Call to War." *VT* 18 (1968): 100–107.

Miscall, Peter D. "Isaiah: The Labyrinth of Images." *Semeia* 54 (1991): 103–21.

—*Isaiah*. Readings: A New Biblical Commentary. Sheffield: JSOT Press, 1993.

Moor, Johannes C. de, ed. *The Elusive Prophet: The Prophet as Historical Person, Literary Character and Anonymous Artist*. OTS 45. Leiden: Brill, 2001.

Moore, G. F. "On יזה in Isaiah LII. 15." *JBL* (1890): 216–22.

Morgenstern, Julian. *The Message of Deutero-Isaiah in its Sequential Unfolding*. Cincinnati: Hebrew Union College Press, 1961. Reprint from "The Message of Deutero-Isaiah in its Sequential Unfolding." *HUCA* 30 (1959): 1–102.

—"The Suffering Servant—A New Solution." *VT* 11 (1961): 292–320, 406–31.

—"Two Additional Notes to "The Suffering Servant—A New Solution." *VT* 13 (1963): 321–32.

Motyer, J. Alec. *The Prophecies of Isaiah: An Introduction and Commentary*. Downers Grove, Ill.: InterVarsity, 1993.

Mowinckel, Sigmund. *He That Cometh: The Messiah Concept in the Old Testament and Later Judaism*. Translated by G. W. Anderson. Nashville: Abingdon, 1956.

Muilenburg, J. "The Book of Isaiah Chapters 40–66: Introduction and Exegesis." *IB* 5:381–773.

—"Form Criticism and Beyond." *JBL* 88 (1969): 1–18.

Mulder, M. J. "Filologische Kanttekeningen Bij Jes. 41:23b. 42:19b en 43:14b." Pages 141–49 in Grosheide et al., eds., *De Knecht: Studies rondom Deutero-Jesaja*.

—"Die Partikel כן im Alten Testament." Pages 201–27 in van der Woude, ed., *Remembering all the Way…*

Mullen, E. Theodore, Jr. "Divine Assembly." *ABD* 2:214–17.

—*The Divine Council in Canaanite and Early Hebrew Literature*. HSM 24. Chico, Calif.: Scholars Press, 1980.

Müller, Hans-Peter. "Ein Vorschlag zu Jes 5310f." *ZAW* 81 (1969): 377–80.

Muraoka, Takamitsu. *Classical Syriac for Hebraists*. Wiesbaden: Harrassowitz, 1987.

—*Emphatic Words and Structures in Biblical Hebrew*. Leiden: Brill, 1985.

Neuberg, Frank J. "An Unrecognized Meaning of Hebrew *Dôr*[1]." *JNES* 9 (1950): 215–17.

Nielsen, Eduard. "Deuterojesaja: Erwägungen zur Formkritik, Traditions-und Redaktionsgeschichte." *VT* 20 (1970): 190–205.

North, Christopher R. "The 'Former Things' and the 'New Things' in Deutero-Isaiah." Pages 11–26 in Rowley, ed., *Studies in Old Testament Prophecy*.

—*The Second Isaiah. Introduction, Translation and Commentary to Chapters XL–LV*. Oxford: Clarendon, 1964.

—*The Suffering Servant in Deutero-Isaiah: An Historical and Critical Study*. 2d ed. Oxford: Oxford University Press, 1956.

Odell, Margaret S. "An Exploratory Study of Shame and Dependence in the Bible and Selected Near Eastern Parallels." Pages 217–33 in Younger, Hallo, and Batto, eds., *The Biblical Canon in Comparative Perspective*.

Olley, John W. "'The Many': How is Isa 53,12a to be Understood?" *Bib* 68 (1987): 330–56.

—*"Righteousness" in the Septuagint of Isaiah: A Contextual Study*. SBLSCS. Missoula, Mont.: Scholars Press, 1979.

Oosterhoff, B. J. "Tot een Licht der Volken." Pages 157–72 in Grosheide et al., eds., *De Knecht: Studies rondom Deutero-Jesaja*.

Orlinsky, Harry M. "'Israel' in Isa. XLIX, 3: A Problem in the Methodology of Textual Criticism." *Eretz-Israel* 8 (1967): 42–45.

—"The So-Called 'Servant of the Lord' and 'Suffering Servant' in Second Isaiah." Pages 1–133 in Orlinsky and Snaith, eds., *Studies on the Second Part of the Book of Isaiah.*

Orlinsky, Harry M., and Norman H. Snaith, eds. *Studies on the Second Part of the Book of Isaiah.* VTSup 14. Leiden: Brill, 1967.

Oswalt, John N. *The Book of Isaiah, Chapters 1–39.* NICOT. Grand Rapids: Eerdmans, 1986.

—*The Book of Isaiah, Chapters 40–66.* NICOT. Grand Rapids: Eerdmans, 1998.

Ottley, R. R. *The Book of Isaiah according to the Septuagint (Codex Alexandrinus).* Cambridge: Cambridge University Press, 1906.

Pardee, Dennis. "The 'Epistolary Perfect' in Hebrew Letters." *BN* 22 (1983): 34–40.

Pardee, Dennis, and Robert M. Whiting. "Aspects of Epistolary Verbal Usage in Ugaritic and Akkadian." *BSO(A)S* 50 (1987): 1–31.

Parry, Donald W., and Elisha Qimron, eds. *The Great Isaiah Scroll (IQIsa^a): A New Edition.* STDJ 32. Leiden: Brill, 1999.

Patrick, Dale. "God's Commandment." Pages 93–111 in Linafelt and Beal, eds., *God in the Fray.*

—"Is the Truth of the First Commandment Known by Reason?" *CBQ* 56 (1994): 423–41.

—*The Rendering of God in the Old Testament.* OBT. Philadelphia: Fortress, 1981.

—"The Rhetoric of Revelation." *HBT* 16 (1994): 20–40.

—*The Rhetoric of Revelation in the Hebrew Bible.* OBT. Minneapolis: Fortress, 1999.

Patrick, Dale, and Alan Scult. *Rhetoric and Biblical Interpretation.* JSOTSup 82. Sheffield: Almond Press, 1990.

Patte, Daniel. "Speech Act Theory and Biblical Exegesis." *Semeia* 41 (1988): 85–102.

Paul, Shalom M. "Deutero-Isaiah and Cuneiform Royal Inscriptions." *JAOS* 88 (1968): 180–86.

Payne, D. F. "Characteristic Word-Play in 'Second Isaiah': A Reappraisal." *JSS* 12 (1967): 207–29.

—"Recent Trends in the Study of Isaiah 53." *IBS* 1 (1979): 3–18.

—"The Servant of the Lord: Language and Interpretation." *EvQ* 42/43 (1970–71): 131–43.

Polk, Timothy. "Paradigms, Parables, and *Měšālîm*: On Reading the *Māšāl* in Scripture." *CBQ* 45 (1983): 564–83.

—*The Prophetic Persona: Jeremiah and the Language of the Self.* JSOTSup 32. Sheffield: JSOT Press, 1984.

Porteous, Norman W. "Jerusalem–Zion: The Growth of a Symbol." Pages 235–52 in *Verbannung und Heimkehr: Beiträge zur Geschichte und Theologie Israels im 6. und 5. Jahrhundert v. Chr.* Festschrift Wilhelm Rudolph. Edited by Arnulf Kuschke. Tübingen: J. C. B. Mohr (Paul Siebeck), 1961.

Porter, Stanley E., ed. *The Nature of Religious Language: A Colloquium.* Roehampton Institute London Papers 1. Sheffield: Sheffield Academic Press, 1996.

Pratt, Mary L. *Toward a Speech Act Theory of Literary Discourse.* Bloomington: Indiana University Press, 1977.

Preuss, Hortst D. *Deuterojesaja: Eine Einführung in seine Botschaft.* Neukirchen–Vluyn: Neukirchener, 1976.

Raabe, Paul R. "The Effect of Repetition in the Suffering Servant Song." *JBL* 103 (1984): 77–84.

Quinn-Miscall, Peter D. *Reading Isaiah: Poetry and Vision*. Louisville, Ky.: Westminster John Knox, 2001.

Rad, Gerhard von. *Old Testament Theology*. Translated by D. M. G. Stalker. 2 vols. New York: Harper & Row, 1962–65.

—"The Theological Problem of the Old Testament Doctrine of Creation." Pages 131–43 in *The Problem of the Hexateuch and Other Essays*. London: SCM Press, 1984.

Récanati, François. *Meaning and Force: The Pragmatics of Performative Utterances*. Cambridge: Cambridge University Press, 1987.

—"Some Remarks on Explicit Performatives, Indirect Speech Acts, Locutionary Meaning and Truth-Value." Pages 205–20 in Searle, Kiefer, and Bierwisch, eds., *Speech Act Theory and Pragmatics*.

Reicke, Bo. "The Knowledge of the Suffering Servant." Pages 186–92 in *Das Ferne und Nahe Wort*. Festschrift Leonhard Rost. Edited by F. Maass. BZAW 105. Berlin: Töpelmann, 1967.

Reid, Stephen B., ed. *Prophets and Paradigms*. Festschrift Gene M. Tucker. JSOTSup 229. Sheffield: Sheffield Academic Press, 1996.

—"Psalm 50: Prophetic Speech and God's Performative Utterances." Pages 217–30 in idem, ed., *Prophets and Paradigms*.

Reider, Joseph. *An Index to Aquila*. Compl. and revised by Nigel Turner. VTSup 12. Leiden: Brill, 1966.

—"On *Mšḥty* in the Qumran Scrolls." *BASOR* 34 (1954): 27–28.

Rembaum, Joel E. "The Development of a Jewish Exegetical Tradition Regarding Isaiah 53." *HTR* 75 (1982): 289–311.

Rendsburg, Gary A. "Morphological Evidence for Regional Dialects in Ancient Hebrew." Pages 65–88 in *Linguistics and Biblical Hebrew*. Edited by Walter R. Bodine. Winona Lake, Ind.: Eisenbrauns, 1992.

Rendtorff, Rolf. The Book of Isaiah—A Complex Unity: Synchronic and Diachronic Reading." Pages 109–28 in Gitay, ed., *Prophecy and Prophets*. Revised ed. of pages 32–49 in Melugin and Sweeney, eds., *New Visions of Isaiah*. Revised and updated ed. of pages 8–20 in Lovering, ed., *SBL Seminar Papers, 1991*.

—"Isaiah 6 in the Framework of the Composition of the Book." Pages 170–80 in *Canon and Theology: Overtures to an Old Testament Theology*. Translated by M. Kohl. OBT. Minneapolis: Fortress, 1993. Trans. of "Jesaja 6 im Rahmen der Komposition des Jesajabuches." Pages 73–82 in *The Book of Isaiah, Le livre d'Isaïe: Les oracles et leurs relectures, unité et complexité de l'ouvrage*. Edited by Jacques Vermeylen. BETL 81. Leuven: Leuven University Press/Peeters, 1989.

—Isaiah 56:1 as a Key to the Formation of the Book of Isaiah." Pages 181–89 in idem, *Canon and Theology: Overtures to an Old Testament Theology*. Translated by M. Kohl. OBT. Minneapolis: Fortress, 1993.

Reventlow, Henning Graf. "Basic Issues in the Interpretation of Isaiah 53." Pages 23–38 in Bellinger and Farmer, eds., *Jesus and the Suffering Servant*.

Riesener, Ingrid. *Der Stamm* עבד *im Alten Testament: Eine Wortuntersuchung unter Berücksichtigung neuerer sprachwissenschaftlicher Methoden*. BZAW 149. Berlin: de Gruyter, 1979.

Rignell, L. G. "Isa. LII 13—LIII 12." *VT* 3 (1953): 87–92.

—*A Study of Isaiah Ch. 40–55*. LUÅ 52/5. Lund: Gleerup, 1956.

Robinson, H. Wheeler. "The Council of Yahweh." *JTS* 45 (1944): 151–57.

—"The Hebrew Conception of Corporate Personality." Pages 25–44 in *Corporate Personality in Ancient Israel*. Rev. ed. Philadelphia: Fortress, 1980. Revised ed. of pages 49–62 in *Werden und Wesen des Alten Testaments: Vorträge gehalten auf der Internationalen Tagung Alttestamentlicher Forsher zu Göttingen vom 4.–10. September 1935*. Edited by P. Volz, F. Stummer, and J. Hempel. BZAW 66. Berlin: de Gruyter, 1936.

Rosenbaum, Michael. *Word-Order Variation in Isaiah 40–55: A Functional Perspective*. SSN. Assen: Van Gorcum, 1997.

Roth, W. M. W. "For Life, He Appeals to Death (Wis. 123.18): A Study of Old Testament Idol Parodies." *CBQ* 37 (1975): 21–47.

Rowley, H. H. *The Servant of the Lord and other Essays on the Old Testament*. 2d ed. Oxford: Blackwell, 1965.

—ed., *Studies in Old Testament Prophecy*. Festschrift Theodore H. Robinson. New York: Scribner's, 1950.

Rubinstein, Arie. "Formal Agreement of Parallel Clauses in the Isaiah Scroll." *VT* 4 (1954): 316–21.

—"A Kethib-Qere Problem in the Light of the Isaiah Scroll." *JSS* 4 (1959): 127–33.

—"Notes on the Use of the Tenses in the Variant Readings of the Isaiah Scroll." *VT* 3 (1955): 92–95.

—"The Theological Aspect of Some Variant Readings in the Isaiah Scroll." *JJS* 6 (1955): 187–200.

Ruiten, J. van, and M. Vervenne, eds. *Studies in the Book of Isaiah*. Festschrift Willem A. M. Beuken. BETL 132. Leuven: Leuven University Press/Peeters, 1997.

Sadock, Jerrold M. "Toward a Grammatically Realistic Typology of Speech Acts." Pages 393–406 in Tsohatzidis, ed., *Foundations of Speech Act Theory*.

Sadock, Jerrold M., and Arnold M. Zwicky. "Speech Act Distinctions in Syntax." Pages 155–96 in *Language Typology and Syntactic Description*. Vol. 1, *Clause Structure*. Edited by Timothy Shopen. Cambridge: Cambridge University Press, 1985.

Saebø, Magne. "Vom Individuellen zum Kollektiven: Zur Frage einiger innerbiblischer Interpretationen." Pages 116–25 in *Schöpfung und efreiung*. Edited by Rainer Albertz, W. Golka Friedemann, and Jürgen Kegler. Festchrift Claus Westermann. Stuttgart: Calwer, 1989.

Sanders, James A. "Adaptable for Life: The Nature and Function of Canon." Pages 11–39 in *From Sacred Story to Sacred Text*. Philadelphia: Fortress, 1987. Reprint from pages 531–60 in *Magnalia Dei: The Mighty Acts of God*. Festschrift G. Ernest Wright. Edited by Frank M. Cross, Werner E. Lemke, and Patrick D. Miller Jr. New York: Doubleday, 1976.

—*Canon and Community: A Guide to Canonical Criticism*. GBS. Philadelphia: Fortress, 1984.

Sandy, D. Brent. *Plowshares and Pruning Hooks: Rethinking the Language of Biblical Prophecy and Apocalyptic*. Downers Grove, Ill.: InterVarsity, 2002.

Satterthwaite, P. E., and David F. Wright, eds. *A Pathway into the Holy Scripture*. Grand Rapids: Eerdmans, 1994.

Sawyer, John F. A. "Daughter of Zion and Servant of the Lord in Isaiah: A Comparison." *JSOT* 44 (1989): 89–107.

Saydon, P. P. "The Use of Tenses in Deutero-Isaiah." *Bib* 40 (1959): 290–301.

Schaller, Joseph J. “Performative Language Theory: An Exercise in the Analysis of Ritual.” *Worship* 62 (1988): 415–32.

Schmidt-Radefeldt, Jürgen. “On So-Called ‘Rhetorical’ Questions.” *JP* 1 (1977): 375–92.

Schmitt, John J. “The Gender of Ancient Israel.” *JSOT* 26 (1983): 115–25.

—“The Motherhood of God and Zion as Mother.” *RB* 92 (1985): 557–69.

Schökel, Luis A. *A Manual of Hebrew Poetics*. Subsidia Biblica 11. Rome: Pontificio Istituto Biblico, 1988.

Schoors, Antoon. “Les choses antérieures et les choses nouvelles dans les oracles Deutéro-Isaïens.” *ETL* 40 (1964): 19–47.

—*I Am God Your Savior: A Form-Critical Study of the Main Genres in Is. XL–LV*. VTSup 24. Leiden: Brill, 1973.

Schreiner, Josef, ed. *Wort, Lied und Gottesspruch: Beiträge zu Psalmen und Propheten*. Festschrift Joseph Ziegler. FzB 2. Stuttgart: Katholisches Bibelwerk, 1972.

Schwarz, Günther. “Jesaja 50:4–5a.” *ZAW* 85 (1973): 356–57.

—“‘...wie ein Reis vor ihm’?” *ZAW* 83 (1971): 255–56.

Scullion, John J. “Righteousness (OT).” *ABD* 5:724–36.

—“*Ṣedeq-Ṣedaqah* in Isaiah cc. 40–66 with Special Reference to the Continuity in Meaning Between Second and Third Isaiah.” *UF* 3 (1971): 335–48.

Searle, John R. “Austin on Locutionary and Illocutionary Acts.” Pages 141–59 in Berlin et al. eds., *Essays on J. L. Austin*. Revised from *PhR* 77 (1968): 405–24.

—“The Background of Meaning.” Pages 221–32 in Searle, Kiefer, and Bierwisch, eds., *Speech Act Theory and Pragmatics*.

—*The Construction of Social Reality*. New York: Free Press, 1995.

—“Conversation.” Pages 7–29 in Searle et al., *(On) Searle on Conversation*.

—“Conversation Reconsidered.” Pages 137–47 in Searle et al., *(On) Searle on Conversation*.

—*Expression and Meaning: Studies in the Theory of Speech Acts*. Cambridge: Cambridge University Press, 1979.

—“How Performatives Work.” Pages 85–107, 288–89 in *Essays in Speech Act Theory*. Edited by Daniel Vanderveken and Susumu Kubo. P&BNS 77. Amsterdam: John Benjamins, 2002. Reprint from *Linguistics and Philosophy* 12 (1989): 535–58.

—“Indirect Speech Acts.” Pages 30–57 in *Expression and Meaning*. Reprint from pages 59–82 in *Speech Acts*. Edited by P. Cole and J. Morgan. Syntax and Semantics 3. New York: Academic Press, 1975.

—*Intentionality: An Essay in the Philosophy of Mind*. Cambridge: Cambridge University Press, 1983.

—“Literal Meaning.” Pages 117–36 in *Expression and Meaning*. Reprint from *Erkenntnis* 13 (1978): 207–24.

—“Meaning and Speech Acts.” *PhR* 71 (1962): 423–32.

—*Mind, Language and Society: Philosophy in the Real World*. MasterMinds. New York: Basic Books, 1998.

—ed., *The Philosophy of Language*. Oxford: Oxford University Press, 1971.

—“Reiterating the Differences: A Reply to Derrida.” *Glyph* 1 (1977): 198–208.

—*Speech Acts: An Essay in the Philosophy of Language*. Cambridge: Cambridge University Press, 1979.

—“A Taxonomy of Illocutionary Acts.” Pages 1–29 in *Expression and Meaning*. Reprint from pages 344–69 in *Language, Mind, and Knowledge*. Edited by Keith Gunderson. Minnesota Studies in the Philosophy of Science 7. Minneapolis: University of Minnesota Press, 1975.

—"What is a Speech Act?" Pages 39–53 in idem, ed., *Philosophy of Language*. Reprint from pages 221–39 in *Philosophy in America*. Edited by M. Black. Ithaca, N.Y.: Cornell University Press, 1965.

Searle, John R. et al. *(On) Searle on Conversation*. P&BNS 21. Amsterdam: John Benjamins, 1992.

Searle, John R., Ferenc Kiefer, and Manfred Bierwisch, eds. *Speech Act Theory and Pragmatics*. Texts and Studies in Linguistics and Philosophy 10. Dordrecht: Reidel, 1980.

Searle, John R., and Daniel Vanderveken. *Foundations of Illocutionary Logic*. Cambridge: Cambridge University Press, 1985.

Seitz, Christopher R. "The Book of Isaiah 40–66: Introduction, Commentary, and Reflections." *NIB* 6:307–552.

—"The Divine Council: Temporal Transition and New Prophecy in the Book of Isaiah." *JBL* 109 (1990): 229–47.

—"How is the Prophet Isaiah Present in the Latter Half of the Book? The Logic of Chapters 40–66 within the Book of Isaiah." *JBL* 115 (1996): 219–40.

—"Isaiah 1–66: Making Sense of the Whole." Pages 105–26 in *Reading and Preaching the Book of Isaiah*. Edited by Christopher Seitz. Philadelphia: Fortress, 1988.

—"On the Questions of Divisions Internal to the Book of Isaiah." Pages 260–66 in Lovering, ed., *SBL Seminar Papers, 1993*.

—" 'You are my Servant, You are the Israel in whom I will be glorified': The Servant Songs and the Effect of Literary Context in Isaiah." *CTJ* 39 (2004): 117–34.

Simian-Yofre, Horacio. "Exodo en Deuteroisaías." *Bib* 61 (1980): 530–53.

Smith, Barry. "Towards a History of Speech Act Theory." Pages 29–61 in Burkhardt, ed., *Speech Acts, Meaning and Intentions*.

Smith, James M., and James Wm. McClendon, Jr. "Religious Language after J. L. Austin." *RelS* 8 (1972): 55–63.

Smith, J. Payne, ed. *A Compendious Syriac Dictionary Founded Upon the Thesaurus Syriacus of R. Payne Smith*. Winona Lake, Ind.: Eisenbrauns, 1998.

Smith, Mark S. *The Origins of Biblical Monotheism: Israel's Polytheistic Background and the Ugaritic Texts*. Oxford: Oxford University Press, 2001.

Snaith, Norman H. "The Servant of the Lord in Deutero-Isaiah." Pages 187–200 in Rowley, ed., *Studies in Old Testament Prophecy*.

—"A Study on the Teaching of the Second Isaiah and Its Consequences." Pages 135–264 Orlinsky and Snaith, eds., *Studies on the Second Part of the Book of Isaiah*.

Soggin, J. Alberto. "Tod und Auferstehung des Leidenden Gottesknechtes: Jesaja 53:8–10." *ZAW* 87 (1975): 346–55.

Sonne, Isaiah. "Isaiah 53 10–12." *JBL* 78 (1959): 335–42.

Spaller, Christina. "Syntaktische und stilistische Relationen im Vierten Gottesknechtslied und deren exegetische Relevanz." Pages 275–92 in *Liebe zum Wort: Beiträge zur klassischen und biblischen Philologie*. Festschrift P. Ludger Bernhard. Edited by Friedrich V. Reiterer and Petrus Eder. Salzburg: Müller, 1993.

Spencer, Bradley J. "The 'New Deal' for Post-exilic Judah in Isaiah 41,17–20." *ZAW* 112 (2000): 583–97.

Sperber, Alexander, ed. *The Bible in Aramaic: Latter Prophets according to Targum Jonathan*, vol. 3. Leiden: Brill, 1992.

Spykerboer, Hendrik C. *The Structure and Composition of Deutero-Isaiah with Special Reference to the Polemics Against Idolatry*. Meppel: Krips, 1976.

Steck, Odil H. "Aspekte des Gottesknechts in Deuterojesajas 'Ebed–Jahwe–Liedern.'" Pages 3–21 in *Gottesknecht und Zion*. Reprint from *ZAW* 96 (1984): 372–90.

—"Aspekte des Gottesknechts in Jesaja 52,13–53,12." Pages 22–44 in*Gottesknecht und Zion*. Reprint from *ZAW* 97 (1985): 36–58.

—*Gottesknecht und Zion: Gesammelte Aufsätze zu Deuterojesaja*. FAT 4. Tübingen: J. C. B. Mohr (Paul Siebeck), 1992.

—"Zion als Gelände und Gestalt: Überlegungen zur Wahrnehmung Jerusalems als Stadt und Frau im Alten Testament." Pages 126–46 in *Gottesknecht und Zion*. Reprint from *ZTK* 86 (1989): 261–81.

Stenning, J. F. *The Targum of Isaiah*. Oxford: Clarendon, 1949.

Stratton, Beverly J. "Engaging Metaphors: Suffering with Zion and the Servant in Isaiah 52–53." Pages 219–37 in Fowl, ed., *The Theological Interpretation of Scripture*.

Strawson, P. F. "Austin and "Locutionary Meaning." Pages 46–68 in Berlin et al., eds., *Essays on J. L. Austin*.

—"Intention and Convention in Speech Acts." Pages 23–38 in Searle, ed., *The Philosophy of Language*. Reprint from pages 380–400 in Fann, ed., *Symposium on J. L. Austin*. Reprint from *PhR* 73 (1964): 439–60.

Strobe, H. J., ed. *Wort—Gebot—Glaube: Beiträge zur Theologie des Alten Testaments*. Feschrift Walther Eichrodt. ATANT 59. Zürich: Zwingli, 1970.

Stuhlmueller, Carrol. *Creative Redemption in Deutero-Isaiah*. AnBib 43. Rome: Biblical Institute, 1970.

—"Deutero-Isaiah (cc. 40–55): Major Transitions in the Prophet's Theology and in Contemporary Scholarship." *CBQ* 42 (1980): 1–29.

—"First and Last and Yahweh—Creator in Deutero-Isaiah." *CBQ* 29 (1967): 495–511.

Suggs, M. Jack. "Wisdom of Solomon 1 10–5: A Homily Based on the Fourth Servant Song." *JBL* 76 (1957): 26–33.

Sukenik, W. L., ed. *The Dead Sea Scrolls of the Hebrew University*. Jerusalem: Hebrew University, 1955.

Sweeney, Marvin A. "The Book of Isaiah as Prophetic Torah." Pages 50–67 in Melugin and Sweeney, eds., *New Visions of Isaiah*.

—"The Book of Isaiah in Recent Research." *CRBS* 1 (1993): 141–62.

—*Isaiah 1–39, with an Introduction to Prophetic Literature*. FOTL 16. Grand Rapids: Eerdmans, 1996.

Talmon, Shemaryahu, and Weston W. Fields. "The Collocation משתין בקיר ועצור ועזוב and its Meaning." *ZAW* 101 (1989): 85–112.

Tate, Marvin E. "The Book of Isaiah in Recent Study." Pages 22–56 in Watts and House, eds., *Forming Prophetic Literature*.

TeSelle, Sallie McFague. *Speaking in Parables: A Study in Metaphor and Theology*. Philadelphia: Fortress, 1975.

Thiselton, A. C. "Authority and Hermeneutics: Some Proposals for a More Creative Agenda." Pages 107–41 in Satterthwaite and Wright, eds., *A Pathway into the Holy Scripture*.

—"'Behind' and 'In Front Of' the Text: Language, Reference and Indeterminacy." Pages 97–120 in Bartholomew, Greene, and Möller, eds., *After Pentecost*.

—"Christology in Luke, Speech-Act Theory, and the Problem of Dualism in Christology after Kant." Pages 453–72 in *Jesus of Nazareth, Lord and Christ: Essays on the Historical Jesus and New Testament Christology*. Edited by Joel B. Green and Max Turner. Grand Rapids: Eerdmans. Carlisle: Paternoster, 1994.

—"Communicative Action and Promise in Interdisciplinary, Biblical, and Theological Hermeneutics." Pages 133–239 in Lundin, Walhout, and Thiselton, *The Promise of Hermeneutics*.

—*The First Epistle to the Corinthians*. NIGTC. Grand Rapids: Eerdmans. Carlisle: Paternoster, 2000.

—*Language, Liturgy and Meaning*. 2d ed. Grove Liturgical Study 2. Nottingham: Grove Books, 1986.

—"The Logical Role of the Liar Paradox in Titus 1:12, 13: A Dissent From the Commentaries in the Light of Philosophical and Logical Analysis." *BibInt* 2 (1994): 207–23.

—*New Horizons in Hermeneutics: The Theory and Practice of Transforming Biblical Reading*. Grand Rapids: Zondervan, 1992.

—"The Parables as Language-Events: Some Comments on Fuchs's Hermeneutics in the Light of Linguistic Philosophy." *SJT* 23 (1970): 437–68.

—"Speech-Act Theory and the Claim that God Speaks: Nicholas Wolterstorff's *Divine Discourse*." *SJT* 50 (1997): 97–110.

—"The Supposed Power of Words in the Biblical Writings." *JTS* 25 (1974): 283–99.

—"Thirty Years of Hermeneutics: Retrospect and Prospects." Pages 1559–74 in Krašovec, ed., *The Interpretation of the Bible*.

—*The Two Horizons: New Testament Hermeneutics and Philosophical Description with Special Reference to Heidegger, Bultmann, Gadamer, and Wittgenstein*. Carlisle: Paternoster. Grand Rapids: Eerdmans, 1980.

Thomas, D. Winton. "A Consideration of Isaiah LIII in the Light of Recent Textual and Philological Study." *ETL* 44 (1968): 79–86.

—"A Consideration of Some Unusual Ways of Expressing the Superlative in Hebrew." *VT* 3 (1953): 209–24.

—"More Notes on the Root ידע in Hebrew." *JTS* 38 (1937): 404–5.

—"A Note on the Hebrew Text of Isaiah XLI. 27." *JTS* 18 (1967): 127–28.

—"The Root ידע in Hebrew." *JTS* 35 (1934): 298–306.

—"Some Observations on the Hebrew Root חדל." Pages 8–16 in *Congress Volume; Strasbourg, 1956*. Edited by G. W. Anderson et al. VTSup 4. Leiden: Brill, 1957.

Tidwell, N. L. "My Servant Jacob, Is. XLII 1: A Suggestion." Pages 84–91 in *Studies on Prophecy: A Collection of Twelve Papers*. Edited by G. W. Anderson et al. VTSup 26. Leiden: Brill, 1974.

Tilley, Terrence W. *The Evils of Theodicy*. Washington: Georgetown University Press, 1991.

Tomback, Richard S. *A Comparative Semitic Lexicon of the Phoenician and Punic Languages*. SBLDS 32. Missoula, Mont.: Scholars Press, 1978.

Torrey, Charles C. "Isaiah 41." *HTR* 44 (1951): 121–36.

—*The Second Isaiah: A New Interpretation*. New York: Scribner's, 1928.

Treves, Marco. "Isaiah LIII." *VT* 24 (1974): 98–108.

Tsohatzidis, Savas L., ed. *Foundations of Speech Act Theory: Philosophical and Linguistic Perspectives*. London: Routledge, 1994.

—"The Gap between Speech Acts and Mental States." Pages 220–33 in idem, ed., *Foundations of Speech Act Theory*.

—"Ways of Doing Things With Words: An Introduction." Pages 1–25 in idem, ed., *Foundations of Speech Act Theory*.

Tucker, Gene M. *Form Criticism of the Old Testament*. GBS. Philadelphia: Fortress, 1971.

Uehlinger, Christoph. "Audienz in der Götterwelt: Anthropomorphismus und Soziomorphismus in der Ikonographie eines altsyrichen Zylindersiegels." *UF* 24 (1992): 339–59.

Urbrock, William J. "Blessings and Curses." *ABD* 1:755–61.

Urmson, J. O. "Performative Utterances." Pages in 260–67 *Contemporary Perspectives in the Philosophy of Language*. Edited by Peter A. French, Theodore E. Uehling, Jr., and Howard K. Wettstein. Minneapolis: University of Minnesota Press, 1979.

Vanderveken, Daniel. "A Complete Formulation of a Simple Logic of Elementary Illocutionary Acts." Pages 99–131 in Tsohatzidis, ed., *Foundations of Speech Act Theory*.

—*Meaning and Speech Acts*. Vol. 1, *Principles of Language Use*. Cambridge: Cambridge University Press, 1990.

—*Meaning and Speech Acts*. Vol. 2, *Formal Semantics of Success and Satisfaction*. Cambridge: Cambridge University Press, 1991.

Vanhoozer, Kevin J. "From Speech Acts to Scripture Acts: The Covenant of Discourse and the Discourse of Covenant." Pages 159–203 in *First Theology: God, Scripture & Hermeneutics*. Downers Grove, Ill.: InterVarsity. Leicester: Apollos, 2002. Revised from pages 1–49 in Bartholomew, Greene, and Möller, eds., *After Pentecost*.

—"God's Mighty Speech Acts: The Doctrine of Scripture Today." Pages 143–81 in Sattherwaite and Wright, eds., *A Pathway into the Holy Scripture*.

—*Is There a Meaning in This Text? The Bible, the Reader, and the Morality of Literary Knowledge*. Grand Rapids: Zondervan, 1998.

—"The Semantics of Biblical Literature: Truth and Scripture's Diverse Literary Forms." Pages 53–104 in *Hermeneutics, Authority, and Canon*. Edited by D. A. Carson and John D. Woodbridge. Carlisle: Paternoster. Grand Rapids: Baker Books, 1995.

Vervenne, Marc. "The Phraseology of 'Knowing YHWH' in the Hebrew Bible: A Preliminary Study of its Syntax and Function." Pages 467–92 in van Ruiten and Vervenne, eds., *Studies in the Book of Isaiah*.

Vriezen, Th. C. "The Term *Hizza*: Lustration and Consecration." Pages 201–35 in *Oudtestamentische Studiën 7*. Edited by P. A. H. de Boer. Leiden: Brill, 1950.

Wagner, Andreas. "Die Bedeutung der Sprechakttheorie für Bibelübersetzungen, aufgezeigt an Gen 1,29, Ps 2,7 und Dtn 26,17–19." Pages 1575–88 in Krašovec, ed., *The Interpretation of the Bible*.

—*Sprechakte und Sprechaktanalyse im Alten Testament: Untersuchungen im biblischen Hebräisch an der Nahstelle zwischen Handlungsebene und Grammatik*. BZAW 253. Berlin: de Gruyter, 1997.

—"Die Stellung der Sprechakttheorie in Hebraistik und Exegese." Pages 55–83 in Lemaire, ed., *Congress Volume: Basel, 2001*.

Wainwright, Geoffrey. "The Language of Worship." Pages 465–73 in *The Study of Liturgy*. Edited by C. Jones, G. Wainwright, and E. Yarnold. London: SPCK, 1978.

Waldow, Eberhard von. "Anlass und Hintergrund der Verkündigung des Deuterojesaja." Ph.D. diss., Bonn University, 1953.

—"The Message of Deutero-Isaiah." *Int* 22 (1968): 259–87.

Walsh, Jerome T. "The Case for the Prosecution: Isaiah 41.21–42.17." Pages 101–18 in Follis, ed., *Directions in Biblical Hebrew Poetry*.

Warnock, G. J. "Some Types of Performative Utterance." Pages 69–89 in Berlin et al., eds. *Essays on J. L. Austin.*

Watson, Wilfred G. E. *Classical Hebrew Poetry: A Guide to its Techniques*. JSOTSup 26. Sheffield: JSOT Press, 1995.

—"Shared Consonants in Northwest Semitic." *Bib* 50 (1969): 25–33.

Watts, James W., and Paul R. House, eds. *Forming Prophetic Literature: Essays on Isaiah and the Twelve.* Festschrift John D. W. Watts. JSOTSup 235. Sheffield: Sheffield Academic Press, 1996.

Watts, John D. W. *Isaiah 1–33*. WBC 24. Waco, Tex.: Word, 1985.

—*Isaiah 34–66*. WBC 25. Waco, Tex.: Word, 1987.

Watts, Rikki E. "Consolation or Confrontation? Isaiah 40–55 and the Delay of the New Exodus." *TynBul* 41 (1990): 31–59.

—"The Meaning of *ʿālāw yiqpeṣû melākîm pîhem* in Isaiah LII 15." *VT* 40 (1990): 327–35.

Webb, Barry G. *The Message of Isaiah: On Eagle's Wings*. The Bible Speaks Today. Downers Grove, Ill.: InterVarsity, 1996.

Wehr, Hans. *A Dictionary of Modern Written Arabic (Arabic–English).* Edited by J. Milton Cowan. 4th ed. Wiesbaden: Harrassowitz, 1979.

Westermann, Claus. *Basic Forms of Prophetic Speech*. Translated by H. C. White. Cambridge: Lutterworth. Louisville, Ky.: Westminster John Knox, 1991.

—"Das Heilswort bein Deuterojesaja." *EvT* 24 (1964): 355–73.

—*Isaiah 40–66*. Translated by D. M. G. Stalker. OTL. Philadelphia: Westminster, 1969. Trans. of *Das Buch Jesaia, 40–66*. DAT 19. Göttingen: Vandenhoeck & Ruprecht, 1966.

—*Prophetic Oracles of Salvation in the Old Testament*. Translated by K. Crim. Louisville, Ky.: Westminster John Knox, 1991.

—*Sprache und Struktur der Prophetie Deuterojesajas Mit einer Literaturübersicht "Hauptlinien der Deuterojesajaforschung von 1964–1979" zusammengestellt und kommentiert von Andreas Richter*. CThM 11. Stuttgart: Calwer, 1981. Reprint from "Sprache und Struktur der Prophetie Deuterojesajas." Pages 92–170 in *Forschung am Alten Testament: Gesammelte Studien*, vol. 1. Tbü 24. Munich: Kaiser, 1964.

Wheeler Stone, Bebb. "Second Isaiah: Prophet to Patriarchy." *JSOT* 56 (1992): 85–99.

White, Hugh C. "Introduction: Speech Act Theory and Literary Criticism." *Semeia* 41 (1988): 1–24.

—ed., *Speech Act Theory and Biblical Criticism.* Semeia 41. Decatur: Scholars Press, 1988.

—"The Value of Speech Act Theory for Old Testament Hermeneutics." *Semeia* 41 (1988): 41–63.

Whitley, C. F. "A Note on Isa. XLI. 27." *JSS* 2 (1957): 327–28.

—"Textual Notes on Deutero-Isaiah." *VT* 11 (1951): 457–61.

Whybray, R. N. *The Heavenly Counselor in Isaiah xl 13–14: A Study of the Sources of Theology of Deutero Isaiah.* SOTSMS 1. Cambridge: Cambridge University Press, 1971.

—*Isaiah 40–66*. NBC. Grand Rapids: Eerdmans. London: Marshall, Morgan & Scott, 1975.

—*The Second Isaiah.* OTG. Sheffield: Sheffield Academic Press, 1997.

—*Thanksgiving for a Liberated Prophet: An Interpretation of Isaiah Chapter 53.* JSOTSup 4. Sheffield: JSOT Press, 1978.

—"Two Recent Studies on Second Isaiah." *JSOT* 34 (1986): 109–17.

Widengren, Geo. "Yahweh's Gathering of the Dispersed." Pages 227–45 in *In the Shelter of Elyon: Essays on Ancient Palestinian Life and Literature.* Festschrift G. W. Ahlström. Edited by Barrick W. Boyd and John R. Spencer. JSOTSup 31. Sheffield: JSOT Press, 1984.

Wieringen, Archibald van. "Jesaja 40,1–11: eine Drama-Linguistische Lesung von Jesaja 6 her." *BN* 49 (1989): 82–93.

Wilcox, Peter, and David Paton-Williams. "The Servant Songs in Deutero-Isaiah." *JSOT* 42 (1988): 79–102.

Wildberger, Hans. "Der Monotheismus Deuterojesajas." Pages 506–30 in *Beiträge zur Alttestamentlichen Theologie.* Festschrift Walther Zimmerli. Edited by Herbert Donner, Robert Hanhart, and Rudolf Smend. Göttingen: Vandenhoeck & Ruprecht, 1977.

—"Die Neuinterpretation des Erwählungsglaubens Israels in der Krise der Exilszeit." Pages 307–24 in Strobe, ed., *Wort—Gebot—Glaube.*

Willey, Patricia T. *Remember the Former Things: The Recollection of Previous Texts in Second Isaiah.* SBLDS 161. Atlanta: Scholars Press, 1997.

—"The Servant of YHWH and Daughter of Zion: Alternating Visions of YHWH's Community." Pages 267–303 in *SBL Seminar Papers, 1995.* Edited by E. H. Lovering. SBLSP 34. Atlanta: Scholars Press, 1995.

Williamson, Hugh G. M, *The Book Called Isaiah: Deutero-Isaiah's Role in Composition and Redaction.* Oxford: Clarendon, 1994.

—"*Daʿaṯ* in Isaiah LIII 11." *VT* 28 (1978): 118–21.

—"First and Last in Isaiah." Pages 95–108 in McKay and Clines, eds., *Of Prophets' Visions and the Wisdom of Sages.*

—*Variations on a Theme: King, Messiah, and Servant in the Book of Isaiah.* The Didsbury Lecture Series 1997. Carlisle: Paternoster, 1998.

Willis, John T. "Alternating [ABA'B'] Parallelism in the Old Testament Psalms and Prophetic Literature." Pages 49–76 in Follis, ed., *Directions in Biblical Hebrew Poetry.*

—"The Juxtaposition of Synonymous and Chiastic Parallelism in Tricola in Old Testament Hebrew Psalm Poetry." *VT* 29 (1979): 465–80.

Wilshire, Leland E. "Jerusalem as the 'Servant City' in Isaiah 40–66: Reflections in the Light of Further Study of the Cuneiform Tradition." Pages 231–55 in *The Bible in the Light of Cuneiform Literature: Scripture in Context III.* Edited by William W. Hallo, Bruce W. Jones, and Gerald L. Mattingly. ANETS 8. Lewiston, N.Y.: Edwin Mellen, 1990.

—"The Servant-City: A New Interpretation of the 'Servant of the Lord' in the Servant Songs of Deutero-Isaiah." *JBL* 94 (1975): 356–67.

Wilson, Andrew. *The Nations in Deutero-Isaiah: A Study on Composition and Structure.* ANETS 1. Lewiston, N.Y.: Edwin Mellen, 1986.

Winkle, Dwight W van. "Proselytes in Isaiah XL–LV? A Study of Isaiah XLIV 1–5." *VT* 47 (1997): 341–59.

—"The Relationship of the Nations to Yahweh and to Israel in Isaiah XL–LV." *VT* 35 (1985): 446–58.

Wittgenstein, Ludwig. *Philosophical Investigations.* Translated by G. E. M. Anscombe. 3d ed. Englewood Cliffs: Prentice–Hall, 1958.

Wolff, Hans W. *Jesaja 53 im Urchristentum.* Basel: Brunnen, 1984.

—"Wer ist der Gottesknecht in Jesaja 53?" *EvT* 22 (1962): 338–43.

Wolterstorff, Nicholas. *Divine Discourse: Philosophical Reflections on the Claim that God Speaks*. Cambridge: Cambridge University Press, 1995.

—"The Promise of Speech-Act Theory for Biblical Interpretation." Pages 73–90 in Bartholomew, Greene, and Möller, eds., *After Pentecost*.

Woude, Annemaricke van der. "Can Zion Do Without the Servant in Isaiah 40–55?" *CTJ* 39 (2004): 109–16.

Wunderlich, Dieter. "Methodological Remarks on Speech Act Theory." Pages 291–312 in Searle, Kiefer, and Bierwisch, eds., *Speech Act Theory and Pragmatics*.

Young, Edward J. "The Interpretation of יזה in Isaiah 52:15." *WTJ* 3 (1941): 125–32.

Younger Jr., K. Lawson, William W. Hallo, and Bernard F. Batto, eds. *The Biblical Canon in Comparative Perspective: Scripture in Context IV*. ANETS 11. Lewiston, N.Y.: Edwin Mellen, 1991.

Zimmerli, Walther. *I Am Yahweh*. Edited by W. Brueggemann. Translated by D. W. Stott. Atlanta: John Knox, 1982.

Zimmerli, Walther, and Joachim Jeremias. *The Servant of God*. Rev. ed. SBT 20. London: SCM Press, 1965.

Indexes

Index of References

INDEX OF AUTHORS